Child
Sexual
Abuse

Also available from Lyceum Books, Inc.

Advisory Editor: Thomas M. Meenaghan, *New York University*

Understanding and Managing the Therapeutic Relationship
by Fred McKenzie

Endings in Clinical Practice: Effective Closure in Diverse Settings
by Joseph Walsh

Children and Loss: A Practical Handbook for Professionals
edited by Elizabeth C. Pomeroy and Renée Bradford Garcia

Therapeutic Games and Guided Imagery:
Tools for Mental Health and School Professionals
Working with Children, Adolescents, and Their Families
by Monit Cheung

The Ethics of Practice with Minors
by Kim Strom-Gottfried

Secondary Traumatic Stress and the Child Welfare Professional
by Josephine G. Pryce, Kimberly K. Shackelford, and David H. Pryce

Adoption in the United States:
A Reference for Families, Professionals, and Students
by Martha J. Henry and Daniel Pollack

Child
Sexual
Abuse

Best Practices for Interviewing and Treatment

Monit Cheung
Graduate College of Social Work,
University of Houston

LYCEUM
BOOKS, INC.

Chicago, IL 60637

Published by
    LYCEUM BOOKS, INC.
    5758 S. Blackstone Avenue
    Chicago, Illinois 60637
    773-643-1903 fax
    773-643-1902 phone
    lyceum@lyceumbooks.com
    www.lyceumbooks.com

Cover image © Lucian Milasan—Dreamstime.com

6 5 4 3 2 1   12 13 14 15 16

ISBN 978-1-933478-43-2

Printed in the United States of America.

Library of Congress Cataloging-in-Publication Data

Cheung, Monit.
    Child sexual abuse : best practices for interviewing and treatment / written by Monit Cheung.
        p. cm.
    Includes bibliographical references and index.
    ISBN 978-1-933478-43-2 (pbk. : alk. paper)
1. Child sexual abuse—Investigation. 2. Interviewing in child abuse. 3. Sexually abused children—Treatment. I. Title.
    HV8079.C48C44   2012
    362.76'65—dc23

                                                                    2011018375

To all professionals who treat and stop child
sexual abuse, and to Lyceum Books, for
believing in practice-based evidence and
evidence-based practice

Contents

Acknowledgments

Child sexual abuse is a hidden problem and a family taboo. All children are at risk if adults do not want to talk about the subject. More than 80 percent of the perpetrators in child sexual abuse cases are known to the child victim. Whose responsibility is it to stop abuse? When a child tells someone in the family about sexual abuse, more often than not, no one wants to act on it out of fear—fear of losing a breadwinner, fear of family breakdown, fear of being punished or further violated.

I started to prepare this book thirty-five years after handling my first child sexual abuse case in a refugee camp. In the 1970s, the case was hard on me because I did not have any guidelines. I immediately acted in my role as a social worker to help the child move to a safe place and to comfort her so that she could trust us enough to tell us what happened. Not only did the child want to recover quickly but we as social workers and helping professionals received from her the message that we must work together to pass through the trauma and help other vulnerable witnesses survive cross-examinations and move forward with their lives. They can most definitely not forget about their trauma, but we can at least help them deal with it and stop further damage. I thank this child for giving us this message.

In preparing this book, I would like to thank my mentors Professor Keith Kilty and Professor Cecilia Chan for their guidance and trust in me; to Siao Fong Fong, president of the End Child Sexual Abuse Foundation, and her entire board and staff, and to Judge Judi Barnes, for their commitment to implementing preventive work in child sexual abuse; to my parents and siblings for their unconditional love; and to my husband, Professor Patrick Leung, and our daughters, Carol and Marie, for their continuous support and encouragement.

I also appreciate all the researchers and practitioners in this field who have been working extremely hard to assist children and their families become strong survivors. More important, with proper guidelines, all of us are taking our responsibility seriously to prevent and stop child sexual abuse. This book could not have been completed without research in evidence-based practice and all of my research assistants and their endless efforts to organize the materials so that I could recognize all the researchers and scholars accordingly. My research assistants include Chi Wa Chan, Whitney Chapman, Elena Delavega, Jacquelynn Duron, Alicia Fletcher, Amanda Ford, Alicia LaChapelle, Scarlet Lee, Joanne Hui-tung Li, Ashlee Marshall, Peter Nguyen, Ashleigh Scinta, Eusebius Small, Xenia Tse, Venus Tsui, Christine Underwood, Corrine Walijarvi, Ada Yip, and Mandy Yu—all at the University of Houston, a Carnegie-designated tier-one public research university. My thanks also go to Katherine Faydash, who has provided her detailed feedback and editorial support.

I also thank Stephen Cheng Se-lim and Ephraem Tsui of the Hong Kong Police Force for providing two examples from the collection of Chinese anatomical drawings to show the use of culturally relevant materials in forensic interviews; Tony Brackett of ABC News for allowing me to reprint transcripts of "From the Mouths of Babes" to address research from experts such as Stephen Ceci to advocate for professional training to improve skills in forensic interviews; and Fiona Remko, program director of the Fort Bend Children's Advocacy Center, for her professional guidance in preparing our demonstration cases.

I also extend my sincere thanks to Cardinal Daniel DiNardo, Bishop Curtis Guillory, Bishop Joseph A. Fiorenza, Bishop Joe Vasquez, Bishop Vincent Rizzotto, Monsignor Frank Rossi, Sister Maureen O'Connell, Christina Deajon, and the Diocesan Review Board in the Archdiocese of Galveston-Houston for their spiritual support and professional guidance. I also thank the experts and professionals in the field of child protection who have provided the research evidence and practice insight that make this book useful. This book shows the importance of interdisciplinary effort in improving our work in preventing and stopping child sexual abuse.

For children's sake, I remain.

Monit Cheung

Preface

Focusing on the recent development of forensic interviews and best-practices research, this book provides practical information for forensic interviews and court preparation as well as treatment suggestions for use in cases involving child sexual abuse. The legal and practice focus of this book and the materials provided are based on research conducted mainly in the United States. Legal mandates vary from country to country, but the materials found here can be used as a reference for other countries based on experiences in the United States with regard to the design of country-specific interviewing protocols and treatment programs. This text provides a comprehensive multidisciplinary guide applicable for the development of interview skills and treatment in work with sexually abused children, allegedly abused children, perpetrators and alleged perpetrators, and other professionals who handle child sexual abuse cases.

The book strongly encourages a team approach, with professionals working together to help child victims and perpetrators (alleged or confirmed) in the most effective ways. Teams may include parents, school personnel, church personnel, law enforcement officers, medical professionals, forensic interviewers, nonforensic interviewers, child welfare workers, child-care workers, child advocates, support persons, and legal prosecutors and defense attorneys. The term *child victim* is used herein to represent the alleged or confirmed victim in the case of child or the survivor of childhood sexual abuse. In other words, the client can be a child, an adolescent, or an adult. "Julie's Case," a case study, is used across the chapters to illustrate many of the elements involved in working with child abuse cases. In addition, each chapter provides helpful tips for parents and professionals in providing the best support possible for the victim or alleged victim.

From both the forensic view and the helping perspective, "skillful forensic interviews are important to ensure the protection of innocent individuals and the conviction of perpetrators" (Cronch, Viljoen, & Hansen, 2006, p. 195). The focus on forensic interviews is intended to promote a systematic approach to working with child victims and perpetrators (alleged or confirmed) at all stages of the disclosure process. A systematic approach is used to integrate research evidence into the forensic interview and treatment processes. This approach involves practical, step-by-step illustrations with case information intended to help professionals work with alleged victims and perpetrators involved in child sexual abuse investigations so that information can be gathered and treatment planned. It is important for professionals and interviewers to be familiar with standardized approaches in work with child victims and perpetrators to avoid any negative ramifications, such as unnecessary documentation errors, false allegations, or unsolved cases. Parents also learn not to take validation in their own hands but trust that professionals will handle the situation by asking appropriate questions to confirm or refute abuse.

With a focus on promoting child welfare, the specific purpose of this book is to offer suggestions for parents, school and medical personnel, church review-board members, and other professionals in the following areas:

- Evidence-based procedures to outline what parents, professionals, and interviewers should be looking for as signs of sexual abuse in children
- Knowledge regarding what questions parents and caretakers can ask alleged child victims and perpetrators before calling Child Protective Services and law enforcement
- Information regarding age-appropriate and developmentally sound questions in the validation and treatment processes
- Knowledge of what is needed to prepare for a formal forensic investigation, court hearings, and advocacy work
- A systematic way to intervene in the delicate lives of sexually abused children and adult survivors and to assist alleged perpetrators in the forensic process, to provide the most helpful services possible.

It is important for interviewers to remain neutral, sensitive, and flexible in their interviews with the alleged victims and alleged perpetrators. When working with children and adolescents, patience and genuine listening skills are needed as the alleged victims disclose, in their own way, their experiences. "Interviewers should maintain an attitude that additional information can be obtained from other sources, which will help the interviewer demonstrate patience and understanding, rather than leading the child to disclosure or false allegation" (Cheung, 2008, p. 142). However, interviewers should not be rigid when asking questions, because a protocol should not dictate how questions are to be asked; a protocol is simply a suggested way to structure an interview so that important validation and follow-up questions are not missed.

A client-focused interview is much more helpful than an authoritative questioning style, which can create fear and concern. The interviewers should use more open-ended than close-ended questions so that respondents can fully disclose important information from their experience and point of view. With a focus on the child victim's perspective, "Julie's Case," a composite case based on several real cases of child and adolescent incest victims, illustrates the major points presented in each chapter. Chapter 4 presents interviewing techniques with alleged perpetrators.

I hope that by using the information suggested in this book, along with adopting an evidence-based approach, readers will be more successful in their approaches to helping child victims describe abuses and overcome trauma by starting the process of recovery as early as possible. I hope that breaking the cycle of child sexual abuse will prevent the recurrence of abuse and the emergence of later abusive behaviors.

Introduction: Child Sexual Abuse as a Rising Concern

Child sexual abuse is a serious crime but has been a topic of public concern only in the past four decades. Before 1970, child sexual abuse was rarely reported. In the twenty-first century, more child sexual abuse cases have been reported; although, the report rate has declined from 232 per 100,000 children in 1992 to 114 per 100,000 children in 2001 (Keuhn, Vericker, & Capps, 2007; Terry & Tallon, 2004). Many studies have attempted to address the prevalence of child sexual abuse. Research indicates that the likely range of incidence of child sexual abuse is between 8 percent and 20 percent of the population (Terry & Tallon, 2004). According to *Child Maltreatment 2007*, of the 794,000 victims of child maltreatment in the United States in 2007, 7.6 percent were sexually abused (Children's Bureau, U.S. Department of Health and Human Services, 2009). Sexual abuse occurs more often among female victims, and the severity of victimization increases with age; as a result of this gender-based difference, interviewing female adolescents has been a focus of skill-based training (Finkelhor, Ormrod, & Turner, 2009). A study published in 1992 indicated that 24 percent of female children have been sexually abused before reaching the age of five (Boyer & Fine, 1992). The most recent statistics in the United States and Canada show that the prevalence rate of sexual abuse for male children before reaching age sixteen is 17 percent (Hopper, 2008). A meta-analysis of child sexual abuse identified a prevalence rate of 13 percent for male children and of 30–40 percent for female children (Bolen & Scannapieco, 1999). Terry and Tallon (2004) used the trend of reported cases to project future incident rates and reported child sexual abuse cases would continue to decline to less than 0.1 percent in the total child population in the United States. In contrast, professionals in the field estimate that there are increasing levels of unreported child sexual abuse although there is no evidence offered to support this concern. These two contradictory reports seem to indicate that there is a gap between the increasing number of child sexual abuse incidents and declining report rates, which is alarming to those who work in child welfare, especially when advocating resources for planning prevention and educational programs to combat this problem.

According to the American Academy of Child and Adolescent Psychiatry (2009), there are more than eighty thousand reports of child sexual abuse each year in the United States. Many other cases go unreported, as a result of fear and difficulties in obtaining legal validation. Statewide prevention programs have mostly focused on teaching children to say no, to be assertive, and to receive adequate sex education and learn preventive measures from parents and schools. Through these programs, children become responsible for being aware of their "sexuality" issues and knowing how to say no to sexual molestation or abuse; however, the emphasis on children's learning and personal responsibility means that adults are not the focus of this type of education. Adults must have the primary responsibility to say no to being abusive or codependent of sexual abuse because of fear and helplessness. The problem of child sexual abuse will continue if adults who abuse children do not know how to stop and if adults who know about the abuse do not take the role of stopping the abuse. It is important for everyone to recognize that "it's the responsibility of adults to protect children" (End Child Sexual Abuse Foundation, 2008, p. 5) and to stop child sexual abuse completely.

History of Child Protection

Using the history of child protection in the United States as an example, we can illustrate how child sexual abuse is included in the national policy agenda as a means to increase public awareness of child abuse and neglect issues (see appendix A).

In the United States, awareness and promotion of child welfare began with the citizens' role in protecting children from abuse and neglect. In the 1900s, child protection activities focused on combating poverty; these activities helped prevent neglect and decrease the high number of abandoned children. In 1935, America's Social Security Act became a landmark piece of legislation by providing abandoned mothers and their children with cash assistance. In 1968, C. Henry Kempe coined the term *battered child syndrome* to provide a formal framework for assessing evidence to prove the seriousness of the physical abuse of children.

The second stage of the history of child protection was the passage of child abuse prevention laws. Between 1963 and 1969, all fifty U.S. states passed child abuse legislation, with most having mandatory requirements for reporting suspected cases to authorities. The enactment of the federal Child Abuse Prevention and Treatment Act in 1974 (P.L. 93-247) provided a national "mandatory reporting law" that granted child welfare professionals authority to intervene when child abuse occurred in a family. The history and dynamics of the act reflected two significant issues: funding and intrusion into family privacy. The need for treatment and prevention was not a major reason for opposition. After the enactment of this law, three components were implemented with high visibility: a working definition of child abuse and neglect (including child sexual abuse), a multidisciplinary focus on intervention, and a set of service eligibility requirements for the states. In 1980, the Adoption Assistance and Child Welfare Act (P.L. 96-272) aimed to prevent system abuse or placement delays by means of the establishment of the reasonable-efforts law, which mandated permanency planning for maltreated children, including helping to reunite the family, so that a permanent placement could be finalized within a reasonable time frame.

The third and most recent stage of the history of child protection is related to child sexual abuse. Although child sexual abuse has always been included in the definition of child abuse, as a part of all child protection laws, it has only alarmed the public's concern since the enactment of the Protection of Children against Sexual Exploitation Act of 1977 (P.L. 95-225) (an expansion of the Mann Act of 1910) to protect children from forced prostitution. The legislative effort was to stop sex-slave trafficking rather than to protect children in their own home environments. Because the number of incest cases reported publicly in the United States during the early 1980s increased, the focus of public education shifted to intrafamilial child sexual abuse. Increasing concerns that children were being abused by known individuals (e.g., teachers, child-care workers, relatives, friends) also facilitated discussions on establishing a child sexual predator registry. The purpose of the registry was to notify the public of the where-abouts of former sexual offenders to prevent them from working with or approaching children and youths in schools, child-care centers, temples and churches, or homes of relatives. In 1990, the first predator registry law, the Community Protection Act, was passed in Washington State, authoriz-ing the release of information regarding former sexual predators to the community. Since then, all fifty states have issued similar legislation to pro-vide such registries. The U.S. Department of Justice and the Federal Bureau of Investigation maintain and update the National Sex Offender Public Registry Web site to help the public determine whether people such as job applicants are listed on the registries in any of the fifty states, the District of Columbia, Puerto Rico, and Guam (see http://www.nsopw.gov and http://www.fbi.gov/hq/cid/cac/registry.htm).

The public today is more aware of the seriousness of child sexual abuse and realizes that the care of a child cannot be entrusted to any indi-vidual on the basis of that individual's appearance. Knowing the character-istics of sexual predators and identifying the behavioral indicators of abused children are what parents need to be able to draw on when they sus-pect the abuse of their child. Denying the problem is not a solution. We must admit that the world is imperfect and protect the children of our future.

Prevention of Child Sexual Abuse

The history of child protection sheds light on the establishment of profes-sional organizations that focus on child sexual abuse issues. In the United States, the Centers for Disease Control and Prevention (CDC) has used a public health model to plan programs to prevent child sexual abuse (Baker, 2009). As with all of its family violence prevention activities, the CDC (2002) has developed evidence-based activities to disseminate effective programs to prevent child sexual abuse through its active Injury Research Agenda, as highlighted in seven main areas of priorities:

1. Evaluate strategies to disseminate science-based parenting inter-ventions.
2. Study risk and protective factors for perpetration (including sub-stance abuse and impacts of stressors).

3. Identify optimal times and settings for prevention.
4. Develop, evaluate, and disseminate interventions and methods to stop and prevent perpetration.
5. Identify and change societal norms that lead to child sexual abuse.
6. Document the health consequences of child sexual assault across the life span.
7. Increase community responses to prevent child sexual abuse.

These priorities have provided incentives to many organizations to plan and implement programs and activities to combat child sexual abuse. The most impressive development is the establishment of children's advocacy centers (CACs) in the United States. The CACs provide interdisciplinary services to help children and their families prevent and/or end child abuse. Funded by the Office of Juvenile Justice and Delinquency Prevention, four regional CACs have been established to coordinate with state and local CACs, which work directly with children's protective services and other professional entities to help abused children and their families. Their function is to coordinate efforts to work with CAC members in assigned states to connect people to appropriate services (see appendix B).

According to the National Children's Alliance (2011), regional CACs provide child-focused information, consultation, training, and technical assistance to facilitate and support coordination among agencies to maximize child protection. Regional CACs also provide support to strengthen the functions of local CACs. Specifically, regional CACs assist their regional and local communities in the following areas:

- Assessing their community's capacity to provide services
- Developing a comprehensive, multidisciplinary response to child abuse, particularly the CAC model
- Developing and negotiating interagency agreements and protocols
- Maintaining open communication and case coordination among community professionals and agencies involved in child protection efforts
- Enhancing professional skills among interdisciplinary partners
- Coordinating and providing training to the disciplines represented on the multidisciplinary team
- Identifying and developing funding and marketing strategies

- Strengthening the organizational capacity of CACs and child abuse programs
- Assisting with plans for program expansion
- Increasing community understanding of child abuse

Regional CACs have set up Web sites that point to specific CACs in their localities (e.g., city, county, state) so that people who need services and professionals who coordinate child protection activities can find CACs in their neighborhood. Many nonprofit organizations and CACs join in working with governmental entities that are assigned to help abused children. Their tasks include interviewing children; helping families work through the judicial system; assisting child victims and their families in locating culturally appropriate services in trauma treatment; and connecting children and families with professionals who work closely with the church, school, police, Child Protective Services, and other entities so that they can receive answers to their inquiries. The primary functions of CACs are to support child victims and their families through professional interviews and interdisciplinary connections.

Organization of This Book

This book has eight chapters, each focusing on a specific topic related to the process of working with child victims in child sexual abuse cases. Chapter 1 describes the first step of fact-finding. The chapter provides background information and research support to describe the functions, processes, and principles of conducting forensic interviews. The chapter includes a summary of evidence-based research to help parents and professionals learn about the dynamics of child sexual abuse that may affect the information-gathering process when a child is suspected of having been sexually abused. Chapter 1 also includes a list of the dos and don'ts when asking questions of an alleged victim so that no false assumptions will be made in the process of validating the suspected abuse. Chapter 2 approaches the problem by outlining a systematic way to learn the facts. The chapter stresses the importance of using a free-narrative approach when in interviews. Chapter 3 provides detailed screening strategies to make sure that children can differentiate between telling the truth and lying. The chapter presents data to support how false positives and false negatives can affect case outcomes. Chapter 4 describes the best approaches in forensic interviews with alleged victims, childhood victims, and alleged perpetrators. The research-based techniques of interviewing two types of alleged victims (disclosure and nondisclosure cases) are further described to accompany the illustrations on the accompanying DVD. In addition, based on recent research evidence, suggestions to modify the transcripts of these two cases are included for practice to improve interviewing skills. Chapter 5 moves into the judicial area and identifies how to prepare child victims and their support persons before court appearances. Chapter 6 describes research-based treatment modalities that have proved helpful in situations in which abuse was substantiated and when it was unfounded. Chapter 7 is a collection of self-care discussions and suggested methods for professionals to deal with secondary trauma resulting from exposure to the sensitive details of child sexual abuse cases. Chapter 8 provides an example of advocacy work in child sexual abuse prevention and draws a conclusion about how people can work together to eliminate child sexual abuse. The chapter also discusses the roles and responsibilities of professionals. Overall, this book aims to be a resource guide for teaching, training, and educational programs that improve the child welfare system so that it can be better equipped to deal with the child sexual abuse crisis.

APPENDIX A

Child Abuse Prevention and Treatment: A Legislative History in the United States

The following are legislative actions that have directly led to, expanded from, or amended the Child Abuse Prevention and Treatment Act of 1974:

- The Social Security Act of 1935 (P.L. 74-271) enacts Title IV for child welfare services.
- The Social Security Amendments of 1962 extends and improves public assistance and child welfare services provided by the Social Security Act.
- The Social Security Amendments of 1969 (P.L. 91-172) adds funds for child protection programs and requires children's protective services statewide under Title IV-B.
- The Child Abuse Prevention and Treatment Act of 1974 (P.L. 93-247) establishes the National Center on Child Abuse and Neglect in the Department of Health, Education, and Welfare; creates funds for a demonstration program that enhances the identification, prevention, and treatment of abuse and neglect; publishes and disseminates research; and creates a task force to aid small communities (subsequent amendments: P.L. 93-644; 95-266; 98-457; 98-473; 99-401; 100-117; 100-294; 101-126; 101-226; 101-645; 102-295; 102-586; 103-171; 103-252; 104-235; 106-177).
- The Protection of Children against Sexual Exploitation Act of 1977 (P.L. 95-225) authorizes the prosecution of both producers

and distributors of child pornography and amends the Mann Act (1910).

- Child Abuse Prevention and Treatment and Adoption Reform Act of 1978 (also known as the Adoption Opportunity Act, P.L. 95-266) expands the definition of child abuse and neglect to include exploitation.
- The Adoption Assistance and Child Welfare Act of 1980 (P.L. 96-272) amended Title IV-B (child welfare services) of the Social Security Act with an emphasis on prevention of child removal and on promotion of family reunification (subsequent amendments: P.L. 96-611; 98-118; 98-617; 99-272; 100-203; 105-89; 106-169; 108-145; 109-113).
- The Child Abuse Prevention and Treatment and Adoption Reform Act of 1981 increases state grants and appropriations for National Center for Child Abuse and Neglect for increased research and demonstration projects, and reviews adoption standards of special needs and minority children (see also P.L. 98-118 and P.L. 102-295, Title IV).
- The Child Abuse Prevention and Treatment and Adoption Reform Amendments of 1983 (P.L. 98-118) increase grants for states for abuse prevention programs and creates the Department of Health and Human Services Advisory Committee.
- The Child Abuse Amendments of 1984 (P.L. 98-457) extends provisions to address child abuse problems in the family; provides additional funds to the National Clearinghouse on Child Abuse and Neglect for medical, nutritional, and social services to infants with life-threatening congenital impairments; and reviews adoption standards for children with special needs (see also P.L. 102-295, Title III).
- The Children's Justice and Assistance Act of 1986 (P.L. 99-401) amends the Child Abuse Prevention and Treatment Act to establish a program to encourage states to enact child protection reforms that are designed to prevent further trauma during administrative and judicial proceedings, and establishes demonstration programs of temporary child care for handicapped

children and crisis nurseries (see also P.L. 101-127 and P.L. 102-295).

- The Child Abuse Victims Rights Act of 1986 (P.L. 99-500 and 99-591) addresses the long-term impact of child abuse and addresses the problem of courtroom assessment of children.
- The Child Sexual Abuse and Pornography Act of 1986 (P.L. 99-682) clarifies the definition of sexual abuse to help in the prosecution of sexual offenders.
- The Child Abuse and Neglect Assistance State Eligibility Requirements Waiver (P.L. 100-117) assists states that are making substantial progress toward compliance with federal requirements.
- The Child Abuse Prevention and Treatment Act Reauthorization of 1988 (P.L. 100-294) reauthorizes appropriations through 1991 for programs aimed at child abuse and neglect prevention; it also establishes the Presidential Commission on Child and Youth Deaths and provides funds for trainings on family violence to local law enforcement agencies.
- The Child Abuse Prevention, Adoption, and Family Services Act of 1988 (P.L.100-294) extends all provisions of P.L. 95-266 (which dealt with adoption issues) and P.L. 98-457 (which was the Family Violence Act) through fiscal year 1991.
- Indian Land Conveyances, Forest Management, Child Abuse Prevention, and Health Care Programs of 1990 (P.L. 101-63) revises reporting laws and helps begin establishing prevention and treatment programs specifically for Native American children.
- The Drug and Alcohol Abuse, Treatment and Prevention Improvement Act of 1990 (P.L. 101-645) improves and expands drug and alcohol abuse prevention programs and social services for drug-abusing parents and their children.
- The Drug Free Schools and Community Act of 1989 (P.L. 101-93) provides funds for the development of drug abuse education and prevention programs in elementary and secondary schools.
- The Steward B. McKinney Homeless Assistance Amendments Act of 1990 (P.L. 101-645) provides funds for health care, child abuse projects, treatment, and education programs for homeless children.

Children's Advocacy Centers in the United States: Accessing Local CACs through National, Regional, and Statewide Support

National CAC	Mission	Function	Web site
National Children's Alliance	Serves as a membership organization providing services to CACs, multidisciplinary teams, and professionals across the country.	Four regional CAC coordinators are identified so that an accredited CAC can be located in a specific region.	http://www.national childrensalliance.org

Regional CAC	Mission	Function	Web site
Midwest Regional Children's Advocacy Center	Assists new communities with program start-up and strengthens prospective and existing centers by supporting their passage through developmental stages. The goal of the intervention is to ensure coordinated, nontraumatizing services to children and their families who are victims of abuse and neglect.	Regional site for 12 states: IL, IN, IA, KS, MI, MN, MO, NE, ND, OH, SD, WI	http://www .MRCAC.org

Regional CAC	Mission	Function	Web site
National Children's Advocacy Center	Models and promotes excellence in child abuse response and prevention.	Regional site for 16 Southern sites and D.C.: AL, AR, DE, FL, GA, KY, LA, MD, MS, NC, OK, SC, TN, TX, VA, WV	http://www.national cac.org/
Northeast Regional Children's Advocacy Center	Strengthens CACs and multidisciplinary teams by promoting and improving a multidisciplinary community response to child abuse.	Regional site for 9 states: CT, MA, ME, NH, NJ, NY, PA, RI, VT	http://www.nrcac .com/
Western Regional Children's Advocacy Center	Strengthens existing CACs and helps communities develop such centers through training and technical assistance in 13 western states.	Regional site for 13 states: AL, AR, CA, CO, HI, ID, MT, NE, NM, OR, UT, WA, WY	http://www.western regionalcac.org

CHAPTER 1

Forensic Interviews in Child Sexual Abuse

This chapter identifies the essential steps in child sexual abuse investigations and assessments. The chapter also provides information from evidence-based research to describe the use of a process approach in forensic interviews. A case ("Julie's Case") is provided (in this chapter and subsequent chapters) to illustrate how to identify major steps involved in forensic interviewers' work with an alleged victim of child sexual abuse. The word *alleged* is used to describe the victim on the basis of the legal procedure of the forensic interview, which is used to find evidence to support or disprove the abuse allegation.

As a first step in child maltreatment investigations, a forensic interview is conducted to validate the complaint (see appendix 1A). In most U.S. cities and counties, the forensic interview of a sexual abuse investigation usually takes place at a children's advocacy center or in a Child Protective Services (CPS) office operated by the state, county, or city government. In other jurisdictions, such as the United Kingdom and Hong Kong, a special homelike location managed by the police force or the governmental Child Protection Unit is used for interviews. This setup is designed to help complainants feel at ease when disclosing their traumatic experiences.

Most recently, through the establishment of review boards, all Catholic dioceses and some other Christian churches have created a committee responsible for the interviewing of priests or spiritual leaders alleged to have committed abuse and childhood sexual abuse victims. This has provided an opportunity for the church to review sexual abuse cases that happened before the expiration of the statute of limitations (SOL). Review boards function to set up and continuously examine policies that safeguard children, to recommend actions to protect children from further harm, and to fulfill the church's responsibility to investigate sexual abuse complaints. Based on recent laws and statutes in the United States, appendix 1B provides a summary of SOLs by state for comparison purposes so that practitioners can determine whether a childhood sexual abuse case can or cannot be presented as a court case under the limit of the law. Practitioners should consult with legal professionals to verify the most recent changes in state law.

Legal Commitments

Since the United States enacted the Child Abuse Prevention and Treatment Act (CAPTA) in 1974 (see the introduction) to implement a national mandatory reporting system for child protection, child welfare workers have continuously encountered overwhelmingly high child abuse and neglect caseloads. Since 1992, the National Child Abuse and Neglect Data System (NCANDS) has reported annual statistics of child abuse and neglect cases from all states and has found that the number of reported cases has increased by 31 percent from 2.66 million in 1997 to 3.48 million in 2006 (Child Welfare League of America, 2009), whereas substantiated cases have decreased from 776,298 in 1997 to 761,692 in 2006 (an almost 2 percent decrease). The U.S. Department of Health and Human Services (DHHS, 2008a) has indicated that 8.8 percent of all the reported abuse cases in 2006 were child sexual abuse cases. Even though increasing government responsibility means that more resources must be allocated to establish child protection laws, the protection of children is achieved only when the laws are enforced.

Section 111 of the Child Abuse Prevention and Treatment Act (1974) mandates standard (or minimum) definitions for child abuse and neglect, including sexual abuse; each state must adhere to these definitions when implementing its reporting system and services. According to U.S. federal law, child abuse or neglect is any recent act or failure to act that results in imminent risk of serious harm, death, serious physical or emotional harm, sexual abuse, or exploitation of a child (usually a person under the age of 18, but a younger age may be specified in cases not involving sexual abuse) by a parent or caretaker who is responsible for the child's welfare.

Specifically, section 111 of the act defines child sexual abuse as

(A) Employment, use, persuasion, inducement, enticement, or coercion of any child to engage in, or assist any other person to engage in, any sexually explicit conduct or any simulation of such conduct for the purpose of producing any visual depiction of such conduct; or
(B) Rape, and in cases of caretaker or inter-familial relationships, statutory rape, molestation, prostitution, or other form of sexual exploitation of children, or incest with children.

By law, it is the responsibility of professionals to report suspected and substantiated child abuse and neglect to authorities. According to the U.S. DHHS (2008b), "All States, the District of Columbia, the Commonwealth of Puerto Rico, and the U.S. territories of American Samoa, Guam, the Northern Mariana Islands, and the Virgin Islands have statutes identifying persons who are required to report child maltreatment under specific circumstances" (p. 1). It is common across all fifty states that the "mandatory reporters" include professionals such as the following:

- Child-care providers
- Law enforcement officers
- Medical examiners and/or coroners
- Mental health professionals
- Physicians and other health-care workers
- Social workers
- Teachers and other school personnel

Also, in eighteen states and Puerto Rico, all adult residents (or "any person") are designated as mandatory reporters, and sixteen of those states also specify a list of professionals who must report. With respect to other types of mandatory reporters, the DHHS further states:

- Some other professions frequently mandated across the States include commercial film or photograph processors (in 11 States, Guam, and Puerto Rico), substance abuse counselors (in 13 States), and probation or parole officers (in 15 States).

- Six States (Alaska, Arizona, Arkansas, Connecticut, Illinois, and South Dakota) include domestic violence workers on the list of mandated reporters.
- Court-appointed special advocates are mandatory reporters in seven States (Arkansas, California, Maine, Montana, Oregon, Virginia, and Wisconsin).
- Members of the clergy are now required to report in 26 States. (p. 2)

According to Smith (2007), anyone who reports suspected child abuse in "good faith" is granted immunity from prosecution (p. 1). However, false allegations or reports without a reasonable basis are subject to civil or criminal liability. Although confidentiality privileges are provided to mandatory reporters, some states offer clergy an exemption if they are told abuse information in the context of a sacred communication or confession, except when they are serving a role outside of their clergy duties, for example, as a health or mental health practitioner. This expectation of mandatory reporting raises a concern for pastoral counselors who simultaneously serve as priest in listening to confession and counselor in providing counseling support at the same time. It is unclear how priests can maintain confidentiality privileges in their multiple roles (Smith, 2007).

For detailed mandatory requirements by state, visit the Child Welfare Information Gateway (CWIG, 2011) Web site (www.childwelfare.gov, search by state under "State Statutes Search") funded by the DHHS (2009). Appendix 1C is from the report *Clergy as Mandatory Reporters of Child Abuse and Neglect* (CWIG, 2011), and summarizes the clergy privileges granted or denied in the case of suspected child abuse and neglect. As cautioned in the report, readers should always verify the statutory content to confirm and update information pertaining to laws that are specific to a state of interest.

Principles Guiding Forensic Interviews

Regardless of the mandatory status, many professionals are responsible for interviewing a child victim in the case of child sexual abuse. Interviews are considered forensic when their purpose is to obtain information for legal and documentation purposes. Because child sexual abuse is a criminal act, it is important to conduct the forensic interview carefully so that information can be accurately gathered for use in legal proceedings.

According to the National Children's Advocacy Center (2009), "a forensic interview is a structured conversation with a child that is designed to elicit accurate accounts of events" (n.p.). The goal of a forensic interview is to obtain statements from the involved individuals in an objective, developmentally sensitive, and legally defensible manner (Davies & Cole, 1996). In child sexual abuse cases, because the purpose of the forensic interview is "to elicit as complete and accurate a report from the alleged victim as possible" (American Professional Society on the Abuse of Children, 2002, p. 2), a set of guiding principles has been proposed in research and practice with the aim of helping professionals assess the information provided and validate whether the child (or adolescent or adult survivor) has been sexually abused. Although the focus of the interview is on the child's account, other involved individuals may be interviewed to obtain additional information to substantiate or disprove the case. It is expected that the forensic interview is legally sound, conducted without subjective judgments from the interviewer, free of leading questions, recorded sensitively with detailed documentation, and a means to provide information to the professionals involved.

Principle 1: Legally Sound

Because sexual abuse of a child is a criminal act, an interview that collects the child's statements must be legally sound; that is, during the process the interviewer can ask only questions that aim to validate abuse and can prepare documentation for use in court or other hearings, such as church childhood abuse hearings. In child sexual abuse investigations, the forensic interview is a means of collecting evidence directly from those who are involved, including the alleged child victim, the alleged perpetrator, the witnesses (if any), the child's family members, and the person who received the child's first complaint, each of whom is interviewed separately. In these cases, the child sexual abuse victim is the focus of attention because the child is often the only person who can provide a firsthand account of the incident.

Principle 2: Without Judgments

In *Forensic Interview Structure*, the National Children's Advocacy Center (2002) suggests that the interviewer must act as a fact finder by maintaining neutrality and applying a hypotheses-testing approach to gather information throughout an interview. Maintaining neutrality means that in the conversations:

- No hints or suggestions are given to mislead the child to say something to please the interviewer or to say what the interviewer wants to hear.
- No assumptions are made in terms of who did what and how; no judgment, negative or positive, is made of the accused.
- No gestures or use of body language that may convey a message of disbelief, taking sides, impatience, or running out of time are used.
- No discussion of consequences should occur, either regarding removal of the child or the accused from home or regarding sentencing or legal actions.

Rapport building is important, but interviewers should not treat the interview in a casual way, which could leave a child with a false understanding that he or she is playing with the interviewer or pretending that something has happened.

Principle 3: No Leading Questions

Many research studies support the use of open-ended questions to elicit descriptions of abuse, rather than the premature use of too many specific questions, which may lead a child to fabricate stories (Sternberg, Lamb, Davies, & Westcott, 2001). A well-planned interview protocol must focus on using open-ended questions to obtain a first-person account from the alleged victim and must not use leading questions in the interview process (Cheung, 2008; Orbach et al., 2000; Vieth, 2008). To avoid leading questions, specific questioning techniques (when, where, who, what, and how) should be used only after a child discloses sexual abuse.

Principle 4: Recorded with Documentation

Documentation is necessary during the process of obtaining information. Video-recorded interviews are highly recommended so that verbal, behavioral, and affective responses can be documented. The validation of child sexual abuse requires evidence from three areas: behavior, content, and affect (Cheung, 1997; Stevenson, Leung, & Cheung, 1992). With a video-recorded interview, interviewers can concentrate on a child's responses and be actively engaged in the interview because they are not forced to record the details. With the alleged victim's detailed descriptions of the situation (or further elaborations on motive), clear documentation can withstand judicial scrutiny.

Principle 5: Working in Collaboration with Other Professionals

As previously advocated, a team approach is critical in handling child sexual abuse cases because a child victim will likely provide information for various professionals in the disclosure process and while testifying in court. The slogan "Working together and trusting each other for the welfare of the child" has been used in multidisciplinary joint-training programs so that professionals from various disciplines can achieve a mutual understanding of one another's roles in cases (Cheung, 1997, p. 274). Interdisciplinary collaboration is essential to helping child victims without further traumatizing them with repeated interviews.

Rationale for Using Forensic Interview Protocol

Research has demonstrated that a four-stage process approach is effective in gathering data in a way that alleviates complainants' fear and the awkwardness of disclosure; instead, the complainants are more likely to provide information based on facts without feeling forced or pushed into immediate disclosure of abuse. After providing information through an interview, the complainant is required to testify through legal channels to prove the allegation. Whether the allegations are true or false, all parties involved must receive intensive counseling after the interviewing process is completed.

It is important not to confuse forensic interviewing with facilitated communication (FC). Facilitated communication is a process in which individuals with communication difficulties, such as those common to autism, are assisted physically, mentally, and emotionally by a facilitator (usually with the aid of a computer) to increase their ability to express thoughts and feelings. Since the 1990s there have been major controversies over the use of FC in legal proceedings. Literature has shown that the validity of FC has not been empirically supported (Dayan & Minnes, 1995; Eberlin, McConnachie, Ibel, & Volpe, 1993; Mesibov, 1995; Minnes, 1993; Prior & Cummins, 1992) and that the facilitator, who is perceived to be in control of the process, becomes the source of resulting messages (Bligh & Kupperman, 1993; Howlin & Jones, 1996; Konstantareas & Gravelle, 1998; Levine, Shane, & Wharton, 1994; Mostert, 2010; Routh, 1994; Shane, 1993; Smith, Haas, & Belcher, 1994). In forensic interviews in cases of child sexual abuse, the interviewer's role is to gather facts, not to lead the child in a particular direction of thinking; in other words, the communications with the child should not be coached or facilitated and must be connected to the facts based on the child's direct view and experience. In general, research has shown that facilitated communication as an interview strategy is not recommended for the purpose of precise communication (Mostert, 2001; Wheeler, Jacobson, Paglieri, & Schwartz, 1993) and is therefore not appropriate for use in legal proceedings or forensic interviews with nonexpressive individuals, including in allegations of child sexual abuse (Gorman, 1999; Myers, 1994; Siegel, 1995). Cheung (1997) affirmed that, in forensic interviewing, no leading questions should be asked and recommended that skilled questions with a focus on the children's five senses (feeling/touching, seeing, hearing, tasting, and smelling) can assist nonexpressive children to talk about past experiences based on their own view, rather than what someone else wants to hear.

The purpose of forensic interviewing is to obtain accurate information (National Children's Advocacy Center, 2009); thus, the interviewer should use a blank-screen or hypotheses-testing approach along with a structured approach so as to maintain objectivity throughout the conversation without feeling compelled to use questions based on option-posing prompts (Sternberg et al., 2001). A blank-screen approach requires that the interviewer make no assumptions or judgments before and during the interview. For example, in a child sexual abuse investigative interview, if the interviewer senses the child's reluctance to disclose, the interviewer may say, "Tell me what's been bothering you or your family." The hypotheses-testing approach is used after the child has disclosed sexual abuse, when the interviewer may ask, "Has anyone asked you to tell or not tell what you just told me?"

Although objectivity is a requirement in forensic interviews, many interviewers find it difficult not to experience emotions when listening to details of sexual activities and the descriptions of sexual abuse. However, any reaction from the interviewer, whether disapproving of the sexual abuse, wanting to support the child, or blaming the perpetrator, may jeopardize the trustworthiness of a child's statements, because a child may seek to distort reality in an attempt to "please the audience." As a result, research has demonstrated that training is essential so that interviewers are adequately prepared to control their emotions during interviews (Cheung & Boutté-Queen, 2000). The main purpose of professional training in forensic interviews is to increase or maintain the integrity of the interviews, to provide support to those interviewers who may feel uncomfortable about listening to sexual abuse details, and to identify evidence-based techniques that have proved effective in working with children.

Accountability

Researchers agree that the forensic interview process must be handled carefully to ensure that further trauma does not occur. It is extremely important that the questioning process be conducted properly and that the interviewer asks only valid questions. The relationship the interviewer builds with an allegedly abused child through rapport can be a significant factor in helping the child provide truthful answers (Hershkowitz & Terner, 2007; Perona, Bottoms, & Sorenson, 2006; Westcott & Kynan, 2006). An allegedly abused child can easily give false answers if certain specific questions are asked or not asked. Research shows that open-ended questions are the most effective in validating a child's account; it is important for the interviewer to keep this in mind to prevent steering the child toward closed-ended questions and away from open-ended ones (Cronch, Viljoen, & Hansen, 2006; Hershkowitz, 2002; Hershkowitz & Terner, 2007; Lamb & Fauchier, 2001). Hershkowitz (2002) found that "facilitators are not necessarily open-ended in nature and are likely to function as opposing or suggestive questions when they follow responses to such questions" (p. 63). According to Cheung (2008), "Interviewers should maintain an attitude that additional information can be obtained from other sources, which will help the interviewer demonstrate patience and understanding, rather than leading the child to disclosure of false allegation" (p. 137). Hershkowitz and Terner (2007) found that if rapport building is incorporated into the interview process, then more than one interview can be done with the client, in which case the interviewer can receive additional information, beyond that obtained from the first interview, without false information resulting. Although there are still debates about how many interviews are appropriate, there is common agreement among professionals that repeated interviews, without the intent to obtain additional information, should not be allowed (National Children's Advocacy Center, 2009). Research on the impact of repeated interviews is addressed in chapter 2.

Research Evidence

Many research projects have supported the use of a systematic approach to gather information about a child or a childhood sexual abuse allegation. Faller (1993) has outlined a comprehensive model of risk assessment and the interviewing process and has identified major issues in assessment and intervention. Recently, more research has focused on the interviewing process and has suggested additional directions for enhancing the accuracy of information gathering in forensic interviews. Appendix 1D provides a summary for professionals and parents of strategies for interviewing an alleged child victim; it is based on techniques with research support.

Cronch et al. (2006) examined the current techniques used in forensic interviews with child sexual abuse victims and provided new directions for research and practice. They found six major techniques to be useful in interviewing:

1. *Blank-screen approach*: Disclosure rates increased when the interviewer had no information about the allegations.
2. *Narrative approach*: Using an open-ended approach to ask the child victim about what happened is the least leading way to get information. Open-ended questions elicit longer, more detailed, and more accurate responses and are less likely to elicit contradic-

tions in children's statements. With younger children, immediate follow-up questions to clarify a cue (e.g., "How did he touch you?") are not as effective as using cued invitations (e.g., "You mentioned that he touched you. Tell me more about that.").

3. *Cognitive validation*: A process approach to interview helps a child use the mental reconstruction of the event so that the child can recall the detail (regardless of perceived importance) from his or her own memory of the sequences and perspectives.

4. *Truth-lie ritual*: The American Professional Society on the Abuse of Children (2002) recommends that interviewers use concrete examples during truth-lie discussions. It is useful to obtain a verbal agreement from the child to tell the truth throughout the interview and to stress the moral consequences of lying. It is also important not to use the interviewer or the child as the subject when providing examples of lying (e.g., instead of saying, "If I told you that X, am I telling the truth or a lie?" it would be best to say, "If someone told you that X, is that person telling the truth or a lie?").

5. *Touch survey*: The touch survey includes a discussion of various touches the child has experienced (e.g., hugging, kissing, hitting, sexual touches), feelings associated with the touches, locations on the body where the child received the touches, and who touched the child. In nondisclosure cases, the touch survey seems to be helpful as an educational and preventive tool.

6. *Use of interviewing aids*: It is important that the interviewer use tools and aids only to clarify unclear information from the child's disclosure, not to solicit undisclosed information. Research indicates that anatomically detailed dolls should be avoided with preschool children, because of the suggestibility and lack of self-representational skills in this age group. Other tools to show anatomy are to be used only to clarify the abuse, position, and/or specific action of the sexual activity, as well as the terminology of sexual parts that a child mentions.

Cronch et al. (2006) identified three models for interviewing that may be useful for practitioners. The first model is the use of structured interviews, a systematic process recommended in the literature. Their function is to

identify the most effective way to interview child victims so that information can be used to validate the account of the child. Research-based protocols include the National Institute of Child Health and Human Development's (NICHD) structured interview protocol (Lamb, Orbach,
Hershkowitz, Esplin, & Horowitz, 2007; Lamb et al., 2009); the Structured
Interview of Symptoms Associated with Sexual Abuse (SASA; Wells,
McCann, Adams, Voris, & Dahl, 1997); and other suggestions posted on the
Web sites of the American Academy of Child and Adolescent Psychiatry,
the American Medical Association, the American Professional Society on
the Abuse of Children, and the American Psychological Association. Common stages used in these protocols include rapport, open-ended narrative
approaches, specific questioning techniques, and closure. In a study about
research-based protocols, Nichols (2009) reported that "the assessment of
a child's knowledge, understanding the importance of 'truth and lie' is
essential to a valid interview" (p. 187).

The second model is extended forensic evaluation, which was developed by Connie Carnes at the National Children's Advocacy Center (2009)
in Huntsville, Alabama, to address the problem of children who do not disclose abuse during the first interview but whose cases include other indicators that abuse has occurred. Goals of the extended forensic evaluation are
to allow the child to disclose over time in a nonthreatening environment,
to determine whether abuse has occurred and by whom, and to gather
information to assist in legal and treatment decision making. As a result of
these findings, the recommended length of the forensic evaluation is six
sessions, including one session with the nonoffending caregiver and five
weekly, fifty-minute sessions with the practitioner and child. Several concerns with this model have been noted. Extending the interview process
over several sessions could potentially pose a risk to the child's safety.
Another concern is related to the risks of repeated interviewing. Research
has shown that repeated interviewing can lead to distortions in reporting,
higher rates of self-contradictions, and increases in children's levels of distress. Before a case is substantiated, clinical and forensic roles of the practitioners must be separated (on potential consequences of repeated interviews, see chapter 2).

The third model is the child-advocacy-center model, which is applied
in a centralized, multidisciplinary child advocacy center to provide a safe,

neutral, child-friendly facility for assessment and treatment. Many cities and counties in the United States are using the child advocacy center model to conduct forensic interviews by trained interviewers, in collaboration with medical examiners, mental health practitioners, victim support advocates, and CPS caseworkers.

Many researchers have cautioned that, regardless of the model of interviewing used, an adult interviewer's questions can easily contaminate a child's statement. The use of a protocol is an important step for all interviews because it can be explained as a standard procedure used in all interviews. Specific questioning techniques are divided into four areas: (1) rapport-building skills; (2) competency testing; (3) obtaining the details of abuse; and (4) closing the interview (Faller, 1996; Lamb et al., 2009). Data show that the interviewer must pay attention to the following advanced skills during the course of the entire interview:

- *Rapport*: When the child has concerns about the process, the interviewer must address those concerns in a child-focused manner.
- *Truth-lie*: When providing examples to differentiate telling the truth and lying (i.e., truth-lie ritual), the interviewer must use another individual (e.g., "someone"), not the child or the interviewer, in the examples.
- *Slang clarification*: Although the interviewer may understand the meaning of slang terms that the child expresses, it is important to tell the child the purpose of clarifying further.
- *Consequences*: In the truth-lie ritual, the interviewer must also determine whether the child understands the consequence of lying.
- *Nonlinearity of the interview stages*: When a child begins to withdraw and/or become silent without disclosing abuse, it is suggested that the interviewer move to the questioning stage of the interview to explore the child's reluctance and concern. Once a child begins to feel comfortable speaking and becomes open to narrating the occurrence of events, the interviewer can return to stage 1 or 2—the child's free narrative—and move with ease between stages (particularly stages 2 and 3) on the basis of the child's level of participation and comfort.

- *Sequence of questions*: The interviewer uses the who, when, and where questions to help the child talk and to reduce embarrassment, anxiety, fear, and further negative feelings that the child may associate with the use of other questions.
- *Nondisclosure*: If a child does not disclose abuse, the interviewer may provide information about body protection. If a child discloses abuse, the interviewer may return to the free-narrative stage.
- *Motivation of disclosure*: As the interview draws to a close, the interviewer may ask the child, "Has anybody told you to say what you just shared with me?" and follow that with validation questions, such as "What did that person tell you?" Such questions clarify that the information is from the child's own experience rather than from prompting.

Regardless of which model is adopted, an introduction of the role of the interviewer and encouragement to the child to talk about factual information is important, as it will also ease the anxiety of the child who can then provide answers based on facts, not to please the interviewer or to repeat a statement from another individual. Techniques to validate follow in a case example ("Julie's Case") to identify major techniques used. Julie's case is a composite case based on many real-life cases used in all chapters in this book to demonstrate the interviewing process.

Julie's Case: The Helping Process

Case: Julie X, fourteen-year-old female

Intake Information

Stephanie Y and Julie X were classmates. Stephanie reported to their homeroom teacher that Julie was pregnant. When the teacher saw Julie privately, Julie tried to explain that she had been absent and couldn't hand in her homework because she was emotionally distressed at home. Upon asking her about the distress, the teacher found that Julie was not very comfortable about telling her about the "stuff" that was happening at home. The teacher referred Julie to the school social worker, who encouraged Julie to talk about her health situation, which prompted Julie to talk about her suspicion of being pregnant.

Julie was a petite adolescent (five feet tall and about ninety pounds) whose affect showed that she might be depressed. She lived with both parents and did not have any siblings living at home. Her eighteen-year-old sister had been a runaway drug addict and was currently staying at a rehabilitation home for girls under probation. Julie said that her stepdad was an alcoholic, and when he got drunk, he would do "weird things." Julie stated that she might be pregnant because she missed her period the previous two months. A possible reason for her pregnancy might be related to her stepdad's weirdness. When asked more specifically about the "weird" things her stepdad did to her, she disclosed that she was doing her stepdad a favor because he and her mom had intimacy problems. Julie said she had been touched sexually since she was ten years old but that recently the touching had become "more sexual." She reported that her stepdad had stopped doing "it" last month, but Julie had been afraid to tell anyone about it.

Referral to CPS

This case was referred to Child Protective Services (CPS), which sent an interviewer to Julie's school to do an investigation. During the investigative interview, Julie's mother, who cried hysterically at the school office while signing the consent form, agreed to a videotaped session. The mother denied having intimacy problems with her husband, stating that it was all in the daughter's head. The mother also mentioned that Julie had not come home in the previous month because she had moved to a friend's apartment after she had said that they had to study for their final examinations. The mother wondered whether her daughter's report of being sexually abused might have been a cover-up for her pregnancy by her boyfriend. She had been dating for a while and had showed a bad attitude toward her stepdad at all times.

Findings

Julie was taken to the county's child advocacy center to be interviewed by a forensic interviewer. During the videotaped forensic interview, Julie disclosed detailed descriptions of sexual activities like touching, mutual masturbation, sexual intercourse, and dry intercourse (genitals rubbing outside the body). She mentioned that the abuse took place at home many times and provided detailed information about the most recent and the earliest incidents. Julie was immediately removed from home and placed in a foster home assigned to her. Her family couldn't see her for the first week during the investigation process. The mother and the stepdad (the alleged perpetrator) were separately interviewed.

Two days later, before the investigator could arrange an interview with Julie's sister, Julie left the foster home without notifying the foster parents. When the CPS worker located her through her best friend in school, Julie stated that she wanted to spend the rest of her life with her boyfriend and recanted her sexual abuse story. She said she was lying and just wanted to end this "weird thing" altogether. However, CPS continued the investigation, fearing that the recantation might be a way for Julie to escape from pressure from her family.

Two days after Julie's recantation, her sister, Wanda, was interviewed at the girls' home. She was shocked to find out that Julie had been sexually abused by their stepdad; her stepdad had promised her that he would not do anything to Julie. She admitted that she had been sexually abused by her stepdad since she was about twelve years old and had an abortion at the age of sixteen. She warned her stepdad not to do anything to Julie or she would tell the police about it. She started abusing cocaine at the age of sixteen.

Skills Demonstrated

This is a typical intrafamilial sexual abuse case that illustrates the dynamics of child sexual abuse, from disclosure to recantation. Interview principles are clearly demonstrated through a comprehensive interview that included, in an appropriate order, interviewing the alleged child victim, removal of the victim while additional investigative interviews were being conducted, interviewing the first point of contact (the teacher and the school social worker), interviewing the nonoffending parent, interviewing the alleged perpetrator, and then interviewing the sibling (if any). Nonetheless, many intrafamilial cases end in recantation. Additional discussions in chapters 2–7 address the various issues involved in this case.

Conclusion

Child sexual abuse remains a pervasive issue in the United States. Together, mandatory reporters and other adults must collaborate and employ the principles of forensic investigation to obtain the most accurate investigative findings in child sexual abuse cases. Evidence-based practice and case studies illustrate the importance of using the blank-screen approach, the narrative approach, cognitive validation, the truth-lie ritual, and the touch survey. Throughout the process of forensic investigation, adult parties must demonstrate accountability to obtain accurate information for the investigative process. With validated information, the alleged victim's healing process can begin as early as possible.

Tips for Professionals and Parents: Interviewing the Alleged Victim

Tips for Professionals

Tip No. 1: Preparing to Interview an Alleged Victim

- Know the basic information before the interview.
  - Intake information on the allegation
  - Former record of accusation(s) from the alleged victim
  - Any prior knowledge of the alleged victim (e.g., personality, psychiatric problem, learning or communication difficulties)
- Meet with the interdisciplinary team to identify specific questions to include in the interview.
- Know the dos and don'ts when asking questions.
- Set ground rules.
  - If more than one interviewer, determine who will invite questions.
  - Do not judge.
  - Do not promise anything you don't know.
  - Set time limit for the interview (depending on the age of the interviewee).
  - Determine support person rules if a support person is present.
- Ensure that the environment is comfortable.
- Be familiar with an interview protocol for the process.

Tip No. 2: Dos and Don'ts in Forensic Interviews

Dos

- Take control of the process.
- Be clear about the report and separate what is in the report from what are you gathering.
- Clarify terms in the alleged report.
- Clarify and analyze the observed facts and statements.
- Address the client's emotion when it blocks the interviewing process.
- Show concern for emotional responses.
- Be nonpunitive and nonjudgmental.
- Be honest.
- Be a listener.
- Use a free-narrative approach to begin the interview (e.g., "Tell me what happened to you").
- Use who, when, where, what, and how questions to clarify.
- Use the client's information to ask further questions.

Don'ts

- Ask leading questions.
- Lose sight of your role and the purpose of the interview.
- Use words that may convey blame or judgments (either positive or negative).
- Take sides.
- Use statements that can reflect false reassurance (e.g., "Everything will be all right").
- Break silence prematurely.
- Use technical terms (e.g., dry intercourse, pedophile).
- Show approval or disapproval of what you hear.
- Ask why questions with an accusing tone.
- Defend the alleged perpetrator.
- Make assumptions or jump to conclusions.

Tips for Parents

Tip No. 1: Handling Your Child's Emotion

- Don't panic; stay calm when hearing about the accusation (e.g., take a few deep breaths, drink a glass of cold water).
- Ask the child to tell you who did it, or to repeat who did it (so you can identify the perpetrator before furthering other questions).
- Ensure that the child is telling the truth: "This is a serious matter. Promise me that you are telling the truth, OK?"
- Provide time for the child to tell you about this "complaint" (repeat the child's word for the event): "Now tell me what happened."
- When your child has told you about what happened, make sure to ask the four *W* questions:
  - *Who*: the full name of the perpetrator (don't make assumptions)
  - *Where*: the location of the (recent or most remembered) abuse to focus on
  - *When*: the date and time of the (recent) abuse
  - *What*: the specific act of the abuse (e.g., if the child said "He touched me there," ask, "Where did he touch you?" "What did he touch you with?" and "Did he do anything else?")
- Call Child Protective Services (or related services if CPS is not available in your area).
- Don't call the perpetrator to verify the child's account (for your own and your child's safety, and to not give the perpetrator a chance to pressure the child). Let the professionals do their job.

APPENDIX 1B

U.S. Statutes of Limitations, by State

State	Statute of limitations	Law
Alabama	• No special SOL. • Suspension of limitation due to disability under § 6-2-8, which applies to individuals younger than 19 and those diagnosed with serious mental illnesses. • Individual has 3 years after termination of a disability or reaching age of majority to initiate action, which must transpire within 20 years of original incident.	Ala. Code § 6-2-8 (2006)
Alaska	• No SOL for felony sexual abuse of a minor or unlawful exploitation of a minor. • Individual must bring action for misdemeanor sexual abuse of a minor, incest, or felony indecent exposure within 3 years. • Individual has two years after reaching the age of majority to initiate action for misdemeanor sexual abuse of minor	Alaska §§ 09.10.065 (2007); 09.10.140(a) (2001); 09.10.140(b) (2001)
Arizona	• No special SOL for child sexual abuse. • Victim younger than age of majority or who has a serious mental disability has 2 years after reaching age of majority or termination of disability to bring action.	Ariz. Stat. §§ 12-542 (1992); 12-502 (1997)
Arkansas	• Suits must be filed within 3 years of attaining full age (21) or 3 years of the discovery of childhood sexual abuse.	Ark. Code Ann. §§16-56-130 (2010); 16-56-116 (2010)
California	• Victims must initiate action within 8 years of reaching age of majority or 3 years from the realization that they have experienced psychological damage due to childhood sexual abuse.	Ca. Civ. Proc. Code § 340.1 (1990)

State	Statute of limitations	Law
Colorado	• Victims must file claims within 6 years of reaching age of majority, 6 years of the realization of abuse or psychological damage caused by childhood sexual abuse, or 6 years of the termination of the disability. • After the victim is 15 years older than age of majority, claims filed for damages may be awarded only for medical and counseling costs.	Added by Laws 1990, H.B. 90-1085, § 1, eff. April 16, 1990; amended by Laws 1993, H.B. 93-1259, § 1, eff. July 1, 1993. Colo. Rev. Stat. §13-80-103.7 (2002)
Connecticut	• No common law provision exists for discovery of sexual abuse. • A victim must file a suit within 30 years of reaching age of majority (18).	Conn. Gen. Stat. § 52-577d (2002)
Delaware	• New legislation repealed SOL for civil suits relating to childhood sexual abuse so that there is no statute of limitations. • Individuals who had been victims of childhood sexual abuse and were not able to bring a suit under former legislation have 2 years to file claims from July 1, 2007.	Del. Code 10, § 8145 (2007)
D.C.	• A victim must bring action within 3 years of the original incident or 3 years of reaching age of majority.	D.C. Code §§ 12-302(a)(1) (1995), 12-301 (1995)
Florida	• SOL does not apply retroactively; came into effect April 8, 1992. • Victim must bring action for alleged abuse or incest within 7 years of reaching age of majority, 4 years after injured party leaves dependency of the abuse, or 4 years of the discovery of the injury.	Fla. Code § 95.11(7) (1992)
Georgia	• Victim must bring civil action within 5 years of reaching age of majority; came into effect on July 1, 1992. • Special provisions for individuals with disabilities.	Ga. Code Ann. § 9-3-33.1 (2007)
Hawaii	• No special SOL exists. • General limitations period for injuries to persons exists; victim must file claims within 2 years of reaching the age of majority or discovery of the injury. • Disability must have been in existence at the time of the original incident.	Haw. Rev. Stat. §§ 657-7 (1993), 657-13 (1995), 657-14 (2009)

State	Statute of limitations	Law
Idaho	• This legislation does not apply retroactively; came into effect July 1, 1989. • Suit must be filed within 5 years of the victim reaching age of majority or 5 years after the victim's discovery of the abuse and the impact the injury caused to the victim.	Idaho Code §§ 6-1704 (2005), 6-1705 (1989)
Illinois	• Action must be brought within 10 years of age of majority or 5 years of the victim's discovery of the childhood sexual abuse and the psychological injury caused from abuse.	735 I.L.C.S. § 5/13-202.2(b)-(d) (2006)
Indiana	• Claims must be filed within 2 years of the original incident, 2 years of reaching age of majority, or 2 years of the termination of a disability.	Ind. Code §§ 34-11-2-4 (1998), 34-11-6-1 (1998), 1-1-4-5 (2002)
Iowa	• For victims older than age of majority, claims must be filed within 4 years of the discovery of abuse and injury and the causal relationship between the injury and the abuse. • Claims against counselors, therapists, or school employees must be filed within 5 years of the last date of treatment by the counselor or therapist or the last day of enrollment at the school. • Claims must be filed within 1 year of reaching the age of majority or 1 year of the termination of a disability.	Iowa Code §§ 614.8 (2009), 614.1 (2008)
Kansas	• This legislation is retroactive. • Claims must be filed within 3 years of reaching age of majority or 3 years of the discovery of the childhood sexual abuse and/or the psychological injury caused from the abuse.	Kan. Stat. Ann. § 60-523 (1992)
Kentucky	• Claims must be filed within 5 years of reaching age of majority, 5 years of the victim's discovery of the childhood sexual abuse, or 5 years of the last act of abuse.	Ky. Rev. Stat. Ann. § 413.249 (1998)
Louisiana	• Claims must be filed within 10 years of reaching age of majority or 1 year of the victim's discovery of the childhood sexual abuse.	La. Rev. Stat. Ann. § 9:2800.9 (2008)

State	Statute of limitations	Law
Maine	• There is no SOL. • This legislation does not apply retroactively.	Me. Rev. Stat. Ann. tit. 14 § 752-C (2008)
Maryland	• This legislation does not apply retroactively; came into effect October 1, 2003. • Victims must file claims within 7 years of reaching age of majority.	Md. Code Ann., Cts. & Jud. Proc. § 5-117 (2008)
Massachusetts	• Victims must file claims within 3 years of the original incident, 3 years of reaching age of majority, or 3 years from the time of discovery of and injury and the causal relationship between the injury and the abuse.	Mass. Gen. Laws ch. 260, § 4c (2008)
Michigan	• No special statutes or rules exist. • General personal injury statute governs claims for childhood sexual abuse. • Claims must be filed within 2 years of original incident, 1 year of reaching age of majority, or 1 year of the termination of a disability.	Mich. Comp. Laws §§ 600.5805(2) (2011), 600.5851 (2006)
Minnesota	• Claims must be filed within 6 years of reaching the age of majority or 6 years of time of discovery of causal relationship between the injury and childhood sexual abuse.	Minn. Stat. Ann. § 541.073 (2008)
Mississippi	• Claims must be filed within 3 years of the original incident, 3 years of reaching age of majority, and 3 years of victim's release from imprisonment.	Miss. Code Ann. §§ 15-1-49 (2008), 15-1-57 (2003), 15-1-59 (1995)
Missouri	• Claims must be filed before victim reaches age 31 or within 3 years of the time of discovery of causal relationship between the injury and childhood sexual abuse. • This legislation is not retroactive; it came into effect on August 28, 2004.	Mo. Rev. Stat. § 537.046 (2009)
Montana	• Claims must be filed within 3 years of original incident, 3 years of reaching the age of majority, or 3 years of the discovery of causal relationship between the injury and childhood sexual abuse.	Mont. Code Ann. §§ 27-2-216 (2007), 27-2-401 (2001)

State	Statute of limitations	Law
Nebraska	• No special SOL exists. • Victims must file claims within 4 years of original incident or 4 years after reaching age 20.	Neb. Rev. Stat. §§ 25-207 (2008), 25-213 (1995)
Nevada	• Victims must file claims within 10 years of reaching age of majority or 10 years of discovery that injury was caused by childhood sexual abuse.	Nev. Rev. Stat. Ann. § 11.215 (2008)
New Hampshire	• Victims must file claims within 12 years of reaching age of majority or 3 years of the time of discovery of causal relationship between the injury and childhood sexual abuse.	N.H. Rev. Stat. Ann. §§ 508:4-g (2005), 632-A et seq. (2009), 639.2 (2009)
New Jersey	• Victims must file claims within 2 years of time of discovery that injury was caused by the childhood sexual abuse.	N.J. Stat. Ann. § 2A:61B-1 (1998)
New Mexico	• Victims must file claims before age 24 or within 3 years of the discovery of causal relationship between the injury and childhood sexual abuse.	N.M. Stat. Ann. § 37-1-30 (1995)
New York	• This legislation does not apply retroactively; came into effect June 23, 2006. • Victims must file claims within 5 years of the original incident or 5 years of reaching age of majority.	N.Y. C.P.L.R. § 213-c (2010)
North Carolina	• Claims must be filed within 3 years of the original incident, 3 years of reaching age of majority, 3 years of the removal of the incompetency, or 10 years of the time of discovery of causal relationship between the injury and childhood sexual abuse.	N.C. Gen. Stat. Ann. §§ 1-52 (5) (1996), 1-52(16) (1996), 1-17(a)(1) (1996)
North Dakota	• Victims must file claims within 2 years of the original incident, 1 year of reaching age of majority, or 2 years of the time of the victim's discovery of the original incident.	N.D. Cent. Code §§ 28-01-18 (1991), 28-01-25 (1991)
Ohio	• Victims must file claims within 12 years of reaching age of majority. • If the defendant concealed facts about the abuse, the claim must be filed within 12 years of the victim's discovery of the facts.	Ohio Rev. Code Ann. § 2305.111(C) (2009)

State	Statute of limitations	Law
Oklahoma	• Claims must be filed within 2 years of the last act of abuse, 2 years of reaching age of majority, or 2 years of the time of discovery of causal relationship between the injury and childhood sexual abuse. • If the abuser is incarcerated, the victim must file a claim within 5 years of the abuser's release. • If the abuser is incarcerated, the victim may file claims at any time during the incarceration within 20 years of the victim reaching the age of majority.	Okla. Stat. Ann. 12, § 95(6) (2008)
Oregon	• Claims must be filed within 6 years of reaching age of majority or 3 years of the time of discovery of the causal relationship between the injury and childhood sexual abuse.	Or. Rev. Stat. Ann. § 12.117(1) (2008)
Pennsylvania	• Claims must be filed within 12 years of reaching age of majority.	42 Pa. Cons. Stat. Ann. § 5533(b)(2) (2008)
Rhode Island	• Claims must be filed within 7 years of the incident of child sexual abuse or 7 years of the time of discovery of causal relationship between the injury and childhood sexual abuse.	R.I. Gen. Laws § 9-1-51 (2008)
South Carolina	• Victims must file claims within 6 years of reaching age 21 or 3 years of the time of discovery of causal relationship between the injury and childhood sexual abuse.	S.C. Code § 15-3-555(A) (2008)
South Dakota	• Claims must be filed within 3 years of the act or 3 years of the time of discovery of causal relationship between the injury and childhood sexual abuse.	S.D. Codified Laws Ann. § 26-10-25 (2008)
Tennessee	• No special SOL exists. • Victims must file claims within 1 year of the original incident, 1 year of reaching the age of majority, or 1 year of the time of discovery of causal relationship between the injury and the childhood sexual abuse.	Tenn. Code §§ 28-3-104 (2008), 28-1-106 (2008)

State	Statute of limitations	Law
Texas	• Claims must be filed within 5 years of the act or 5 years of reaching age of majority. • Texas Supreme Court applies case-by-case discovery rule for cases in which individuals may have had delayed realization of abuse and its attendant injuries.	Tex. Civ. Prac. & Rem. Code §§ 16.0045 (2008), 16.001 (2008)
Utah	• Victims must file action within 4 years of reaching age of majority or 4 years of the time of discovery of causal relationship between the injury and childhood sexual abuse.	Utah Code Ann. 1953 § 78B-2-308(2) (2008)
Vermont	• Victims must file action within 6 years of the act, 6 years of reaching age of majority, 6 years of the discharge of a disability, or 6 years of the time of discovery of causal relationship between the injury and child-hood sexual abuse.	Vt. Stat. Ann. tit. 12, §§ 522(a) (2003), 560 (1994), 551 (1997)
Virginia	• Victims must file action within 2 years of the act, 2 years of reaching age of majority, 2 years of the discharge of a disability, or 2 years of the time of discovery of causal relationship between the injury and the childhood sexual abuse.	Va. Code §§ 8.01-243 (2003), 8.01-229 (2003), 8.01-249
Washington	• Claims must be filed within 3 years of the act, 3 years of reaching age of majority, or 3 years of the time of discovery of causal relationship between the injury and child-hood sexual abuse.	Wash. Rev. Code Ann. § 4.16.340 (1995)
West Virginia	• No special SOL exists. • Claims must be filed within 2 years of reaching age of majority or 2 years of act. • To file after the SOL has expired, victims must demonstrate they were prevented from knowing of the claim at the time of the injury due to concealment, inability to comprehend the injury, or extreme hardship.	W. Va. Code § 55-2-15 (2011)
Wisconsin	• Claims must be filed before the victim reaches age 35.	Wis. Stat. Ann. § 893.587 (2005)

State	Statute of limitations	Law
Wyoming	• Claims must be filed within 8 years of reaching age of majority or 3 years of time of discovery of causal relationship between the injury and childhood sexual abuse.	Wyo. Stat. §1-3-105(b) (1999)

APPENDIX 1C

Clergy as Mandatory Reporters of Child Abuse and Neglect: Summary of State Laws

	Privilege granted but limited to pastoral communications	Privilege denied in cases of suspected child abuse or neglect	Privilege not addressed in the reporting laws
Clergy enumerated as mandated reporters	AL, AZ, AK, CA, CO, IL, LA, MA, MS, MO, MN, MI, NV, NM, ND, OH, OR, PA, SC, VT, WI	NH, WV	CT, MS
Clergy not enumerated as mandated reporters but may be included with "any person" designation	DE, FL, ID, KY, MD, UT, WY	NC, OK, RI, TX	IN, NE, NJ, TN, PR
Neither clergy nor "any person" enumerated as mandated reporters	VA, WA	Not applicable	AS, DC, GA, GU, HI, IA, KS, MP, NY, SD, VI

Source: CWIG (2010).

Note: All abbreviations listed are standard postal abbreviations. AS = American Samoa, GU = Guam, MP = Northern Mariana Islands, PR = Puerto Rico, and VI = U.S. Virgin Islands.

Selected Research Evidence, 2001–2010: Forensic Interviews in Child Sexual Abuse

A. Based on literature review

Author	Background	Recommended interview process and considerations
Colangelo, 2007	Based on controversy over recovered memories of childhood sexual abuse since 1990	• Avoid memory retrieval techniques that have been shown to foster the creation of false memories. • Discuss legal ramifications of specific memory retrieval strategies with the client. • Avoid interpreting behavioral symptoms alone as an indication of sexual abuse without other supporting documentation. • Verify the veracity of any recovered or recalled memory whenever possible, provided it is the desire of the client to do so. • Educate clients as to the pitfalls of memory work. • Avoid recommending clients to confront perpetrators or family members. Clinicians must be conscious of two concerns: • Relentlessly pursuing the recovery of abuse memories may do more harm than good, as it creates a greater possibility of the formation of false memories and forces clients to deal with affect that they may already feel unable to handle.

Author	Background	Recommended interview process and considerations
		• It is helpful to work with clients on how to deal with the inner images and feelings they may be experiencing, not necessarily with what historically may or may not have happened to them.
Cronch, Viljoen, & Hansen, 2006	Based on literature review of factors influencing disclosure during interviews and techniques used in forensic interviews, including allegation blind interviews, open-ended questions, cognitive interviewing, truth-lie discussions, touch survey, and anatomically detailed dolls	• Use a wide variety of definitions for various types of interviewer utterances. • Address the child's developmental tasks. • Examine issues specific to adolescents in relation to forensic interviewing. • Examine other variables (e.g., absence of self-contradictions, number of details elicited, length of child responses) to determine the effectiveness of various ones.
Faller, Cordisco-Steele, & Nelson-Gardell, 2010	A description of the state of knowledge about extended forensic assessments that provides a critical review of literature that describes two models and presents descriptive survey findings	• Problematic cases can be resolved approximately two-thirds of the time using extended assessments. • Substantial and substantive abuse-related disclosure information can be obtained in more than a single interview. • Children who are young, have certain cognitive and physical limitations, and are cultural minorities may benefit most from extended forensic evaluations. • A challenge to implementing extended interview mechanisms is cost. • Further research is needed to clearly articulate sequencing and techniques in extended assessments.
Fontes & Plummer, 2010	Because of the vast array of cultural differences represented by clients, understanding and developing ways to conduct forensic interviews with respect to cultural influences is of utmost importance.	• Individual professionals should endeavor for proactive learning about cultures, their dynamics, and the role of the family. • Professionals must be aware of expectations, biases, agency policies, countertransference, and interventions as they are informed by culture and affect culturally diverse clients in different ways. • Culture is a factor in all cases in which children are considering disclosure, not solely when minority status is noticeable.

Author	Background	Recommended interview process and considerations
		• Cultural learning is an ongoing process that requires the interviewer to remain flexible and aware of its ever-changing dynamics.
Kuehnle & Connell, 2010	The importance of defining and maintaining professional roles during the investigative process is vital to reducing harm to children who have made allegations of sexual abuse.	• A neutral therapeutic environment may be most useful in working with children who have unknown abuse status; first responders should not assume that abuse-specific therapy is an appropriate intervention for an alleged victim. • Victims of child sexual abuse may perceive investigative therapists as untrustworthy because many victims have been taught to distrust figures of authority and other professionals. • Family members may benefit from therapeutic support during the investigative process.
Perona, Bottoms, & Sorenson, 2006	Study based on the experience of authors, criminal prosecution, psychologists, and social workers and researchers.	

B. Based on evidence-based research

Author	Subjects	Procedure	Findings
DeVoe & Faller, 2002	• 47 girls and 29 boys, age 5–10 years. Possible sexual abuse age between 5 and 10 years. • Children come from a project in public child welfare agencies with concerns about possible sexual abuse.	• Standard procedure in the study was to interview each child twice. • Because of the experimental nature of the first interview, a second interview was conducted to ensure that clinical issues were not compromised because of the research design.	Findings suggest the following: • Individual children require unique approaches as a function of their histories, developmental capacities, abuse allegation characteristics, and current circumstances. • Interview procedures that include a flexible interview protocol are warranted.

Author	Subjects	Procedure	Findings
		• Nine categories of interviewer behavior and child response were coded: (1) type of question the interviewer asked, (2) child's response, (3) type of disclosure, (4) how the child presented the information, (5) type of sexual behavior, (6) identity of victim, (7) identity of alleged offender, (8) details of sexual abuse, and (9) context of sexual abuse.	• CPS workers and others who are charged with investigating child sexual abuse allegations must be supported in their work with specialized and ongoing training and consultation in the dynamics of sexual abuse and disclosure. • Most preferred are open-ended questions: general, focused, repeat and/or clarify, empathic response. • Closed-ended questions that cannot be used are leading and coercive or persuasive.
Faller & Nelson-Gardell, 2010	98 females and 39 males comprised the sample from 22 professionals at 18 agencies.	The Disclosure Credibility checklist was used to determine whether cases should be referred for extended evaluations of either 4 or 8 interviews.	• Cases assigned to the four-interview protocol were less likely to be classified as "credible disclosure." • Variables that predicted likelihood of sexual abuse included older victim age, caretaker belief in allegation, and the eight-session protocol. • By the sixth session, 95% of new disclosures had occurred.
Hershkowitz, 2002	• 50 forensic interviews with alleged victims of child sexual abuse. The sample included 40 girls and 10 boys, age 4–13 • All alleged perpetrators were not family members.	The procedure followed the National Institute of Child Health and Human Development (NICHD) investigative protocol. Interviewer's utterances were classified into five categories—(1) invitation, (2) facilitator, (3) directive, (4) option posing, and (5) suggestive—and the number of words and details provided in each child's responses were tabulated.	Findings suggest the following: • Facilitators are not necessarily open-ended in nature and are likely to function as option-posing or suggestive questions when they follow responses to such questions. • Facilitators in the fifth part of the substantive phase and facilitators following responses to open-ended invitations were most effective.

Author	Subjects	Procedure	Findings
Hershkowitz & Terner, 2007	40 alleged victims of sexual abuse, by an extrafamilial suspect, age 6–13 years.	NICHD investigative protocol is used: rapport-building phase, transitional phase, free-recall phase • The children were reinterviewed after a short break. • The second interview started with a free-recall substantive phase.	Studies indicated the following: • Repeated open-ended interviews are not necessarily harmful and may have advantages. The information obtained in the second interview was almost 25% new. • Older children repeated more information than younger ones. • The data suggest that a repeated forensic interview may elicit new information.
Hlavka, Olinger, & Lashley, 2010	10 female forensic interviewers and 500 written questionnaires that were synopses of videotaped forensic interviews; the 500 questionnaires were completed for interviews with 500 children (age 2–17)	• The CornerHouse RATAC semistructured forensic interview protocol was used, which included the use of drawings and/or anatomical diagrams based on the child's developmental level. • 24 Teach a Bodies anatomical dolls were available but were not introduced to the child unless he or she verbally disclosed sexual abuse. • After the interview (only when sexual abuse was disclosed), the interviewer completed a questionnaire. • Interviewers were instructed to provide a written rationale when dolls were not used, and primary prompts were provided when dolls were used.	• Although dolls were often introduced for more than one function, clarification was reported to be most frequently followed by communication, consistency, distancing, and "other." • Clarification was used more frequently (77%) when the victim was female, Caucasian, and school aged, and when the case involved penetration by an alleged intrafamilial offender. • Interviewers also introduced dolls for purposes of consistency with female and male children.

Author	Subjects	Procedure	Findings
		• The outcome measure, interviewer perceived value, was used to identify which of the five functions were useful in relation to the dolls: clarification, consistency, distancing, communication, or other.	
Korkman, Santtila, Drzewiecki, & Sandnabba, 2008	Interviews with 29 girls and 14 boys, age 3–8, were included in the study.	• The first 30 substantial utterances from the interviews were transcribed as pairs (question and answer); thus, 1290 pairs were coded. • The pairs were coded on the basis of utterance level (linguistic complexity, concepts of touch and time, informativeness of responses, interrater reliability) and interview level (topic and topic changes).	• Multiple questions with language including long and complex sentences were often used with unclear references to persons and situations before allowing the child's answer. • All of the above were associated with fewer child-given details. • Interviewers often introduced the topic of abuse in unclear ways that could be characterized as leading, and fluctuation between on- and off-topic discussions fuels further concerns. • Further research about conducting age-appropriate forensic interviews is needed to translate research to practice.
Krahenbuhl, Blades, & Westcott, 2010	Children (ages 4–11) who made allegations of abuse.	95 police transcripts were examined for repetition of questions.	25% of all questions were indicative of question repetition, which led to changes in 75% of children's responses in forensic interviews; thus, the implications are weighty.

Author	Subjects	Procedure	Findings
Lamb & Fauchier, 2001	• 2 boys and 5 girls (age 66–107 months) in a day-care center are included in the study. • The average time between the first and last interviews was 5 months.	Interviewer utterance types and details were defined and coded as in Lamb et al. (1996). All interviews were video-taped and profession-ally transcribed.	Results showed the following: • Open-ended prompts are the most desirable and directive questions are supe-rior to option-posing prompts with respect to the accuracy of the information elicited. • This study strongly supports the professional consensus that interviews should be conducted using as many open-ended and as few focused prompts as possible.
Patterson & Pipe, 2009	66 interviews with 24 children (age 3–6) were examined.	• Each child was inter-viewed 2–4 times, and questions were categorized in terms of topic, openness, and degree of inter-viewer input. • Children's responses were coded for amount of informa-tion and type of response (on task or off task).	• Children respond to most questions, regardless of type or topic. • Failure to respond to a question was generally related to abuse-specific rather than non-abuse-related questions. • More than a single investiga-tive interview may be re-quired, and best-practice guidelines should be developed.
Sayfan, Mitchell, Goodman, Eisen, & Qin, 2008	47 males and 77 females age 3–16 who disclosed some form of abuse or neglect during a forensic interview were studied.	The 124 videotaped forensic interviews were coded for emo-tional displays, global adaptive functioning, children's trauma-related symptoms, and abuse type and fre-quency.	• During disclosure, most children displayed neutral emotion. • Indices of psychopathology were linked to stronger negative reactions. • The quantity of abuse experiences was inversely related to negative emo-tional displays. • Maltreated children may not evince strong emotions.

Author	Subjects	Procedure	Findings
Westcott & Kynan, 2006	• 70 interview transcripts from a previous study of questioning practice by 12 police forces (Sternberg et al., 2001) were used. • 51 females and 19 males, age 7–12.	Each transcript was coded for several features relating to the four areas of interest to the research: • The presence of the four memorandum phases • Components of the rapport phase • Ground rules discussed in rapport • Components of closure	Findings suggest that interviewers find it difficult to maintain and implement the knowledge and skills they should have acquired during training.

CHAPTER 2

Assessing Child Sexual Abuse

This chapter identifies research findings that contribute to the development of effective skills and techniques useful in performing initial interviews and/or assessments. It also provides guidelines for working with alleged child victims in a nondisclosure situation when the initial reporter is not the child victim; in other words, when the child who does not initiate the report or disclose having been sexually abused may deny the abuse. It is important that the investigator ask appropriate questions, without using any leading questions, to gather factual information during the interview process. Discussions based on "Julie's Case" (see chapter 1) address assessment difficulties.

Various issues associated with child sexual abuse disclosure have been discussed in the literature, including the correlation between decision making and the child victim's disclosure (Wharff, 1998), gender differences in disclosure (Spataro, Moss, & Wells, 2001), factors influencing disclosure (Alaggia & Kirshenbaum, 2005; Paine & Hansen, 2002), facial expressions in nondisclosing sexual abuse survivors (Bonanno et al., 2002), interviewer utterances (Korkman, Santtila, & Sandnabba, 2006), and question strategies used in disclosure cases (DeVoe & Faller, 2002). However, the literature has seldom addressed interviewing skills for nondisclosure cases. This chapter provides information based on the author's experiences and findings from research regarding both disclosure and nondisclosure situations.

Disclosure Cases

At initial disclosure, whether there is an outcry for help or a suspicious case of abuse, a report must contain information that describes whether the sexual abuse has occurred and the name of the known (or alleged) perpetrator. Because more than 80 percent of sexual abusers are known to the child victim, the dynamics of the relationship between the victim and the perpetrator may interfere with the child's willingness to report. On the basis of Faller's (1993) assessment model, the dynamics of child sexual abuse and the characteristics of the offender must be observed and evaluated. At intake, the investigator must consider the developmental level of the child victim and the risks associated with the child's age, number of siblings and reported victims, number of alleged offenders, the alleged offender's reaction, the relationship between the accused and the child, the type of abuse, and the child's family functioning. These factors can increase risk or create a protective shield for the child, depending on how helpful the family is in the process of disclosure (Faller, 2002, 2006).

Because multiple abuses may occur in any child abuse situation, the general risk assessment form may be used to assess the child's safety (see appendixes 2A–2C; appendix 2D provides a summary of risk assessment factors for the initial assessment of child sexual abuse). It is essential to develop a good rapport with the child victim and the family to achieve maximum protection.

Dynamics of Child Sexual Abuse

If a stranger sexually molests a child, a child's fear of not reporting is often mainly related to the child's feeling of having done something wrong or of having disobeyed parents' advice of not talking to strangers. When parents notice the child's sudden change in behavior, their concern about the well-being of their child will decrease the child's fear and guilt, which will then encourage the child to report the incident.

In intrafamilial sexual abuse situations, or in cases when the child knows the abuser, the child victim may not disclose the abuse until a later time. This delayed disclosure is mainly due to relationship dynamics. Secrecy, coercion, and progression of abuse can delay the effect and confuse the child's desire for affection from the abuser.

Child victims who suffer a love-hate relationship with their abuser often do not step forward to seek help. In many cases, children abused by a parent may have shared the secret with the nonoffending parent but do not receive the parent's trust and support; thus, they give up hope. Fear, love-hate conflict, mistrust, and feelings of powerlessness and hopelessness are the most common feelings that block children from reporting abuse. When they suspect child sexual abuse, professionals must understand the dynamics of child sexual abuse as the first step in making an accurate assessment. Many factors from each time period of disclosure—before, during, and after—can complicate the dynamics of the victim-perpetrator relationship.

Before Disclosure

Although the perpetrator may demonstrate a desire to feel important, powerful, dominant, authoritarian, knowledgeable, admired, and wanted, the child victim may feel a need to find a logical explanation for the sexual engagement, progression of abuse, and secrecy of intimate activities. Usually the child victim is not willing to continue involvement and does not feel safe being alone with the perpetrator, but the child keeps the abusive relationship a secret because of rewards, threats, and/or lies from the abuser; thinking it is a family matter; having too-low self-esteem to step forward; and wanting to protect others in the family. These grooming factors that contribute to the child victim's unwillingness to disclose include the following:

- *Rewards*: Feeling good from temptations; initially enjoying the pleasurable sexual stimulation; feeling good about the relationship; feeling like the "favorite" child, which enhances self-esteem; feeling important to another person in a special grown-up fashion; receiving a monetary reward
- *Threats*: Experiencing physical violence and psychological trauma (e.g., avoiding being beaten or physically violated); believing that disclosure will anger the nonoffending parent, other family members, or the known perpetrator; feeling that disclosure will cause family separation; believing that the abuse was caused by the child; thinking that the abuser will harm someone else (e.g., a younger sibling); believing that the abuser will self-harm

- *Lies*: Believing that the abuse is not abuse (e.g., the child's own fault, a secret passage to adulthood, a religious ritual, a punishment as a result of the child's mistake)
- *Family matter*: Not wanting to upset the family; agreeing with the abuser that it is a family issue that should not be publicly disclosed; feeling confused about how to disclose and to whom
- *Low self-esteem*: Not knowing what to do; thinking no one will believe a child over a trusted adult; denying the problem; feeling hopeless; developing an internal defense (or mental disorder) to dissociate oneself from the abuse
- *Protective of others*: Wanting to protect the nonoffending parent and/or siblings

Disclosure

Disclosure can take many forms and routes. In many incidents, intrafamilial abuse (or abuse by a known adult) is not easily discovered because the child victim does not report as a result of personal safety issues and the reasons previously stated. In some child abuse situations, because the child is too scared of the abuser or too young to know what abuse is, disclosure may take years. In general, disclosure can be accidental or purposeful.

Accidental disclosure. Reasons for accidental disclosure may include observation by a third party, physical injury to the child, sexually transmitted disease in the pediatric age group, pregnancy, precocious sexual activities initiated by the child, sudden change in behavior, and fearful response to staying alone with the abuser. Other forms of relationship problems may cause these activities or events, but these behavioral indicators provide a clue to further the investigation.

Purposeful disclosure. In incidents when the abuser is a known adult, sexual abuse is disclosed when the child cannot tolerate the abuse, has an opportunity to talk to a trusted person about the abuse, is pregnant, or knows that having a sexual relationship with an adult is a problem. Because sexual abuse is traumatic, many psychological and traumatic symptoms may surface: expressing emotional extremes (e.g., fear, guilt, excitement), feeling distressed from keeping a secret for too long, trying to escape (e.g., running away from home), or looking for a magical solution to the problem. In this stage, the child victim has reached the point of thinking, "I must tell, or I will die." The assessment must address the motive and purpose of the report, especially when the child has already been acting out or has had sexual relationships with others.

After Disclosure

The psychological effects of the disclosure on the victim are hard to measure. After disclosure, the child feels like he or she is in a state of chaos, with high anxiety, hostility, and fear. Depending on whether the child has a support person, the child may withdraw from reality. The perpetrator may further threaten the victim to recant. The victim may try to seek help from a trusted person but may not want to see or talk with the perpetrator or other family members.

Family reactions to disclosure. It is common that the perpetrator, who will face criminal charges, is extremely afraid of losing social status and employability. As a result, he or she will deny the problem, show hostility toward the child and the family, want to gain full control of the situation, try to persuade the entire family of the negative consequences of the child not recanting, and blame everything on the child. Siblings typically react defensively, fear disruption of family life, fear the unknown and possible separation, and feel torn between siding with the perpetrator or with the victim.

The nonoffending parent often has reactions ranging from disbelief (denial) to covering up the problem by lying to the child about personally protecting the child and accepting the complaint because of prior knowledge of the abuse. Specifically, the characteristics of mothers in father-daughter incest cases include the following:

- Denial of the incest, possibly because of her own incestuous experience, passivity or dependency, and/or fear of abandonment
- Depression, with poor self-image and a deep sense of personal inadequacy (as a mother, wife, and woman)
- Feelings of tiredness and being worn out

- Emotional immaturity and display of childlike behaviors
- Aversion to sex and sexual rejection of her husband
- Role reversal with the daughter
- Blaming of the child and holding the child responsible
- Feelings of being weak and powerless
- A strained relationship with her children

Suppression stage. The child's immediate and extended families may react by suppressing publicity, denying information, or refusing intervention. Sometimes this suppression extends to denial of the significant disturbances that the child victim suffers as a result of the sexual abuse to discourage further intervention by outsiders. Based on experiences handling cases of child sexual abuse, the author found forty-two reasons for child victims' recantation (table 2.1). These reasons are consistent with the findings Marx (1996) has reported, which can be broadly categorized into ten reasons for recantation:

1. Lack of family support
2. Pressure from family or others
3. Blame from family or others
4. Feelings of not being trusted
5. Isolation
6. Use of recantation to solve the problem
7. Giving up hope
8. Unfair treatment
9. Not getting help
10. Other factors (e.g., disruption of life)

Sexual Activities Involving Children

Secrecy, coercion, and progression of sexual activities are three main indicators that validate the occurrence of child sexual abuse. According to Sgroi (1982), children's knowledge and detailed descriptions of sexual terms and activities that do not match with their age are indicators of sexual abuse, either with the child's cooperation or because of coercion. In addition to

Table 2.1 Recantation Reasons

Personal reasons	Family reasons	External and/or social reasons
I don't like how this case was handled.	I feel that no one would understand my dilemma.	I want to avoid the media.
I am embarrassed.	I can't trust anyone.	I don't want everyone in the world to blame me.
I am fearful.	I decided to leave my family anyway.	I'm disappointed in the social system.
I can solve my own problem.	I don't want to see the accused (e.g., my dad) go to jail.	I can't continue my normal life.
I don't like myself; people dislike me.	I like the accused (e.g., my dad) and don't want to see him suffer.	I can't deal with reality.
I don't want to go to jail.	I was influenced by others and therefore made a mistake.	I dislike the interviewer's attitude.
I don't want to talk about it anymore.	I was separated from my family because of this.	I don't want to see a judge.
I feel hopeless; I want to give up.	I wasn't trusted anyway.	I hate this world.
I forgive the person who abused me.	If I said it didn't happen, the whole matter would go away.	It's society's fault.
I lied.	It's my family matter.	No one can really help, so why proceed?
I misunderstood the accused (e.g., my dad)	I would make my family lose its source of financial support and a breadwinner.	The police don't trust me.
It's my fault.	My abuser has already been punished; there's no need to further complicate my life.	Social workers or CPS workers are not helpful.
It's in my imagination, not real.	My family pressured me.	The system has been unfair to children (and adolescents).
I feel tremendous pressure from within myself.	Someone told me to say so; someone brainwashed me.	What I reported was against my own will (because I was misled or coached).

giving explicit, age-inappropriate information regarding sexuality, children who talk about the abusive environment and the changing types of abuse over time—especially expressing adult sexual activities from the eyes of a child—are likely to have experienced sexual abuse. Progression of sexual activities can take many forms, which can be related to the severity and intensity of exposure to sexuality. The following lists these activities in progressive order (Sgroi, 1982):

1. *Nudity*—The adult parades nude around the house in front of all or some family members.
2. *Disrobing*—The adult disrobes in front of the child, generally when the child and the adult are alone.
3. *Genital exposure*—The adult exposes his or her genitals to the child. Here the perpetrator directs the child's attention to the genitals.
4. *Observation of the child*—The adult surreptitiously or overtly watches the child undress, bathe, excrete, or urinate.
5. *Kissing*—The adult kisses the child in a lingering and intimate way. This type of kissing is reserved for adults. Even very young children sense the inappropriateness of this behavior and may experience discomfort about it.
6. *Fondling*—The adult fondles the child's breasts, abdomen, genital area, inner thighs, or buttocks. The child may similarly fondle the adult at his or her request.
7. *Masturbation*—The adult masturbates while the child observes, the adult observes the child masturbating, the adult and the child observe each other while masturbating themselves, or the adult and child masturbate each other (mutual masturbation).
8. *Fellatio*—The adult has the child fellate him, or the adult will fellate the child. This type of oral-genital contact requires the child to take a male perpetrator's penis into his or her mouth or the adult to take the male child's penis into his or her mouth.
9. *Cunnilingus*—This type of oral-genital contact requires the child to place mouth and tongue on the vulva or in the vaginal area of an adult female, or the adult will place his or her mouth on the vulva or in the vaginal area of the female child.

10. *Digital (finger) penetration of the anus or rectal opening*—Perpetrators may thrust a finger or inanimate objects (e.g., crayon, stick) inside the child's anus or rectal opening. Preadolescent children often report a fear of "things being inside them" and "being broken."

11. *Digital (finger) penetration of the vagina*—This involves penetration of the vagina by a finger. The perpetrator may also insert inanimate objects.

12. *Penile penetration of the anus or rectal opening*—This involves penetration of the anus or rectal opening by a male perpetrator's penis. A child can often be rectally penetrated without injury as a result of the flexibility of children's rectal openings.

13. *Penile penetration of the vagina*—This involves penetration of the vagina by a male perpetrator's penis.

In some sexual abuse cases with adolescent girls, dry intercourse may happen in between the times that other activities occur when a male abuser tries to avoid direct penile penetration for reasons of pregnancy prevention or psychological defense against immorality. *Dry intercourse* is a slang term describing an interaction in which a man rubs his penis against the child's genital-rectal area, inner thighs, or buttocks. The typical scenario of progression is the sexual engagement from less intimate types of sexual activity (e.g., exposure, self-masturbation) to actual body contact (e.g., fondling), to some form of penetration. Oral penetration can be expected to occur early in this progression, and it is often followed by digital penetration of the anus or vagina. Ejaculation by a male, sometimes against the female's body, can occur at any time in the progression.

It is important to obtain information from the referral person about the child's initial complaint. This first point of contact may be a parent, a sibling, or another person to whom the child first reported the incident so that information about progression, coercion, and secrecy can be verified.

Nondisclosure Cases

Nondisclosure often occurs for one of two reasons: the child does not want to disclose or has been forced not to disclose, or sexual abuse did not occur.

DeVoe and Faller (2002) have confirmed that alleged victims did not readily disclose their experiences, but that disclosure did occur in response to
nonleading and focused questions. In addition, they found that victims
who disclosed their sexual abuse experiences were asked approximately
sixty-one more questions than those who only partially disclosed or did
not disclose at all. The interviewers used more repeated clarifying questions with children who disclosed than with children who did not disclose.

In a study of twenty-eight children who did not reveal or refused to
divulge any child sexual abuse experiences, Cheung (2008) found that the
children who did not disclose tended to be younger than those who disclosed. These younger children may not have expressed their child sexual
abuse experiences because of their limited ability to verbalize, their lack of
readiness to express concerns, their lack of understanding of the problem,
and their lack of support from the nonoffending parent (Malloy, Lyon, &
Quas, 2007). In addition to being associated with young age, nondisclosure
was also associated with male children, which may reflect a common phenomenon observed in child sexual abuse cases of male children often being
confused about the reason for sexual abuse and not wanting to report their
experiences. Spataro et al. (2001) have attributed reasons for the underreporting of male child sexual abuse to fear, self-reliance, and male sexuality
issues. Other research has demonstrated that male victims may feel more
responsible for their sexual abuse than female victims do, viewing themselves as participants in rather than victims of the sexual activity; they
often feel sexually involved because of their own erection or ejaculation or
have concerns about homosexuality (Alaggia, 2004; Alaggia & Kirshenbaum, 2005; Romano & De Luca, 2001; Rusinoff & Gerber, 1990).

In nondisclosure cases, the interviewers tended to use more what and
how questions with the children who disclosed and more close-ended
questions with children who did not disclose. The finding that disclosure
occurred after being asked what and how questions was consistent with
DeVoe and Faller's (2002) conclusion that open-ended questions usually
do not evoke specific information from the victims about sexual abuse
accounts but that additional use of nonleading and focused questions can
encourage more descriptive responses. The use of closing questions was
likely related to using nonleading questioning strategies. When substantiating information could not be obtained from the child to validate an

alleged report, the interviewer may have felt obligated to address the child's concerns, answer the child's questions, give the child an opportunity to ask further questions, or provide educational materials about abuse and future contacts. To avoid the appearance of leading or suggestive questioning in a nondisclosure situation, the interviewer tended to pose additional closing questions as a technique to address the child's concerns.

Protocol Used in Disclosure and Nondisclosure Cases

This section presents an interview protocol for practice purposes. The interview process generally goes through four stages: rapport building, encouraging the child to freely describe, asking specific follow-up questions, and closing the interview (see appendix 2E; on skills associated with the interview process, see chapters 3–4). In many states or countries, the law may require the interviewer to determine three things: (1) whether the alleged victim knows whether the perpetrator has abused anyone else, (2) whether anyone else has abused the victim (as an alternative hypothesis), and (3) the reason for reporting the incident now.

The differences between the protocols used in a disclosure case versus a nondisclosure case occur in stage 3 when the specific questions are related to the disclosed abuse in a disclosure case and when the specific questions are related to child protection in a nondisclosure case. It is important not to ask leading questions, such as "Has your stepdad ever sexually abused you?" Doing so allows for an argument in court that the child has been coached to provide an answer. In nondisclosure situations, the child will answer questions related to body protection as a general educational routine used by the interviewer or the agency (see appendix 2E).

Protocol in a Disclosure Case

Stage 1: Rapport
    Identification: Name, agency, position or role of the interviewer, purpose of the videotaped interview.
    Competency: Who, when, where, what, how, home situation, discipline method, family relationship, free narration of a nonabuse event.

Truth and lies: State the importance, assess differentiation between truth and lie, understand consequences of not telling the truth or telling a lie, use a direct approach, use two examples (e.g., a lie and a truth example), conclude the importance of telling the truth.

Ground rules: Ensure truth telling, accept "don't know," clarify terms.

Stage 2: Free-Narrative Account

What happened; dolls appropriately used; come back to this stage later when needed.

Stage 3: Questioning

Who: Alleged perpetrator's (AP) name, relationship, description, who else was there, first person told, reaction, who else knew, other people involved.

When: Date, time (if exact date not remembered, then year, month, day of the week, season, school day or not, holiday).

Where: Location, address, description of abuse place, where other people were.

What: Most recent occurrence first, what AP did, what child did, what AP was wearing, what child was wearing, what child saw, what AP said, what else happened in this incident.

How: Methods, tools, frequency, duration and/or length, use of child's terminology, clarification of terminology, the physical and emotional feelings associated with being touched, any changes in the relationship with the AP.

Progression of sexual activity: What else happened, what was it, how often, four *W* questions (who, when, where, what) and how questions for first and recent incident and other incidents.

Other: Other known victims, alternative hypothesis (see protocol in appendix 2E).

Avoid the use of why, leading, and judgmental questions.

Don't initiate any touching, as when comforting the child.

Stage 4: Closing the Interview

What is next, confirm truth telling, address client's questions and concerns, ask additional questions, thank and reassure.

Protocol in a Nondisclosure Case

Stage 1: Rapport

Identification: Name, agency, position or role of the interviewer, purpose of the videotaped interview.

Competency: Who, when, where, what, how, home situation, discipline method, family relationship, free narration of a nonabuse event.

Truth and lies: State the importance of truth telling, assess differentiation between truth and lie, understand consequences of not telling the truth or of telling a lie, use a direct approach, use two examples (e.g., a lie and a truth example), conclude the importance of telling the truth.

Ground rules: Ensure truth telling, accept "don't know," clarify terms.

Stage 2: Free-Narrative Account

What happened; dolls appropriately used; come back to this stage later when needed.

Stage 3: Questioning

Additional rapport: Ask about likes and dislikes.

Emotions: Address child's discomfort or uncertainty.

Body protection: Body parts can and can't be touched by others; knowledge about body private parts.

Follow-up: Use referral information to follow up with child.

Avoid the use of why, leading, and judgmental questions.

Don't initiate any touching, as when comforting the child.

Stage 4: Closing the Interview

What is next, confirm truth telling, address client's questions and concerns, ask additional questions, thank and reassure.

These two protocols show that stages 1, 2, and 4 are the same for disclosure and nondisclosure cases. The only difference occurs in stage 3 for nondisclosure situations when no specific information about sexual abuse has been obtained from stage 2, and therefore, the interviewer is to build in additional rapport in order to understand how the child relates to the alleged perpetrator or the reporter who suspects that sexual abuse has occurred. If no abuse has been indicated after the interviewer's additional rapport questions, then the interviewer can provide educational materials about body protection, starting with knowledge about body parts and then ways to protect one's body.

This four-stage protocol should not be used rigidly (for some practical examples, see chapter 4). Whether or not the child has disclosed before the forensic interview, the interviewer is advised not to make any assumptions and should take a blank-screen approach to listen first and ask later. The interview process should be similar across all interviews, except when a child shows difficulties because of a special need (e.g., speech and hearing difficulties, intellectual challenges). There are three main steps to determine the differences between a disclosure case and a nondisclosure case:

1. *Checking reluctance versus no knowledge*—During the free-narrative stage, the interviewer generally asks the child what happened. In a disclosure situation, the child would either describe a problem or indicate a reluctance to share through emotions or behaviors. The interviewer usually encourages the child to talk about the concern so that the interviewer can find ways to help the child. In a nondisclosure situation, the child may not know what to say and may simply say, "I don't know." In this case, the interviewer must assess whether the child has no knowledge or reluctance by saying, "What do you know?" or using questions such as, "What has been bothering you [or your mom]?" and "Did anything happen that you should tell someone you can trust?"

2. *Listen patiently*—If no information can be gathered from the general questions such as "Tell me a problem that has bothered you" or "What did you tell your teacher that you can tell me directly?" then the interviewer can say, "I am here to listen to you." Then the interviewer can return to the rapport-building stage to allow the child more room to talk about personal experiences and feelings.

3. *Use educational materials and questions*—If nothing can be generated from the general questioning process, then the interviewer can initiate a talk about body protection. It is helpful to educate nondisclosing children about inappropriate behavior before they leave the interview room. When asking a child about his or her

knowledge about body protection, the interviewer can say, "I am here to address body protection with children. Now, tell me which part of your body no one can touch." "Who can touch your body?" and "What would you do if someone touched you inappropriately?" It is a professional's responsibility to use body protection materials to prevent sexual abuse. As long as the interviewer clarifies the intent of using these educational questions and materials, it is not regarded as guiding or leading.

Case Scenarios and Transcripts for Practice

Case scenarios from actual child sexual abuse cases have been composed and transcribed into two categories: disclosure and nondisclosure cases (see chapters 3 and 4). They were role-played by social workers to demonstrate the use of the interview protocol to obtain information from a child who has disclosed sexual abuse and from another child who has not disclosed sexual abuse. The two cases can be used in the development of practice skills and in the critique of skills. Readers should pay attention to the evidence-based suggestions and then practice with the cases to gain a better understanding of how to apply the interview protocols. In this chapter, readers can review the interview protocol (see appendix 2E), use questions to validate abuse (appendix 2F), and practice interviewing techniques with practical examples extracted from real cases (appendix 2G). Assessment points used in the protocols have been developed through evidence-based research.

Evidence-Based Research

There are three main reasons that videotaped interviews should be used to obtain information from a child who alleges sexual abuse or an alleged victim of sexual abuse. First, sexual abuse is a sensitive issue that requires the interviewer's full attention to the child. Using paper and pencil to record verbatim is not a sensitive method. At the beginning of the interview, the interviewer should inform the child that the purpose of videotaping is to ensure that the interviewer can pay attention to the child by not writing down every word he or she says.

Second, it is important that the interviewer not repeat the same questions, because repeated questions may confuse the child and make the child think that he or she has said something wrong for the interviewer to ask the same question again or for another interviewer to ask about what a previous interviewer has asked. Using a videotaped interview to document information already obtained from the child can eliminate duplication of effort. Also, when repeated questions are asked, the interviewer must clarify his or her intent (e.g., "I forgot what you have told me about X. Can you tell me again?") in order to eliminate any of the child's misconceptions of the interviewer's intent.

Third, a child's attention span is short, and a structural interview can help shorten the interview time. In a videotaped interview, a clear procedure will help the interviewer make sure that he or she has asked all required questions for validation from a multidisciplinary perspective so that no additional interviews will be required. If more interviews are used, children may not want to participate or may not have the focus required to answer additional questions.

Avoiding Repeated Interviews

According to Dr. Stephen Ceci, repeated interviews have been shown to confuse children, interfere with children's memory-recall process, and increase the chance of false allegations among younger children. Three of Ceci's research studies were introduced on the ABC program *20/20*: the Sam Stone Study, the Mousetrap Story Study, and the Anatomical Doll Study. These studies identified that people representing positions of authority can easily influence very young children (for the transcripts of the program, see appendix 2H). The segment supported three lessons learned for conducting effective child sexual abuse interviews:

1. *No repeated questions*—Do not use a suspicious tone of disbelief that leads the child to think that he or she must give or make up answers.
2. *No guiding hints or suggestive, leading questions*—Do not use suggestive statements or questions to guide the child. Do not direct the child to believe that something might have happened.

3. *No suggestive tools*—Do not use anatomical dolls or other suggestive tools before a child discloses the abuse. Use dolls or tools only
after disclosure to clarify the action, position, or gesture that the
child could not explain verbally.

Interviewing Very Young Children

Because preschool-age children have difficulty with spontaneous recall,
Gardner (1995) has recommended specific questions to trigger their
responses, such as the following:

- An initial response: "So what's been happening to you lately?"
- A follow-up description: "What was the next thing that happened?"
- Place and location: "Tell me exactly where each of these things
  happened."
- Specific inquiries of the abuse recall: "What was [the alleged per-
  petrator] wearing?"
- Noticeable details: "What else did you see?"
- Other specific corroborative details: "Who was the first person
  you ever told about what X did to you? How did it come about
  that you told Y about what X did to you? What did Y then say?"

Interviewing Nondisclosing Children

Cheung (2008) suggests the following practical recommendations:

1. Take children's short attention span into consideration: fifteen- to
   thirty-minute interviews are the norm for both disclosure and
   nondisclosure cases.
2. Younger children are less likely to disclose sexual abuse than older
   children: demonstrate patience and understanding, and obtain
   additional information from other sources rather than asking
   leading questions.

3. Hire more male interviewers to help male victims express their concerns about sexuality.

4. Do not first ask what and how questions of reticent children, but instead ask who, when, and where questions to gather initial information.

5. Avoid accusatory why questions during the interview. For practical use, aside from the most commonly utilized questions cited earlier, other examples include:

- "Who would you talk to when you have a problem?"
- "You said you could be in trouble if you told me. Who can get you in trouble?"
- "You said that you didn't want to talk about *it*. Who shouldn't know about *it*?"
- "Where do you go when you are feeling happy?" (pause for answers) "Where do you go when you are feeling sad?"
- "You said that your mom wanted you to talk about something. Where were you when your mom told you that?" (pause for answers) "When did this *something* happen?"
- "You said that you came here to talk about something you did. When did it happen?"

Generally, most of the accusatory *why* questions should be avoided during investigative interviews, but the question "Why are you here today?" seems to help reticent children feel at ease and opens up the conversation. Many of these children did not respond initially to the open-ended "Tell me what happened" question, so the "Why are you here today?" question is often a viable alternative.

When interviewing children who have no intention of disclosing sexual abuse, interviewers should not quickly ask specific what and how questions that hint at sexual abuse; rather, they can use who, where, and when questions to understand the child's current situation. These questions place the children at ease and allow them to divulge information and their feelings about the alleged perpetrator. During situations when the interviewer does not obtain specific sexual abuse information, it is still important that he or she use closing questions to create a safe and comfortable environment for the child on that day and for any future inquiries. As a final point, the Cheung (2008) study implied that the use of leading questions should always be avoided and that interviewers should use techniques to help children talk about their experiences, whether related to sexual abuse or to other matters.

Julie's Case: Assessment Difficulties

Assessment

Fourteen-year-old Julie met the forensic interviewer at the Child Advocacy Center; her homeroom teacher was her support person. Julie's mother was informed about the interview, and she came to the center to sign the consent for Julie to be videotaped during the interview. The purpose of videotaping the interview was to minimize repeated interviews and to ensure that the content could be used for further assessment. A Child Protective Services (CPS) caseworker interviewed Julie's mother at the school; Julie's mother explained that Julie was not a good child and had been displaying totally unacceptable behaviors. She also mentioned that Julie was a liar who stole money from her mother's drawer and didn't come home for almost a month. She initially refused that Julie's interview be videotaped, but she later agreed that Julie must be interviewed to validate or disprove the case.

When Julie met with the forensic interviewer, she showed signs of distress and tiredness. Being patient with Julie, the interviewer used rapport-building skills to make sure that Julie was comfortable with the interview: the interviewer offered Julie opportunities to ask questions, ensured that she understood the meaning of telling the truth, and had Julie promise to tell only the truth. However, when the interviewer asked, "What happened?" Julie became silent and didn't want to tell anything. The interviewer suggested ways that Julie could relax, such as by taking a few deep breaths with her and offering her a bottle of water. Julie was finally able to tell the interviewer that her father had touched her and that she had had sexual intercourse with him from the time she was ten years old until a week before the interview.

Difficulties

One difficulty in the assessment process was that Julie did not feel comfortable with the interviewer at the beginning of the interview. She noted that people wouldn't believe her complaint, which was why she wasn't ready to share anything with the interviewer. Her distress was somewhat lifted when the interviewer said that it was important for Julie to speak directly about her "complaint" so that the interviewer could find ways to help her. Julie had experienced many difficulties in her life since she was ten years old. She mentioned that she told her mother about the first inappropriate touch when her father was drunk on a night that her mother was sick in bed. Her mother did not believe her and scolded her. Ever since, her father advanced the sexual touches from kisses and body touches to sexual intercourse, and he warned Julie not to tell anyone—or else he would send her to the girls' home to live with her sister and other criminals.

Another difficulty in assessing the information Julie provided was her current behavioral problems, exhibited both at home and in school. Although it is known that behavior of acting out sexually is one behavioral outcome of child sexual abuse, there is no evidence that a child who sexually acts out and who has reported having been sexually abused is always telling the truth. Some people believe that an adolescent's disclosure with detailed sexual intercourse information from a first-person perspective might come from a sexual relationship with a boyfriend or girlfriend. Even physical examination by the forensic examiner would not be able to provide evidence to support that the father was the abuser. Here, the information from Julie's pelvic exam and laboratory results indicated that she was not pregnant; she did not have a sexually transmitted disease; her external genitalia showed no lesions, bruises, abrasions, blood, or seminal fluid; and her rectal exam was normal. The medical report noted that having no injury did not mean the absence of sexual abuse.

Yet another difficulty was related to Julie's recantation (for more information on recanting, see chapter 1). Another difficulty was that Julie's sister was not interviewed because she was under the supervision of the state for her record of delinquency. Finally, the alleged perpetrator's (Julie's father) denial and the unsupportive attitude of the nonoffending parent (Julie's mother) complicated validation of the case. Risk factors could help the interviewer to recommend removal of the child, but a protective order that was granted was only temporary, especially when Julie's recantation blocked further investigations. With the presence of significant risk factors, CPS followed up on Julie's case even though it would not continue in court. However, the caseworker could conduct only two more follow-up visits. The caseworker did so and then closed the case.

Conclusion

Responsible adult parties involved in child sexual abuse investigations must be sensitive to the dynamics involved in child sexual abuse. In addition, professionals must adjust their interview protocol for disclosure and nondisclosure cases. In general, forensic interviewers should adopt a line of open-ended questions, use age-appropriate interviewing techniques, and avoid repeating the interview process with the child. Through the use of videotaped interviews and the incorporation of recommendations derived from evidence-based practice, forensic interviewers will minimize trauma to the alleged victim and increase the accuracy of the forensic interview.

Tips for Professionals and Parents

Tips for Professionals: Using the Child Sexual Abuse Protocol

Tip No. 1: Knowing the Differences between Disclosure and Nondisclosure Cases

Disclosure

Disclosure can be accidental:

- Observation by a third party
- Physical injury to the child
- Sexually transmitted disease
- Pregnancy
- Precocious sexual activities initiated by the child
- Sudden change in behavior
- Fearful response to stay alone with the abuser

Disclosure can be purposeful, as when the child

- Cannot tolerate the abuse
- Has a chance to talk to a trusted person about abuse
- Is pregnant
- Knows that having a sexual relationship with an adult is a problem

Nondisclosure

- Subjects who disclose sexual abuse experiences are asked more questions than subjects who only partially or do not disclose.
- Nondisclosure subjects tend to be asked more closing questions instead of what and how questions.
- Nondisclosing children tend to be younger, perhaps because of their limited ability to verbalize, lack of readiness to express concerns, lack of understanding of a problem, and lack of support from the nonoffending parent.
- Male victims are less likely to disclose for reasons of fear, self-reliance, and sexuality issues.

Tip No. 2: Interview Protocol

Interview protocols help make sure that the interviewer address all appropriate questions and concerns in the interview. Interviews generally go through four stages, although the protocol differs in stage 3 depending on whether the child has disclosed abuse.

Interview Protocol

Stage 1: Rapport building

Stage 2: Encouraging the child to freely describe

Stage 3: Asking specific questions to follow up (with disclosure, ask questions about abuse; with nondisclosure, ask questions related to child protection)

Stage 4: Close the interview

Tip No. 3: Steps to Differentiate Disclosure and Nondisclosure Cases

1. Check reluctance versus no knowledge using questions like "What has been bothering you?"
2. Listen patiently; return to rapport building if no information is gathered from the general questions.
3. If disclosure does not take place, initiate a talk about body protection and educate the child about inappropriate behavior.

Tip No. 4: Knowing What and What Not to Do During an Interview

- Avoid repeated questions, as they may be confusing to the child or interfere with the memory-recall process.
- Do not use suggestive tools (e.g., dolls, toys) until after disclosure has taken place.
- Use specific questions to help young children with specific recall.
- Keep the interview short—fifteen to thirty minutes is the norm.
- Avoid accusatory why, what, and how questions.
- Videotape the interview, which helps the interviewer give full attention to the child, avoid repeated questions and additional interviews, and shorten the interview time.

Tips for Parents: Understanding Sibling Abuse versus Childhood Sex Play

Recently, more cases of sexual abuse have occurred in which the abuser is a minor. Assessment with cases of child or adolescent abusers must address three main points: (1) whether sexual abuse is a form of bullying and misuse of power; (2) whether abuse is intentional, habitual, and/or psychopathological; and (3) whether sexual touching is a form of childhood sex play. Among adolescents, trial sex can happen as a means to test curiosity, to fulfill sexual desire and romance, and to overpower the partner. Parents can assess childhood sex play with the following tips.

Tip No. 1: Questions to Be Considered (Health Canada, Family Violence Prevention Division, 1994)

- Is this behavior developmentally appropriate?
- How long has the behavior been happening?
- Does it seem that one of the children involved is being forced or feeling discomfort to participate?
- What is the purpose of the behavior?

Tip No. 2: Definitions and Examples

Sexual abuse	Sex play
Definition: Sibling abuse is an abuse of power between sibling dyad, including sexual behaviors that are developmentally inappropriate and not motivated by age-appropriate curiosity. It may involve physical touching, fondling, forced intercourse, unwanted sexual conversation, forcing a sibling to take or view pornographic pictures, and forcing a sibling to observe others' sexual behavior (Haskins, 2003).	*Definition:* Sex play is a normal part of a child's development; children of similar age or size participate voluntarily in normal sexual exploration. Common behaviors may include kissing, hugging, peeking, and touching and exposing genitals (Horton, 1996).
Examples • Frequently rubs genitals instead of playing • Persists in watching other children in the bathroom • Forces other children to undress when playing doctor • Pretends or tries to have intercourse • An adolescent boy wants to look at his five-year-old sister's genitals and forces his sister to perform oral sex	*Examples* • Rubs genitals before falling asleep • Is interested in watching another child go to the bathroom • Plays doctor with other children • Plays mommy and daddy roles • A four-year-old girl touches her baby brother's penis out of curiosity

Tip No. 3: Teaching Parents and Educating Youths

If parents see their children engaging in inappropriate sexual behavior, they should stay calm and ask the children to stop and get dressed. Parents should never overreact!

Sexual Curiosity
- If the children's intent is sexual curiosity, ask them to play in a place where a third party is present so that their "game" does not go over the limit.
- Monitor television programs and videos that the children watch.
- Be willing to talk about sexuality. Take this opportunity to teach children about their body parts, differences between boys and girls, and being respectful to others' body.
- Be aware of any signals from a child who has been sexually abused.
- Join a parenting support group for encouragement.
- Seek consultation from professionals such as doctors, nurses, psychologists, and social workers. Parents can also contact counseling centers.

Sibling Incest
- If the witnessed behavior is considered sexual abuse, call Child Protective Services or the police.
- Understand the victim's emotions.
- Ask who, when, where, and what, as well as how it happened and how the child feels. Never ask why, because it will make the child defensive!
  - Who was this person?
  - When did it happen?
  - Where did it happen?
  - What happened?
  - What do you feel (e.g., when he put something inside your body)?
  - How did it happen?
  - How do you feel?

- Be aware of any indicator of abuse from a child who has been sexually abused.
- Be supportive! Encourage nonsexist attitudes and behaviors.
- Arrange counseling for the victim and the perpetrator.
- Closely work with the counselor and/or social worker to help the children.

Documentation of Risk Assessment: Risk Assessment Factors

Risk Assessment Factors

Past and Current Abuse and/or Neglect and Risk

Characteristics, Intent, and Motivation

- Child used to meet parent's needs
- Deliberate intent to hurt or harm
- Intent to teach or discipline
- Lack of knowledge of child's capabilities
- Parent lost control
- Result of omission
- Other (specify)

Nature of Abuse or Neglect

- Alcohol or drug related
- Child death
- Cruel, bizarre
- History of emotional abuse
- History of physical abuse or neglect
- History of sexual abuse
- Refusal to protect child
- Other (specify)

Child Factors

Parental and/or Caretaker View of Child

- Bad
- Provoking
- Special or different
- Troublesome
- Other (specify)

Child Characteristics and Functioning

- Delinquent behavior
- Depression or mood problems
- Drug-affected birth
- Drug or alcohol usage
- Emotionally disturbed
- Fearful
- Learning problems
- Low self-esteem
- Mental retardation
- Peer interaction problems
- Physical injuries
- Physical limitations
- Provocative
- Restricted or flat affect
- Sexually acting out
- Suicide ideation or attempt
- Other (specify)

Adult History, Current Functioning, and Parenting Ability

Parents' or Caregivers' Predominant Behaviors

- Apathetic, low energy
- Depression or mood problems
- Drug and/or alcohol dependency or abuse

- Diagnosed mental illness
- Generalized anger
- Inability to manage stress
- Low empathy for others
- Low self-esteem
- Self-centered
- Other (specify)

Parents' or Caregivers' Predominant Ways of Parenting

- Aversion to parenting role and/or demands
- Failure to provide basic needs
- Provision of inappropriate discipline
- Insensitive to child's needs, inappropriate age expectations
- Lack of appropriate bonding or attachment
- Lack of knowledge and/or skills in child development practices
- Unrealistic or rigid
- Other (specify)

Parents' or Caregivers' History

- Abused or neglected as a child (history of sexual abuse)
- Criminal involvement
- Diagnosed mentally retarded
- Emotional instability
- Few close friends or lack of emotional support
- Health problems
- Perpetrator of spousal abuse
- Victim of spousal abuse
- Other (specify)

Family Functioning

- Financial problems
- Health problems
- Housing problems
- Lack of education or training

- Family recently relocated
- Several preschool-age children
- Single parent and/or caretaker
- Young, immature parent(s)
- Other (specify)

Family Unit Operation

- Absence of household routines
- Can't talk about problems or solutions
- Child-rearing disagreements
- Crisis lifestyle
- Deals poorly with stress
- Interpersonally or socially distant
- Lack of support from extended family members
- Marital conflict
- No emotional bonding between family members
- Role boundary problems
- Scapegoating of child or others
- Unsupportive extended family
- Other (specify)

Developing a Service Plan

Consider the following areas in developing a service plan with the family.

Strengths

- Ability to learn from problems
- Able to communicate needs
- Capable of behavior change
- Capable of understanding new ideas
- Capable of accessing resources
- Committed to child and the family
- Has awareness of problem

- Has support systems or relationships
- Motivated to work for change
- Willingness to cooperate

Changes Needed

- Ability to identify child's strengths
- Communication skills
- Gives and receives affection
- Impulse control
- Parenting skills
- Personal responsibility
- Problem solving
- Protective skills toward children
- Stress management
- Use of resources

Documentation of Risk Assessment: Assessment of Caretaker

Assessment Questionnaire (Used with the Risk Assessment Factors Form)

Name of Caretaker: _____

Age of Caretaker: _____

1. Tell me about your family when you were growing up.
   Probe: How many members? Where did you live? What do you remember about your childhood?
2. How did your parents discipline you as a child breaking the rule in the family?
   Probe: Describe your parent's parenting method. How did your parents look after your basic needs?
3. Tell me about any past marriages or relationships you have been in. What have been some good points about your past and/or present relationships? Some bad points?
4. To plan services for you and your family, tell me about any drinking or drug use in the past or present. Has it ever caused problems for you, your family, or on the job?
5. What do you like best about yourself? What would you like to change?
6. When something is bothering you, how do other people know it?
7. What is your physical health like these days? When was the last time you saw a doctor? What was it for?
8. Who do you call when things are in a crisis? What do they do to help you?

9. How did you learn about being a parent?
10. What are some of best things you have done for your child and/or children?
11. What would you like to do differently with your kids?
12. Tell me about each of your children.
13. What is a typical day for you?
14. Who is your best friend? Who are you closest to in your family?
15. What do you like to do for fun? How about for relaxation?
16. How are your finances right now? Has anything changed recently with your job or money?
17. How do you make decisions about where to live and how to spend your money? Who do you consult with, or do you do it all by yourself?
18. What is your biggest concern about your child and/or children right now?
19. What makes you feel good about your children right now?
20. Have you thought of ways that our agency can assist you with your family right now? How do you feel about having a child welfare worker coming to your home and working with you?
21. What is your view about child abuse, neglect, and child sexual abuse?
22. What can you do to protect your children?

Risk Assessment of Child Sexual Abuse

Check all that apply to the child's situation:

1. History of child abuse in this family:
   ___ Physical abuse
   ___ Emotional abuse
   ___ Neglect
   ___ Sexual abuse
2. Child's age:
   ___ Infant (0–11 months)
   ___ Toddler (12–35 months)
   ___ Preschooler (3–5 years)
   ___ School age (6–10 years)
   ___ Adolescent (11–17 years)
3. Offender's age: ___
4. Offender's relationship with the child:
   ___ Parent
   ___ Relative
   ___ Sibling
   ___ Friend and/or neighbor
   ___ Teacher and/or coach
   ___ Someone known to the child but not in a listed category
   ___ Stranger
5. Offender's reaction to the allegation:
   ___ Admitting to the problem
   ___ Blaming the victim for the wrongdoing
   ___ Labeling the victim as a liar

___ Cooperating with the investigation
___ Emotional breakdown
___ Strong denial
___ Trying to find out the cause of allegation
___ Other (specify)

6. Characteristics of the sexual abuse as reported:

   a. Has sexual abuse occurred more than once?
      ___ More than once ___ Only once ___ Not sure
      If more than once:
      Frequency: ___ times per week
      Duration of each abuse: ___ minutes, hours, or days

   b. Sexual abuse first occurred when the child was ___ years old

   c. Secrecy of sexual abuse:
      ___ Reported immediately
      ___ Did not report immediately because
         ___ Don't know what to do
         ___ Felt threatened and/or frightened
         ___ Felt ashamed
         ___ Gift and/or money was given
         ___ No one would believe
         ___ Was told to keep it secret

   d. Did the abuse situation change over time?
      How? _____
      ___ Decreased frequency and/or intensity
      ___ Increased frequency and/or intensity
      ___ No sexual contact after the child reached a certain age (___)
      ___ Type of sexual abuse changed from ___ to ___

   e. Did the abuse change the relationship between the child and the accused?
      How? _____

   f. Who was the first person the child told about the abuse?
      Name and relationship to child: _____
      What was this person's reaction and action? What did this person say at that time? _____

7. Family Functioning
   a. Does the family ever have these problems?
      ____ Alcohol and/or other substance abuse
      ____ Chronic illness
      ____ Family violence
      ____ Financial problem
      ____ Mental retardation or intellectual challenges
      ____ Mental illness
      ____ Physical limitations or disabilities
      ____ Prostitution
      ____ Others (specify)
   b. What was the nonoffending caretaker's reaction to the allegation?
      ____ Admitted to the problem
      ____ Blamed the victim for the wrongdoing
      ____ Labeled the victim as a liar
      ____ Cooperated with the investigation
      ____ Experienced emotional breakdown
      ____ Experienced strong denial
      ____ Tried to find out the cause of allegation
      ____ Other (specify)

Child Sexual Abuse Interview Protocol (CSAIP)

Child Sexual Abuse Interview Protocol (CSAIP): For Use in Forensic Videotaping Interviews

Stage 1: Rapport

Tell the child who the interviewer is
    ( ) Name   ( ) Agency   ( ) Position/Role

Briefly identify the purpose
    ( ) Inform the child about videotaping purpose and the presence of accompanying adults
    ( ) Address the child's concern regarding being videotaped
    ( ) Obtain consent from the child (if required by the law)

Establish rapport with the child

Ask the child about a specific nonabuse event for event narrative practice

Also assess the child's competency in answering the following questions:
    ( ) Who   ( ) When   ( ) Where   ( ) What   ( ) How

Optional questions:
    ( ) Home situation ( ) Discipline method ( ) Family relationship

Set up the ground rules (may be viewed as a separate stage)
    ( ) State the importance of telling the truth
    ( ) Assess the child's ability to differentiate the truth and a lie
    ( ) Encourage the child to define what is telling the truth and what is lying

If the child can't define:
    ( ) Check competency with one example of the truth and one example of a lie
    ( ) Include what happens when people tell truth or lie

( ) Specify the ground rules
( ) Ensure that the child promises to tell the truth
( ) Accept "I don't know" or "I don't understand" as answers
( ) Say "Correct me if I get anything wrong"
( ) Clarify the reasons that the child may need to further explain slang or unusual terms

Stage 2: Free-Narrative Account

What happened
( ) Encourage the child to tell what happened in his or her own words
Use dolls (or drawings) appropriately
( ) Use dolls (if needed) only after the child has disclosed content of child sexual abuse
Use open-ended questions
( ) Come back to this free-narrative stage whenever needed

Stage 3: Questioning

If the child is reticent:
Before disclosure
( ) Ask what happened lately with the child
( ) Show patience to listen
( ) Encourage the child to use own words to describe what has happened
( ) Try more rapport building (e.g., ask about home and school situations)
( ) Ask the child about the purpose of this visit
( ) Ask whether there is anything that someone asked the child to tell or not to tell
( ) Refer to any signs of silence or emotional distress
( ) Ask whether there is anything else the child needs help with
( ) In the case of no disclosure:
    ( ) Follow up on the child's statements with the 4WH questions (when, where, who, what, and how).

( ) Provide information about body protection and further
     assistance

After disclosure

( ) Encourage the child to tell what happened in his or her own words
( ) Focus on one recall at a time (e.g., start with the most recent
     abuse or the most remembered abuse)

If the child has disclosed, use follow-up questions for validation:

When

( ) Date (e.g., year, season, holiday)
( ) Time (if not exact time, day or night)

Where

( ) Abuse location (e.g., bedroom, game room)
( ) Address of the location
( ) Brief description of the location (if address not given)
( ) Where were other family members during the abuse?

Who

( ) Full name of the alleged perpetrator
( ) Relationship of the alleged perpetrator to the child
( ) Brief description of the alleged perpetrator (if relationship
     unknown)
( ) Who else was there when the abuse occurred?
( ) Who else knew about the abuse?

What (also determine coercion and secrecy)

( ) Focus on events before, during, and after the abuse
( ) What did the alleged perpetrator do?
( ) What did the child do?
( ) What was the perpetrator wearing?
( ) What was the child wearing?
( ) What was the body position of alleged perpetrator and child?
( ) What did the child see, hear, say, feel, or sense?
( ) What did the alleged perpetrator say?
( ) What else happened in this incident?

How

Follow up on the child's description of abuse, but be aware that this
may be difficult for young children.

( ) Determine methods of abuse

( ) Frequency of the specific act (e.g., "How many times did he or she do this to you?")

( ) Duration and/or length of this incident (e.g., "How much time did s/he spend doing it?")

( ) Clarify the child's terminology for private body parts

( ) Clarify the child's terminology for sexual acts
(specify) _____

( ) Use the child's terminology to ask further questions about the abuse

( ) How did the child feel before, during, and after the abuse?

( ) How does the child usually get along with the alleged perpetrator? (Check their relationship before and after the abuse)

( ) Determine the progression of abuse

( ) What else happened?

( ) How often have similar incidents occurred?

( ) Ask about the first incident in multiple abuse cases

( ) Ask about the most recent incident in multiple abuse cases (if not disclosed yet)

( ) Ask about other incidents between the first and the most recent incident

( ) Ask about other sexual acts

( ) Ask about being exposed to or forced to participate in pornography

Additional information (may be required by law)

( ) Do you know if the perpetrator has done this to anyone else?

( ) Has anyone else done something like this to you? (alternative hypothesis)

( ) Determine the motive to report (e.g., reason to report the abuse now)

( ) Who was the first person the child told about the abuse?

( ) This person's reaction or action?

( ) What made the child decide to report?

( ) Don't use inappropriate techniques

( ) Don't use why questions (which may be perceived as accusing)

( ) Don't use leading questions

( ) Don't be judgmental

( ) Don't touch the child

( ) Don't be tense (be child focused)

Stage 4: Closing the Interview

( ) Confirm the name of the perpetrator and the type(s) of abuse

( ) Ask the child to confirm that the disclosed content is what has happened

( ) Confirm that no one has forced the child to tell or not to tell what has been told

( ) Be honest with the child about what will happen next

( ) Give the child an opportunity to ask questions

( ) Address the child's concerns

( ) Thank and reassure the child

( ) Formally close the interview by stating that the interview has ended or reporting the time

Checklist of Child's Credibility in Child Sexual Abuse Interviews

The items in this checklist are based on the author's research and practice experience in the field of child sexual abuse. The checklist aims to help the investigative team determine the reliability of a reported case through interviews with the child victim. Some items may be irrelevant to your case (circle NA if the item is not applicable). Extract only the relevant information for your documentation (the examples that follow derive from Myers, 1992; National Training Program on Effective Treatment Approaches in Child Sexual Abuse, 1993; Schetky & Green, 1998; Stevenson, Leung & Cheung, 1992).

The child was able to describe the content of the sexual abuse:

Verbal   Behavioral

_____ _____ NA   Describes sexual knowledge beyond what is to be expected for the child's developmental age.

_____ _____ NA   Describes sexual behavior from a child's viewpoint.

_____ _____ NA   Describes explicit details of sexual acts.

_____ _____ NA   Describes sexual activities with progression if the abuse has occurred more than once.

_____ _____ NA   Describes specific content of the abuse even though the child does not understand what it means.

_____ _____ NA   Uses age-appropriate language, vocabulary, or terminology to describe the abuse.

The child was able to describe the context of the sexual abuse:

_____ _____ NA When it happened.
_____ _____ NA Where it happened.
_____ _____ NA What the alleged perpetrator did.
_____ _____ NA What the alleged perpetrator said.
_____ _____ NA Where other family members were during the time of abuse.
_____ _____ NA What the child was wearing.
_____ _____ NA Whether clothing of the child was removed.
_____ _____ NA How the clothing of the child was removed.
_____ _____ NA What the perpetrator was wearing.
_____ _____ NA Whether clothing of the perpetrator was removed.
_____ _____ NA How the clothing of the perpetrator was removed.
_____ _____ NA Describes the coercive nature of sexual abuse.
_____ _____ NA Describes the elements of secrecy.
_____ _____ NA Whether the child told anyone about the abuse.
_____ _____ NA Describes the reactions of the person the child told.

The child's affect when recounting the sexual abuse:

Verbal **Behavioral**
_____ _____ NA Reluctance to disclose
_____ _____ NA Embarrassment
_____ _____ NA Rage and/or anger
_____ _____ NA Disgust
_____ _____ NA Fear

The child's behaviors before and after disclosure:

Verbal **Behavioral**
_____ _____ NA Guarded somatic complaints
_____ _____ NA Sexually acting out behavior or socially withdrawn
_____ _____ NA No secondary gain from disclosure
_____ _____ NA Recantation
_____ _____ NA Other behavioral indicators of child sexual abuse (specify)

Example Questions for Conducting Videotaped Interviews in Child Sexual Abuse Investigations

Phase 1: Introduction and Rapport Building

The numbers used next to each question aim to identify specific questions for training purposes and do not reflect a fixed sequence of questioning techniques. When the child does not want to talk about the abuse details, the interviewer may add other questions, such as "Is something making you uncomfortable?"

1. Specific introduction of your role, agency, purpose of interview, and so on.
2. "What is your name?"
3. "What do your friends call you?"
4. "May I call you _____?"
5. "How old are you?"
6. "When is your birthday?"
7. "What grade are you in?"
8. "What do you like most at school?"
9. "What time do you go home from school?"
10. "What is your favorite color (fruit, television program)?"
11. "Who lives at home? Tell me their names."
12. "Who helps you with your homework?"
13. "Who is your best friend?"
14. "Who else do you like to play with?"

15. "How did you come here today?" If multiple choices are given to encourage an answer, the provided choices must be exhaustive such as "Someone drove you here? by bus? or other means?"

Explain the Ground Rules

Truth and Lies

16. "Today, you and I are going to talk about something that is very important. Before we begin, I need to know that you understand the difference between telling the truth and telling a lie."

Direct approach (for older children)

17. "Tell me in your own words what the word *truth* means."

18. "Tell me what a lie means to you."

Conceptual approach

19. Give an example of a lie and check for competency: "Is it raining inside this room?" (If child answers no). "If someone said, it's raining in this room, would that be the truth or a lie?" (If child answers yes to the question "Is it raining inside this room?", then the interviewer can say, "Saying yes to this question is not a truth; it is considered a lie or a made-up thing. It cannot rain inside this room. OK?").

20. If the child does not answer, ask the question in a different way: "Is raining in this room a fact, or is it a fantasy (or did someone just make it up)?" Provide the accurate answer and use another example.

21. Also give an example of the truth and check for competency: "What color is my jacket?" (child answers "red," which is the truth): "If someone said my jacket is red, would that be the truth or a lie?"

22. If the child is unable to differentiate between the truth and a lie, the interviewer should attempt to define the difference in simple terms, such as "The truth is something that really happened. It represents the fact. Lies are things that don't really happen, things or fantasies that are made up."

Acceptability of saying, "I don't know" or "I don't understand"

23. "If you really don't know the answer to my question, it's OK to say, 'I don't know,' and when you don't understand my question, say, 'I don't understand,' and I will ask the question in a different way. Don't make up answers."

Conclusion about telling the truth

24. "What would happen if someone is not telling the truth?"

25. "Everything we talk about today must be only the truth, nothing made up or pretended. Also, don't leave anything important out. OK?"

Phase 2: Free-Narrative Account

26. "Now tell me what happened." (Use silence to show your patience)

27. "Has anything bothered you lately?"

28. "Did someone tell you not to tell what happened to you?"

29. "If you tell me what happened, I could find ways to help you. OK?"

Phase 3: Questioning

Trigger Questions (If Child Is Reticent)

30. "Why are you here today?" ("What brought you here?")

31. "You appear to be upset (or another observation). Tell me what happened."

32. "Earlier today at school, you told (someone) that something happened to you. Tell me about that."

33. If the child is reluctant to tell, say, "I received a phone call (or report) that something has happened, and I would like to be able to help. I first need to know, in your own words, exactly what has happened."

34. "Has anyone done something to you that you should tell?"

35. "Has anyone told you to keep a secret?"

36. Clarify the child's terminology and use the child's language to ask questions (avoid using questions such as "Do you remember" or "Can you tell me" that the child can simply answer yes or no to evade the second part of the question).

Detailed Information of the Most Recent Incident

Use who, when, and where questions to identify whether abuse occurred. Once abuse is disclosed, encourage the child by saying, "Now tell me the details of what happened."

Who

(*Daddy* is used here to illustrate the questioning techniques, but an alleged perpetrator may be another person, male or female, known or unknown to the child.)

37. "Who is Daddy?"
38. "What is Daddy's full name?"
39. "How many daddies do you have?"
40. "Where does Daddy live?"
41. (If more than one daddy) "Which daddy did you say put his hand in your pants?"
42. (If gender of the perpetrator cannot be identified) "Is your music teacher a man or woman?"
43. "How old is he or she?"
44. "Describe how he or she looks."

When

45. "When did it happen?" (Determine time and date.)
46. "You said you were watching TV when it happened. What was on TV at that time?"
47. "You said you couldn't remember the date. Did you go to school that day?"
48. "What did you do at school that day?"
49. "You said it happened the night before. Today is (date). What date was the 'night before'?"

50. "Was it dark outside, or was it daylight?

51. "You said you were sleeping when Daddy came in. What time did you go to bed that day?"

Where

52. "You said something happened when Mommy was not home. Which home are you referring to?"

53. "Where were you when Daddy touched you?"

54. "You said it was at home. What is the address of your home?"

55. "How many rooms does your house (apartment) have?"

56. "Which room were you in when Daddy touched you?"

57. "Whose bedroom was it?"

58. "Describe what was inside that room."

59. "When you stepped in this place, what did you see?"

60. "How did you go to this place?" (if the place is not a familiar place)

61. "You said that Daddy takes you to the third floor of an apartment building. Was there anything such as a number posted on the apartment door?"

What (general questioning)

62. "What happened to you?"

63. "Tell me more about that."

64. "Tell me the most recent incident."

65. "Go on."

66. "What else happened?"

67. "What happened next?"

68. "You said that Daddy did something bad. Tell me what Daddy did."

How (follow-up questions to investigate specific details)

69. "You said it was dark in the room, how did you know it was Daddy?"

70. "You said he said something to you and you recognized it was Daddy, what did he say?"

71. "How did he make you 'uncomfortable'?"
72. "What did Daddy touch you with?"
73. "You said he put something in your bottom part. What is your 'bottom part'?"
74. "Tell me another name for 'sh-sh.'"
75. "What do your mom and doctor call 'sh-sh'?"
76. "What were you wearing when he touched you?"
77. "What was Daddy wearing when he touched you?"
78. "How did Daddy touch your bottom part with your pants on?"
79. "You said Daddy put his pee-pee in your mouth. Did he say anything before (when, after) he did that?"
80. "When he put his pee-pee in your mouth, what did you see?"
81. "Describe his pee-pee."
82. "What else did you see?"
83. "What happened to him after he touched his pee-pee in front of you?"
84. "What did you feel when he put his pee-pee in your mouth (or what the child just described)?"
85. "How did he move his body?"
86. "You said he shook his body. Show me how he did it."
87. "How many times did he shake?"
88. "How long did it last?"
89. "How much time did he spend with you?"
90. "You said he gave you some toilet paper to wipe yourself. Where did you wipe?"
91. "After you wiped yourself, what did you see on the toilet paper?"
92. "Where did you put the toilet paper?"
93. "You said you felt something wet on your bottom. Did you see what that was?"
94. "You said the 'candy' from his pee-pee tasted really bad. What did you do with it?"
95. "Where did you spit it?"
96. "What color was it?"
97. "What was the smell?"
98. "Did he do anything else to you?"
99. "What did he say afterward?"

Coercion and/or Secrecy

100. "What else did he do (or say) when he put his pee-pee in your mouth?"
101. "You said he pushed you against the wall and made you kneel down. How did he make you kneel down?"
102. "When he grasped your right shoulder with his hand, what did he do with the other hand?"
103. "Before Daddy left your bedroom (or wiped your legs), did he say anything?"
104. "Who else knew about what you've just told me?"
105. "When you told Mommy about this, what did she say?"

Who Else

106. "Who else was in the bedroom when Daddy came in?"
107. "Who else was in the house (apartment) when this happened?"
108. "You mentioned your brother was also in the bedroom. Did he say anything at that time?" "How about afterward. Did he say anything about what Daddy did to you? How about to him?"

Progression of Abuse

109. "What else happened?"
110. "Has this kind of thing happened in the past?"
111. "How many times did it happen?"
112. "Tell me what happened in the first time." (Focus on the who, when, where, what, and how questions for the first incidence after asking questions of the most recent incidence.)

Phase 4: Closing the Interview

Brief Summary

113. "You just told me that Daddy touched your pee-pee and you were scared to tell. Is there anything else you would like to tell me?"

Alternative Hypotheses

114. "Do you know if Daddy has done this to anyone else?"
115. "Has anyone else done something like this to you?"

Answer Questions from Child

116. "I have asked you a lot of questions today. Do you have any questions you would like to ask me?"

Comfort and Thank Child

117. "I know this may have been difficult for you to talk about. Thank you very much for telling me about it."
118. "You seem to be anxious to go. Before we go, I would like to thank you for coming."
119. "I want you to know that I will try to help you to go through this process. If you have any questions for me later, please let me know. I will leave my phone number for you (or the relative of a young child). Thank you for coming."

Research Supporting Admissibility of Forensic Interview Videotapes

Research Studies on Supporting Videotaping Interviews in Child Sexual Abuse Investigations

The following is extracted from the transcript for "The Mouth of Babes," a television interview from ABC TV's *20/20*; the square brackets indicate background dialogue occurring separately from the narrator and interview subjects; headings have been inserted to separate the three research studies discussed.

TV HOST: Cornell University Professor Stephen Ceci read the testimony of some well-known molestation cases and concluded that the interviewer had led the kids on by asking suggestive questions. The interviewer could say, "How else can we get this information out because the kids won't volunteer it?"

CECI: The problem is that from a research standpoint, we are now discovering that if you put kids who are not abused to the same kind of highly leading repetitive interview, some of those children will also disclose events that seem credible but in fact that they are not warranted in actuality.

I. Sam Stone Study

[Dr. Ceci] planned an experiment known as the "Sam Stone Study." He told the classroom full of 4 or 5 or 6 year olds that a man named Sam Stone would come to their class and he was very clumsy. Then the man came in, stayed a few minutes and left; that's it. He didn't do anything clumsy. Then three or four times in the next few months, half the kids were asked leading questions about the man's visit.

CECI: "Remember when Sam Stone came to the school and he broke that toy? Did he do it on purpose or was it an accident?" Well, he didn't break a toy, so it is a highly suggestive, erroneously suggestive question.

After that, another interviewer simply asked, ["I wasn't there that day and I want to know everything that happened the day that Sam Stone came to visit. Can you tell me what happened?"]

This little boy said that Sam Stone was reading a book during the visit to the classroom.

["He was doing it so fast that he ripped one of the pages."
"Really?"]

This girl said that Sam Stone threw dolls and books in the air when he was in the class.

["Well, when your teacher saw that he was throwing things in the air, what did she say?"
"Then you need to go."
"You need to go?"
"Yes, 'cause he kept ripping up stuff."]

Just asking leading questions inspired most of the kids to make stories up.

After the fact [the children] repeatedly been asked questions like this: ["Do you remember that time when Mr. X asked you to stick his penis in your mouth? OK?"]

[None of the child abuse investigators would agree to be interviewed for this story.]

Some clearly go too far.

CPS WORKER: ["You are pressing your pee-pee against me, you know. It feels good when you do that."]

CHILD: ["I'll stick it up your butt."]

CPS WORKER: ["Is that what they did too?"]

Stephen Ceci said that the questioning in the Kelly Michael's case was just as leading as this. They said to the child, "We want you to tell us what Kelly did."

The kid says ["I don't remember."]

["Oh yes you do. You remember."]

["No, I don't remember."]

["You do so[;] we know you remember."]

At this point the child's crying. ["I want to get out of here."]

["You are not going anywhere until you tell us what we know you know."]

II. Mousetrap Story

Here a researcher asked four- and five-year-olds to pick a card out of a deck of ten. On each card there was a question.

INTERVIEWER: ["Okay, Derek. Have you ever seen a baby alligator eating apples on an airplane?"]

CHILD: ["No." "No?"]

INTERVIEWER: ["Have you ever had your finger caught in a mousetrap and had to go to the hospital?"]

CHILD: ["No." "No?"]

At first almost all of the kids say 'No.' But then once a week for the next ten weeks they ask the question again. No coercion, no leading questions as in the child abuse cases. They just gently repeat the question.

INTERVIEWER: ["You went to the hospital because your finger got caught in a mousetrap. Did that happen?"]

CHILD: ["Ah . . . ha . . ."]

By week four or six or ten most of the children were saying yes, it happened. Some were not just saying yes, but giving such precise information about it that you think it must have happened.

INTERVIEWER: ["Did it hurt?"]

CHILD: ["Yeah."]

INTERVIEWER: ["Who took you to the hospital?"]

CHILD: ["My daddy, my mommy, my brother."]

INTERVIEWER: ["So where in your house is the mousetrap?"]

CHILD: ["It is somewhere down in the basement."]

INTERVIEWER: ["Down in the basement. What is it next to in the basement?"]

CHILD: ["It's next to the firewood."]

CECI: "I think it is fair to say that my colleagues and I were absolutely shocked that by the tenth week not only were they consenting to some of these things that did not occur, but they were giving very coherent narratives. Highly elaborative narratives that are, I think, quite persuadable."

TV HOST: By the time I met the same boy, it was weeks after the experiment, but he still could give lots of convincing details about things that never happened.

TV HOST: ["Was there a time when you got your finger caught in a mousetrap and you had to go to the hospital?"]

CHILD: ["Mm-hmm"]

TV HOST: ["Wow. Which finger was it?"]

Remember, this was the result after researchers simply asked the question once a week for ten weeks. In real abuse cases, kids are questioned for years, often by parents, doctors, then by the investigator, perhaps by a therapist, then by a lawyer.

TV HOST: ["Who went with you to the hospital?"]

CHILD: ["Uh, my mom and my dad and my brother Collin. But not my baby. It was in my Mom's tummy."]

TV HOST: ["Your baby"]

This boy's testimony was even more remarkable because just a few days earlier his father had discussed the experiment with him. He explained that it was just a test and that the whole mousetrap event had never happened. The boy agreed that it was just in his imagination. Still, listen to this.

TV HOST: ["Let me ask you. Did your father tell you something about the mousetrap finger story. Is it true? Did it really happen?"]

CHILD: ["It wasn't a story. It REALLY happened."]

TV HOST: ["It really happened. You really got your finger caught. It really happened."]

CHILD: ["Yeah."]

TV HOST: I assume the child isn't lying. They aren't intentionally making up stories.

CECI: "Absolutely. I think they have come to believe it. It is part of their belief system."

III. Anatomically Correct Dolls

TV HOST: Some experts believe that they would come closer to the truth using anatomically correct dolls. With dolls, they wouldn't have to ask so many questions. But Ceci's colleague, Dr. Maggie Bruck, conducted a test that led her to conclude using dolls also leads kids on.

TV HOST: ["I would think anatomically correct dolls would be a good neutral way to ask questions."]

BRUCK: ["I thought the very same way. After having this experience, I am not quite sure how you do that."]

TV HOST: Bruck and this pediatrician add some extra steps to his routine physical examination of pre-school kids. He measures the child's wrist with a ribbon. He puts a little label on the child's stomach. He tickles the child's foot with a stick.

Never does the doctor go anywhere near the child's private parts.

Then, right after the exam, using an anatomically correct doll, Bruck asks leading questions about the doctor's exam.

BRUCK: ["Can you show me on the doll how the doctor touched your vagina?"]

CHILD: ["No, he didn't touch my vagina"]

BRUCK: ["He didn't?"]

The child tells the truth. But just a few days later, Dr. Bruck and the child's father asked again about the doctor's visit, it is a different story. Before Bruck has a chance to even bring out the doll, the child shows how the doctor had strangled her with the ribbon.

CHILD: ["He did this."]

Father: ["He put that around your neck?"]

CHILD: ["Tight . . . so tight."]

Watch what happens when the doll's brought out. She is asked to explain what the doctor did that day.

["So what did he do?"]

CHILD: ["He put a stick in my vagina."]

["He put a stick in your vagina?"]

CHILD: ["Yeah."]

["Just like that?"]

It gets even more violent. She claims that the doctor hammered the stick into her vagina. Then she shows how the doctor examined her.

BRUCK: ["He was where?"]

CHILD: ["My hiney."]

BRUCK: ["He did look in your hiney?"]

TV HOST: Of course, none of it is true. Dr. Bruck found that when dolls were used, half the kids who had never had their private parts touched claimed the doctor had touched them.

These tests made Dr. Bruck bring questions about the testimony made by children in court.

"Do you think there are dozens of people in jail now who are totally innocent?"

"Yes, I do." [END OF TRANSCRIPT]

Lessons Learned

1. No repeated questions—particularly with suspicious tone of disbelief that leads the child to think he or she must give or make up answers.

2. No guiding, suggestive, or leading questions—that lead the child to believe something might have happened because of what you said.

3. No suggestive tools—don't use anatomical dolls before any disclosure of abuse.

CHAPTER 3

Screening Stage
Truth or False Allegations

This chapter describes the process of validation by identifying methods to check a child's competencies in answering questions and describing protocol to help the child differentiate between telling the truth and lying. In child sexual abuse investigations, it is important to create a team of professionals who have had clinical experiences with children to help the victim deal with the trauma. Such trauma is often caused by the abuse, but it may also be caused by the disclosure itself, whether it is a truthful disclosure or a false memory. Children who are afraid of the perpetrator may not tell the truth to other adults, whereas children who have been coached by others to lie may not know how to tell the truth. As a result, it is essential to handle the investigative and intervention process in a way that can help the child disclose the whole truth without causing more trauma. Some important points for practice are highlighted in "Julie's Case," described in chapter 1. Because multidisciplinary collaboration occurs during the process of both child sexual abuse investigation and intervention, professionals from different disciplines, such as social work, law enforcement, psychology, forensic investigation, medicine, and the legal field, must work together to achieve the goal of getting the whole truth.

In the past decade, many childhood sexual abuse cases have come from religious institutions, and significant publicity has focused on abuse by priests in the Catholic Church. This chapter also describes procedures to validate child sexual abuse allegations and provides policies established by religious institutions to examine needed actions to protect both children and individuals who are falsely accused. The case of Julie is used to identify techniques to validate abuse.

Crisis Intervention

Before seeking help to deal with a crisis, families often experience internal chaos, and family members tend to be reluctant to report the problem to the outside world. In cases of child sexual abuse, however, the perpetrator typically tells the child victim to keep the abuse a secret, and the child is therefore coerced to maintain the sexual relationship without showing emotions or any other observable trace of the abuse. As a result, it is possible that the family can seem quite peaceful, and its members may not be aware of the abuse. When the crisis is reported, either accidentally or purposively, the family will enter a stage of emotional shock, denial, and/or refusal to cooperate. Because of their inability to deal with a sudden crisis, the family members, especially the nonoffending parent, will find a way to persuade either themselves or the child that the allegations of abuse are not an accurate reflection of the facts. Not only will they deny the allegation after a report has been made, but they will also pressure the child victim to withhold information or recant the complaint. If the child perceives that recanting can put the family in a better and more stable position, particularly if the alleged perpetrator (AP) is the sole breadwinner in the household in the case of intrafamilial abuse, he or she will deny the abuse even after a formal complaint is filed with Child Protective Services or the police (for a better understanding of recantation, see figure 3.1).

Many workers who have experience with abused children have observed that children in abusive situations fear the negative consequences of reporting and feel that the family will be broken if the report is pursued in the legal system. Child victims may feel ambivalent about punishing the abuser and may even want to protect the AP. A careful and sensitive investigation must take place in order to avoid both type I (identification of abuse when it does not exist) and type II (failure to identify abuse when it does exist) errors that can arise because of the mix of truth and false allegations.

Type I and Type II Errors

According to a study conducted by Oates, Jones, Denson, Sirotnak, Gary, and Krugman (2000), a review of 551 cases of child sexual abuse reported to the Denver Department of Social Services over twelve months found

Figure 3.1 Recantation in Child Sexual Abuse Investigation

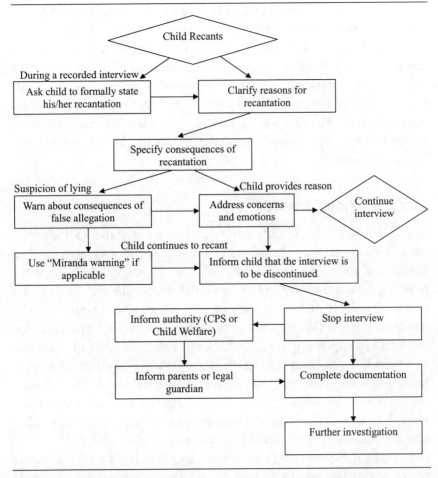

four groups of cases: substantiated (43 percent), not sexual abuse (34 percent), inconclusive (21 percent), and erroneous accounts by children (2.5 percent). Although the erroneous cases represent only a small proportion of the investigated cases, it was found that, among the fourteen erroneous cases, three were reported as a result of collusion with the parent, three were the child's misinterpretations, and eight were false allegations.

According to Baker (1998), investigators may find two types of false allegation errors: type I and type II. Type I is a false-positive error, which occurs when the child reports abuse that has not occurred. Type II is false-negative error, which occurs when the child does not report abuse that has actually occurred. There is a higher probability that the child will not report having been sexually abused than that the child will report falsely. Neoh and Mellor (2009) suggest that whether false allegations are well intentioned, genuinely believed, or maliciously motivated, professionals must always pay attention to case handling, alternative reasons behind the complaint, confirmation bias, and repercussions of allegations. It is the responsibility of the professionals involved to handle these types of cases with sensitivity. The first step in an interview is a competency check, to ensure that the child is able to answer questions in a logical, rational, and consistent manner.

Competency Checks

In previous research, the author and a colleague found that multidisciplinary professionals view the interview protocol as a tool to serve the dual function of collecting forensic data and assessing the child's competency (Cheung & Boutté-Queen, 2009). In another study, Cheung (2003) found that professionals consider the use of who, when, where, what, and how questions (i.e., the 4W1H questions) a good rapport-building tool that also serves as a competency check for the child before the start of a forensic interview. It is absolutely essential to follow evidence-based interview protocols when interviewing alleged victims and perpetrators. The literature does support that when a child victim is interviewed, the introduction serves two major roles: rapport building and competency checking (Cheung, 2008; Lamb, Orbach, Hershkowitz, Esplin, & Horowitz, 2007).

Competency checking includes checking the child's ability to answer the 4W1H questions. The first step is to increase professional awareness through three major tasks:

Task 1: Understand your role and responsibilities.
If you are not the right person to conduct the interview, it is important to refer the client to the appropriate person by stating, "I understand your concern. In this kind of situation, X is the most appropriate person to address this concern. If you would prefer, I can go with you to talk with X."

*Task 2: **Be sensitive without overreacting.***

If you interpret what the client said as sexual abuse, but those are not exactly the client's own words, clarify it first (e.g., "What do you mean?" "What is X?").

Ask for more information to validate (e.g., "What did he do?" "This seems to be a serious matter. Tell me more about it." "When did it happen?" "Where?" "You said you told X; what did X say at that time?").

Know the dos and don'ts when asking questions (see chapter 4).

If you are the appropriate person to hear this concern, use the appropriate interview protocol (see chapter 4).

*Task 3: **Know the use of 4W1H questions in checking the child's competency.***

As a basic principle, questions used in the rapport-building stage can test whether the child knows how to answer when, where, who, what, and how questions. Because sexual abuse questions are sensitive to the child, most interviewers start interviews with rapport-building questions:

- *When*: "When is your birthday?" "When do you usually leave your house to go to school?"
- *Where*: "Where do you usually like to go if you eat out with your parents?"
- *Who*: "Who is living with you?" "Who is your favorite teacher (singer)?" "Who came with you today?" "Who is X you just mentioned? How is he related to you?"
- *What*: "What do you like to eat?" "What color is this?" "What color do you like?"
- *How*: "How did you get here? By bus or car?" "How did you feel when you first sat down? How about now?"

These questions are used in a relaxed way so that the child becomes accustomed to the environment before answering questions. These questions are used to evaluate the child's ability to answer specific questions. Professionals must also be skilled when asking specific questions. These competency-check questions help professionals warm up and assess the reactions of the child. Later, when asking questions about sexual abuse, the interviewer can use questions about time and place to begin the inquiry, as the child will often perceive these questions as less threatening. The who question is also a good rapport-building question if the child has already provided some information about the abuse before the interview. The interviewer may check whether the child can say the full name of family members, including the AP in intrafamilial abuse. It is critically important to obtain the exact name of the AP in a forensic interview. Never assume that you know the name of the AP without asking, and never think that the child is referring to the same person you are thinking about.

The Truth-Lie Ritual

In the rapport-building stage, an interviewer will check to determine whether the child understands the difference between telling the truth and lying. The truth-lie ritual serves three major functions. First, it is used as a transition method to link the relaxing rapport stage to the more serious free-narrative reporting stage. Second, it allows the interviewer to assess whether the child is able to differentiate between telling the truth and telling a lie and between fact and fantasy. Third, it provides an opportunity for the interviewer to explain to the child the importance of telling what really happened and not making anything up, even when a child, either because of age or because of developmental ability, does not understand the examples that the interview gives.

In a study of ninety randomly selected videotaped forensic interviews with alleged child sexual abuse victims, comparisons of techniques were made between disclosure and nondisclosure cases (Cheung, 2008). In these interviews, interviewers in 95 percent of the disclosure cases helped the child to understand the importance of telling the truth. A direct approach was used in forty-eight cases (77.4 percent); that is, the children were asked to define the truth and a lie in their own words. In forty-four cases (71 percent), at least one example was used to assess the child's competency in differentiating between telling the truth and telling a lie. A balanced perspective of using one truth example and one lie example was represented in forty-one cases (66.1 percent).

Whether or not the child disclosed, the interviewer went through a truth-lie ritual in all interviews. A content analysis of 111 truth and lie examples used in these sixty-two interviews was conducted. These examples can be categorized into five groups:

1. Nonspecific definitions given by the interviewer (fifty-two examples given): real, honest, made up, not real, good thing, bad thing
2. Child's information (twenty-six examples given): the child's age, name, clothes, shoes
3. Incident-specific examples (twenty-one examples given): money stolen, cookies eaten, broken toy, a child hitting someone, milk spilled on the floor
4. Observations (eight examples given): wallpaper color, who is in the room, whether it is raining in the room, birds flying in the room
5. Imaginary examples (four examples given): an elephant on your hand, a cup on your hand, dinosaurs flying through the window

Most of these examples were used as either a truth or a lie example, depending on what the interviewer had used to illustrate the point. Some of the nonspecific definitions the interviewers gave were evaluated as judgmental or confusing, such as, "It is a bad thing to tell a lie, isn't it?" The interviewers also used imaginary items as examples of telling a lie. Because children can usually respond to a question regarding their own personal data but not to a question about an unfamiliar scenario, the literature supports the use of concrete examples when questioning children. For example, questions about the child's age, name, or clothing color are helpful in assessing the child's understanding (Cheung, 1997). Also, when the interviewer gives an example, it is helpful to first check the correct answer with the child before asking the child whether the example illustrates the truth or a lie. In addition, it was not helpful to use either the child or the interviewer as the person to illustrate the example of telling a lie; doing so might confuse the child about his or her own ability to tell the truth and the truthfulness of the interviewer.

According to the analysis, some of the examples were considered helpful in determining the children's understanding of telling the truth or telling a lie, including the following:

Information based on the child:
"What is your name?" (The child answered correctly.) "If someone said your name is [correct or wrong name], would it be the truth or a lie (mistake)?"

"How old are you?" (The child answers correctly.) "If someone said you're [correct or wrong age], would it be the truth or a lie?"

"I noticed that you are wearing blue jeans today. If someone said you're wearing [blue jeans or a dress] today, would this person be telling the truth or telling a lie?"

Incident-specific examples:
"A friend ate all the cookies from the cookie jar and he said he [did or didn't], would this friend be telling the truth or telling a lie?"

"A girl took money from her mom's purse and said she [did or didn't], would she be telling the truth or telling a lie?"

"A boy broke his toy and told his mom [he did it or his sister did it], would he be telling the truth or telling a lie?"

Observations:
"Is it raining inside this room?" (The child answers no.) "If someone said it [is or isn't] raining inside this room, is this person telling the truth or telling a lie?"

"Do you see birds flying inside this room?" (The child answers no). "If someone said there is a bird flying inside this room, is this person telling the truth or a lie?"

Imaginary examples:
"If someone said that there is an elephant sitting on my hand, is this person telling the truth or making things up?"

"If someone said two dinosaurs were just flying out through this room, would that really happen?" (The child answers no.) "If someone said it really happened, would this person be telling the truth or telling a lie?"

Best-Practice Principles in Assessment

Children are typically not willing to talk with a stranger. After the interviewer builds rapport with a child, if the child asks, "Will you believe what I'm going to tell you?" the interviewer must use a blank-screen approach to be an active listener in order to gather information for assessment. The interviewer's reaction to this question must encourage the child to tell the truth. Possible answers may include encouraging disclosure (e.g., "Tell me—I'm here to listen"), motivating truth telling (e.g., "If you are telling the truth, of course I will believe you"), understanding the motive (e.g., "What do you want to tell me?"), reflecting feeling (e.g., "I feel that you are concerned about something—tell me what it is), hearing it first (e.g., "You haven't told me what it is—how about telling me first?"), and providing an answer later (e.g., "I don't have an answer now; how about letting you know later?").

After the child tells, the child may ask, "Now tell me, do you believe what I just told you?" If the interviewer's role is to gather information, then answers may include the following:

- *Address feeling*: "You seem to be concerned. How do you feel now after telling me about this problem?"
- *Share genuineness*: "Yes, what you told me seems to be true" (particularly if the child has a trustworthy character); "I'm not sure because I wasn't there"; "It seems to be impossible"; or "I have a mixed feeling—I believe in some part but cannot understand how it might happen."
- *Interpret the meaning*: "I heard something was very wrong. Are you concerned about what you can do now?"
- *Identify intent*: "What exactly do you want me to do to help you?" or "Why did you tell me this?"
- *Divert to a related issue (by not answering the question directly)*: "You told me earlier that you wanted to tell your mom but she was not around; would you like me to help you talk to your mom?"
- *Disclose your role*: "My role [as a social worker] is to hear your concern, not to judge you."
- *Ask about past experience*: "Did someone not believe in your story [disclosure] before? What was their reaction?"

- *Ask about the child's concerns*: "What are you worried about?"
- *Share your concern*: "When you asked me this question, I sensed something was not right."
- *Stress the importance of telling the truth*: "I believe you if you have told the truth. Do you know what the truth is?"
- *Reverse the question*: "I am shocked by this. What do you expect me to say?"
- *Use specific questioning technique*: "When you ask for a belief, what do you want?"
- *Set priorities*: "It is more important to address your problem now, not whether I believe in you."
- *Identify who*: "Who should believe in this [but didn't]?"
- *Take a new perspective*: "If someone told you something that is extremely traumatic, would you believe? Why or why not?"
- *Confront the speaker*: "Do you think that I would not believe in you? Tell me how you got this impression"; or if doubtful, "Why should I believe in you? Tell me a reason to support you."
- *Find meanings*: "Tell me what 'believe me' means to you."
- *Praise the speaker*: "It's hard to share something like this with a stranger [someone you just met]. You are brave."
- *Determine the outcome*: "What do you think would come out from this sharing?"
- *Discuss the future*: "What is your next step? What can we do together to resolve this problem?"

Role of Religious Organizations

When assessing the truthfulness of an allegation, professionals must be aware of the setting in which the abuse took place. One recent focus is on clergy abuse in the church. Among all religious institutions, the Catholic Church has received the most media coverage regarding sexual abuse by the clergy, particularly when the abuse took place in church or during the time when the child participated in activities with the clergy or in a religious setting.

First, when a complaint comes in about a member of the clergy or religious leader, the interviewer first assesses the abuse setting. If the abuse took place in the Catholic Church, the interviewer must be knowledgeable about the Charter for the Protection of Children and Young People, a set of procedures established by the U.S. Conference on Catholic Bishops (USCCB) in June 2002, with updates for addressing allegations of sexual abuse of minors by Catholic clergy. Similar charters have been established in other countries. Second, the interviewer must find out when the abuse took place, because there may be a statute of limitations in the state or country (see appendix 1C in chapter 1).

In 2005, the charter was revised to add specific guidelines for reconciliation, healing, accountability, and prevention of future acts of abuse (USCCB, 2009). The charter directs action with respect to creating a safe environment for children and young people, healing and reconciliation of victims and survivors, providing prompt and effective responses to allegations, cooperating with civil authorities, disciplining offenders, and providing a means of accountability for the future to ensure that the problem continues to be effectively dealt with through a national secretariat of child and youth protection and a national review board.

In the United States, the ad hoc Committee on Sexual Abuse provides a comparison based on the 157 policies submitted by the nation's dioceses to the USCCB in 1992–1993 and suggests that church policies should include seven components: accountability and written guidelines, prevention education programs, administrative guidelines, policies regarding victims, policies regarding the accused (e.g., timing of administrative leave during investigation), reassignment of the accused, and media coverage (e.g., assignment of a spokesperson; USCCB, 2009). Appendix 3A shows a comparison of the actions taken by some of the dioceses in the United States, based on information available online. The following are the common themes discovered from the comparisons:

- Forming national and local review boards—with experts in crime fighting and dealing with the emotional, psychological, and spiritual fallout of clergy sexual abuse. Victims of clergy sexual abuse, priests, retired police officers, judges, lawyers, psychiatrists, psychologists, educators, social workers, doctors, and nurses.
- Notifying local law enforcement agency and child protective agencies

- Clearly defining the child victim according to the statutes
- Naming bishops and archbishops as the final decision makers to determine whether the accused priest is to be suspended or expelled
- Creating the Safe Environment Program, an annual education program of diocesan and parish personnel on the awareness and prevention and reporting of child abuse
- Providing assistance to victims and their families
- Carrying out all investigations according to the essential norms and charter of the canon law of the Catholic Church 1717–1719

Appendix 3B summarizes policies from selected religious organizations, so users can retrieve a clear process from the relevant Web site should they need to consult with the organization about what needs to be done or what has been done during an investigative process.

Best-Practice Principles in Multidisciplinary Collaboration

There are many settings other than churches in which child abuse takes place. However, few empirical studies focus on multidisciplinary team collaboration in child sexual abuse, such as working with teachers, child-care workers, Child Protective Services (CPS) workers, police, counselors, and social workers. Nevertheless, studies have investigated the ways in which law enforcement personnel and CPS have worked together. An evaluation of joint law enforcement and CPS investigations over three and a half years found that "caseworker response time was significantly shorter in joint investigation cases than in independent [traditional—each agency goes its own way] investigation cases" (3.3. days versus 1.6 days in joint investigation, as those were severe cases that received higher priority; Tjaden & Anhalt, 1994, p. 15). Usually, the joint approach takes longer, but the investigation is more thorough and can lead to better outcomes for children and families.

In the United States, the concept of child advocacy centers (CACs, or multidisciplinary interview centers) to conduct assessments and deliver treatments under one roof has been tested and found to be both effective and efficient. Research findings indicate that such centers have reduced the number of interviews and interviewers (Martone, Jaudes, & Cavins, 1996). The following represents the collaborative process in a CAC.

First is casework. The worker receiving intake information gathers as much information from the complainant, and possibly additional collateral contacts, as is necessary to determine whether a child appears to have been at risk or still be at risk of abuse or neglect, or is at risk of abuse or neglect in the foreseeable future.

Second is the supervisor's review. In this review, priorities are set for investigation purposes. Some CACs have a two-level priority system, for example, priority 1 is to investigate within twenty-four hours, in cases of immediate risk or death and/or serious harm, and priority 2 is to investigate within ten days of receiving a report.

Third is the administrative review. In this review, the CAC will help CPS determine how to handle the case and will consider staff assignment on request of the AP or the family. An administrator who has not directly supervised or been involved in the investigation must conduct the review within a short period of time (e.g., forty-five days) after the receipt of such request (the review may be postponed until court proceedings are completed). Others can attend the review at the discretion of the reviewer.

Fourth is the release review. It has become more common for an AP to request a release review, which is a request to the CAC to reconsider a decision to release information about him or her to people outside the investigation who have control over access to children. The request must be filed within an allotted time (e.g., fifteen days) after receiving the notice of the AP's right to a release hearing, assuming that the child has been removed from home. The AP has a right to appear in person at the review, to invite a representative to speak on his or her behalf, and to submit relevant written material. Other attendees may include an interpreter and the regional director for protective services (families and children) or his or her designee. Emergency release is authorized when the department has evidence that the risk of harm to one or more children outside the family of the alleged victim is both substantial and immediate. To determine whether an AP poses a substantial risk to children outside the family of the alleged victim, staff will typically consider the following:

- The nature of the abuse or neglect
- Past patterns of behavior
- Attempts to seek employment or offer volunteer services at agencies or organizations that provide services to children
- The AP's level of maturity and psychological functioning
- The age, physical condition, level of maturity, psychological functioning, and other characteristics of the children to whom the AP has or might have access
- The nature of the AP's access to children
- The presence or absence of adults who can supervise the AP's access to children
- All other relevant information

Fifth is the CAC's multidisciplinary team (MDT) review. In the United States, some states provide for the execution of a memorandum of understanding with participating entities so that a CAC can serve two or more contiguous counties. In such cases, the CAC's functions include investigation, prosecution, and provision of victim services. A multidisciplinary team consists of persons who are involved in the investigation or prosecution of child abuse cases or the delivery of services to child abuse victims and their families. Services include forensic interviews, medical examinations and treatment, community outreach, and public education. Key elements in the formation of successful investigative MDTs are the following (adopted from Bilchik, 2001):

- Committed members who have the support of their agencies for the MDT approach
- An initial meeting during which each member's role and previous experience in investigating child abuse and neglect are respectfully heard
- The development of a mission statement that clearly sets forth the purpose of the team, the scope of its activities, and its guiding principles
- The subsequent creation of a team protocol that specifies the types of cases that will be investigated, the responsibilities of team members, and the procedures for conducting investigations

Key elements in the successful operation of an MDT include confidentiality policies that accord with legislative mandates, agency policies, professional practices, and the best interests of the abused children; conflict resolution practices that ensure that core issues are aired and resolved satisfactorily on the basis of mutual respect and recognition that child abuse investigations are complex, demanding, and frustrating but also important, meaningful, and rewarding; and periodic self-analysis and outside evaluation of how the team is working so that it continues to achieve the purposes for which it was formed.

Sixth is the initial service plan. The purpose of an initial service plan is to help children find a placement during the investigation period. Usually within forty-five days of a child's placement in substitute care, CPS must develop a written plan for services to the child. Moreover, CPS must ask the following individuals to participate in developing the child's service plan: the child's worker in the conservatorship unit; the worker supervising the placement, if different from the worker in the conservatorship unit; the child, unless he or she is too young to participate; the child's parents, unless they cannot be found, have had their parental rights terminated, or have executed an affidavit of relinquishment and have indicated that they do not want to participate in the child's case; the substitute caregiver (e.g., foster parent, residential group-home director, relative); the attorney or guardian ad litem, or both; and other professionals and volunteers who are providing services to the child or the child's family, when appropriate.

An effective service plan should include the following:

- A description of the type of home or facility in which a child is placed
- A discussion of the safety and appropriateness of the placement
- Plans to carry out the judicial determination made with respect to the child
- A plan to ensure that the child receives safe and proper care
- A plan to ensure that services are provided to the child and foster parents (or caregivers) to facilitate return of the child to his or her own safe home or the permanent placement of the child
- A plan to address the needs of the child while in foster care (or substitute care)

- A discussion of the appropriateness of the services that have been provided to the child under the plan
- Health and education records of the child, to the extent available and accessible
- A written description of the programs and services that will help the child prepare for the transition from foster care to independent living, if available
- Documentation of the steps the agency is taking to find and place the child with an adoptive family, a fit and willing relative, a legal guardian, or other planned permanent living arrangement for the child and the steps to finalize the adoption or legal guardianship (for children whose permanency plan is adoption or placement in another permanent home)
- A plan to achieve placement in a safe setting that is the least restrictive, consistent with the best interests and special needs of the child
- An explanation of the reasons such a placement is in the best interests of the child (if the child has been placed in a foster family home or child-care facility a substantial distance from the home of the parents of the child or in another state in which such home is located)

During the investigative process, professionals such as mental health or health-care practitioners, parents, and teachers must pay attention to the behaviors of the alleged child victim and understand the child's emotional state and intent to report (for tips for professionals, parents, and teachers, see appendix 3C).

Julie's Case: Telling the Truth or Lying?

In fourteen-year-old Julie's case, during the videotaped forensic interview, the interviewer asked Julie whether she could differentiate between telling the truth and lying. Julie answered vaguely that she understood. When specifically asked what telling the truth meant, Julie said, "Telling what's been actually happening." Julie was able to define *actual* when the interviewer stressed that she must tell only the truth and nothing made up.

In a forensic interview with children under the legal age of taking an oath in court, it is the responsibility of the interviewer to determine that the child understands the importance of telling the whole truth, without guessing or imagination, because the videotaped interview, which is forensic in nature, may be admissible in court. In most cases involving very young children, specific examples must be used to illustrate the child's competency in telling the truth. For example, use of the child's name, color of hair or dress, or grade of the child's schooling could help a young child understand the concept of truth telling. In cases involving an adolescent as the alleged victim, however, when the answer provides very abstract information, interviewers should not quickly accept the answer without making sure that the adolescent understands the difference between reality and fantasy; it is crucial to determine whether to move on to the next stage by asking the alleged victim to promise to tell only the truth. In Julie's case, the interviewer used a four-step approach of the truth-lie ritual to determine whether Julie was indeed competent to continue with the next stage of questioning:

1. *Check the answer about truth and lie*—"What does telling the truth mean to you?" "What does lying mean to you?"
2. *Use two examples: one truth and one lie*—"I'm going to give you two simple examples to help me understand your answer better. First, what is your name?" (Julie.) "If someone said, 'Your name is Julie,' is this person telling the truth or lying? I'll use another simple example: are we sitting here now?" (Yes.) "If someone was talking to another person outside of this room and said, 'Monique [interviewer] and Julie are not inside,' is this person telling the truth or lying?" The interviewer did not use herself or the child in the example to avoid any confounding effect of having an authority telling a lie or putting the child in the position of a liar.
3. *Explain the importance of telling the truth*—"Although simple examples are given, I just want to make sure that you agree the meaning of telling the truth—again, nothing made up or imaginary. It is very important to tell only the truth."
4. *Obtain a promise*—"You understand that what we are talking about today should be the whole truth, nothing partial, and nothing made up. Can you promise me to tell only the truth based on your own experience?"

This truth-lie ritual is similar to the oath-taking procedure in court. In a forensic interview, this ritual represents a friendly reminder that what the child will testify is a serious matter, and only the truth should be revealed. As a result, in the case when the child has been coached to accuse someone, the interviewer can then use questions such as "Has anyone told you to say what you've just told me?" "What did that person say?" "You said that your mother told you to tell me about this; how do you know what you told me was the whole truth?" and "You said that it happened on such-and-such date; how do you remember this so clearly?" to provide an opportunity for the child to provide additional information to verify the credibility of the child's statement. If the child has not been coached to say anything, then he or she will affirm, such as "I knew it because I was there" or "I was in pain because I just came home from grandmother's funeral, and that's why I remember the date," and so on. In general, providing this opportunity for the child to understand the importance of telling the truth is an important step to help the child make statements that are not based on hearsay or speculation.

If a child is very young or an adolescent with the mental and cognitive capacity of a very young child, he or she may not understand the examples given or the questions asked to determine his or her understanding. In an incident involving an alleged child victim who was only three years old, even after a few lying examples were given, the child still said that everything was the truth; in this situation, it would be important to provide a clear answer to affirm to the child that the example did not represent the truth and to provide the correct answer, such as "If this person said your name is something else, this person may be lying and is definitely not telling the truth." It is the duty of the interviewer to provide affirmative answers to correct the child when the child provides a wrong answer in this ritual. The purpose is to help the child understand the importance of telling the truth, not to force the child to define a concept that may be difficult for the child to clarify in words (chapter 4 addresses further investigative techniques to validate abuse).

Conclusion

To conduct a competency check on the alleged victim and avoid type I and type II errors, professionals must understand their roles and responsibilities, be sensitive without overreacting, and competently use the 4W1H questions. To ensure the apprehension of the perpetrator and the admissibility of a child's statement in court, forensic interviewers should employ the truth-lie ritual. The truth-lie ritual should incorporate information based on the child, incident-specific examples, observations, and/or imaginary examples. When working with a diverse client population, professionals must modify their assessment of child abuse allegations for certain settings, particularly sexual abuse perpetrated by clergy. Multidisciplinary teams and multidisciplinary service centers provide the best avenue for professionals working collaboratively to obtain information from the alleged victim in order to minimize repeat traumatization.

Protocols and Procedures for Handling Child Sexual Abuse Allegations in Different U.S. Dioceses: Examples

Diocese	Allegations first reported to . . .	Persons and/or parties to be notified	Points to consider	Interview factors
Oakland, CA	Chancellor and Victim Assistance Coordinator	Bishop will receive report and convene the Diocesan Review Board to review each reported case.	Diocesan Review Board assists the Bishop in the investigative process. Accused cleric will be placed on administrative leave during investigations.	The alleged victim shall select the meeting place and is offered to select two members from the Diocesan Review Board for an interview. When deemed necessary, the Review Board may invite a qualified professional investigator or researcher to assist in this process.
San Francisco, CA	Victim Assistance Coordinator (VAC)	Archbishop will work closely with the VAC and hire an investigator to conduct the investigation.	The Archbishop will consult with an Independent Review Board to review cases and policy regarding sexual abuse reporting.	None mentioned.

Diocese	Allegations first reported to ...	Persons and/or parties to be notified	Points to consider	Interview factors
Fort Wayne-South Bend, IN	Victim's Assistance Coordinator and General Vicar	Vicar will notify the Bishop and the Diocesan Review Board.	If a child is a victim, immediate report to appropriate civil authority is required. Review Board can confer and ask questions regarding the assessment and investigation. The Bishop will hear recommendations from the Review Board and report to the members about his final decision.	With reasonable suspicion, the priest will receive a psychological evaluation and therapy. If the priest is subject to legal action, he is responsible for hiring his own attorney.
Detroit, MI	Victim Assistance Coordinator or Archbishop's Delegate	All allegations of sexual abuse of minors and criminal sexual conduct involving priests or deacons will also be reported to 1) Department of Human Services (Michigan); 2) appropriate law enforcement agencies as required by law; and 3) the Delegate. Any communications between the Archdiocese and civil officials will be made by the Delegate through legal counsel.	The Review Board shall consist of 7–10 professionals to provide support and advice to the Archbishop regarding the alleged report and investigations. In the event civil authorities decide not to investigate a complaint, or in other special circumstances, the Archbishop may involve an independent investigator to provide a report to the Board.	The Review Board will make initial assessment and subsequent recommendations to the Archbishop regarding credibility of the allegations (Cf. cc. 1717-1719). The alleged victim and/or the accused may request to meet with the Board.

Diocese	Allegations first reported to ...	Persons and/or parties to be notified	Points to consider	Interview factors
Gaylord, MI	Assistance Coordinator	An investigator will assist the Review Board; collect information from other authorities or agencies; conduct an investigation; prepare a report to the Review Board with a recommendation of substantiated or unsubstantiated, unless good cause may be shown for extending the investigation. If the investigation is "substantiated," the Review Board shall provide advice to the Bishop with its recommendations concerning assistance to the victim, the accused, and others.	The board must have at least 5 persons "in full communion with the church." A majority of the board members must be lay people not employed by the diocese. One member should be a priest who is a respected pastor. At least one member should have expertise in treating sexual abuse of minors. Members are chosen for a 5-year term.	The board is to advise the Bishop on the credibility of allegations, the suitability for ministry of accused priests.
Brooklyn, NY	District Attorney or the Chancellor	Diocesan Review Board assists the Bishop in making his assessment. An Assistance Coordinator will manage counseling assistance.	The Diocesan Review Board serves as an advisory council to the Bishop. A policy regarding false accusation is also stated to empower the Review Board if further recommendations are to be made to the Bishop.	Specialized training is required for clergy, along with religious and lay employees and volunteers who interact with children; all are required to undergo background checks.

Diocese	Allegations first reported to ...	Persons and/or parties to be notified	Points to consider	Interview factors
New York, NY	Victim's Assistance Coordinator (VAC)	According to the penal law of the state of New York, sexual abuse of a minor is a crime and must be reported to the local authorities. In addition to phone calls to the diocese, a Web-based form is designed for the VAC to receive written reports of sexual abuse through the Internet.	Advisory Committee of clergy and laity (attorney, judges, former prosecutors) assists and provides advice to the Bishop regarding an alleged report.	Any single act of sexual abuse of a minor, the offending priest will be permanently removed from ministry.
Rockville Centre, NY	Director for the Office of Protection of Children and Young People	The complainant should report abuse to legal authorities. After having done that, report should be made to the director of Protection of Children and Young People. The alleged offender will be encouraged to retain the assistance of civil and canonical counsel.	When evidence is sufficient, the Diocesan Bishop, in writing, shall remove the accused priest or deacon from his assignment and prohibit the public exercise of ministry, pending the outcome of the process. The Congregation for the Doctrine of the Faith shall be notified. All directions given by the Holy See for each case will be followed.	No interview information is offered on the website. The Review Board is established by the Diocesan Bishop to provide advisory support about all aspects of the case.

Diocese	Allegations first reported to …	Persons and/or parties to be notified	Points to consider	Interview factors
Cleveland, OH	Victim Assistance Coordinator	Response team includes two licensed mental health professionals and one certified pastoral minister. Members of the Review Board include: two clinicians, a survivor of child sexual abuse, a parent, a parish priest, a canon lawyer, an attorney and individuals with experience in investigation, human resources and administrative law/dispute resolution.	Website is connected to the Office for the Protection of Children and Young People	Archbishop may also designate Vicar General to work with civil authorities and initiate a process of healing for those who are affected.
Providence, RI	Local authority (Agency Director, Pastor, Principal); Area of Mission Secretary; Moderator of the Curia; Coordinator of the Office of Education and Compliance (COEC)	COEC will notify the Coordinator of the Office of Human Formation and Outreach for the immediate pastoral care of the individual communicating the allegation; Bishop will meet with Diocesan Review Board to consider further actions.	The Bishop can exercise his executive power of governance to remove an offending cleric from office, to remove or restrict his faculties, and to limit his ministry duties.	The Review Board assists the Bishop to review child sexual abuse allegations both retrospectively and prospectively and provides advice.

Diocese	Allegations first reported to ...	Persons and/or parties to be notified	Points to consider	Interview factors
Galveston-Houston, TX	Victim Assistance Coordinator (VAC)	The VAC will report the allegation to the Archbishop and the chairperson of the Diocesan Review Board. The Archbishop will convene the Review Board to assess the allegation. The Review Board will discuss the credibility of the allegation and advise the Archbishop regarding the need for an investigation. During investigation, the alleged cleric will be on leave.	If the cleric admits the allegation, the Archbishop will consult with the Review Board regarding appropriate actions. If the accused cleric denies the allegation, the Archbishop shall convene a special panel (3–5 persons, including at least one priest and two members of the Review Board) to interview the alleged victim and cleric in accord with canon law (Canon 1717-1719).	Interviews will focus on the substantiation of the allegations and credibility of the alleged victim.
San Antonio, TX	Archbishop or Auxiliary Bishops, or the Vicar General	Archbishop will work with the Crisis Intervention Committee (CIC) (clergy and laity) to begin a prompt and thorough investigation. CIC will report findings directly to the Archbishop.	Allegations of abuse are reported according to the law of Texas.	If the case is found credible, the CIC will meet with the Archbishop and the Justice Promoter to present its findings. It is the Archbishop's responsibility to initiate the action phase and implement final recommendations. If it is unfounded, the Archbishop will make his final decision regarding case dismissal.

Diocese	Allegations first reported to ...	Persons and/or parties to be notified	Points to consider	Interview factors
La Crosse, WI	Bishop	The Bishop will meet with the Diocesan attorney, the accused, and the alleged victim. If the alleged perpetrator does not admit the abuse, the Bishop will appoint a liaison (qualified professional) to conduct further investigations.	Review Board will be asked to provide advice about the investigative assessments.	The Diocese may provide assistance for the alleged victim even if the case is not substantiated. The form and extent of the assistance will depend upon the nature of the case.

Source: Relevant information is summarized in part from the Web sites of respective dioceses. For accuracy, check current Web pages, which are revised periodically.

Examples of Policies Established by Religious Institutions on Child and Youth Protection

Religious organization	Affiliations and Web sites
Anglican Church policies	■ The Diocese of the Northeast, Anglican Church in America (http://conwayanglicans.org/.pdf%20files/Promise%20to%20 Protect.doc) ■ Child Protection in the Anglican Church Diocese of Sydney (http://www.psu.anglican.asn.au/images/uploads/RESPONSE_ to_child_abuse.pdf)
Baptist Church policies	■ Myers Park Baptist Church Children and Youth Protection Policy (http://www.google.com/#sclient=psy-ab&hl=en&site=&source =hp&q=Myers+Park+Baptist+Church+Children+and+Youth+ Protection+Policy+&pbx=1&oq=Myers+Park+Baptist+Church+ Children+and+Youth+Protection+Policy+&aq=f&aqi=&aql=1& gs_sm=e&gs_upl=1280l1280l0l1981l1l1l0l0l0l0l116l116l0.1l1l0& bav=on.2,or.r_gc.r_pw.,cf.osb&fp=869f99effd7195f2&biw=959& bih=480) ■ Child Protection Policy of San Jacinto Baptist Association (http://www.sjbaptist.org/index.php/about-us/administration/ constitutionpolicies/childrens-protection-policy) ■ Altrincham Baptist Church Youth and Children's Ministry Child Protection Policy (http://www.altrinchambaptist.org/Child ProtectionPolicy.pdf) ■ Sexual Misconduct Policy of Grace Baptist Church of Stillwater, MN (http://www.stillwaterbaptist.net/library/SEX_PREVENTION.pdf)
Catholic Church (Australia)	■ Towards Healing: Principles and Procedures in Responding to Complaints of Abuse against Personnel of the Catholic Church in Australia (2007) (http://www.acbc.catholic.org.au/documents/ 200711231131.pdf)

Religious organization	Affiliations and Web sites
Catholic Church (The Philippines)	■ The Holy See and the Convention on the Rights of the Child in the Republic of the Philippines (2004) (http://www.catholics forchoice.org/topics/international/documents/2005shadow reportphilippines.pdf)
Catholic Church (United States)	■ Charter for the Protection of Children and Young People (2002, revised 2005) (http://usccb.org/issues-and-action/child-and-youth-protection/charter.cfm) ■ Restoring Trust: Response to Clergy Sexual Abuse (http://old.usccb.org/comm/restoretrust.shtml) ■ The Five Principles to Follow in Dealing with Accusations of Sexual Abuse (1992) (http://old.usccb.org/comm/kit4.shtml) *Selected Dioceses* ■ Archdiocese for the Military Services, USA: Policy to Address Claims of Sexual Abuse of a Minor (http://www.milarch.org/resources/docs/ams_abuse_policy.pdf) ■ Archdiocese of Atlanta: Updated Policy of the Archdiocese of Atlanta Concerning the Protection of Children and Vulnerable Individuals from Sexual Abuse by Church Personnel (2003) (http://www.georgiabulletin.org/local/2003/08/07/policytext/) ■ Archdiocese of San Antonio: Policy of Sexual Misconduct on the Part of the Church Personnel of the Archdiocese of San Antonio (2003) (http://docs.google.com/viewer?a=v&q=cache:TPcnab 97FQEJ:www.bscc-sa.org/upload/faith/docs/Archdiocese% 2520of%2520San%2520Antonio%2520Policy%2520on%2520 Sexual%2520Misconduct.pdf+Archdiocese+of+San+Antonio: +Policy+of+Sexual+Misconduct+on+the+Part+of+the+Church +Personnel+of+the+Archdiocese+of+San+Antonio+%282003% 29&hl=en&gl=us&pid=bl&srcid=ADGEEShVLS_BVngF5PZGhQy Xl_OkbwCwmuqv461-JYzg676c6FSSKtQDBfqk9WtOE16yp BNCXXafkOAHmw4udCg-yqQznexDlTFCzKTgzpN4eZoH5p NXFW—I7caF2d7IJuUViRRwk2G&sig=AHIEtbT0vw8gXRfiBiQ-LJNOGWgUXEOIOA) ■ Archdiocese of New York: Safe Environment Policy (http://www.archny.org/pastoral/safe-environment-program/) ■ Diocese of Albany: Sexual Misconduct Policies and Procedures Manual (http://www.albanyepiscopaldiocese.org/documents/forms/misconduct.html)
Christian Church (Disciples of Christ) in Illinois and Wisconsin	■ Clergy Ethics Policy and Procedures (www.cciwdisciples.org/component/remository/func-startdown/89/)

Religious organization	Affiliations and Web sites
Church of God and Christ policies	■ Sexual Exploitation, Ministerial Conduct, and Youth Protection Policy with Procedures in Cases of First United Church of Christ Royersford, PA (www.firstuccroyersford.org/index.../SafeChurch Policy1stUCC.RTF)
Episcopalian Church policies	■ Safe Church Policy of the Episcopal Diocese of Western Massachusetts (http://www.diocesewma.org/parishmatters/ safechurch.html) ■ St. Paul's Episcopal Church Holyoke, MA: Policy for the Protection of Children and Youth (www.stpaulsholyokema.org/.../41070/ safe_church_policy_9_06.pdf)
Jehovah's Witness Church policies	■ Jehovah's Witnesses (WTS) Policies & Examples of Child Sexual Abuse (http://www.religioustolerance.org/witness7.htm)
Jewish policies	■ Jerusalem Protection Center for Children and Youth, an Innovative Service for Initial Intervention with Child Victims— Evaluation Study (http://brookdale.jdc.org.il/?CategoryID=192& ArticleID=20_)
Lutheran Church policies	■ Evangelical Lutheran Church in America: Questions about Protecting Children, Youth and Adults from Abuse (http://www .elca.org/Who-We-Are/Our-Three-Expressions/Churchwide-Organization/Office-of-the-Secretary/Congregation-Administration/Legal-Issues-for-Congregations/Questions-About-Protecting-Children-and-Adults-from-Abuse.aspx)
Methodist Church policies	■ First United Church Methodist Church of Keller Child/Youth Protection Policy (http://www.kellerumc.com/docs/Safe%20 Sanctuary%20policy.pdf) ■ Child/Youth Protection Checklist Summary Developed by the Virginia Conference United Methodist Church Office of Children's Ministries and Discipleship (http://www.vaumc.org/ repository/Children/ChildProtectionChecklist.doc) ■ Child/Youth/Adult Safety Procedures Tarrytown United Methodist Church (http://www.tarrytownumc.org/safety procedures.htm)
Muslim policies	■ Child Protection in Faith-Based Environments: A Guideline Report (http://www.muslimparliament.org.uk/Documentation/ ChildProtectionReport.pdf) ■ Muslim Child Advocacy with UNICEF/Muslim Women Advocacy (http://www.unicef.org/policyanalysis/index_29678.html)

Religious organization	Affiliations and Web sites
Russian Orthodox Church Outside of Russia	■ The Policy and Procedures of the Synod of Bishops of the Russian Orthodox Church Outside of Russia Regarding Sexual Misconduct by Clergy (http://www.russianorthodoxchurch.ws/ 01newstucture/pagesen/rules/smisconduct.htm)
Pentecostal Church policies	■ Policies and Procedures for Working with Youth: Pentecostal Church of God, Central California District Section 1 (http://www .ccalyouth.com/Forms/Child%20Abuse%20Prevention%20 Program/CCD%20Youth%20Policy%20Procedure/Teaching% 20Binder/Full%20Binder%20060605/Section%20One.pdf)
Presbyterian Church policies	■ Sexual Misconduct Policy and Its Procedures Adopted by the Twentieth General Assembly (https://www.pcusa.org/oga/ publications/sexual-misconduct-policy.pdf) ■ Taking Care—Child Protection Guidelines (http://www.presbyterianireland.org/takingcare/index.html) ■ News: Child and Youth Protection Policy in Place (http://www.stillwaterfpc.org/#/resources/forms) ■ The Presbytery of Prospect Hill Child and Youth Protection Policy (http://www.prospecthillpresby.org/forms/CHILDAND YOUTHPROTECTIONPOLICYI.pdf) ■ Policy to Prevent Abuse of Children and Youth (http://www.feautor.org/uploads/contributions/37.rtf)
Protect My Ministry	■ Sexual Misconduct Policy (http://www.protectmyministry.com/ sampleforms/Sample_Screening_Policy1.pdf)
Seven Day Adventist Church policies	■ Code of Conduct Child Protection Policy and Procedures, Lilydale Seventh-Day Adventist Church
Trinity Church policies	■ Trinity United Methodist Church: Safe Sanctuaries Policy: Reducing the Risk of Child Abuse in our Church (http://www.tumcif.org/SafeSanct/Policy.pdf) ■ Trinity Church Lime Rock: Policies for the Protection of Children and Youth (http://www.trinitylimerock.org/2007/PDFs/Policy% 20for%20protection%20of%20children%20and%20youth.pdf)
United Church of Canada	■ Sexual Abuse (Sexual Harassment, Pastoral Sexual Misconduct, Sexual Assault) and Child Abuse: Official Policy and Procedures Document (http://www.united-church.ca/files/handbooks/ sexualabuse.pdf)
United Church of Christ, Chelmsford, MA	■ Safe Church Policy and Procedure (http://www.firstchurchsandwich.org/)

Note: Web sites may change periodically; check Internet for accuracy and updates.

Tips for Professionals, Parents, and Teachers

Tips for Professionals: During the Screening Stage

Tip No. 1: Know the Importance of Interdisciplinary Collaboration

- Appreciate that most investigations involve a multitude of professionals who conduct thorough interviews, which can produce better outcomes.
- Find data to support the roles of CACs (or centralized child advocacy units) in providing effective and efficient services in assessments and treatment.

Tip No. 2: Increase Professional Awareness

- Understand your roles and responsibilities.
- Be neutral to the allegation and do not overreact.
- Use the 4W1H (who, when, where, what, and how) questions to build rapport and determine the child's competency.
- Document the date and time and event with the reporter or alleged victim.

Tip No. 3: Use the Truth-Lie Ritual

- Use the truth-lie ritual to help transition from the rapport stage to the free-narrative stage.
- Assess whether the child knows the difference between telling the truth and telling a lie, and provide an opportunity to explain the importance of telling the truth.

- Use concrete examples (e.g., name, color, gender) that the child can understand.
- Check the correct answer with the child before asking if the example is the truth or a lie.
- Do not use either the child or the interviewer as the person who is telling the lie in the example.
- Make sure that the child promises to tell only the truth.

Tips for Parents or Teachers: At Abuse Disclosure

Tip No. 1: Show Your Concern for the Child

Show your concern to the child by asking sensitive questions about what happened (e.g., "I would like to know more about what happened; can you describe to me the entire incident?" or "You seem upset; what's been bothering you?").

Tip No. 2: Use the 4W1H Questions to Obtain Further Information about the Abuse

After the child discloses abuse (physically and/or sexually), use the 4W1H questions to ask the child about what happened:

- "Where did the incident occur?"
- "Who was doing that to you?"
- "When did it occur?"
- "What did the abuser do or say after he did [use child's word for abuse]?"
- "How did the abuser do it [use child's word for abuse]?"
- "Who was with you when this happened?"

If the child doesn't disclose directly but you suspect sexual abuse, pay attention to the clues the child provides to ask questions that focus on when, where, who, what, and how:

- "When you said, 'Someone's doing something I dislike,' tell me who that person is."

- "When you said, 'Nothing happened' but you seem to be upset, when did you start feeling this way?"
- "I hear you say that you don't know how to say it; how about just tell me where you were when this thing happened in the most recent past?"
- "When you said, 'I just feel helpless [mad or upset],'" what made you feel that way?"
- "I hear you say that you're not feeling well. How is your well-being affected by the thing you are about to tell me?"
- Do not use misleading or leading questions during the questioning process:
- Don't say, "I think X is not a good guy and he is the abuser, am I correct?"
- Don't say, "X had a lot of bad records in the past; he must be the abuser, right?"
- Don't say, "Did X have sex with you?"
- Do not use why questions to make the child feel that you are not trusting him or her.

Tip No. 3: Understand the Child's Response

Understand how the child responded to the incident, such as by asking the child about his or her feelings and actions at the time or comparing the feelings between then and now:

- "How did you feel at that time?"
- "What did you say or do after the abuser touched [or use child's word for abuse] you?"
- "How do you feel now?"
- "What do you want us to do with X [abuser]?"
- "What do you want X [abuser] to do or not to do in the future?"

Tip No. 4: Analyze the Situation

Ask further questions to find out details and clarify aspects of the child's account:

- "What did X [abuser] do to you?"
- "How did his or her behavior make you feel?"
- "Did you try to stop him or her, or hint to him or her that it's not OK to do it?"
- "What was his or her response after you indicated [physically or verbally] that you didn't want to do it?"

Tip No. 5: Always Provide Encouragement after Questioning

Make sure that the child understands that it is the right thing to talk to you and that you are glad that the child shared information and feelings with you:

- "Thank you for telling me about this incident. It will help me find ways to stop the problem."
- "I will always be supportive of you and help you in the future."

Educate the child about body protection and stand up to others:

- "You can always say no if you don't feel comfortable about the situation."
- "Your body is very private, and you have the right to protect it."
- "If you don't like someone's actions, you can tell that person about your disappointment and ask him or her to stop it."
- "You can ask people to be respectful to you."
- "It's important that you tell your parents or teachers about your concern."

CHAPTER 4

Best-Practice Interview Protocols

This chapter describes three interview protocols for use in the forensic interview process with the alleged victim, the alleged childhood victim (i.e., an adult who was abused during childhood), and the alleged perpetrator. All protocols address the importance of using the free-narrative approach, which allows the interviewee to describe the event, complaint, recollection, or justification using general open-ended questions rather than too many specific close-ended questions. In addition to a set of general questions, the chapter demonstrates techniques used in the specific questioning phase with respect to the use of anatomical drawings and/or dolls to verify the type of abuse after disclosure (see figure 4.1). Also included are questions to use when interviewing a nonoffending parent, as well as current techniques used in court to protect vulnerable witnesses. In a disclosure or a nondisclosure situation with an alleged child victim, the reader can use the transcripts provided in this chapter to practice step-by-step techniques (the two DVDs that accompany this book also record that process). The transcripts in this chapter cover the most recent research-based techniques to enhance the effectiveness of the interviewing process.

Interviewing the Alleged Child Victim

During a forensic interview, a skilled interviewer must be aware that children of different developmental levels may show differential abilities in handling the following: being separated from the caretaker, talking with a

Figure 4.1 Two Human Figure Drawings Used in Hong Kong

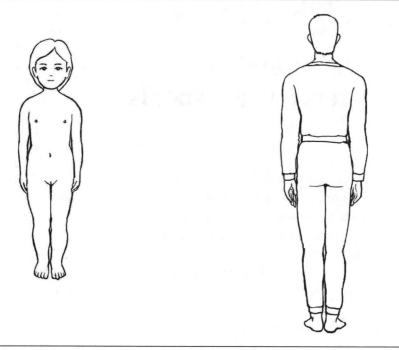

Source: Hong Kong Police Force, copyright 2009. Reprinted with permission.

stranger, using specific terminology to identify abuse, describing a situation, expressing or suppressing emotions, reacting to specific questions, and recalling a memory. The interviewer must be equipped with knowledge of child development before conducting a professional interview. Because a minor does not have the legal obligation to present an oath before making a statement, it is important to use the truth-lie ritual to ensure that the child understands the importance of telling only the truth. To prepare for the interview, the interviewer must obtain consent from at least one of the child's legal guardians (in the case of a child under a child protection order, the legal guardian is the state).

In this chapter, specific examples from chapter 2 are placed into the protocol and analyzed by interviewing stages (see also "Julie's Case"). In addition, appendix 4A provides tips for parents of interviewed alleged child victims.

Stage 1: Rapport Building Stage

In the rapport-building stage, an interviewer must assess the child's developmental level; the child's ability to recall details; and the child's perceptions of time, date, frequency, and descriptions of a person or an event. The interviewer can determine the child's competencies in responding to these concepts through general questions, such as "What is your name?" "How many minutes does one hour have?" "How do you know if someone is telling the truth [or lying]?" "Who can make you happy [or sad]?" and "What is something you did during the last summer vacation?" The concepts for developmental competence testing include the following:

Self-identity: Name, age, birthday, address or district of residence, family members (name and relationship), occupation, favorable subjects, and regular activities

Gender and sex: Male or female, boy or girl, men and women, same sex or opposite sex, feminine, masculine, boyfriend, girlfriend

Time: Year and date; day of the month or week; timing (hours, minutes, seconds); calendar (regular and lunar); time indicator (digital clock or regular clock reading); seasons; public holidays; school terms; school breaks (winter, summer, spring); exam week; before, after, and during

Numeric: Counting from one to ten (verbal or clapping counts), even- or odd-number counting (one to twenty), how many times (frequency), how long (duration in time unit), a dozen

Color: Concrete color, mixed color, color in pattern, dark and light colors, transparent (no color but not white)

Weight: Light, heavy, specific unit of weight (pound, ounce, kilo, gram)

Dimension: Shapes (round, rectangle, irregular), length (long, short), width, depth, size, angle, front and back, left and right, in and out, up and down

Physical body: Body parts (name and location), internal organs (location and function), how to protect body, physical and sexual touching

Health: Birth, death and dying, illness, breathing, bleeding, animate versus inanimate objects

Truth and lie: Fact and fantasy, cartoon, make-believe, secrets, consequences of lying

Value: Money, knowledge, being a child versus an adult, religious values, family values, punishment versus reward, being helpful, being
helped by others

Emotion and feeling: Mad, sad, happy, glad, guilt, embarrassment,
bored, depressed, fearful, released

When establishing a child's competencies during the rapport-building
stage, the interviewer will ask, "What is . . . ?" or simply say, "Tell me . . ."
to determine whether the child can express content related to the concept
the interviewer is asking about. In this stage, the interviewer should not ask
complicated questions or questions that have direct implications of sexual
abuse. Complex questions may confuse the child and defeat the purpose
of testing the child's competencies. Also, as professionals we want to give
the child a chance to show competencies in answering general nonabuse
questions first.

Some U.S. state laws and laws of other countries require that the
interviewer demonstrate the child's ability to differentiate telling the truth
from lying. In addition, the interviewer must state the ground rules up
front to ensure that the child promises to tell only the truth. Moreover, the
interviewer should accept "I don't know" or "I don't understand" as
answers, say "Correct me if I get anything wrong," and clarify the reasons
that the child may need to further explain slang or unusual terms. The
ground-rules stage is usually considered part of the rapport-building stage,
but sometimes it is considered a separate stage to highlight its importance.
In this example, ground rules are included in stage 1 to be consistent with
the literature (box 4.1).

Box 4.1 Stage 1: Rapport—Specific Techniques with Examples

Principles

- Provide a relaxing environment for the client.
- Assess the child's competency to answer questions
- Identify the purpose and process of the interview.

- Emphasize the importance of telling the truth.
- Provide ground rules.

Identification

Identification of the Interviewer

- Introduce the name, role and position, and agency of the interviewer(s).
  - "My name is X and I am a (job title) at (agency or employer). I am here to listen to you."
- Verify the name of the child victim.
  - "What's your name? Please write your name down on this paper for me."
- Check what name (or nickname) the interviewee prefers to be called during this interview.
  - "What does your teacher (friends) call you? May I call you that?"

Purpose and Nature of the Interview

- Identify the purpose of this interview (e.g., fact-finding, reporting to the agency or review board).
- Stress the importance of telling the truth and staying focused.
  - "We are videotaping this interview so that I can focus on what you will tell me instead of writing everything down."
  - "I (we) will spend about one hour listening to your concern. If you need a break, please let me know. If you need more time, let me know, too."

Explain the Interview Process

- Give directions and specify whether a protocol is to be followed.
  - "I will use a standard procedure in this interview. In other words, I will ask you questions that I ask every child who comes to this type of interview."

- • "When I ask you specific questions, it doesn't mean I don't understand your answer, but it's important to make sure all things are clearly understood."
- Inform the child about note-taking or recording the interview, and explain reasons and dispositions of notes and records.
  - • "We will be videotaping this interview. Only those who are working with me on this case will have access to the tape."
  - • "I will be taking notes, but I'll use the notes only to recall my memory when I prepare my report. Once my report has been written, my notes will (may) be destroyed."
- Briefly identify the steps of this interview: listening, questioning, and answering additional questions at the end.
  - • "Next, I'd like you to tell me about your concern. Then I will ask you some specific questions to clarify what you have said. You can ask questions any time or at the end."

Competency

Rapport Building

- Ask the child about a specific nonabuse event experienced for event narrative practice.
  - • "Tell me how you came to this place."
  - • "What is a favorite TV show of yours? Can you describe one of its main characters?"
- Assess the child's competency in answering when, where, who, what, and how questions.
  - • "When is your birthday?"
  - • "Where do you live?" (If the alleged place of abuse is at home, then "Tell me your home address.")
  - • "Who lives with you?"
  - • "How do you make yourself comfortable when you are talking to a stranger?"
- Identify home situation to check current and past relationships with alleged perpetrator (AP).
  - • "When did you move into this address? Is it a house or an apartment, or something else?"

- "How does your dad usually react when you do something wrong?"
- "What does your family do when you have a day off from school?"
- "Can you describe your current relationship with your step-dad?"

Truth-Lie Ritual (for Children Younger Than Eighteen Only)

- State the importance of telling the truth.
  - "Today, you and I are going to talk about something that is very important. Before we begin, I need to know that you understand the difference between telling the truth and telling a lie."
- Use the direct approach to assess whether the child can differentiate between telling the truth and lying.
  - "Tell me in your own words what the word *truth* means."
  - "Tell me what a lie means to you."
- Use a lie (or made-up) example and a truth example to assess the child's competency in differentiating the truth from lying.
  - A lie example: "Is it raining inside this room?" If the child answers no: "If someone said that it's raining in this room, would that be the truth or a lie?" If the child answers yes: "That would not be a truth because it's not raining inside this room. It would be making something up if someone said it is raining inside this room. Do you understand? I will use another example to see if you really understand."
  - If the child does not answer, ask the question in a different way: "Is it a fact that it is raining in this room or is it a fantasy (or, did someone just make it up)?"
  - A truth example: What color is my jacket? Child answers red, which is the truth: "If someone said my jacket is red, would that be the truth or a lie?"
  - If the child is unable to differentiate between the truth and a lie, the interviewer should make an attempt to define the difference in simple terms (e.g., "The truth is something that really happened. It represents the fact. Lies are things that haven't really happened, things or fantasies that are made up").

- Provide a conclusion and/or summary.
  - "Everything we talk about today must be only the truth, nothing made up or pretended. Also, don't leave anything out. OK?"

Ground Rules

- "It's OK to ask me to clarify if you don't understand any of my questions."
- "It's OK to say, 'I don't understand' if you don't understand my questions. I will try to rephrase them for you."
- "It's OK to say, 'I don't know' if you really don't know the answer."
- "It would be helpful if you would say your answer instead of shaking your head or nodding."
- "Correct me if I get anything wrong."
- "I may ask you to explain some slang or unusual terms so that I will not have any misunderstanding."

Check questions before proceeding (e.g., "Do you have any other questions about this interview? If not, we will proceed").

Stage 2: Free Narrative

In stage 1, after using general questions to build rapport and determine the child's competence in answering questions, the interviewer can determine whether the child has any concerns about the interview (including the setting) before disclosure. It would be a logical flow in stage 2 to check whether the child has any of the following beliefs and concerns by asking a general question, "Has anyone told you something or done something that bothered you?" It is likely that the child has the following beliefs and does not want to talk to you:

Belief 1: Children will become orphans and lose their belongings if their parents leave them.
Belief 2: Adults know more than children do.
Belief 3: Adults have money and power.
Belief 4: I must obey adults or else I will be punished.

In the free-narrative stage, open-ended questions can help the child disclose abuse (box 4.2). These questions include the following:

- "Can you tell me what happened?"
- "I heard something had happened to you. Would you tell me about it?"
- "Your mom (or someone) told me you had something important to tell me. Would you tell me about it now?"
- "After you told your mom (or someone) something, she asked me to help. I would like to hear it directly from you. What is it?"

Box 4.2 Stage 2: Free Narrative—Specific Techniques with Examples

Principles

- Encourage the child to tell in his or her own words.
- Use open-ended questions.

Free Narrative

- Begin with a general question
  - "What happened?"
  - "What has made you upset?"
- Use additional rapport questions if the child is silent.
  - "What would you like to do when you have a vacation?"
  - "Who is your favorite teacher (or best friend)?"
  - "How do you feel when you talk to a stranger like me?"
- Use questions that are less threatening.
  - "Who made you feel the way you are feeling now?"
  - "Where did that happen?"
  - "When did it happen?"
- Use anatomical dolls or drawings only to clarify the disclosed information. When a child mentions a sexual act but is not able to tell the body part involved, or when a child can't describe the position or action of the sexual act, then take out a set of dolls (usually a boy, a girl, a man, and a woman) and follow this protocol:

Introduce the dolls:
- "You said he touched you. Which part of your body did he touch? How about choosing some dolls to show me where?"
- Rule 1: Do not touch the dolls once the child starts to use the dolls to demonstrate.
- Rule 2: Do not name the dolls for the child. Let the child show you what happened before clarifying what the child did.

Ask specific questions:
- "When you showed how he touched you, which doll represented you? Who did the other doll represent?"
- "What do you call that part of your body that he touched? What does your mother call that body part? Have you heard another name for that body part from someone?"
- "When you showed how he touched you, where were you when it happened?"
- "How did he do what you just showed me? Did he use anything else?"
- "Is there anything else you want to show me that happened?"

Close the doll interview:
- "Let's put the clothes back on the dolls. Do you need help?"
- "Let's put the dolls away first. I would like to ask you a few more questions."

For recommendations of anatomically correct dolls, see the Teach-a-Bodies Web site (http://www.teach-a-bodies.com) and figure 4.1.

Stage 3: Questioning

The role of the interviewer is to clarify the narrative provided. Especially in intrafamilial abuse cases, children are usually afraid of the abuser and do not initiate a conversation about the abuse. It is the responsibility of the interviewer to use information from the free narrative to ask specific questions for validation purposes. Even if the child has answered clarification questions, the interviewer can always encourage the client to complete the description instead of continuing to ask too many specific questions. Encouragement can include things such as "Tell me more," "Then what happened?" and "Go on." It is important not to assume; rather, the interviewer should clarify terms the child uses for sexual acts or activities. If the child is not willing to clarify further, address the child's feelings and tell the child that it is typical not to talk about it. Doing so, however, is essential to understand the exact meaning of everything the child has said so that the interviewer can find a better way to assist the child and the family.

In this process, the interviewer collects additional information, such as evidence that is material, competent, and relevant. The focus of this stage is to clarify and use specific questions to find validation points: detailed description of the sexual offense, progression, secrecy, coercion (threat or reward), first complaints (e.g., psychological or psychiatric evaluations after the incident, corroborating information from others, behavioral indicators), and terminology used. Before the end of the interview, it is essential that the interviewer ask the full name of the abuser, determine the child's relationship with the abuser, and seek to understand the child's perception of the alleged abuser's role (e.g., authority, friend). It is also important to check the child's motive for reporting and to identify the reaction of the first person the child told about the abuse. This stage also provides an opportunity for the child to share anything else that has not been asked but is highly relevant to this case (box 4.3).

Box 4.3 Stage 3: Questioning—Specific Techniques with Examples

Principles

- Identify reasons for further questioning.
- Provide an opportunity to teach the nondisclosing child about body protection.
- Address the child's emotions.
- Avoid using why or leading questions.
- When the child can tell more about the abuse, go back to the stage 2 and encourage the child to describe the abuse without asking closed-ended, specific questions.

Questioning

When? (gathering information on date and time)
- "When did it (the child's word for abuse) begin?"
- "When did it happen last?"
- "How many times did these kind of bad touches (the child's language) happen between you and your father?"

Where? (gathering information on location)
- "Where did it (the event) take place?"
- "Where were you when it happened?"
- "Where were other people (e.g., your mom) when it happened?"

Who? (gathering information on people involved)
- "Who picked the place (of contact)?"
- "Who told you about this place?"
- "Who knew about what happened?"

What? (gathering information on the details of the abuse)
Encourage the child to describe the situation or problem in his or her own words:
- "Tell me what happened."
- "What word would you use to describe the contact?"
- "What were your thoughts then? What are your thoughts now?"
- "What did you see (or hear, touch, smell, feel)?"

How? (gathering information on interviewee's emotions and feelings)
- "How would you describe yourself in the time you were in contact with (name of the accused)?"
- "How would you describe (name of the accused) during the time he or she was in contact with you?"
- "How was (name of the accused) dressed at the time of abuse?"
- "How old were you at the time of the first contact?"

Additional Information (May Be Required by Law)

- "Do you know if (name of the accused) has done this to anyone else?"
- "Has anyone else done something like this to you?" (alternative hypothesis)

Other Questions

- "Did anyone comment on your contacts? What did he or she say?"
- "Did you tell anyone about what was happening? What was that person's reaction? What did that person do or say?"
- "Were you forced to do anything you did not want to do?"
- "What made you stand up to report the abuse (use the child's word)?"
- "Was there use of alcohol or drugs?"

Stage 4: Closing the Interview

Closing an interview is an essential step in a forensic interview for three major reasons. First, an interview with formal closure will make the child feel respected. Second, the child who has perceived him- or herself as a passive subject in a formal interview can have an additional opportunity to address what has not been addressed in the interview protocol. Third, the interviewer can provide a sense of safety for the child when the interviewer is sincerely interested in what the child has to say on top of what the interviewer has planned to ask. During closure, if the interviewer asks the child what else he or she would like the interviewer to know, this sends a message to the child that it is all right to share a concern even if that concern has not been revealed or asked earlier. Role modeling an attitude of positive regard is an important principle in this stage (box 4.4).

**Box 4.4 Stage 4: Closing the Interview—
                      Specific Techniques with Examples**

Principles

- Provide the child with a formal closure.
- Confirm the child's knowledge of telling the truth.
- Verify that no coaching has been involved.
- Provide a chance to ask questions that have not been asked.
- Answer what is next and provide an opportunity for the child to ask questions and share concerns.
- Close the interview with reassurance.

Closing the Interview

Summarize
- Highlight facts revealed by the child and summarize the points.
  - "You just told me that Daddy touched your pee-pee, and you were scared to tell. Is there anything else you would like to tell me?"

Confirm the Truth (May Be Required by Law)
- Make sure the alleged victim is telling what has actually happened and no coaching was involved.
  - "Let me ask you two more important things before we go. Did anyone tell you what to tell or not to tell me?"
  - "Was everything you just told me everything that had happened to you?"

Answer Questions from the Child
- "I have asked you a lot of questions today. Do you have any questions you would like to ask me?"

Comfort and Thank Child
- "I know this may have been difficult for you to talk about. Thank you very much for telling me about it."
- "You seem to be anxious to go. But before we go, I would like to thank you for coming."

- "I want you to know that I will try to help you to go through this process. If you later have any questions for me, please let me know. I will leave my phone number for you (or relative for a young child)."

Future Action Plan
- Check what the child would want to see happen next (with respect to the future of the AP, self, family, church, work, counseling).
- Ask whether the child wants the interviewer to accompany him or her to talk with the parent(s) about the disclosure.
- Discuss possible future actions (if needed).

Address Emotional Concerns
- Check on the child's current feelings and concerns.
- Open an opportunity for the child to ask questions.

Ending
- Provide a phone number and name to be contacted.
- Thank and reassure the child.
- Formally close the interview by stating that the interview has ended or report the ending date and time in a videotaped interview (if needed).

Interviewing the Alleged Childhood Victim and/or Survivor

When obtaining information from a childhood victim (i.e., an adult survivor of childhood sexual abuse), the interviewer must use a narrative approach before checking on intent, an earlier complaint, mental health, methods of memory recall, and so on. Because false memory syndrome has been an issue for individuals recalling childhood victimization, the interviewer must determine how the survivor remembered some of the detailed information that he or she could have forgotten in normal circumstances. When the survivor describes an incident for which he or she can remember specificities (e.g., the exact date of the first abuse, the clothes the abuser was wearing at the time of abuse), the interviewer may ask questions such as, "What makes you so sure about this specific date?" or "Describe how you could remember the color (pattern, design) of his clothes." In the case that the survivor sought counseling after the abuse, it is important to obtain such information through a signed consent (see appendix 4B).

Interviewer's Preparation

- Sign the confidentiality statement relevant to the agency policy (see appendix 4C).
- Know basic information before the interview:
  - Intake information about the allegation
  - Former record of accusations from this alleged victim (AV; survivor)
  - Any knowledge about the survivor (e.g., personality, psychiatric problem)
- Meet with the interview team to identify specific questions to ask.
- Know the dos and don'ts of asking questions (appendix 4D).
- Set ground rules (e.g., inform the client that you will take notes and obtain consent if you will record the interview, do not judge, do not promise anything you don't know, set a time limit for the interview, determine support person rules).
- Ensure a comfortable environment.
- Use the interview protocol (see appendix 4E).

Interviewing the Nonoffending Parent

It is important to interview the nonoffending parent (NOP) before interviewing the alleged perpetrator (AP) so that the AP cannot press the NOP to lie. In research, no standard protocol has been established to be used for NOP interviews. The author's practice experiences have demonstrated that it is important to normalize the feeling that the NOP does not believe in the alleged victim's report. For example, the interviewer might say, "It is hard to believe that sexual abuse actually happened in your own family." However, it is also important to persuade the NOP to give the child an opportunity to express his or her concerns so that professionals can then validate or disprove the case. Specific questions are listed here for reference. In interviews, the interviewer should use the name of the AP or child:

Determine NOP's belief in the allegation:
- Do you believe that the child has been sexually abused?
- Who may place blame on the child?
- Do you have prior knowledge of the sexual abuse?
- Have you checked with the child and/or the AP regarding the sexual abuse allegations, and if so, did you report this to Child Protective Services (CPS)?
- Are you aware of any past allegations of sexual abuse by the AP?
- Has the child previously displayed possible indicators of sexual abuse?
  - Avoiding the AP?
  - Receiving special treatment from the AP?
  - Complaining about the AP's behavior?
  - Sexually acting out?
  - Running away from home?
  - Playing in a sexually inappropriate way with other children?
  - Having frequent nightmares or other emotional problems?
  - Experiencing physical indicators of sexual abuse, such as bleeding or bladder infections?

Verify specific information from the child's allegation:
- Did the AP take the child camping last weekend (as indicated in the victim's report)?
- Where were you on that date (abuse date as indicated in the child's allegation)?
- When was the first time the child told you about the sexual abuse? What was your first reaction? What did you say at that moment?

Check history of physical abuse and/or neglect:
- Have you or the AP ever been involved with CPS for problems with parenting?
- Have you witnessed physical abuse, emotional abuse, or neglect of your child?
- Who is afraid of the AP (before this allegation)?
- Who dislikes the AP?
- Have you been abused by the AP? Tell me the details.

Identify past history of sexual abuse:
- Have you had any difficulties understanding your child's expressed needs?
- Is there a history of sexual abuse in the family?
- Was the child a victim of domestic violence (e.g., trying to protect the NOP)?

Assess current living situation:
- Can you think of any other potential child sexual abuse victims in the family?
- Do you have any social support (from family or friends)?
- Do you or the AP have weapons in the home?
- Does the AP have access to other children alone?
- What are your household rules for determining how family members behave about privacy in bedrooms and bathrooms; sleeping arrangements in the home, bathing rituals, bedtime rituals, dressing rituals, and the degree to which family members are dressed in one another's presence?
- Have the AP and the child always had opportunities to stay together alone (particularly during the time frame of the alleged sexual abuse)?

Assess education and employment history:
- How do you assess your ability to be independent of the AP, to support yourself and your children?
- Are you often physically absent from the home? Do you work long hours or night shifts?
- Do you go out often and/or assign responsibility for child care and other household chores to the AP or to other older children?

Assess parenting responsibilities:
- How do you provide for the needs of the child (including nurturance and protection)?
- Has your child been taking care of the house when you are not there? Who makes decisions in the family?

Check on discipline methods:
- Have you noticed any signs of possible punitive, abusive, or neglectful treatment?
- Has the AP ever blamed the child for something not his or her fault?
- Has the child received any special treatment from the AP?
- Is there a history of physical abuse in the family?

Assess partner relationship:
- Tell me about your marital history. First, are you married?
- Tell me about any history of marital problems.
- Tell me about any history of domestic violence.

Assess substance abuse:
- Have you or the AP ever used alcohol?
- Have you or the AP ever used drugs?
- Has the AP ever been influenced by alcohol or drugs so that he or she could not control him- or herself?

Assess mental health:
- Tell me about your perception of the mental functioning of each individual in your household.
- Are you emotionally ready and able to protect the child?
- Are you emotionally detached from the family?
- Have you experienced any history of emotional abuse in the family?
- Is there any history of mental illness in your family (including mental health treatment for any family member)?
- Do you have any family members with mental retardation?

Assess criminal history:
- Does the AP have any history of criminal arrests?
- Do you have any history of criminal arrests?

Most of these questions aim to assess the ability of the NOP to protect the child and the risk factors involved. It is essential to identify all strengths in the family in order to provide proper support to the NOP. Therefore, beyond the investigative questions listed, the interviewer must also ask about strengths in protecting the child and family from harm and about how the interviewee protects the child from any physical, emotional, and sexual molestation. If through the questioning process the interviewer finds that the NOP has strengths that he or she is not able to verbalize, the interviewer can identify those strengths and encourage the NOP to protect the child. Most strengths come directly from a person's willingness to accept parental responsibilities and access to informal support networks, such as family and religious community. It is essential to highlight the NOP's strengths, including protective factors such as what the NOP can provide for the child, the NOP's understanding of the child's difficulties, and the NOP's acceptance of the role of protector. With empowerment, the child can be further protected during the course of investigation (for tips for parents, see appendix 4A).

Interviewing the Alleged Perpetrator

It is important to interview the alleged perpetrator (AP) alone, with a focus on mental health, childhood abuse, past incidents with children, and any past records as an AP of child sexual abuse. According to Goldstein (1999), it is not necessary for law enforcement to give the Miranda warning immediately when interviewing an alleged offender "until you are ready to interview the offender about the crime" so that you can obtain "spontaneous statements/admissions/denials" (pp. 294–295). One strategy used in this process is "to disprove the statements made by an offender rather than to try to prove he is a molester" and "the basic principle . . . is to produce circumstances under which it is most likely the accused person will tell the truth" (Goldstein, 1999, pp. 303, 317).

In the four-stage interview process, the interviewer can use an assessment tool to evaluate the AP if the AP denies all allegations (see appendix 4F). The interview protocol for the AP is similar to that for the alleged victim or survivor (see appendixes 4G–4I). The following sections provide a brief summary of the protocol.

Stage 1: Introduction and Rapport Building

Introduction of the Interviewer
- Introduce each interviewer's name, role, and position.
- Verify the name of the interviewee.
- Check what name (nickname) the interviewee prefers to be called during this interview.

Purpose and Nature of the Interview
- State that the reason or purpose is to interview the AP to obtain information about an allegation.
- Ask the client whether he or she understands fully what is being alleged and the implications.
- Emphasize the use of a blank-screen and neutral approach (i.e., not knowing much of the report but wanting to find out the facts directly from those involved).

Explaining the Interview Process
- Give directions and specify the protocols to be followed.
- Inform the AP about note taking or recording the interview; explain reasons and dispositions of notes and records.
- Determine the AP's understanding of the purposes and procedures by asking for clarifications.

Rapport Building
- Provide opportunity for the client to express feelings and release tensions.
- Be nonpunitive and nonjudgmental in the approach.

Others
- Check feelings and emotions.
- Check current relationships with the alleged victim and/or survivor and/or other youths.
- Stress the importance of telling the truth and staying focused.

- Make sure the AP understands his or her legal rights, confidentiality issues, and so on.
- Set a time limit and ground rules for the interview.
- Ask whether there he or she has any questions about the purpose of the interview.

Stage 2: Free Narratives

- Encourage the AP to describe the situation and/or problem in his or her own words.
- Collect basic facts related to the allegation.
- Use exact wording from the AP in your notes.
- Ask open-ended questions.
- Be aware of the intent for asking specific questions and avoid leading.

What?

- "Tell me what you know about this allegation."
- "I am here to listen to your side of the story."
- "Tell us about your relationship with (the person who accused you)?"

How?

- "Tell us how you are feeling right now."
- "How did it make you feel when you first heard about this report against you?"

Stage 3: Specific Questioning

Clarify the Narrative

- Allow the AP to finish his or her version before asking specific questions to clarify what the AP just said.
- Use information from the free narrative to ask specific questions for validation purposes.
- Clarify and analyze the AP's observed facts and statements.
- Clarify terms in the report regarding sexual acts or activities.

Additional Information
- Collect evidence that is material, competent, and relevant.
- Focus specific questions to find validation points: detailed description of the sexual offense, progression, secrecy, coercion (threat or reward), first complaints (e.g., psychological or psychiatric evaluations after the incident, corroborating information from others, behavioral indicators), and terminology used.

Check AP's Knowledge of Alleged Victim (AV) and Prior History
- Determine whether AP knows the full name of the AV.
- Determine whether AP knows the AV's family.
- Determine whether AP knows the age of the AV (or school grade) at the reported incident period.
- Ask about prior history of being molested by others, prior history of activities with youths, prior history of being alone with youths, and ways of handling conflicts with youths.

Others
- Obtain corroborator's name, phone, e-mail address, and address.
- Obtain release-of-information statement (with signature and date).
- Determine whether there is information to be added.

Stage 4: Closing the Interview

Summarize
- Highlight facts revealed by the AP and review decisions made during the interview.
- Don't conclude (just summarize main points).
- Ask the AP to make a written statement.
- Ask whether additional persons should also be interviewed if time allows.

Future Action Plan
- Discuss possible future actions.

Address Emotional Concerns
- Ask about the AP's concerns (e.g., self, work, children).
- Acknowledge the difficulties of being interviewed about this matter.
- Allow the AP to ask questions.

Closing
- Provide a phone number and name to be contacted.
- Thank the person for coming.
- Formally close the interview by stating that the interview has ended.

Interviewer Etiquette and Behavior Standards

Using the who, what, when, where, and how questions, interviewers can demonstrate techniques that are appropriate for interviewing others involved and other children, such as the alleged victim's siblings or peers who knew about the complaint. It is also important to stress that an investigative or forensic interview be conducted with a blank-screen approach, without assumptions and biases against the AP or NOP but looking for facts and possible abuse indicators. With children, the use of these techniques must focus on behavioral indicators of neutrality, comfort, trust, and affect. Some examples are illustrated as follows:

> *Clarify emotional cues*: Because sex and sexual abuse are taboo subjects, it is important to show your concern when the child shows hesitation to describe the incident or its details:
> - "When you said, 'I don't remember,' is it that you really don't have any memory of it, or you just don't want to talk about it? It's OK if you don't remember or don't want to talk. Just let me know how you feel."
>
> *Clarify terminology for private body parts*: Because children typically do not use sexual terms in their conversations, when they use a term to describe the sexual activity or the body part that was violated, they tend to whisper or use the term that is easy to say without much

embarrassment. In some incidences, very young children tend to mimic the terms the abuser uses to describe his or her demand of sexual acts. It is important to patiently listen to the child before clarifying the term(s) such as using one of the following questioning strategies:

- "When you said he told you to touch his or her X, where is X?"
- You just said used the word X when you described his or her action. I want to make sure I understand. Can you spell the word for me?"
- "What is another term for X? What is the biological name of it? What is the normal function of X?"

Show empathy: When the child shows further hesitation or feels uncomfortable providing additional information, it is important to comfort the child before moving on to the next question:

- "I understand that it is hard to spell it out this way. It's OK. How about telling me what your mom would call this word?"
- "You said that the X is on his or her body, and when you pointed at the lower part of your body, and you seem to have some feelings about that. Are you feeling OK? Do you know the formal term of this body part on his or her body?"

Show nonpossessive warmth and understanding: Abused children do not feel comfortable being touched by stranger. When a child shows extreme distress, the interviewer should not initiate touching. It is inaccurate to think that the child needs a hug when feeling emotional. In general, it is more appropriate to use noncontact gesture to show your concern:

- "Nobody here will be upset with you because you don't remember or don't want to talk about it."
- "I can feel something here. Can you tell me how you feel?"

Admit making mistakes and model acceptable behaviors: To not leave the child with the impression that you do not believe him or her, if you repeat a question by mistake, admit that it is your mistake:

- "Thank you for reminding me that you told me already. Sometimes if I forget something, you just let me know, OK?"
- "Sorry that I forgot the answer. Would you mind telling me once more?"

Summary of Stages

Stage 1: Rapport

The initial stage of a forensic interview lays the foundational ground rules that will be useful throughout the interview process and works toward building rapport with the interviewee. Rapport building is established through open-ended questioning about a nonabuse event or experience for event narrative practice, using the 4W1H questions: who, when, where, what, and how. Likewise, informing the child of the interviewer's name, affiliation, and specific role during the process and addressing the child's concerns, obtaining consent, and discussing the purpose of videotaping are of utmost importance at the onset of this stage of forensic interviewing. Ground rules for the working relationship include a statement of the importance of telling the truth and assessing the child's competency in differentiating the truth from a lie. When testing for competency, the interviewer must change the subject to an individual other than the child to place the burden on the other rather than on the child or the interviewer. The DVD demonstrations that accompany this book suggest that the burden is placed on another to create an objective ground for establishing competency. A child is then asked to promise to tell the truth and to reply, "I don't know" or "I don't understand" when items are unclear and/or unknown. The interviewer should establish the appropriate use of slang or unusual terms, especially when working with teenagers. The interviewer should state that, although the interviewer might know or understand the meaning of slang, the child may be asked to specify what the term means to add clarity to the content of the interview (Cronch, Viljoen, & Hansen, 2006; Lamb et al., 2003; Lamb, Orbach, Hershkowitz, Esplin, & Horowitz, 2007; Lyon, 2005, 2010; Lyon & Ahern, 2010; Lyon & Matthews, 2006; Saywitz, Lyon, & Goodman, 2010; Washington State Criminal Justice Training Commission & Harborview Center for Sexual Assault and Traumatic Stress [WACJTC & HC], 2006).

Stage 2: Free-Narrative Account

During the free-narrative stage of the interview process, as shown on the accompanying DVDs, a limited number of open-ended questions are asked of the child. The child is encouraged to use his or her own words to tell a narrative account of what has happened. Anatomical dolls and other methods of assistance are used only for clarification purposes after an initial disclosure has been made. When a child begins to withdraw and/or become silent without disclosing abuse, it is appropriate for the interviewer to move to the questioning stage of the interview, stage 3, as to explore further when the child indicates reluctance because of a secret. Once a child begins to feel more comfortable speaking and becomes open to narrating the occurrence of events, the interviewer can move back into stage 2 with the child (using free narrative, such as, "Tell me the details"). Thus, the interviewer is able to move with ease between stages 2 and 3 on the basis of the child's level of participation and comfort level as they pertain to the interview process (Anagnostaki, Wright, & Bourchier-Sutton, 2010; Cronch et al., 2006; Deblinger, Thakkar-Kolar, Berry, & Schroeder, 2010; Hershkowitz, Orbach, Lamb, Sternberg, & Horowitz, 2006; Lamb et al., 2003; Lamb et al., 2007; London, Bruck, Wright, & Ceci, 2008; Lyon, 2005, 2010; Lyon & Ahern, 2010; Lyon & Matthews, 2006; Patterson & Pipe, 2009; Saywitz et al., 2010; WACJTC & HC, 2006).

To explore further when the child asks the interviewer to keep information a secret, the interviewer can use the following strategies:

- *Check feeling*: "It seems that you are keeping something inside. When you mentioned it is a secret, how does this secret make you feel right now?"
- *Gain trust*: "I will listen to you and help you. I can help you figure out which part of this secret can be told or not be told."
- *Understand causes*: "What is a secret?" "Tell me a reason that I must keep our conversation a secret." "Is there a reason that your parents shouldn't know?" "Who should and should not know about this secret?"
- *Identify problem*: "How has this secret affected you?" "Tell me a problem that is related to this secret."
- *Analyze consequences*: "What will your parents do (or think) if they know about what you tell me?" "How would keeping your secret help you?"
- *Identify secret*: "What is one thing that your parents should not know?" "Is it something that your parents should know but you prefer them not to know? Tell me more about it."

- *Disclose obligation*: "In some situations, whether related to your well-being or my legal commitment, I will have to tell your parents. Help me understand the situation first."
- *Assist in disclosure (after child's disclosure and assessment of readiness to disclose to family)*: "I think your parents should know about X," or "You said you want to share this with your parents. How can I help you tell your parents?" or "How can you help me tell your parents?" "How about if we figure out a way that your parents will listen to you?" "Would you like me to be there when you tell your parents?"

Stage 3: Questioning

During the questioning stage, specific questions are used to elicit information from the child. The first line of questioning should include the use of who, when, and where. The aforementioned questions are used before asking what questions because they more readily elicit clarity and specificity of responses. In addition, the who, when, and where questions help the child talk and reduce embarrassment, anxiety, fear, and further negative feelings that may be associated with the use of other questions. If this stage is entered before disclosure, the interviewer should maintain patience and continue to build rapport with the child. If the child does not disclose abuse, the interviewer should provide information about body protection and related services. If a child discloses abuse, the interviewer should reenter the free-narrative stage (i.e., ask the child to tell more about it) and reserve the 4W1H follow-up questions for further validation only. Additional information that may also be required by the law may include the possibility of other victims (e.g., "Do you know if the AP has done this to anyone else?") and alternative hypothesis testing (e.g., "Has anyone else done something like this to you?"). The importance of using appropriate techniques is invaluable to this stage of the interview process, and the interviewer should avoid using why questions that may sound accusatory and leading, as well as judgmental tones and mannerisms and physically touching the child (Bottoms, Najdowski, & Goodman, 2009; Cronch et al., 2006; Lamb et al., 2003; Lamb et al., 2007; London et al., 2008; Lyon, 2005, 2010; Lyon & Ahern, 2010; Lyon & Matthews, 2006; Lyon, Saywitz, Kaplan, &

Dorado, 2001; Saywitz et al., 2010; Tishelman & Geffner, 2010; WACJTC & HC, 2006).

Stage 4: Closing the Interview

During the final stage of the interview process, the interviewer must ensure that the most important pieces of information have been received. Confirmation of the alleged perpetrator's name and the type(s) of abuse should be established. The interviewer should be honest with the child about what will occur and should give the child an opportunity to ask questions. The interviewer should also reassure and thank the child for being there, and address the child's concerns. As the interview draws to a close, the interviewer should ask, "Has anybody told you to say or not to say what you just shared with me?" and follow that with other validation questions, such as "What did that person tell you?" This question clarifies that the information is from the child's own experience rather than from the prompting of another individual. At this point, the interviewer should formally close the interview by stating that the interview has ended and/or by reporting the time (Cronch et al., 2006; Lamb et al., 2003; Lamb et al., 2007; Lyon, 2005, 2010; Lyon & Ahern, 2010; Saywitz et al., 2010; Tishelman & Geffner, 2010; WACJTC & HC, 2006).

Special Caution When Using an Interview Protocol

An interview protocol should be used as a guidepost rather than a rigid policy. The interviewer must pay attention to application of the protocol in three areas: children's use of language, techniques to obtain information regarding motive to report, and interviewers' flexibility. In Cheung's (1997, 2003, 2008) studies, what and how question items were accompanied by open-ended spaces to remind the researchers to record the children's terminology of private body parts and sexual activities. In an interview protocol, the interviewer should be reminded to clarify the terms and then to use the child's terminology to ask further questions in the interview.

Motive to report is another issue that researchers have identified as requiring special attention (Wakefield & Underwager, 1988). Because a direct question about motive is likely to be formulated as an accusing why question, the interviewer should use the 4W1H questions to determine motive. Examples include the following: "Who was the first person you told about this incident?" "Who else knew about this?" "What was that person's reaction?" "What happened with your daddy (abuser) after you told this person?" "When did you decide to tell this person about it?" "What did this person say?" "How did you get along with your daddy (abuser) before this happened?" "How do you get along with him now?" The most direct but less threatening question is "What made you decide to report?" It is important that the interviewer use a neutral tone of voice when asking these questions.

Flexibility is another important point to remember when using an interview guide. A forensic interview protocol should serve mainly as a tool to coordinate interview efforts. It can also be used to train and remind interviewers of what specific questions to ask, such as the full name of the alleged perpetrator, a brief description when the AP's name is not given, and the full address or descriptions of the abuse location. Additional items that are helpful can be added according to the case situation presented by the child. Last, and most important, the interviewers should believe that "working for the welfare of the child" is the most important goal of the interview (Cheung, 1997, p. 274). An interview guide should be used with sensitivity to children's needs and concerns (Saywitz & Goodman, 1996).

Conclusion

It is essential to use a blank-screen approach in a forensic interview process so that the interviewer does not make any assumptions about the child sexual abuse incidents. The interviewer, whether representing a child advocacy center, the child protective services, a church, or the court, must know that the interviewer's role is a fact-finding one. Research has not supported the use of touch as a means to comfort the victim in the forensic interview or the use of why questions to validate the child's statements to avoid wrong impressions or misinterpretations of the interviewer's motive. The evidence-based protocols presented here encourage interviewers to use a narrative approach to collect data from the respondents so that a first-person perspective can be obtained and hearsay responses avoided. All techniques proposed in this chapter are based on two key ideas in the achievement of an effective forensic interview: neutrality and fact-finding.

Tips for Parents

Tip No. 1: How to Help Your Child

- Children can express themselves with feelings, words, and behaviors. Your child may need your help to talk.
- Listen. Respect your child's feelings.
- Remember, whatever your child is feeling is normal for your child.
- It may be hard for your child to talk to you about things that are personal, painful, or embarrassing. It's OK if your child needs to talk to other helping adults. Help your child identify safe people to talk to.
- It is difficult for families when children are harmed. It is important to express your feelings without confusing or frightening your child. It may be helpful to talk about your feelings with adults who will listen. You and your family may find counseling helpful.

Tip No. 2: Monitor Your Response

There are four typical parent responses:

1. Protective—responds quickly without blaming the child; anger directed at offender
2. Reflective of role conflict—conflicted in allegiance to child and spouse, difficulty taking strong action, may be angry with the child or ambivalent
3. Overwhelmed, deny abuse or significance—shows only moderate concern for child
4. Rejecting or unprotective—sides with partner and takes no action

Research has demonstrated that children who feel supported and believed experience less psychological difficulties (adapted from Protective Services for Children and Young People, 1993).

Tip No. 3: Familiarize Yourself with the Investigative Process

By knowing about the investigative process, you can help your child to understand each stage of the investigation and make them feel more comfortable.

The Forensic Interview

- The purpose is to obtain a statement from a child, in a developmentally and culturally sensitive, unbiased, and fact-finding manner to support accurate and fair decision making by the involved multidisciplinary teams in the criminal justice and child protection systems.
- Forensic interviews are child centered and coordinated to avoid duplication.
- Children can get tired of answering questions. Please don't question your child before coming to your appointment.
- You can tell your child that the appointment is a safe place to talk about what happened.
- During the interview, children are spoken to alone. Parents, caregivers, and other interested parties are not allowed to observe the interviews.

The Medical Examination

- Conducted by trained medical providers who are familiar and keep current with published research studies on findings in abused and nonabused children, sexual transmission of infections in children, and current medical guidelines and recommendations from national professional organizations such as the American Academy of Pediatrics Committee on Child Abuse and Neglect and the Centers for Disease Control and Prevention.

- The medical examinations are noninvasive and child friendly.
- The examinations can often relieve any anxiety that the child or parents may have about the health of the child's body.

Tip No. 4: Know What Happens to the Interview Information

- Your child's interview and medical examination reports are part of a child protection and/or police investigation.
- Confidentiality laws protect any information provided.
- Only the investigative team authorized to watch the interview can receive information about the interview and medical examination.
- The interview and medical examinations are confidential. The videotaped interviews and written reports are sometimes used as evidence in criminal, juvenile, or family court.

APPENDIX 4B

Signed Consent

Confidential Agreement by Support Person or Translator

By signing this statement I affirm that I will strictly observe and respect confidentiality of the information given by _____ (interviewee) to _____ (name of institution). I also agree that I will remain silent during this interview unless I have been formally asked to be a translator in this interview. I further agree that I will not talk about the information with anyone about the content of this interview unless it is required by the law.

If I am here to provide translation services to the interviewee, I am informed that the integrity of the interview demands that the translations be accurate and as expressed by the interviewee during the interview itself, and not based on any prior communication or experiences with the interviewee or other individuals.

_____   _____
Name of Support Person   Signature of Support Person
(or Translator) (PRINT NAME)

_____
Translator's Affiliation (if applicable)

_____
Relationship to the Interviewee

_____   _____
Witness (PRINT NAME)   Signature of Witness

_____
Date

Confidentiality Statement

Special Investigative Team
Confidentiality, Indemnity and Conflicts of Interest Statement*

This statement made by and between _____
(administrator in the institution) acting on behalf of _____
(name of institution) (hereinafter referred to as "X") and _____,
a member of the Special Investigative Team of _____ (name of
institution) (hereinafter referred to as "Y").

Sensitive and personal information will be provided to each special
investigative team member as a part of the investigative process. This information must be treated with strict confidence within the limit of the law
and with full respect of the privacy rights of the individuals involved. All
notes will be destroyed after the final written report has been prepared.

It is an understanding that while the written report is considered confidential and privileged, the communications between "X" and the Special
Investigative Team may not be recognized as privileged communications in
a court of law. All team members are to refrain from professional or personal relationships with the individuals involved in this and all cases
assigned. Additional requests from these individuals should be directed to
the staff of the _____ (name of institution) who has been assigned as
case manager/caseworker of this case.

Although the _____ (name of institution) will not
anticipate that services for the Special Investigative Team will cause any
legal claim against any team member, prudence requires that this potential
be addressed. In the event if "Y" is being named as a defendant in a lawsuit
or compelled to testify in a court proceeding, the _____
(name of institution) shall indemnify, defend and hold harmless "Y" from
and against any and all claims, liability, causes of action, lawsuits and

judgments, including costs and attorneys fees and expenses related thereto which arise out of, or is any way connected with this service to the _____ (name of institution).

   I hereby attest that I have read this statement with no personal or professional conflict of interest with any parties or individuals involved in this case. Should any potential conflict of interest occur in the future, I will inform the _____ (name of institution) immediately and terminate my involvement in this case. With my signature below, I agree to conduct myself in a manner consistent with the policies and procedures written in the Handbook of Special Investigative Team (or other policy). I understand my continuing obligation to respect the confidentiality of information and perform my role in a professional manner.

_____   _____
Special Investigative Team Member   Witness (PRINT NAME)
(PRINT NAME)

_____   _____
Signature of Special Investigative   Signature of Witness
Team Member

_____
Date

*Check with your legal counsel before adopting this statement

Dos and Don'ts When Interviewing Survivors of Childhood Sexual Abuse

Dos

- Take control of the process.
- Be clear about the report and separate what is in the report from what you are gathering now.
- Clarify terms in the alleged report.
- Clarify and analyze the observed facts and statements.
- Address the emotion when it blocks the interviewing process.
- Show concern for emotional responses.
- Be nonpunitive and nonjudgmental.
- Be honest.
- Be a listener.
- Use a free-narrative approach to begin the interview.
- Use who, when, where, what, and how questions to clarify.
- Use the survivor's information to ask further questions.

Don'ts

- Don't ask leading questions.
- Don't lose sight of your role and the purpose of the interview.
- Don't use words that may convey blame or judgments (positive or negative).
- Don't take sides.
- Don't use statements that can reflect false reassurance (e.g., "Everything will be all right").
- Don't break silence prematurely.
- Don't use technical terms.
- Don't show approval or disapproval of what you heard.
- Don't ask why questions with an accusing tone.
- Don't defend the alleged perpetrator.
- Don't make assumptions or jump to conclusions.

Interview Protocol for Alleged Victim of Childhood Sexual Abuse

Stage 1: Introduction and Rapport Building

Steps	Examples
Introduction	
• Introduce each interviewer's name, role, and position.	• Thank you for coming. Let's introduce myself/ourselves.
• Verify the full name of the survivor.	• My name is X and I am a (position) at (institution).
• Ask the adult survivor to sign a Statement of Truth form (see appendix 4J). If the survivor is a minor, a signature on this form may not have legal power.	In a church setting when internal review is conducted:
	• My name is X. As a volunteer, I am a review board member of (church or diocese). My role is to assist the church in examining child sexual abuse cases and review policies on this matter. By profession, I am a (title). Today I am chairing this meeting. This interview panel is formed by three members, including myself; Mr. X, another review team member; and Rev. X from the church.

- Before we start, we would like to ask you to sign this statement that you will be telling the whole truth in this interview.
- Let's begin. What is your full name?

Purpose and Nature of the Interview

- State the purpose.
- Ask the AV whether he or she fully understands the purpose of this interview.
- Identify the purpose of note taking during the interview and specify when the notes will be destroyed.
- Stress the importance of telling the truth and staying focused.
- Understand legal rights, confidentiality issues, etc.
- Set time limit and ground rules.

- In this meeting, we will ask you to describe your report and then will take turns asking additional questions. We would like to end the meeting in X hours. If you need a break before we end, please let us know.
- We will be taking notes during the interview to help us prepare our report. Once the report is prepared and submitted, we will destroy our notes (or other policy).
- Let us know if you don't understand any of our questions or if you have additional information that you would like to add.

Rapport Building

- Provide opportunity to express feelings and release tensions.
- Be nonpunitive and nonjudgmental in your approach.
- Determine the AV's feelings.

- Do you have any questions about the purpose of this meeting?
- We understand that this is a serious matter that has caused tension and anxiety. We appreciate your willingness to meet with us. Please feel free to ask us questions during the meeting.

- We also would like you to know that we are here to collect information for (the institution); we are here not to judge but to listen.
- How are you doing? Would you like some water? Let's take a deep breath before we continue.
- Let's start with a brief description of how you knew the AP (or your involvement in AP's parish, church, or organization).

Stage 2: Free Narrative

Steps	Examples
Allow Free-Narrative Time	
■ Encourage AV to describe the situation or problem in own words.	■ Tell us what happened.
	■ Tell us more about it. Go on.
■ Use exact wording from the AV in your notes.	■ (If emotional) It's OK to take your time. We are here to listen.
■ Ask open-ended questions.	■ How about telling us about how you met and knew the AP?
■ Address emotions.	■ How are you feeling right now?
	■ How did it make you feel when you decided to come forward to disclose this report?
	■ Tell us about your relationship with the AP now. How about X years ago when you were a member of (the institution, e.g., as parishioner, client, student).
	■ We know you may feel uncomfortable talking about this, especially with strangers. We can assure to you that we are fact finders and will listen to you.

Stage 3: Specific Questioning

Steps	Examples
Clarify the Narrative ■ Allow the AV to finish the abuse complaints before asking specific questions to clarify what AV has said.	■ Use active listening techniques. ■ Do not use leading questions such as "Did the AP sexually abuse and/or touch you?"
■ Use information from the free narrative to ask specific questions for validation purposes. ■ Use who, when, where, what, and how questions. ■ Don't ask why questions. ■ Validate the report by asking about a detailed description of the sexual offense, progression, secrecy, coercion (e.g., threat or reward), first complaints (e.g., psychological or psychiatric evaluations after the incident, corroborating information from others, behavioral indicators), and terminology used.	*Who?* ■ Who is the AP (name, nickname)? • What is or was your relationship with him? • Which parish, organization, or school did you know him from? *When?* ■ When did it happen (e.g., grade, season, holiday)? *Where?* ■ Where did it take place? ■ Describe that place. ■ What other functions usually take place in this place? *What?* ■ What did the AP do (or say) before (during, after) he did X? ■ What were you and the AP wearing at that time? ■ What else happened during that time? Afterward? ■ What did the AP do to make you go along with his request? *How?* ■ How did the AP come into your room? ■ How did AP do X (use AV's own words)?

- How did you feel about the AP's request (action) at that time?
- Did you notice any difference in the AP when he did that?
- How did you know it was (sexual abuse, but use the AV's own words)?
- How many times did something similar happen to you (to determine frequency, duration, type, who, when, where, what, and how)?

Who else?

- Who else knew about this?
- When did you tell that person? What did you say?
- What was that person's first reaction?
- What did that person say or do at that time?
- Did anyone ask you to keep this a secret?

- Clarify meanings of sexual terms or activities.

- Because sexual abuse is a sensitive subject, when we ask you something that is related to sex or intimacy, please be specific and understand that our role is not to judge but to get the exact information from your perspective or experience.
- What is the formal or anatomical name of X?
- Has the AP ever talked with you about sex or sexual matters?
- What did you do or say when AP asked you to do X (use AV's own word)?

- Tell us about your personal view or values about these kinds of sexual activities. What are your views and values about them now (to determine whether there is a difference)?

Motivation	- Did you or anyone confront the AP about this incident at that time? Afterward? - What did the AP say, or how did he react? - What did you say or do? - How did that make you feel? - What made you come forward to report now?

Others

- Obtain additional evidence.
- Identify past history.
- Obtain corroborator's name, phone, e-mail address, and address.
- Obtain Release of Information form (with signature and date; appendix 4K)
- Determine whether there is information to be added.

- Do you keep a diary or journal? Did you write down what happened during that time? Can we have a copy of what you wrote?
- You mentioned earlier that X knew what you did that night. Would you like us to contact him or her if we need further information?
- You mentioned that you went to see a mental health professional after the incident. We would like to contact this professional. Would you please sign a release form before you go?
- Have you ever been sexually abused by others? By whom (relationship)? When did it happen? What did you do about it?
- Have you ever had a drinking or substance abuse problem? When?

- Have you ever had a mental or psychiatric problem? When?
- Can you tell us about your current relationship with men (or women)?
- Tell us about your style of showing affection (before and after this incident).
- Do you have anything to add?

Stage 4: Closing the Interview

Steps	Examples
Summarize - Highlight facts revealed. - Don't conclude (just summarize main points).	- Let's summarize some main points here. - Did I miss any important points? - Are you willing to make a written statement about what you just told us? - Are you willing to be connected to a lie detector when you make this statement?
Future and Concerns - Discuss possible future actions. - Ask about concerns (self, church, children, parishioners). - Allow questions.	- Let's talk about our next steps. We will write up our report to the institution. The case manager (or caseworker) will contact you about our next steps.
Ending - Provide a phone number and name to be contacted. - Thank the person for coming.	- Before we go, we would like to know what concerns you might have about the AP.

- What would you like us (the institution) to do? (For you? To the AP?)
- What concerns do you have about yourself? The media?
- Do you have any questions for us?
- Again, thank you for coming to meet with us. If you have any information to add or questions to ask, please contact X. He (or she) will relate the information to us.

Evaluation Protocol of the Accused Male of Child Sexual Abuse

The following protocol is developed by the author, based on Gardner (1995).

Evaluation Protocol
Client's Name: _____
0 = not evident
1 = minimal level of evidence
2 = some evidence
3 = strong evidence

0 1 2 3   1. History of family influences conducive to the development of significant psychopathology
        • Trouble with the police
        • Drinking problems
        • Drug abuse problems
        • Psychiatric problems
        • Suicide or attempted suicide in the family

0 1 2 3   2. Long-standing history of emotional deprivation
        • Childhood problems with parents
        • Childhood problems in peer relationships

0 1 2 3   3. Intellectual impairment
        • Academic problems
        • Disparity between clinical impression and IQ score

0 1 2 3   4. Childhood history of sex abuse

0 1 2 3   5. Long-standing history of very strong sexual urges
- Age of first sexual urges or masturbation
- Sexual experience with other children
- More sexual urges than the average man of same age

0 1 2 3   6. Impulsivity
- Rage outbursts
- Court restraining order
- Presence of impulsive feelings

0 1 2 3   7. Narcissism
- Always compare to others
- Need to extract comments of praise

0 1 2 3   8. Coercive-dominating behavior
- Conflicts with others
- Forceful marital relationships
- Impose own will on others

0 1 2 3   9. Passivity and impaired self-assertion
- Not speaking up
- Not asserting self enough in life

0 1 2 3   10. Substance abuse

0 1 2 3   11. Poor judgment
- Inability to make a sound judgment
- Quickly entered into a relationship with a stranger

0 1 2 3   12. Impaired sexual interest in age-appropriate women
- Not competent to pursue involvement with women of own age

0 1 2 3   13. Presence of other sexual deviations
- Premature or retarded ejaculation
- Attracted by women with immature body configurations

0 1 2 3   14. Psychosis
- Strange or bizarre experiences in life
- Felt like he or she was being picked on
- Inner voices
- External voices

0 1 2 3   15. Immaturity and/or regression
- Enjoyed child-type activities
- Weak ego strength
- Insensitive to others' feelings
- Low frustration tolerance

0 1 2 3   16. Large collection of child pornographic materials

0 1 2 3   17. Career choice that brings him or her in contact with children

0 1 2 3   18. Recent rejection by a female peer or dysfunctional hetero-sexual relationship

0 1 2 3   19. Unconvincing denial
- No evidence of helplessness
- Weak denials

0 1 2 3   20. Use of rationalizations and cognitive distortions that justify pedophilia
- Not able to profess the normative attitudes toward child abuse

0 1 2 3   21. Utilization of seductivity

0 1 2 3   22. Attitude toward taking a lie-detector test

0 1 2 3   23. Lack of cooperation in the evaluative examination

0 1 2 3   24. Duplicity unrelated to the sex-abuse denial and psycho-pathic tendencies
- Shows little sensitivity to the effect of the abuse on the child victim
- Deceitful when denying the pedophilia
- Deceits that are not related to the allegation of pedophilia

0 1 2 3   25. Moralism
- Rigidly moralistic
- Condemns in others behavior that one wishes to engage in oneself but cannot permit oneself to do
- Inability to accept the opposite position

0 1 2 3   26. Numerous victims

Total Score:

0 ------ 10 ------ 20 ------ 30 ------ 40 ------ 50 ------ 60 ------ 70 ----- 78

Comments: _____

_____   _____

Assessed By: Date:

Interview Protocol for Alleged Perpetrator in a Religious Setting

Stage 1: Introduction and Rapport Building

Steps	*Examples*
Introduction - Introduce each interviewer's name, role, and position. - Verify the full name of the AP. - Ask the AP to sign the Statement of Truth form (appendix 4J; this step can be done at the time when a case manager receives the AP before the interview).	- Thank you for coming. Let's introduce ourselves. - My name is X and I am a (position) at (institution). In a church setting when internal review is conducted: - My name is X. As a volunteer, I am a review board member of (church/diocese). My role is to assist the church to examine child sexual abuse cases and review policies on this matter. By profession, I am a (title). Today I am chairing this meeting. This interview panel is formed by three members, including myself; Mr. X, another review team member; and Rev. X from the church.

- Before we start, we would like to ask you to sign this statement that you will tell the whole truth in this interview.
- Please introduce yourself by stating your full name.

Purpose and Nature of the Interview

- State purpose.
- Ask the client whether he or she understands fully what is being alleged and the implications.
- Emphasize the use of a blank-screen and neutral approach.
- Identify the purpose of note taking during the interview and specify when the notes will be destroyed.
- Stress the importance of telling the truth and staying focused.
- Understand legal rights, confidentiality issues, etc.
- Set time limit and ground rules.

- Our meeting today is to share with you a report of the allegations made against you and to provide you with the opportunity to respond.
- We realize that these allegations are severe, with adverse consequences. You have the right to seek legal counsel if you so choose.
- We uphold strict confidentiality, however, we will share our findings with the archbishop, and the archdiocese may work with the law enforcement if necessary.
- We will ask you to describe what you know and then will take turns asking additional questions. We would like to end the meeting in X hours. If you need a break before we end, please let us know.
- We will take notes during the interview to help us prepare our report to the archbishop. Once the report is prepared and submitted, we will destroy our notes.

| | ■ Let us know if you don't understand any of our questions or if you want to add any information. |

Rapport Building	
■ Provide opportunity for the client to express feelings and release tensions.	■ Do you have anything you would like to ask before we proceed?
■ Be nonpunitive and nonjudgmental in your approach.	■ We understand that this is a serious matter that has created tension and anxiety. We appreciate your cooperation and willingness to meet with us. Please feel free to ask us questions during this meeting.
■ Determine the AP's feelings.	
	■ We would like you to know that we are here to collect information for the review board and the archbishop; we are not here to condemn or judge you.
	■ How are you doing? Would you like some water?
	■ Let's start with a brief description of activities that you have organized or participated in with youth parishioners.

Stage 2: Free Narrative

Steps	*Examples*
Allow Free-Narrative Time	
■ Encourage the AP to describe the situation in own words.	■ Tell us what you know about this allegation.
■ Use exact wording from the AP in your notes.	■ (If emotional) It's OK to take your time. We are here to listen.

- Ask open-ended questions.
- Always be conscious about why you are asking certain questions.

- Can you tell us how you met and knew the AV?
- How are you feeling right now?
- How did it make you feel when you first heard about this report against you?

Stage 3: Specific Questioning

Steps	Examples
Clarify the Narrative	
- Allow the AP to finish telling his or her side of the story before asking specific questions to clarify what the AP just said.	- Use active listening techniques. - Do not use leading questions such as "Did you sexually abuse the AV?"
- Use information from the free narrative to ask specific questions for validation purposes. - Use who, when, where, what, and how questions. - Don't ask why questions.	*Who?* - Who knows about this allegation? *When?* - The report indicated that sexual abuse occurred during (event). Can you tell us about that function and your role in it? *Where?* - Where is that place? - Describe that place. - What other functions usually take place in that place? - Is there any alcohol in this place? - Where were you when the alleged event took place? *What?* - The AV said you did X. What did you do to make her believe that you abused her?

How?
- How did the AV come into your office?
- How did you feel about the AV's request at that time?

- Clarify terms in the report regarding sexual acts or activities.
- Question inconsistencies (e.g., in the AP's words; the AP's version versus the AV's version).

- Because sexual abuse is a sensitive subject, when we ask you something that is related to sex or intimacy, please be specific and understand that our role is not to judge or accuse but to get the exact information from your perspective or experience.
- Had the AV ever talked with you about sex or a sexual matter?
- What did you do or say when the AV asked you to X (use AP's word)?
- When you heard about this sex act, which the AV told us, what was your first reaction? How do you feel about it now?
- Tell us about your personal view or values regarding these kind of sexual activities.

- Be aware that some clients may use defense mechanisms.
- Return to the main investigation by using transition or bridging statements.

- If the AP is loud and hostile or faults you for accusations of sexual abuse, don't take it personally. Just say, "Calm down."
- You have given me information regarding why you were there alone with AV; now tell me what you and the AV did during that encounter.

Determine the AP's Knowledge
of AV
- Determine the history with the
  AV to verify the AV's report.

- What is the full name of the AV?
- Do you know the AV's family?
- How old was the AV (or school
  grade) at the reported period?

Prior History
- Find additional validation points
  through patterns of behaviors.

- Are there any prior allegations
  against you?
- Do you have a history of being
  molested?
- Describe your prior activities
  alone with youths.
- How do you handle conflict with
  youths?
- Have you ever been drunk
  before? How did you handle
  your behavior when you became
  drunk? How do you know?
- Do you have a history of drinking or substance abuse?
- Tell us about your style of showing affection (with adults,
  youths, and young kids).

Others
- Obtain corroborator's name,
  phone, e-mail address, and
  address.
- Obtain information release (with
  signature and date; appendix
  4K)
- Determine whether there is
  information to be added.

- You mentioned earlier that X
  knew what you did that night.
  Would you like us to contact
  him or her if we need further
  information?
- You mentioned that you saw a
  mental health professional after
  this incident; we would like to
  contact this professional. Would
  you please sign a release form
  before you go?
- Do you have anything to add?

Stage 4: Closing the Interview

Steps	Examples
Summarize ■ Highlight facts revealed. ■ Don't conclude (just summarize main points).	■ Let us summarize some main points here. ■ Did I miss any important points? ■ Are you willing to make a written statement about what you just told us? ■ Are you willing to be connected to a lie detector to make your statement?
Future and Concerns ■ Discuss possible future actions. ■ Ask about concerns (self, church, children, parishioners). ■ Allow questions.	■ Let's talk about our next steps. We will write up our report to the archbishop, who may consult with the review board to make a decision. He will inform you of his decision.
Ending ■ Provide a contact name and phone number. ■ Thank the person for coming.	■ Before we go, we would like to know what concerns you might have about the AV. ■ What concerns do you have about yourself? ■ Do you have any questions for us? ■ Again, thank you for coming to meet with us. If you have any information to add or questions to ask, please contact X, who will relate the information to us.

Comparing the Interview Protocols for the Child Victim, the Childhood Victim, and the Alleged Perpetrator

Protocol item	Child victim	Childhood victim	Alleged perpetrator
Stage 1	**Rapport**	**Introduction**	**Introduction**

- Introduce each interviewer's name, role, and position (e.g., a review board member of X Diocese, professional's job title and agency).

- Verify the name of the interviewee.
- Check what name (nickname) the interviewee prefers to be called during this interview.

	Serve as a competency test	Help start memory recall	Understand the purpose
	Check for secondary gain (e.g., discipline, divorce)	Determine reason to come forward now	Check for feelings
	Identify home situation to check current and past relationships with AP	Determine current relationship issues with men (or women).	Determine current relationships with the AV and/or other youths.
	Determine truth-lie understanding	Understand the possible consequences: media, confidentiality, etc.	Understand legal rights, confidentiality issues, etc.

- Identify the purpose of the interview (e.g., fact-finding, reporting to the agency or review board).

184

Protocol item	Child victim	Childhood victim	Alleged perpetrator
	■ Emphasize the use of a blank-screen and neutral approach (i.e., not knowing much of the report but wanting to find out the facts directly from the involved). ■ Stress the importance of telling the truth and staying focused. ■ Briefly identify the steps of this interview: listening, questioning, and answering additional questions at the end. ■ Identify the purpose of note taking (or taping) during this interview and specify when these notes or tapes will be destroyed. ■ Set time limit and ground rules. ■ Ask if there are any questions about the purpose of this interview.		
Stage 2	**Free narrative**		**Information gathering**
	■ Encourage to describe the situation or problem in own words.		
	Tell me what happened.	Tell me about your report of "sexual abuse as a child" (use AV's term).	Tell me what you know about this allegation.
	What has made you happy or upset?	I am here to listen to you.	I am here to listen to your side of the story.
	■ Concern about emotional responses.		
	E.g., "I received this report about you being "abused" (use AV's term) and I know it is difficult to talk about it. How about taking a deep breath and then telling me what it is? One, two, three ..."	"I know you may feel uncomfortable talking about this, especially in front of strangers. I can assure you that we are fact-finders and will listen to you."	"Tell us how you are feeling right now." "How did it make you feel when you first heard about this report against you?"
Stage 3	**Questioning**		**Clarification**
	■ Allow the person to finish the "story" before asking specific questions to clarify what the person just said. ■ Use information from the free narrative to ask specific questions for validation purposes. ■ Use 4W1H questions to clarify: who, where, when, what, and how. ■ Collect evidence that is material, competent, and relevant. ■ Focus specific questions to find validation points: detailed description of the sexual offense, progression, secrecy, coercion (threat or reward), first complaints (e.g., psychological or psychiatric evaluations after the incident, corroborating information from others, behavioral indicators), and terminology used.		

Protocol item	Child victim	Childhood victim	Alleged perpetrator
	■ Make sure to clarify sexual acts, sexual parts, or other terminology. Don't assume (e.g., "What is the formal or anatomical name of X?") ■ After clarification, you can use the person's terminology. It is also ok to use the newly clarified term. ■ Even if clarification questions are asked, the interviewer can always encourage the client to complete the story ("Tell me more," "Then what happened?" and "Go on"). ■ Don't ask leading questions. ■ Don't make assumptions. ■ Don't judge. ■ Be a patient listener.		
	■ Verify the AP's name. ■ Determine AP's relationship with AV. ■ Determine reactions of the first person told. ■ Ask about content and reaction of confrontation, if any.		■ Determine whether AP knows the full name of the AV. ■ Determine whether AP knows the AV's family. ■ Determine whether AP knows the age of the AV (or school grade) at the reported incident period.
	■ Determine AV's senses in reaction to the incident (hear, say, feel, smell, think). ■ For multiple incidents, recall the most recent and the first incidents, then count how many in between, if any. ■ Ask AV's perception of the AP's role (authority, friend) in her family.	■ Any note-taking habit (e.g. diary, journal, or correspondence about this incident). ■ Obtain corroborator's name, phone, email address, and address. ■ Obtain release of information statement (with signature and date; see appendix 4K).	Ask about ■ Prior history of being molested by others ■ Prior history of activities with youths ■ Prior history of being with youths alone ■ Ways of handling conflict with youths
	■ Determine whether there is information to be added.		

Protocol item	Child victim	Childhood victim	Alleged perpetrator
Stage 4		**Closure**	

- Don't conclude (just summarize main points).
- Don't promise if you don't know.
- Don't take sides.

	■ Ask if the child wants the interviewer to accompany him or her to talk with the parents about this disclosure. ■ Confirm what has been told is true and no coaching is involved.	■ Ask if the person wants to make a written statement.	

- Don't touch the child even if you want to comfort him or her.

	■ Determine what the AV would want to see happen next (the AP, self, family, church, work, counseling).		■ Ask about the AP's concerns (self, work, children).

	■ Acknowledge how difficult it may be to disclose this kind of information.		■ Acknowledge courage and willingness to come forward.

- Check on current feelings.
- Allow the person to ask questions.
- Provide a phone number and name to be contacted.
- Thank the person for coming.

Two Cases Demonstrating the Use of a CSA Interview Protocol: Evidence-Based Information for the Two Cases Demonstrated on the Accompanying DVD

Monit Cheung, Amanda Ford, and Jacquelynn Duron

The following two cases, with personal identifiers masked, are based on many real-life cases, and the specific nature of the problem has been altered to protect confidentiality. Pay attention to the dynamics of child sexual abuse in the disclosure case (e.g., relationship issues, progression, secrecy, cohesion, disclosure, denial of the problem, motivation to report) and the use of body protection information in the nondisclosure case. In both cases, the interview is considered to be conducted in a professional manner if the interviewer relies mainly on the use of open-ended questions to assist the child's disclosure without leading the child to disclose while using only specific questioning techniques (or tools) to follow up and clarify the child's earlier statements. Although the examples provide an introductory model for applying the child sexual abuse interview protocol, suggestions to modify the protocol have been made according to guidelines from the most current empirical research. In training, the two cases can be role-played with the additional questions and/or techniques suggested so that trainees understand the importance of including evidence-based questions or modifying existing questions in an interview. These examples are used as a reference, not as a rigid procedure.

The cases can also be used to highlight the use of a standardized protocol with suggestions as constant reminders from research evidence that substantive changes may be deemed necessary for improvement. For each suggestion, we provide literature and research support in the chapter text that explains the suggested procedures and/or strategies and provides further insight into the aforementioned modifications to the videotaped protocol.

Case 1: Case of Disclosure of Child Sexual Abuse (Fourteen-Year-Old Female)

Stage 1: Rapport

Inform about the Interviewer

INTERVIEWER: Hi, my name is Sophia Anderson. You can call me Sophia. What is your name?

CHILD: Julie Michaels.

I: What do people usually call you?

C: Julie.

I: Can I call you Julie?

C: (Nods.)

Identify the Purpose

I: Julie, I am a social worker at the Children's Assessment Center, and I work with kids to find out what is going on and make sure everything is OK. I would like to ask you some questions today and you can ask me questions too. Is that OK?

C: (Nods.)

State the Purpose and Obtain Consent

In a forensic interview, the interviewer should mention the purpose of videotaping the interview and obtain consent when necessary.

I: Julie, you may have noticed that there is a video camera in the room (behind the mirror) and we are recording our conversation today. We use the recording so that we don't have to ask you the same questions. Do you have any questions about the video camera?

C: Does it have to video record us?

I: It is really important that we record our conversation so that other people won't have to ask you these same questions so that you don't have to repeat yourself.

C: What are you going to do with it?

I: Well, other people that are involved in the case may watch it to help some that might include the police.

C: But I don't want my mom to watch it.

I: Tell me why you don't want your mom to watch it.

C: I don't know.

I: OK. I'll try my best to help you, is that OK?

C: (Nods.)

I: Let's continue.

C: (Nods.)

I: It's really important when I ask you a question if you would say yes or no rather than nodding your head, so that I know if that nod means yes or if that nod means no. Is that good?

C: OK.

Establish Rapport and Check Competency

I: Julie, how old are you?

C: Fourteen.

I: When is your birthday?

C: December 20, 1996.

I: That's close to Christmas, huh?

C: Yes.

I: Julie, where do you live?

C: 1212 Fair Drive.

I: Julie, is that a house, an apartment, or something else?

C: A house.

I: Whom do you live with?

C: My mom, Lisa; my stepdad, David; and my little brother, John.

I: Tell me a little bit about them. How old are they?

C: My mom is forty. My little brother is five. And I'm guessing that David is like thirty-five or something.

I: OK, when you don't know something I want you to say, "I don't know." So rather than guessing David's age, you can just say, "I don't know." OK?

C: OK.

I: Julie, what grade are you in?

C: Eighth.

I: Do you like school?

C: Yes.

I: Tell me what you like about school.

C: I like my friends there.

I: What do you like to do with your friends?

C: We just like to hang out.

I: OK.

Assess Competency: Truth versus Lie

I: Julie, thank you for telling me a little about your family and school. Now we are going to talk about some other very important things. Can you tell me what the difference is between a truth and a lie? (*A conceptual approach for older children.*)

C: Yes. The truth is something really happened and a lie is when it didn't happen.

Eliminate Burden and Establish Consequences of Lying

In this example and the following, current literature recommends that, especially when the interviewer uses a lie example, the burden is placed on another individual rather than on the child or the interviewer, who is perceived not to be a liar. Thus, the subject of a truth-and-lie example would be changed from the client (Julie) to another person (someone).

I: If someone said you were in eighth grade, would that person be telling the truth or a lie?

C: The truth.

I: What if someone said Julie is not here in this room—would that person be telling the truth or a lie?

C: A lie.

I: What usually happens if someone tells a lie?

C: They get in trouble.

I: When we talk today it is very important to only tell truths. Can you promise to only talk truths?

C: Yes.

Set Up Ground Rules and Clarify Terminology

As part of the ground rules, the interviewer should also clarify the reasons that slang terminology or unusual terms may need to be explained.

I: Julie, if I ever ask you a question and you don't know the answer, I want you to just say "I don't know." If I say something you don't understand and you need me to repeat it in a different way, I want you to just say, "I don't understand." And if you hear something wrong, I want you to correct me, so I get the right thing, OK?

C: OK.

I: Julie, sometimes you might use words that are slang or a word that you might use and others might use differently, and I might ask you to clarify that, so I might ask you, "What do you mean by that?" and that is just so I understand. Like I said, some people use the same word to mean different things, OK?

C: OK.

Stage 2: Free-Narrative Account

I: Tell me why you came here today.

C: (Silence.)

I: It's OK. Take your time.

C: (Sighs.)

Move between Stage 2 and Stage 3

When a child does not respond to the free-narrative portion of the interview, the interviewer can move to stage 3, questioning, to ask some non-threatening questions first. When the child feels more comfortable, the interviewer is encouraged to return to stage 2 to allow time for the child's own narrative.

I: Julie, who brought you here today?

C: My mom.

I: What did she say about coming here?

C: Hmm. That I was going to talk to you.

I: Did she say what you are going to talk about?

C: (Sighs.)

I: How have you been?

C: Not good.

Handle Secrecy

If the child mentions that this is a secret and asks the interviewer not to tell anyone, the interviewer could use practical strategies to help the client disclose the secret.

I: What hasn't been good?

C: Well, it's a secret. If I tell you, can you not tell anyone?

I: Julie, I talk to lots of young boys and girls, and I can help you figure out what you can tell and what you can't tell.

C: (Silence.)

Return to Stage 2

I: You said you haven't been good. Tell me about this.

C: I have been having problems with my stepdad. Sexual problems. (Pause.) He makes me do things I don't want to do.

Case 2: Nondisclosure Case (Ten-Year-Old Female)

Stage 1: Rapport

Inform about the Interviewer

I: Hi, my name is Amy Johnson. You can call me Amy. What is your name?

C: Erin McGeese.

I: What do people usually call you?

C: Erin.

I: Can I call you Erin, too?

C: Yes.

Identify the Purpose

I: Uh, I wanted to let you know that we do have video camera in the room that is recording us, so that you don't have to repeat what you say and so that other important people can listen to what we have to say. Is that OK?

C: Yes.

State the Purpose and Obtain Consent

I: Uh, I wanted to let you know that we do have video camera in the room that is recording us, so that you don't have to repeat what you say and so that other important people can listen to what we have to say. Is that OK?

C: Yes. Is it on? (Child leaves the seat)

I: Yes, it's on. And they can see us, but I need you to come sit back down. I have some really important questions that I need to ask you. OK?

C: OK. (Returns to chair)

Establish Rapport

I: Erin, can you tell me how old you are?

C: I am ten years old

I: When is your birthday?

C: July 4, 2000.

I: What school do you go to?

C: Thompson Elementary.

I: Do you like school?

C: I love school.

I: What are some of the things you like to do in school?

C: I like to . . . I like recess.

I: Recess, that is your favorite. OK.

I: Where do you live?

C: I live at 1111 Kelly Street.

I: OK, who do you live with?

C: I live with my mom, my dad, my sister, and my brother.

I: Is it a house, an apartment, or something else?

C: A house.

I: Tell me about your family. What are their names?

C: My mom's name is Sarah. My dad is Bob. My sister's name is Julie, and my brother's name is Peter.

I: Erin, can you come sit up here for me so everybody can see. We want to make sure we can see everything. OK? Thank you.

C: OK.

I: Erin, what may happen if you get in trouble at home?

c: Well, I get punished and can't go outside for a week.

i: You probably don't like that, huh?

c: Uh-huh.

Assess Competency: Truth versus Lie

i: Erin, I want to thank you for telling me about your family, and there are some questions I wanted to asked you, but before we get started I wanted to make sure you understand the difference between the truth and a lie. OK? Can you tell me the difference between the truth and a lie?

c: I don't know.

i: How about telling a lie—what does it mean?

c: (Silence.)

Eliminate Burden and Establish Consequences of Lying

i: Let's use an example. Is your name Erin?

c: Yes.

i: If someone said your name is Erin, would this person be telling the truth or a lie?

c: (Mumbles.)

i: Is it the truth or not that your name is Erin?

c: Yes.

i: So when you say yes—what does yes mean?

c: Yes, my name is Erin; it's the truth.

i: Let's use another example. If someone says its raining in this room is that a truth or a lie?

c: A lie.

i: Can you tell me what usually happens if someone tells a lie?

c: They get in trouble.

Set Up Ground Rules

i: Today we are going to talk about things that are very important, and we are talking about things that really happened. . . . And when we are talking about lies, we are talking about things that didn't really happen. But today you have to promise me that you will only talk about true things. Can you promise that to me?

c: Yes.

I: I also want to let you know that when we are talking about things, if I ask you a question and you do not know the answer, you can say, "I don't know."

c: OK.

I: I also want to make sure we understand each other very clearly, so if I say something that you don't understand I want you to say that you don't understand. And then maybe I can say it more clearly so that you will understand. OK?

c: OK.

Clarify Terminology

As part of the ground rules, the interviewer should also clarify the reasons that slang terminology or unusual terms may need to be explained.

I: In order for us to understand each other better, sometimes you may use slang words that I don't know, and I want to make sure I understand everything that you say, so whenever you say a word that I don't know, I may ask you a question about it. And one other thing—sometimes you may say a word that is slang or something I don't know. I may ask you what that means. Or I may ask you to repeat something. This is just to make sure I know what you are telling me. Sometimes people use the same word to mean different things. OK?

c: Yes.

Stage 2: Free-Narrative Account

I: Erin, tell me why you came here today.

c: (Silence.)

I: Is there anything that you want to tell me?

c: No.

I: Erin, I know I am a stranger, but I talk to lots of kids and I am very concerned. I am here to listen to you. I will do my best to help you.

c: (Nods.)

I: What happened lately with you?

c: Nothing happened.

I: Has anything been bothering you lately?

C: I don't know.

I: You don't know, or you can't talk about it?

C: I don't know.

I: Did anyone tell you not to talk about things?

C: No.

I: Erin, it's very important that I understand what you mean when you say, "I don't know." Erin, it's OK if you feel more comfortable later, you can talk to me. Later if you feel like telling me what has been bothering you, I am here to listen.

C: (Silence.)

Move between Stage 2 and Stage 3

When a child does not respond to the free-narrative portion of the interview, the interviewer can move to stage 3, questioning, to ask some nonthreatening questions first. When the child feels more comfortable, the interviewer is encouraged to return to stage 2.

I: Earlier you said you liked to play with your friends. Tell me about what you like to do.

C: Oh! I like to play basketball. I'm really good!

I: Do you have any pets?

C: I have a dog. His name is Monster.

I: Thanks for telling me about your friends and your dog, Monster. Now, tell me something about what happened lately with you. Do you know why your mom brought you here today?

C: Mom said I had to come talk to you.

Stage 3: Questioning

Use Nonthreatening Questions

Throughout stage 3, the three nonthreatening questions—who, when, and where—should be used before introducing the what question, because they help reduce the experience of negative emotions and offer clarity to the acquired information, particularly when interviewing a reticent child.

I: What is your mom's name?

C: Sarah.

I: Do you live with your mom?

C: Yes.

I: Previously, you had said you lived in a house. Do you know how many bedrooms do you have in your house?

C: Four.

I: Thank you, Erin. You're doing a great job. I really appreciate you sitting so nicely.

I: Who sleeps in your bedroom?

C: Me.

I: At this center, we like to talk to children and make sure they understand how to protect their bodies. What are the areas on your body that no one is supposed to touch? Tell me the places on your body that no one should touch.

C: Here, here, here.

Provide Body Protection Knowledge

If the child does not disclose abuse, the interviewer should provide information about body protection and further assistance. The following series of questions demonstrate this concept.

I: You pointed to certain areas on your body, and I just want to make sure I understand. Do you have another name for the areas that you pointed to?

C: My chest, my butt, and my tee-tee.

I: What's another name for tee-tee?

C: Um . . . vagina.

I: Who is allowed to touch those areas?

C: Doctors.

I: Who shouldn't touch you there?

C: Other people.

I: If those other people tried to touch you, what would you say or do?

C: I'll run away really fast!

I: What else would you do?

C: I'll tell my mom.

I: Yes, if someone did try to touch you, telling your mom is the right thing to do. Has anyone ever touched you or tried to touch you in your chest, butt, or tee-tee?

c: No.

I: Has someone ever looked at your privates or tried to look at your privates?

c: No.

Use Follow-Up Questions

I: Earlier when I asked you about things that have been bothering you, you were kind of quiet. Tell me about that.

c: Well, nothing really happened. My mom told me to come here because she didn't want me playing with Tim next door.

I: Who's Tim?

c: My friend.

I: How old is Tim?

c: He's also ten.

I: Did Tim do anything to you?

c: No, we are friends. My mom just doesn't like him.

I: Tell me why your mom doesn't like him.

c: She just doesn't like him.

I: Did anything happen to where your mom doesn't like Tim?

c: No.

I: Erin, is there anything else you would like me to help you with?

c: Tell my mom not to yell at me anymore.

I: What did your mom yell at you about?

c: She just didn't like me going over to Tim's house.

I: What happened at Tim's house?

c: Nothing, we were just playing.

I: Tell me about that.

c: I played with Tim and his dad. We played doctors but nothing happened.

I: What did you play?

c: Tim put a stick in my mouth, and his dad came and grabbed me and said no. Then my mom came in and started yelling at me.

I: How did he grab you?

c: He took the stick out of my mouth.

I: What else happened?

c: Mom thought that Tim pulled down my pants. But he didn't.

I: Do you want to tell your mom about this?

C: She is angry at me now.

I: How about we talk with your mom together? I'll help you to tell your mom about what you just told me. OK?

C: OK.

Stage 4: Closing the Interview

Thank and Reassure the Child, Give the Child an Opportunity to Ask Questions, and Formally Close the Interview

I: Erin, I have been asking you a lot of questions. I think you've done a great job. Do you have any questions for me before we go?

C: No.

I: Just so I make sure I heard everything you said, I want to repeat what you said. You told me that you were playing with Tim and his dad. And you guys were playing and Tim stuck a stick in your mouth. Is that right?

C: Yes.

I: Remember that if you ever have any worries or ever get scared about something, I want you to always tell a grown up. OK?

C: OK.

I: Well, Erin, Thank you for talking with me. I don't have any more questions. Are you ready to go?

C: Yes. Let's go.

Statement of Truth of Testimony

Special Investigative Team
Statement of Truth of Testimony*

By signing this statement I pledge and affirm that the testimony I have given to the Special Investigative Team of _____ (name of institution) is true, accurate, and complete, to the best of my knowledge and recollection. If I remember additional information that would be necessary for the Special Investigative Team to possess or if, upon recollection, I believe that any aspect of my testimony is incorrect, I will notify the Case Manager/Caseworker no later than the next one to five working days.

_____   _____
Interviewee (PRINT NAME)   Witness (PRINT NAME)

_____   _____
Signature of Interviewee   Signature of Witness

_____
Date

*Check with your legal counsel before adopting this statement

Release of Information Form

Release of Confidential Information

_____ (name of professional or institution) has authorization to obtain psychological, educational, medical, legal, oral testimony and other relevant information regarding the person named below. This information is to be used to assist _____ (name of institution) in the process of investigating a case of child sexual abuse.

This authorization applies only to the following individual/institution (a separate form will be required for each individual or institution):

Name:

Address:

Phone/Email Contact:

I understand that by requesting this release of information, my record from _____ (date) to _____ (date), or its entity if these dates are not specified, will be sent to the professional/institution above. I also understand that I may revoke this consent at any time except to the extent that the release has been taken in action. In any event, this consent will expire automatically 90 days from the signing of this consent.

Name on Record to be Released (PRINT): _____

Authorized Signature (parent/guardian, if minor): _____

Date: _____

CHAPTER 5

Court Preparation

Preparing for the judicial process can be a meticulous task full of many uncertainties for experienced and inexperienced individuals alike. The goal of this chapter is to provide a brief description of the judicial process for allegedly sexually abused children and those who work with them. "Julie's Case" is used to illustrate the court process when a child victim is involved.

Mellor and Dent (1994) state that "children benefit from the involvement of their [caregivers] in the process of preparation, so that both [caregiver(s)] and child develop an understanding of the court system and know what to expect" (p. 169). The caregivers are not limited to family members and friends but also include the professionals and support persons who prepare the child witness to feel comfortable testifying in court. Preparation can help greatly in informing the child witness and those working with the child about the various roles of judges, attorneys (prosecutors or defense lawyers), law enforcement officers, forensic interviewers, support persons, witnesses, and expert witnesses in the judicial system. It is imperative that the child understands the process of being a witness before going to court.

It is also just as important for the court to take the child witness's needs into consideration before court proceedings to eliminate further harm to the child in the pursuit of ensuring that the child gives accurate information. However, in this process of protecting the child victim, it is impossible to exclude the child victim from his or her role of being present in a court setting to provide evidence. According to Mellor and Dent (1994), "Emphasis on obtaining unequivocal, uncontaminated evidence at the expense of the witness, when both evidence and witness are inextricably linked, does not make good sense" (p. 170). In addition to providing specific judicial preparatory steps for the allegedly abused child and those who work with the child, this chapter also includes tips for testifying in court to ensure that persons called to testify in child sexual abuse cases know what to expect and how to answer and ask questions. The chapter also describes techniques for documentation, identifies how to prepare court testimony, explains defense tactics, and prepares professionals and support persons to assist the witness in court.

Understanding the Court System

According to Jones (2006), working with the courts—including "preparing for and conducting themselves in court" (n.p.)—is considered a major component in casework for all Child Protective Services (CPS) workers. In addition to CPS workers, other professionals who work with children are not exempt from appearing in court if the case involves civil or criminal legal actions. Because child sexual abuse is a criminal offense, additional parties, beyond judges and attorneys, are involved in court proceedings, including the alleged victim, the alleged perpetrator, any witnesses other than the child victim, the person(s) presenting the first-point-of-contact information, the CPS worker in charge of the case, other professionals involved in the case, and any expert witnesses. Some of these individuals may play multiple roles in the judicial process.

Because child sexual abuse is a criminal act, cases are handled in criminal court. Many times these cases are initially presented as physical or other types of abuse and neglect; therefore, it is common for the case to first appear in civil or family court. When the sexual abuse is compounded by the child's conduct that involves violations of the law (e.g., curfew violation, running away from home, truancy, substance abuse), the case must also be heard in juvenile court. This type of hearing may not continue after the child reaches the age of an adult, unless the state statutes allow continued jurisdiction past a certain age, such as twenty-one.

Children's Rights to Due Process

The U.S. Supreme Court's decisions in *Kent v. United States* (1966) and *In re Gault* (1967) provide minors the basic rights of procedural due process to receive counsel, notice, fair hearing, confrontation, and cross-examination of witnesses. A subsequent decision in *In re Winship* (1970) further constitutionally guarantees to minors the requirement of proof beyond a reasonable doubt for conviction of crimes. When a child has made child sexual abuse allegations and is in the process of providing evidence, the child not only is subjected to cross-examination but also is legally granted the right to due process, particularly when accused of making false allegations.

Timing of Psychotherapy

In the context of legal proceedings, counseling professionals who work with the child victim must be aware of timing, especially regarding when it is most appropriate to provide intensive psychotherapy for the victim. The author's experience indicates that an intensive counseling process, particularly group work, memory recovery work, or hypnotic assessment, should not start until the child has been interviewed by a forensic expert to determine whether the child's statements can be used in court. It is important that the child's account not be influenced or contaminated by professional judgment provided in the child's memory recovery process. This does not mean that the child victim should not be immediately treated, but the initial support and counseling should not contain tactics that can contaminate or bias the disclosure process by skewing the child's view of the matter (e.g., forgiveness, spirituality, aspects of punishment, discussions that address consequences and uncertainties of child placement). In initial counseling sessions, the counselor must allow the child to talk openly using a narrative approach, by not leading the child to think about outcomes or possible recantation issues. As professionals help child victims prepare for a court appearance, best practices call for documentation of disclosure information and clinical observations of the child and the alleged abuser, instruments or assessment tools used in the forensic interview or counseling, case history regarding family dynamics (e.g., parent-child or sibling relationships), and assessment of the child's reactions to abuse as well as how disclosure has affected their psychological well-being.

Many defense lawyers use counseling outcomes as a means to attack the child's intent to falsify reports because "the bias of a therapist can impact the focus of sessions involving children who were allegedly abused" (Mapes, 1995, p. 37). To avoid unnecessary accusations of the therapist biasing the child witness, it is important that counseling professionals do not help the child prepare any written court testimony, which can be viewed as being biased by the counselor's words or views. Assessment should be conducted to gather facts and treatment to help the child victim relax before the victim discloses the abuse to law enforcement or CPS.

Roles of the Courts in Child Sexual Abuse

Because the court system varies from country to country, the description of the court process in this chapter is based on the court system in the United States, where child abuse and neglect cases are handled by one or two courts—civil court and criminal court. Sexual abuse cases frequently involve both courts.

Civil Court

Child protective proceedings are typically processed in the civil court, either family court or juvenile court. In civil court, the primary issue is the protection and best interest of the child, not punishment of the abuser. Jurisdiction is limited to providing services and treatment for the family, including assigning counsel to the accused and guardian ad litem to the child and suggesting treatment for the child, the accused, and/or the entire family.

When a child protection case is referred to the civil court, an abuse petition is filed to determine whether emergency removal of the child is warranted, and then a preliminary hearing is scheduled to determine custody. A pretrial conference is held before a fact-finding hearing is scheduled. After the dispositional hearing has been processed and has yielded sufficient information, the judge then determines the dates of periodic reviews. During any time in this hearing process, the abuser's counsel can file an appeal. The focus of these conferences and hearings is to address child protection for the best interests of the child.

Criminal Court

When the juvenile or family court determines that an abuse case involves child sexual abuse or incest, the case is referred to criminal court for further investigation. The criminal process starts with a thorough investigation that involves testimony of forensic interviewers, social workers, and law enforcement officers. If sufficient evidence is present, the case is filed with the local or county attorney's office; in other words, charges are filed in the criminal court against the alleged adult perpetrator. If the alleged perpetrator is a minor, the case does not proceed to criminal court and remains in juvenile court, unless the accused is to be charged as an adult. The criminal process is far more complicated than the civil or juvenile court process. First, it involves a grand jury in several rounds of trials. Second, the focus of the trials is to address fact-finding with the presentation of evidence to prove the criminal allegations against the alleged perpetrator. Figure 5.1 illustrates this judicial process from the initial report to investigation and the court process.

Prosecutor's Role

In general, a prosecutor is assigned after child sexual abuse charges are filed. In most cases, police, social workers, and/or clinical psychologists have conducted a forensic or investigative interview to evaluate the abuse complaints or situations and to provide the court with detailed information. It is not necessary to conduct another specialized interview, except to prepare the child victim and advocate to understand the court process and to not be afraid of the people present or the court setting. The purpose of this specialized interview is threefold: to test the competency of the child to testify, to establish trust with the child, and to prepare the child for the court process and find any answers the child may have. Suggested approaches include the following:

- *Introduce who you are*: "My name is X, and I'm a prosecutor who represents the Department of Justice in the handling of this case. Although I'm not representing you, I'm here for you. When you are ready to tell what happened to you in court, I will be there."

Figure 5.1a Judicial Processes in Child Sexual Abuse: Stage 1

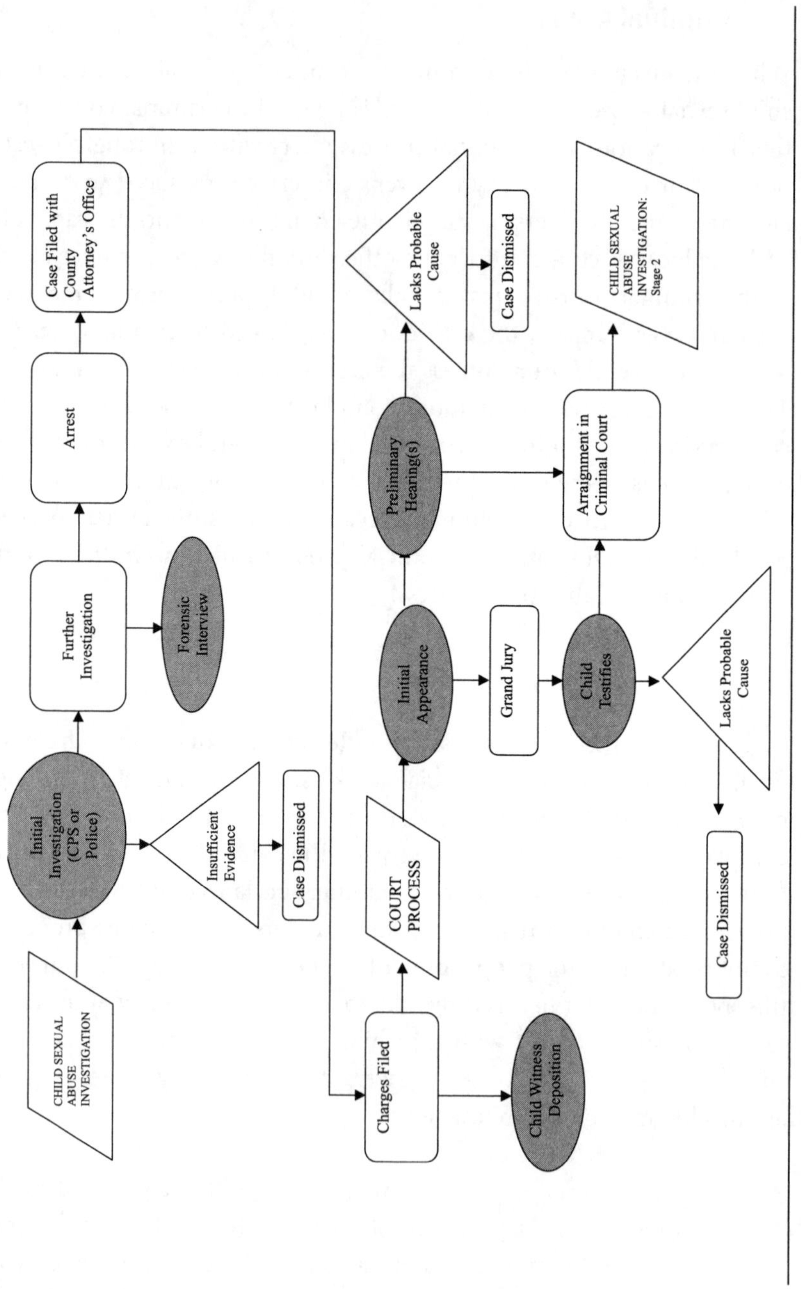

Figure 5.1b Judicial Processes in Child Sexual Abuse: Stage 2

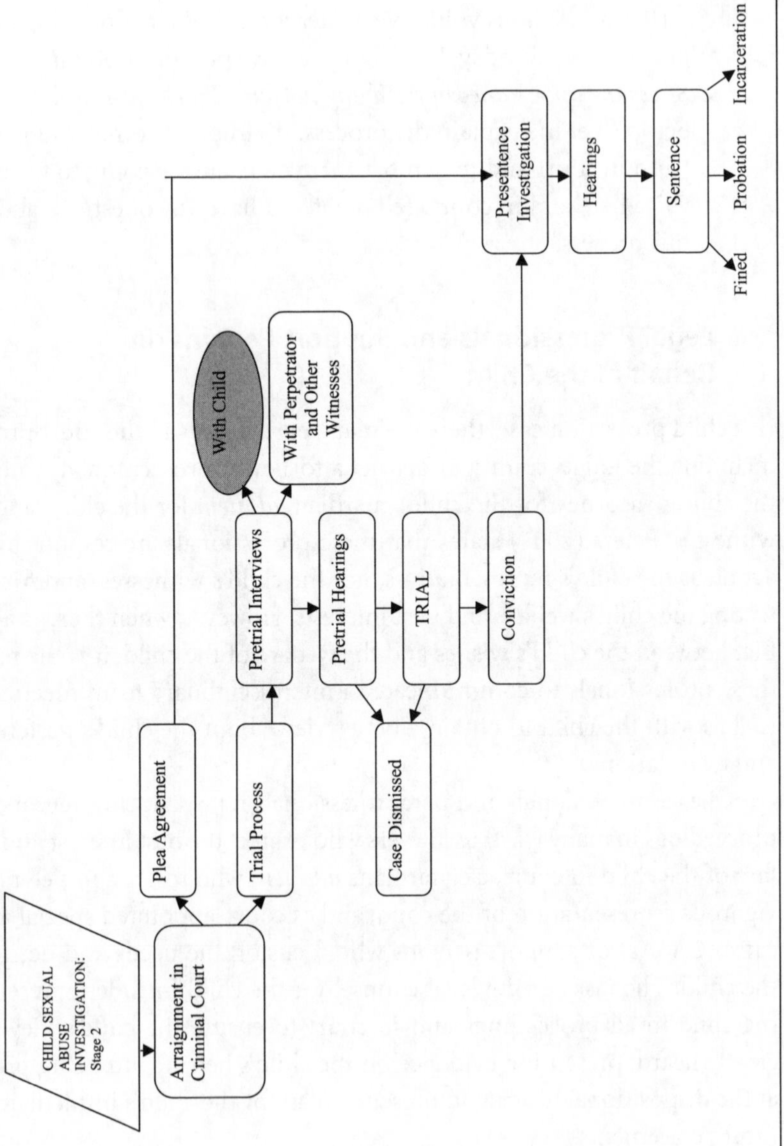

- *Build rapport with competency-testing questions*: "How old are you?" "What is your favorite subject in school?" "When is your birthday" "Who is your favorite teacher?" "Where do you usually like to go on Sundays?" or "Do you have pets or hobbies?"
- *Stress the importance of testifying in court*: "Have you been to court before? Let me explain the process. It's important that you tell the truth in court and remember that you're always going to have a voice here and in court. Tell me if you have any questions about this process."

Legal Professionals and Support Persons on Behalf of the Child

In a child protection case, there are many participants in the court process, including the judge, county or district attorney or prosecutor, attorney for the abuser, attorney for the child, guardian *ad litem* for the child, and any witnesses. Peters (2001) states that these professionals are responsible for acting as the child's representatives, not the child's witnesses, and for protecting the child's welfare and best interests. However, when there is a conflict between the child's wishes and the welfare of the child, it is the role of these professionals to communicate in interdisciplinary team meetings as well as with the child to obtain a better view about the child's preferences and expectations.

Legal professionals and paraprofessionals represent children in court proceedings in many ways: as lawyers who protect the best interest and welfare of the child in court, as guardians *ad litem* who foster competent and vigorous representation of the child, and as court-appointed special advocates (CASAs) or support persons who focus on the needs and desires of the child. The tasks of the legal counsel for the child include representing the child in all proceedings and in court to ensure the child's views are clearly heard, presenting evidence on the child's behalf, and being present at the dispositional hearing to present a plan for the child's immediate and future placements.

In the United States, the Child Abuse Prevention and Treatment Act (1974) requires that a state appoint a guardian *ad litem* for each child in child protection proceedings in order to be eligible for federal funds for child abuse and neglect programs. The tasks of the guardian *ad litem* include the following:

- Conducting face-to-face contacts and interviews with the child to observe the child's safety and assess the child's developmental ability to testify
- Performing independent assessments based on facts
- Informing the child about his or her rights and explaining the nature of all proceedings in a language that the child can understand
- Assessing the child's needs and ensuring that the child receives appropriate attention and resources to meet these needs
- Acting as a mediator in working with the parties involved to reach a consensus before court hearings
- Reducing trauma to the child and establishing a continuous relationship with the child
- Preparing the child to testify when appropriate
- Appearing in court and presenting appropriate materials or recommendations for court purposes
- Communicating with other professionals involved in the case without losing independence
- Advising the child of the court's decision and answering the child's questions or concerns

In most cases, a support person will accompany the child to attend legal hearings and court proceedings. The judge may appoint a volunteer (acting in the role of a support person or child advocate) to help the child deal with the logistics and emotional preparations for these activities. This support person's tasks include examining available records about the case and the child; interviewing the child or the family to build rapport and obtain additional information; putting the child at ease by explaining the situation and process and visiting courtrooms to prepare for the child's court appearance; attending all conferences, meetings, and proceedings with the child; and following up with the child to ensure that recommendations are implemented correctly.

Documentation Skills

There are three main types of evidence that are used in court for the substantiation of child sexual abuse. Direct evidence is based on personal knowledge, such as the testimony of an eyewitness. Demonstrative evidence includes items such as medical examination documents of the alleged victim's contraction of a sexually transmitted disease. Circumstantial evidence is indirect evidence from which an inference can be drawn, such as bruises on the child's private parts. For example, if a four-year-old girl as the eyewitness said that she was asked to "suck the pee-pee" of the alleged perpetrator, her babysitter, she provides direct evidence about the sexual abuse. A photo showing the naked body of this girl on the computer of the babysitter is also direct evidence. If the photo does not show this particular girl but shows another girl that the alleged perpetrator said he downloaded from the Internet, the photo may become circumstantial evidence to support the idea that the accused may have a tendency to sexually desire children.

In most intrafamilial child sexual abuse cases, when the child is the only eyewitness to the abuse, the investigator's documented notes represent additional evidence to support or to not support the child's account. As a result, it is advised that the case record include the following components:

- Demographic information (e.g., names, addresses, relationships, age, contacts, school, and place of work); time and dates of the complaint, including what was seen or heard; quotations; and description of the complaint
- Phone calls and details
- Home visits or interviews with facts recorded
- Physical injuries and photos (including date, time, location, and name of the photographer)
- Medical examination results (including date, time, facility, name of examiner, and accompanying adult)
- Nature of abuse (e.g., types, frequency, time period and progression in multiple forms of abuse, coercion, secrecy, continuity, patterns, multiple victims)
- Risk assessments (e.g., child, siblings, nonoffending parent, family functioning)

- Physical appearance and emotional state of the child victim at each interview
- Information about the first person the child complained to about the abuse and that person's reaction to the abuse
- Child's reason for reporting
- Relationship and behavioral change between the child and the accuser before, during, and after the abuse
- Changes in circumstances after disclosure, including inconsistencies in statements

Admissibility of Evidence

Evidence must meet three major criteria to be admissible: material, relevance, and competence. Material evidence has a clear and logical connection to the presented issue in the case. Relevant evidence must increase the likelihood that the presented facts are true. Competent evidence is material, relevant, reliable, and not in violation of evidentiary rules (e.g., hearsay) related to truth seeking and subject to the protection of extrajudicial interests of society (e.g., privilege not to testify). In the United Kingdom, under the Youth Justice and Criminal Evidence Act of 1999, and in Hong Kong, under the Criminal Procedure Ordinance, cap 221, video-recorded evidence may be admissible even though the normal rules of evidence require witnesses to attend and give their evidence at the time of the trial. In the United States, a videotape of a professionally conducted interview of the child victim may be admissible in court if there is no hearsay in the accusation.

In a short television interview conducted by ABC News, Dr. Stephen Ceci of Cornell University testified that it is absolutely essential to provide the best training for the interviewer in cases of child sexual abuse so that the video-recorded interview can be admissible in court (see chapter 2).

Testifying in Court

Being a Caseworker

Because child sexual abuse does not always involve physical violence and the child's report of the incident is often delayed as a result of fear, confusion, and other reasons, the child victim may not have physical injuries that typically connect to other types of sexual assault. A caseworker who testifies in court presents materials based on the investigations with the child victim, the reporter of the case, family members, and collaterals. Caseworkers with CPS are vulnerable to both civil and criminal liability in the course of their job performance. The most important liability lies in taking precautions to protect a child from potential harm. Under criminal law, the worker's responsibility to determine the removal of a child from harm must be documented with visitation and other means of contacts with the child, as well as assessment of the child's safety. In the case of sexual abuse, removal is necessary when the child, as the sole eyewitness, makes an outcry of sexual molestation even though there is no physical evidence.

In contrast, caseworkers must also be aware of their liability if they wrongfully or unlawfully remove a child from his or her home. As a precaution, they must affirm the child's statement by establishing that the child understands the importance of telling the truth. In child protection agencies, guidelines are set up to determine child removal to safeguard staff when a decision is made against the parents' rights and wishes. These fundamental principles and guidelines must be observed to achieve professional competence as attested in professional training or educational programs, acceptable standards as presented in the agency's investigation procedures, thorough documentation as presented in observation and assessment records, and communication with the parties involved as part of the investigative routine. It is always important to document that these guidelines have been achieved before a child is removed from a home. A caseworker must possess good documentation skills that create a systematic record for the case to be presentable in court. The document must contain five major areas of information:

1. Observation notes of the child's safety and risk assessment (see appendixes 2B and 2C in chapter 2)
2. Detailed interactions with the child and the family
3. Input from supervisors and other collaterals
4. Supporting evidence to reach the removal decision
5. A specific plan of actions and recommendations

Before testifying in court, the caseworker must prepare these documents with a summary. The testimony is effective if the caseworker follows the testifying guidelines in these areas:

- Be prepared and avoid being nervous or defensive.
- Answer only the question that is asked.
- Ask the question be repeated if it is not understood.
- Answer "I don't know" when the answer is not known.
- Be exact in the answer by providing exact date and time, number and frequency, names, and other specificities.
- Think before providing an answer, or ask for time to refer to the presented case record if the answer can be retrieved.
- Show respect for the court (e.g., dress appropriately, be knowledgeable about court etiquette).
- Address the judge as "Your Honor" or "Judge" when opening a statement that requires the judge's attention. However, when the testimony requires the attention of the court, it is better to say, "The court's attention is directed to . . ."
- Be objective and nonjudgmental; avoid personally taking sides in the testimony.
- Limit testimony to the presentation of factual materials unless opinions are specifically asked for.

The caseworker and all witnesses are subject to cross-examination. Most caseworkers are competent in presenting their case materials but may feel stressed when cross-examined. To perform well under cross-examination, caseworkers must be aware of the following skills on how to survive cross-examination:

Skill 1: Be Prepared

Prepare a copy of your resume or a business card that contains your current job title and responsibilities.

Complete your documentation about the case assessment and action plan.

Be on time for the court hearing and notify your supervisor about your court schedule (because your cell phone will not work).

Dress appropriately (and bring a sweater because feeling cold will affect your mood).

Skill 2: Be Calm

Be attentive to the question; take a deep breath to relax if needed.

Do not answer unless you understand the question.

Do not allow yourself to be rushed.

Do not get angry or emotional about the question or the counsel.

Skill 3: Be Positive and Affirmative

Be certain about your answer; if you do not know, answer "I don't know."

Do not get caught by a trick question; ask for clarification.

If a question has two parts that require two different answers, answer it in two parts (e.g., "This question has two parts. I will answer the first part first").

Allow additional information to be presented at a later time when interrupted.

Skill 4: Be Patient

Take time to answer a question even though it was asked rapidly.

Ignore mispronunciation of your name and focus on the question.

Ignore the counsel's staring (in your eyes) or being too close to you; concentrate on the question.

Wait for the next question even though the counsel seems to be waiting for more answers from you.

Skill 5: Be Alert

Be aware that counsel uses tactics to lower your confidence.

Ask for the question to be repeated if improperly phrased.

Be firm in your answer.

Disregard any suggestion from the counsel; keep your answer based on the facts.

Skill 6: Be Consistent

Be consistent in your answers and show confidence even when using *approximately* to describe something when you don't know or remember its exact measurement (e.g., time of day).

Listen carefully when the counsel repeats your answer and correct if the repeated answer has any error by saying, "Your Honor, may the court please note that there is an error in this statement?"

Tell the court if you have just answered a repeated question instead of providing the answer twice to avoid being inconsistent.

Provide answers in your own words based on facts even if a yes or no answer is requested; pause if your answer is being challenged, and wait until the court instructs you on whether you can answer the question in your own words.

Prepare the witness to be calm during the cross-examination process and pay attention to tactics used by defense counsel during cross-examination (see appendix 5A).

Being a Support Person for a Child Witness

To prepare a child for court proceedings, the court may appoint a child advocate or support person for the child. The role of a child advocate is to assist and support the child in order to eliminate any possible fear or harm generated from the litigation process. Many child advocates are volunteers who donate their time and effort for the benefit of children who have been abused. In the United States, these volunteers must register with a court-appointed special advocates program, attend an orientation, and complete the required training program to be eligible to assist children through court order. A typical training program, which requires about thirty hours of time, provides training in areas of child abuse and neglect issues, child developmental milestones, legal issues pertaining to child abuse and neglect, and cultural diversity, as well as skills training in establishing cultural competency, enhancing communication skills, and handling court requests.

Many informational brochures are designed for the child to read before testifying in court. Based on these child-focused materials, a summary of tips on how to prepare the child is provided in appendix 5B (which also provides tips for professionals and parents). The focus of the hints and tips is related to content, process, and psychological preparation before a child testifies in court.

Being an Expert Witness

Professionals can testify in a child sexual abuse case if they are involved in the investigation, assessment, and treatment processes. They can also testify regarding their knowledge based on their expertise in the subject area related to child sexual abuse. According to rule 702 of the Federal Rules of Evidence (2011), "If scientific, technical, or other specialized knowledge will assist the trier of fact to understand the evidence or determine a fact in issue, a witness qualified as an expert by knowledge, skill, experience, training, or education, may testify thereto in the form of an opinion or otherwise." An attorney invites an expert witness to testify to provide support for a specific court case. An expert witness representing the mental health profession may focus on social or family issues based on research and practice experiences related to child abuse and neglect, child development, family reunification, divorce, child custody, foster care, adoption, drug abuse, education, juvenile treatment, and other social work issues. An expert witness must have credentials in the following areas: education, practice, courtroom, communication, and knowledge about the specific needs of the clients presented in the case.

Daubert *standard,* **Daubert** *motion, and* **Daubert** *trilogy.* The *Daubert* standard is a legal precedent set in 1993 by the U.S. in *Daubert v. Merrell Dow Pharmaceuticals,* 509 U.S. 579, regarding the admissibility of expert witnesses' testimony during federal legal proceedings. As a gatekeeping procedure, the *Daubert* motion is raised before or during trial to exclude the presentation of any unqualified expert witness to the jury, including scientific or nonscientific expert opinions, as supported by the U.S. Supreme Court's 1997 decision in *Kumho Tire Co. v. Carmichael,* 526 U.S. 137 (1999). As cited in *General Electric Co. v. Joiner,* 522 U.S. 136 (1997), appellate courts must defer to the lower trial court's decision regarding the admissibility of expert testimony unless the previous ruling is strikingly wrong.

In 2000, the Supreme Court approved amendments to the Federal Rules of Evidence relating to opinion evidence and expert testimony to conform to the *Daubert* trilogy—*Daubert, Kumho,* and *Joiner* (see Bernstein & Jackson, n.d.), which is also called the *Daubert* rule (including *Weisgram v. Marley Co.*, 528 U.S. 440 (2000)), to provide guidelines for admitting expert witnesses in federal courts (see Shields & Bryan, 2005).

When a *Daubert* motion is called, trial judges must evaluate an expert witness to determine whether the person's qualifications are relevant and reliable. Either party may raise evaluative questions in the courtroom to support or reject the presence of a particular expert witness in the trial process. To determine whether a witness's qualifications are relevant, ask, "Does the expert have a relevant educational background? Knowledge about this particular case? Related case and/or practice experiences? Experience conducting studies regarding this type of inquiry? Information that fits the fact of the case?" To determine whether a witness is reliable, ask, "Can the expert show scientific testing of the testimony in practice situations? Objective assessment of the testimony? The use of supportive materials that are subject to peer review and publication? The potential rate of error that may be presented in the materials? The theory or practice inference used in the testimony has been accepted in the relevant scientific community?"

Requirements for the expert report. In the United States, under rule 26 of the Federal Rules of Civil Procedure, an expert's report may include the following:

- A complete statement of all opinions the witness will express and the basis and reasons for them
- Data or other information considered by the witness in forming them
- Any exhibits that will be used to summarize or support them
- The witness's qualifications, including a list of all publications authored in the previous ten years
- A list of all other cases in which, during the previous four years, the witness testified as an expert at trial or by deposition
- A statement of the compensation to be paid for the study and testimony in the case

Timing for the expert report. If the *Daubert* motion is raised before the expert discovery is closed, the nonmoving party may use a Rule 56(f) affidavit to explain why the expert testimony is not available until a later time or may use "supplementation" to include the expert's opinions after such expert discovery is available and timely (Nordberg, 2006). In most cases, a complete report is not required after the expert has testified in court. Before the testimony, to qualify the expert's evidence, it is essential to provide a copy of the expert's curriculum vitae that lists educational and professional qualifications, major accomplishments, and scientific-based publications. If there is a published research article that identifies the expert's knowledge and theory being tested with random sampling of subjects and other commonly accepted scientific research procedures, a copy of the publication should be provided to the judge and all legal counsel involved.

Tasks of an expert witness. Before trial, the expert witness should clarify what expertise is expected; review the case file and relevant information; ask for the trial time and location, and time commitment; provide a current curriculum vitae that lists all the relevant credentials, experiences, and research publications; and determine legal protection for testimony. At the trial, determine whether the expert witness can hear the trial before giving testimony; bring the curriculum vitae, literature, and expert report if requested; be prepared to answer questions about the scientific basis of the expert opinion; answer questions in plain language based on professional knowledge; answer what is asked; leave the stand only when asked by the judge; and return to the stand to testify if asked by the judge.

According to Clifford (2008), there are many ways legal counsel can attack an opponent's expert witness. These tactics include pretrial challenges to the expert's experience or scientific testimony to exclude the expert witness from testifying in courtroom. Counsel can identify relevant grounds for disqualifying the opposing expert, provide objections to the expert's direct testimony, show that the expert's testimony is based solely on personal opinion and not scientific facts that can pass the commonly accepted scientific requirements, or restrict the expert from providing demonstrative evidence in the courtroom. In child sexual abuse cases, gynecologists, medical examiners, psychologists, nurses, social workers, and other mental health professionals have testified as expert witnesses to present evidence and research-based findings regarding symptoms and family dynamics in child sexual abuse situations. However, no research has attested to the effectiveness of expert evidence in assisting the child, especially when he or she is the only eyewitness in the child sexual abuse case.

Wilson (2005) cautions professionals who are called to be expert witnesses to prepare for their roles in advance. He reviewed two child fatality cases and said that the expert witnesses contributed to injustice to the accused because of errors such as inadequate use of scientific methodology, poor forensic methods, and use of inconsistent findings or opinions. It is crucial that the expert witness has conducted scientific evidence-based research that can withstand test-retest reliability before it can be used as expert evidence.

Julie's Case: Testifying in Court

Before Julie testified in court, she was interviewed by a social worker in the presence of a police officer through a one-way mirror. Her interview was videotaped based on the four-stage interview protocol. Julie clearly identified the offender and described the details of sexual abuse. Julie was removed from the home and stayed in a foster home. She was not allowed to go home, and her stepdad was not allowed to see her. The day before she went to the foster home, she saw her mother under the caseworker's supervision.

Julie was seen by her caseworker and child advocate during her stay at the foster home. Her case was heard the second day after the removal without her presence when the judge ordered psychotherapy for her and her stepdad. In her counseling session with the therapist, Julie reviewed her videotaped interview. Her caseworker then accompanied her to complete her deposition in an attorney's office. In this process, Julie still attended school and found it difficult to concentrate. Her best friend in school who knew about the abuse was also interviewed by CPS.

The child advocate accompanied Julie to the courthouse to see the courtroom. Julie expressed that she did not feel comfortable testifying against her stepdad. The court date, however, was set, and she could not have another psychotherapy session. Julie testified in court without the use of closed-circuit television because the judge determined that Julie was mature enough to be cross-examined. Julie was not able to tell anything about the sexual abuse when the defense attorney questioned her in court. When she was asked whether she was lying to make her stepdad and mother feel miserable, Julie was silent. When asked about her sexual intimacy with her boyfriend, she suddenly said that she was lying about the accusation against her stepdad. She cried hysterically and did not answer any further questions. The judge gave her another chance to testify, but she told the caseworker that she would rather not go to court again.

Recantation is a typical reaction to the traumatic experience in court. In this case, Julie, who had been sexually acting out for one year, did not feel comfortable describing her sexual relationship with her stepdad. She felt socially isolated and alone in the legal process, even though she had support from the caseworker, the child advocate, and her psychotherapist. She also felt that she bore all the blame because her stepdad denied all the accusations. She was alone because her mother was not supportive of her. Because she went to see her boyfriend without the permission of the foster parents, she lost trust and was determined to be a "bad" child by her mother and foster parents.

Psychologically, she recanted because she thought everything would be fine without prosecuting her stepdad. She believed what her mother told her when her mother said she would protect her and leave her stepdad. She also believed that the recantation would end her nightmare of being away from home. In addition, she felt that the court experience was intimidating, and she did not want to go through it again. Because of her recantation, no further action could be taken, except returning her home with her mother and stepdad. Then, CPS continued with two additional home visits and terminated the case.

Recantation is a questionable move. Adolescents under these circumstances are often not willing to disclose their problems for fear that the consequences are more traumatic than the sexual abuse. It is the responsibility of the professionals involved (including the judge) to better prepare children and adolescents to testify in court so that they will not feel intimidated and will be able to tell the truth without fear. A closed-circuit television testimony could have been helpful to allow the child to testify without seeing the alleged perpetrator. As a final recommendation, the judge ordered that Julie, her stepdad, and the entire family continue with individual and family psychotherapy. The case finally closed at court after ten weeks of psychotherapy.

Conclusion

Prosecutors, guardians ad litem, and child advocates bear the responsibility for preparing and familiarizing the child victim with the impending court proceedings both at the civil and at the criminal court levels. The court also must act in a manner that is sensitive to the child witness's needs to avoid inflicting further psychological harm on the child. Similarly, legal professionals must review the types and admissibility of evidence to ensure the presentation of a strong case in court. Caseworkers and expert witnesses must prepare themselves as witnesses to testify in an effective and competent fashion.

Responding to Tactics Used in Cross-Examination

Tactics and purpose	Example	Suggested response
Rapid-fire questions—Purpose: To confuse witness; an attempt to force inconsistent answers.	One question after another with little time to answer.	Take time to consider the question; ask to have the question repeated; remain calm.
Condescending counsel questions—Purpose: To give the impression that the witness is inept, lacks confidence, or may not be a reliable witness.	Benevolent in approach, oversympathetic in questions to the point of ridicule.	Give firm, decisive answers, asking for the question to be repeated if improperly phrased.
Friendly counsel questions—Purpose: To lull the witness into a false sense of security where he or she will give answers in favor of the defense.	Very courteous, polite; questions tend to take witness into his or her confidence.	Stay alert; bear in mind that purpose of defense is to discredit or diminish the effect of your testimony.
Badgering and belligerent—Purpose: To make witness angry so that he or she loses sense of logic and calmness (generally include rapid-fire questions).	Counsel staring you right in the face, shouts, "That is so, isn't it?"	Stay calm, speak in a deliberate voice; give prosecutor time to make appropriate objections.
Mispronouncing—Purpose: To draw the witness's attention to the error in pronunciation rather than enabling concentration on the question asked so that the witness will make inadvertent errors in testimony.	Witness's name is Jansen; counsel calls him Johnson.	Ignore the mispronunciation and concentrate on the question counsel is asking.

Suggestive question—Purpose: To suggest an answer to a question in an attempt to confuse or to lead the witness.	Wasn't the mother always willing to talk?	Concentrate carefully on the facts; disregard the suggestion; answer the question.
Demanding a yes or no answer to a question that needs explaining—Purpose: To prevent all pertinent and mitigating details from being considered by the jury.	Did you open this case seeing the child?	Explain the answer to the question. If stopped by the counsel's demanding a yes or no answer, pause until the court instructs you to answer in your own words.
Reversing witness's words—Purpose: To confuse the witness and demonstrate a lack of confidence in the witness.	Witness answers, "The neighbor was inside the house, Mrs. Doe and the child were outside." Counsel says, "Now you say that the neighbor was outside and Mrs. Doe and the child were inside."	Listen intently whenever counsel repeats back something you have said; correct any errors.
Repetitious questions—Purpose: To obtain inconsistent or conflicting answers from the witness.	The same question asked several times slightly rephrased.	Listen carefully to the question and state, "I have just answered that question."
Conflicting answers—Purpose: To show inconsistency in the investigation (normally used on measurements, times).	"But Mrs. Smith, Mrs. Brown just said X."	Remain calm. Conflicting statements have tendency to make a witness extremely nervous. Be guarded in your answers on measurements, times, etc. Unless you have exact knowledge, use the term approximately. Refer to your notes.
Staring—Purpose: To use a long pause to provoke the witness into offering more than the question.	After the witness has answered, counsel just stares as though there were more to come.	Wait for the next question.

Source: American Association for Protecting Children, 1988.

Tips for the Support Person and Parents

Tips for the Support Person: Court Preparation

Role of a Child Advocate or Support Person

"To assist in reducing the formality of the courtroom, and in that way countering the stress and feelings of intimidation associated with the courtroom and the judicial process....The support person will provide the child witness with emotional support by identifying when the child is feeling stressed and informing the court of this" (Hollely, 2002, pp. 14–15).

Child-friendly court preparation tools	How to obtain the tool
☑ *Home Court Advantage DVD: Court Preparation for Children*	The National Children's Advocacy Center (http://www.nationalcac.org/professionals/index.php?option=com_content&task=view&id=118&Itemid=61)
☑ *Sexual Abuse: What Happens When You Tell—A Guide for Children*	National Clearinghouse on Family Violence, Public Agency of Canada (http://dsp-psd.pwgsc.gc.ca/collection_2008/phac-aspc/HP20-6-4-2007E.pdf; http://www.phac-aspc.gc.ca/nc-cn)
☑ *What's My Job in Court?*	Ministry of Attorney General, Ontario, Canada (http://www.attorneygeneral.jus.gov.on.ca/english/ovss/programs.asp#vwap)
☑ *Just in Case You Visit… The Children's Court*	Victoria Legal Aid: Children's Court (http://www.legalaid.vic.gov.au/600.htm)

Precourt hearing	Suggestions
☑ Introduce the court room to the child.	☑ Introduce your role as a support person to accompany the child to appear in court (and other hearings).
	☑ A court tour will ease the overwhelming feelings associated with the hearing and help the child gain some sense of independence and control.

☑ The courtroom can be a very intimidating place for a child, so it is important to reduce that intimidation by briefing the child about the various stages of the court process (e.g., waiting room, courtroom, closed-circuit television room).

☑ Children who have special needs may be more nervous about the court visit. It is important to identify the child's role as a witness, not as a criminal, even though he or she may be questioned by the attorneys there.

☑ Brief the child about things he or she should know.	☑ Assure the child that if he or she needs to use the restroom, he or she can make the request.
	☑ It is important that the child feels comfortable asking any questions before or on the court day. If the child is quiet, remind the child that he or she can ask questions at a later time.
	☑ Questions should be answered in few simple but truthful details. The support person should not ask the child any questions about the child's testimony (Hollely, 2002).

☑ Encourage questions and calm emotions.	☑ Encourage the child to ask questions and let the child know that you may not know all the answers.
	☑ Tell the child if you don't know the answer, you will try to find it out.
	☑ Check the child's concern if a question is related to the allegation.
	☑ Calm the child if the question or answer brings strong emotions.
	Questions the child may ask and/or be curious about
	• Who will be in the courtroom?
	• What is their function (job)?
	• Where will people sit? (not to identify where the accused will sit)
	• Where will I sit?
	• Will I sit?
	• Will people be wearing wigs and gowns?
	• Where will I wait?
	• Who can come in with me?
	• How will I know when I am finished?
	• Who will question me?
	• How long will I wait? (Scottish Government, 2004, p. 7)

☑ Provide adequate answers but not false hope.	*Possible Responses to the Child:*
	• No need to be nervous or worried about attending the courts, just tell the facts to the judge.

- If someone asks, "Why are you here at the court?" you can simply answer, "I am going to be a witness."
- Please be on time.
- When you arrive at the court, you will have time to stay in the waiting room to relax or take a rest.
- The staff will arrange a seat for you when everything is ready. Take your seat when you are asked to.
- Listen to the question carefully and answer clearly.
- If you do not remember the fact, just say, "I don't remember." There is no need to make a guess.
- If you do not understand the question, say, "I don't understand."
- If you become emotional (or are not able to continue), you can request a rest.
- When the question requests a yes or no answer and if you know the answer, say yes or no. Speak the answer clearly instead of shaking or nodding your head.
- If you have any problem or concern (e.g., want to change your answer, drink water, go to the washroom), just raise your hand and wait for the judge to respond.
- If you testify in a closed-circuit television room, the judge and the appropriate people the judge decides on will be able to see and hear you directly through the system.
- After providing the testimony, the jury will make a judgment about whether the defendant is guilty or not. After the decision is made, the judge will make a final judgment. You must know that it is not your mistake if the jury doesn't judge according to what you want them to judge or if the defendant is determined to be not guilty (Social Welfare Department, 2009).

During court hearing

☑ Be supportive	☑ The support person will accompany the child and help with the logistics.

Postcourt Hearing

☑ Conduct a debrief question-naire with the parent and the child over the court process to process their observations and feelings from beginning to end.	*My Day In Court* pilot research program (conducted by Pamela Hurley, Dawn Lashbrook, Alison Cunningham, and Lynda Stevens) gives questionnaires that are help-ful to use after court hearings (http://www.lfcc.on.ca/my_day_in_court_project.pdf).

Tips for Parents and Practitioners: Court Preparation

Knowing the Legal Terminology Used in Child Sexual Abuse Cases

Allegation	A charge or statement of fact in a petition or complaint, which must be proved to be found true.
Deposition	A prerecorded statement and testimony from the child witness under oath for use in court at a later date.
Due process	Both juveniles and adults in legal actions have the rights to counsel, notice, fair hearing, confrontation, and cross-examination of witnesses in court.
Evidence	The means by which an allegation before the court is proved or disproved. The rules of evidence that apply to all cases must show that evidence is material (facts must have direct bearing on issue before the court), competent (facts do not violate any admissibility rules), and relevant (the facts are not too remote from the issue).
Fifth Amendment	In the United States, the Fifth Amendment of the U.S. Constitution guarantees certain individual protections. In child sexual abuse defenses, the accused may invoke this amendment to obtain privilege against self-incrimination and refuse to answer a question on the basis that the answer might incriminate him or her.
Forensic interview	A structured interview (e.g., video recorded) with the child victim to obtain detailed information about the allegation.
Hearsay evidence	Oral or written evidence that is not based directly on the witness's own personal knowledge or observations but on conversations or written materials provided by someone other than the parties before the court. Hearsay evidence is not subject to cross-examination and in most cases is not admissible as evidence except under special exceptions, such as excited utterance (statements made under the stress of excitement caused by the situation or incident, such as emotion expressed after the abuse), present-tense impression (statements made immediately after the situation or incident, such as escaping from the abuse and reporting the incident to a parent), state of mind (statements made regarding the emotion or physical condition of the situation or incident, such as fear of the abuser), or statements for purposes of medical diagnosis and treatment.

Tips for Professionals: Court Preparation

Precourt hearing	Advice
☑ Dress professionally. ☑ Consider visiting a court hearing to hear how others testify and to know what to expect. ☑ Be on time. ☑ Make sure to have victim's file with relevant documents. Be fully knowledgeable of the documentation you bring on the day of the trial.	• "Dress neatly and conservatively, and be courteous....You want to be sure that your appearance and manner do not distract the judge or jury from careful consideration of your testimony. Police officers should be in uniform, or in at least a sport coat and tie. No tinted glasses or flashy jewelry" (Clark County Prosecuting Attorney [CCPA], 2011, n.p.). • "Make it a point to visit the Court and listen to others testify" (CCPA, 2011, n.p.). • "All reports, statements or other evidence in the case should be brought to the attention of the Prosecutor well in advance of trial so that he/she may adequately comply with Court ordered discovery. The Court may exclude from the trial any evidence where the defendant is not notified before trial of its existence" (CCPA, 2011, n.p.).

During court hearing	Questions that you could be asked
☑ Stay seated until the judge addresses you by name to come to the stand (York County, 2011). ☑ Remember to remain relaxed and to be yourself (CCPA, 2011). ☑ Use "Your Honor" or "Judge" when addressing the judge at all times (York County, 2011). ☑ Be consistently truthful. "If you tell the truth and tell it accurately, nobody can cross you up. Do not guess or make up an answer. If you do not know the answer it is best to say, 'I don't know.' If you are asked about details that you do not remember it is best to say, 'I don't remember'" (CCPA, 2011, web page). ☑ Keep language simple and keep yourself from feeling rushed. ☑ Make sure to be heard loud and clear. Keep your hands away from your mouth. Since all testimony is recorded, do not nod your head yes or no.	"Please tell the court your name and your occupation or profession." "Where are you presently engaged in the practice of (your profession)?" "Where do you maintain your offices?" "Are you licensed to practice (profession) in this state?" "When did you receive your license to practice (profession)?" "What professional degrees have you been awarded?" "When were these degrees received and from what schools were they received?" "Following your graduation from (name of school most recently graduated from) have you received any additional professional training?" "Please tell the court when this training was received, the nature of the training, its duration, and the place of the training?" "Are you a member of any professional associations?"

☑ Avoid using humor in the court room. Beware of hallway and bathroom conversations.

☑ Be reasonably sure about the information you bring with you as a witness. Avoid using any uncertain phrases, such as "my judgment," "my opinion," and "my prediction."

☑ Answering questions directly is important. Answer only the questions asked, then stop. Never ask the Judge if you have to answer.

☑ Remain alert at all times. "Use good posture, do not slouch" (CCPA, 2011).

☑ Keep your emotions intact. "Do not fence or argue with the attorneys" (CCPA, 2011, web page).

☑ Questions should be carefully answered. "Beware of questions asking why you don't like the defendant" (CCPA, 2011, web page).

"Have you ever taught or written in professional journals?"

"Following your graduation from (name of school most recently graduated from), where have you engaged in the practice of (profession) and for what periods of time?"

"During this time, how many (evaluations have you performed or children have you treated) in the practice of (profession)?"

"Have you ever been qualified as an expert before? In what capacity?"

"When and before what court? What was the nature of the case(s) you testified"

Postcourt hearing	Advice
☑ Debrief with alleged abused child about experience (if appropriate given your relationship with the child). ☑ Debrief with the parents if they also served as a witness (if appropriate given your relationship with the parents). ☑ Follow up on progress of the case. ☑ Continue to document in the child's file all transactions that take place.	• Address confidentiality. • Address the issue of family relationships. • Leave with contact information for further questions or future issues.

CHAPTER 6

Evidence-Based Practice Treatment

In child sexual abuse, treatment must be provided to the child victim (or childhood abuse survivor), the perpetrator (or alleged perpetrator), the nonoffending parent or partner, and other family members, because all of them have been affected by the report of sexual abuse. Whether or not sexual abuse can be substantiated, an ordeal has occurred and negatively affected the daily routines and psychological well-being of each individual involved. This chapter highlights the essential idea that all individuals in the family should be provided with appropriate treatment and services, both individually and as a family. "Julie's Case" is used as an example to demonstrate clinical techniques in engaging the individual and her family in the treatment process.

As presented in the literature (appendix 6A), evidence has been provided to support the use of psychotherapy to help these individuals recover from trauma, process their emotions and feelings, be aware of their reactions to the trauma and the impact of its aftermath, develop strategies to stop and prevent abuse, understand the socioeconomic and cultural issues involved, and identify recantation reasons and the impact of blaming. Psychotherapy takes many forms, and the most effective treatment takes into consideration the needs of the clients.

After sexual abuse disclosure, it has been found that posttraumatic stress disorder (PTSD) symptoms frequently occur among child victims, survivors of childhood sexual abuse, and nonoffending parents (Chard, 2005; Hembree & Brinen, 2009; Hernandez et al., 2009; Owens, Pike, & Chard, 2001; Ross & O'Carroll, 2004). Posttraumatic stress disorder manifests as mental health problems and psychological distress, including depression, externalizing, internalizing, behavioral problems, aggression, and anxiety disorders (Brown, Brack, & Mullis, 2008; Corcoran & Pillai, 2008; Trowell & Kolvin 2002; Winder, 1996). Research results found that males tend to externalize symptoms through aggression and that females tend to internalize symptoms through depression. Male victims of sexual abuse may also suffer from gender role dissonance, as well as confusion related to gender roles and sexual preference. However, the same techniques that help female victims have been used to treat males (Winder, 1996).

Among the victims, both male and female children also may exhibit sexual behaviors that are more frequent and intense than those of nonabused children. Sexual behaviors can include sexual aggression, public masturbation, promiscuity, and sexual physical contact with others (Kools & Kennedy, 2001). Victims of sexual abuse, however, do not exclusively manifest these symptoms; nonabused children can also exhibit similar sexual behaviors as a result of other emotional problems.

In child sexual abuse cases, most female clients are victims or survivors, whereas most male clients are perpetrators or alleged abusers. However, this does not mean that boys are not victims too, or that female perpetrators are nonexistent. Some treatment methods such as recognition of the impact of abuse can be used, but these methods must be individualized to help the client acknowledge the blaming factor. For example, it is important to stress that it is always the fault of the perpetrator because of the threat of power, whether or not the abused victim has differently perceived or agreed to engage in the sexual relationship. Reestablishing a safe environment for the victim who may feel fear, anxiety, and out of control is an important first step in therapeutic interventions (Brown et al., 2008).

There is evidence throughout the literature that treatment of victims of sexual abuse has provided relief, rational thinking, and acceptance of self. Cognitive and behavioral techniques appear to be favored because these future-oriented techniques focus on healthy thinking patterns and appreciation of self-directed behaviors to live a healthy life. It is essential to examine rational thinking that contributes to recovery including acceptance of self, no self-blame, and strategies to protect self and others.

For Child Victims

The four most common goals of treatment for victims include symptom relief, destigmatization, increasing self-esteem, and preventing future abuse (Lev-Wiesel, 2008). According to a study by Saywitz, Mannarino, Berliner, and Cohen (2000), more than 50 percent of child victims of sexual abuse have exhibited symptoms of PTSD. Adding to the difficulty associated with the inability to concentrate and potential depression, child victims are often misdiagnosed with attention-deficit/hyperactivity disorder, conduct disorder, or other behavioral problems, as many of these symptoms overlap (Lev-Wiesel, 2008). The symptomatological continuum runs from the asymptomatic to the severely psychologically distressed. To accurately assess the needs of these victims, professionals must first ask them questions regarding their symptoms so that the children can pay attention to warning signs and use relaxation techniques taught by the professionals to reduce symptoms.

Cognitive-behavioral therapy (CBT) has significantly reduced the behavioral symptoms in child victims of sexual abuse (King et al., 2000; Ross & O'Carroll, 2004). Nolan et al. (2002) showed that both individual therapy and a combination of individual and group therapy have been effective in alleviating symptoms, including modifying attention problems, aggression, depression, internalizing and externalizing, somatization, and anhedonia. However, Trowell and Kolvin (2002) found that both group and individual therapy are effective in reducing mental distress arising from sexual abuse, and individual therapy is more effective in treating child victims of sexual abuse suffering from PTSD. Another study also found that individual therapy was equally as effective as combined group and individual therapy after six months when the focus was related to reducing psychological symptoms (Nolan et al., 2002). The main goal of many of these treatment programs is to help victims rebuild their body image, to grieve losses, to build self-esteem, and to prevent future abuse.

Child victims of sexual abuse who do not receive treatment are at an increased risk of developing symptoms of PTSD as time passes (Trowell & Kolvin, 2002). It is extremely important that child victims be treated as soon as possible so that the effect of therapy can be delivered to them without delay. Appendix 6B demonstrates an example using puppet therapy in individual treatment, which is designed to help reticent children express their concerns and release anxiety. Age-sensitive therapeutic techniques, such as puppet therapy, must be incorporated into individual treatment to assist child victims in relaxing and voicing their concerns through the healing process.

An important point in child sexual abuse treatment is regarding sexually acting out behaviors. When child victims exhibit overly or inappropriate sexual behaviors as a result of sexual abuse, caretakers may feel inclined to limit the child's contact and closeness with others. When young children exhibit sexual symptoms, it does not help if caretakers ask them to explain their sexual behaviors. These types of questions are too abstract for young children, and posing such questions will not aid the situation but place blame on them (Kools & Kennedy, 2001). It is important to remember, however, that all children have a need for physical expressions of warmth and love; therefore, these children must learn stress reduction methods when dealing with their anxiety that may connect to sexual stimuli.

Although research shows that a combination of group and individual therapy appears to be most effective (Saywitz et al., 2000) when treating the child, psychotherapists may not treat the entire family at the same time because of two factors. First, the child may have been placed in foster care. Second, many child-focused components are possible only when the child is being individually treated. Helping the family is an essential component in helping the child victim of sexual abuse. Psychotherapy, whether group or individual, must be provided to the family as well as the child victim (Grosz, Kempe, & Kelly, 2000; Saywitz et al., 2000).

For Childhood Abuse Survivors

Treatment for childhood abuse survivors usually has the goals of symptom relief, destigmatization, increase of self-esteem, and providing strategies to prevent further abuse (Lev-Wiesel, 2008). Cognitive behavioral and spirituality-based therapies have delivered effective outcomes. A case study by Beveridge and Cheung (2004) has shown that distorted beliefs based on an erroneous understanding of religion may lead to psychological distress in survivors of childhood sexual abuse. Spirituality, not necessarily related to any specific organized religion, may help survivors recapture what they have lost with the abuse.

In control-group random assignment experiments, cognitive-behavioral therapy has been shown to be an effective way to help survivors of sexual abuse (Chard, 2005). It is suggested that the severity of cognitive distortion can affect the severity of symptoms for survivors of childhood sexual abuse (Owens et al., 2001). Cognitive restructuring is part of treatment focusing on spirituality that stresses safety, self-awareness, and self-development (Beveridge & Cheung, 2004). Spirituality can help the victim find meaning and move forward. Assessing spiritual beliefs, restructuring distorted beliefs, and focusing on the strengths that spirituality provides are important phases. The ultimate goal of treatment is to help form a more integrated self.

Current research has shown that trauma-focused cognitive behavioral theory is effective in child sexual abuse treatment (Lev-Wiesel, 2008). Trauma-focused cognitive behavioral theory integrates CBT and stress management techniques to deal with the posttraumatic symptoms of abuse survivors. Treatment of these survivors can be difficult as a result of varying symptoms, degrees of symptoms, and whether or not disclosure has taken place. Experts in treating childhood sexual abuse survivors agree on three main goals for treatment. First, the client's wishes should take priority in the treatment plan. Second, the therapist should focus on the client's progress to determine the involvement of other family members. Third, it is helpful if therapy focuses on the survivor's present functioning before asking him or her to describe abuse details (Cohen, Berliner, & Mannarino, 2010; Cohen, Deblinger, Mannarino, & Steer, 2004; Cohen & Mannarino, 2008; Deblinger, Mannarino, Cohen, & Steer, 2006; Kerig, Sink, Cuellar, Vanderzee, & Elfstrom, 2010; Kessler & Goff, 2006).

In terms of reducing cognitive distortion symptoms in adult women survivors of childhood sexual abuse, cognitive processing therapy as a cognitive-behavioral approach has also been shown to be an effective therapeutic intervention with survivors of childhood sexual abuse (Chard, 2005; Kambouridis & Jevtic, 2003). After the clients have an opportunity to challenge their distorted views about self and others, they can participate in support groups to address common strategies to rebuild self-confidence. Group therapy appears to work well with sexual abuse survivors because the group provides peer support and encouragement (Kambouridis & Jevtic, 2003). With a three-month follow-up, Hebert and Bergeron (2007) found that group therapy is effective in alleviating psychological distress among survivors of sexual abuse.

In group psychotherapy, gestalt therapy and psychodrama have been effectively used in treating adult survivors because survivors can express emotions without any perceived notion of being judged (Winder, 1996). There are techniques that allow survivors to express their inner feelings without openly discussing the concerns with other participants, such as writing journals, expressing themselves artistically through clay or drawing, or engaging in bibliotherapy, which all aim to facilitate cognitive restructuring. Appendix 6C provides an example of using empty-chair techniques based on the gestalt approach. Bibliotherapy is another such technique; it involves a structured interaction based on mutual sharing from books or other readings. Bibliotherapy helps clients disclose and reveal their feelings through projection and storytelling. It also includes questioning techniques to reflect the client's experiences, in order to find solutions for the future. Therapeutic questions used in bibliotherapy focus on feelings, thoughts, issues, and solutions. Appendix 6D presents a list of suggested bibliotherapy books that can be used with young children. Chapter books such as *Just before Dawn* by Jan Hindman (1989) and self-help books such as *Chicken Soup for the Teenage Soul* (Canfield & Hansen, 1998) are good examples of books to share for adolescents and adults.

Depending on the age of the client, there are many ways to read together: the professional can read to the client and ask questions throughout to elicit the client's responses; the professional can read the first page and encourage the client to read the second page, and then take turns to continue reading and ask questions throughout; the professional can ask the client to read and then initiate questions when appropriate; both can read together and ask questions at the end; or the professional can ask the client to read silently and ask questions at the end.

Bibliotherapy can be used in a five-step process to achieve the therapeutic goal of healing:

1. *Relationship*: Establish a therapeutic relationship through trustful involvement in the client's personal development and understanding of the client's emotions, feelings, and behaviors.
2. *Assessment*: Assess the client's conflict and choose the counseling method that will address such conflict; encourage sharing of concerns.
3. *Selection*: Select reading materials based on four major criteria: knowing the client, recognizing the client's conflict, previewing the literature, and applying questioning techniques in the story-telling process.
4. *Treatment*: Focus on the child's identification and insight gained from reading or listening to the story; combine reading with discussion and follow-up activities; create new endings with possible and positive solution(s).
5. *Evaluation*: Use a conflict-resolution approach to identify solutions; encourage verbalization, interpretation, confrontation, and creativity; identify possible changes based on insight from the story and reality.

Although hypnosis, visualization, and guided imagery can be used in treating survivors of childhood sexual abuse, there is controversy surrounding these techniques. Therefore, these techniques must be used with extreme caution, especially when used with patients with extreme emotions or dissociative or other psychiatric disorders (Winder, 1996). Also, drug treatments are effective only with a small number of survivors of sexual abuse suffering from dysfunctions stemming from the abuse (Berman, Berman, Bruck, Pawar, & Goldstein, 2001).

For the Family

Helping the family is an essential component in helping the child victim of sexual abuse. Effective treatment of child abuse victims must include the entire family of the victim (Grosz et al., 2000). Parental level of distress and parental support are important variables in predicting how well a child victim of sexual abuse will respond to treatment. However, treating the family at the same time as the child may not always be possible, because the child may have been placed in foster care or may not be available for therapy (Saywitz et al., 2000).

King et al. (2000) found that treating the family optimizes the positive effects of cognitive-behavioral therapy for the child victim of sexual abuse and emphasizes the importance of treating the nonoffending parent, who may have feelings of guilt, incompetence, anxiety, and depression. It is important to note that King et al. (2000), in their study, found that a large number of nonoffending mothers were abused during their childhood.

Cognitive-behavioral interventions are useful in treating the entire family because they aim to improve the overall family functioning in addition to helping the family cope with the victim's situation (Hernandez et al., 2009). Interventions for the family can take the form of individual or group therapy (Lev-Wiesel, 2008). Trauma-focused cognitive-behavioral and psychoeducational or other supportive interventions have been used with some success with nonoffending parents (Hernandez et al., 2009).

Specifically for the nonoffending parent, treatment research has shown that the nonoffending parent is another victim in child abuse cases. Meta-analysis has shown that interventions with nonoffending parents are effective when they address self-blame, feelings of parental incompetence, denial, and other transference issues (Corcoran & Pillai, 2008; Hernandez et al., 2009). Although some research states the importance of treating the nonoffending parent or caregiver of the child sexual abuse victim at the same time as the child (Trowell & Kolvin, 2002), individualized treatment that is designed for the parent and/or caregiver separately from the child's treatment is necessary. The nonabusive parent has been shown to benefit significantly from cognitive-behavioral therapy, which greatly reduces the symptoms of PTSD arising from the sexual abuse of a cared-for child at the hands of the other parent (Ross & O'Carroll, 2004).

In a chapter written about nonoffending mothers, Cammaert (1988) notes that many of the articles written about nonoffending mothers have characterized the mothers in highly pejorative ways, claiming that the mothers either deliberately ignored incestuous relationships between their husbands and daughters, or even encouraged the incestuous relationship to avoid having a sexual relationship with the husband or partner. Cammaert (1988) proposes an alternative explanation for the nonoffending mother's behavior, stating that mothers in incestuous families often have no power and are highly dependent, both psychologically and financially, on the husband. In many incestuous families, the man uses violence to enforce his control over the family and also isolates his children and wife from the external world to solidify his dominance. Women in incestuous families often hold very traditional views about the importance of family and put a higher value on holding the family together than on protecting their children from the father's or partner's abuse.

Nonoffending mothers do have strengths, principally the strength of enduring highly dysfunctional family situations and continuing to feed and clothe their children. Cammaert (1988) states, "In treatment of the nonoffending mother, it is important to build on her survival skills and to enlarge her skill repertoire to include the ability to provide more effective protection for her daughter, more behaviors conducive to increased self-worth and independence for herself, and skills to heal the mother/daughter split that may have occurred" (pp. 318–319). Individual and/or group therapy for the nonoffending parent, a mother in particular, can help that parent understand the dynamics of child sexual abuse, develop a clearer picture of the family dynamics that contributed to the sexual abuse, and begin the psychological healing that will enable her to become strong enough to be able to protect both herself and her daughter.

Self-help groups for nonoffending mothers have been formed. The benefits of these groups include the sharing of knowledge and experience regarding the legal system and community service programs. Most cognitive-behavioral therapy treatment programs focus on expression of emotions, discussion of irrational thinking about the abuse, development of supportive connections among mothers, assistance with practical aspects of coping, and discussion of repairing the mother-child relationship.

For Perpetrators

The main goal of treatment for perpetrators is to stop abuse and to modify the psychological distortion regarding using power over children. Treatment modalities for adult and adolescent perpetrators differ in terms of the focus on sexual gratification control and sex education expansion. Teenage offenders must learn social skills to control sexual impulses and delay gratification. Adult abusers must understand the distorted view of sex and power misuse. Using the words from male perpetrators, they have expressed the following distorted views and defenses: denial (e.g., "I didn't do it," "I don't remember what happened, but it definitely wasn't me," "I was only trying to be nice to her," "I gave her money (gifts) just to make her happy, nothing else," "She did it to me, and I was the abused"), minimization (e.g., "I only kissed (touched) her neck, not her mouth or any place near her sexual parts," "I only showed her a book (video) to provide sex education; I didn't touch her," "I only touched her breasts once, but it was an accident," "She was curious about my body part, and we only talked about it," "She would not know this is about sex," rationalization (e.g., "I showed her my body part for sex education," "She is little and won't know the difference," "It was normal sex; I wasn't doing anything to harm her," "I was sick that day and wasn't sure what I did," "It came from love, nothing violent"), blaming (e.g., "I can't find age mates to have sex with," "I can't control myself (there's a demon within me)," "She didn't refuse or say anything," "She seduced me and asked for it," "She always wants to marry me," "I was drunk and thought she was my wife," "It's because my wife didn't fulfill her wifely duty," "My wife didn't stop me and should take the full responsibility," "My friends told me that I could do this to teach my kids about sex," "It was the porno video that made me do it"), and power (e.g., "I love my child and therefore teach her how to love me," "She loves me and therefore wants to have sex with me," "She is my child, and I can do whatever to her," "I am her father (stepdad, mother, teacher, grandfather, uncle), and she did this to please me").

Usually, offenders deny their mistakes. They may complain that the child was making things up, lying, or trying to get at them. They use these psychological defenses to protect themselves. In addition to using defenses to shield their wrongdoing, some offenders may not realize that they have psychological disorders. Therefore, it is important to assess whether the offender has any characteristics of a pedophile. Other than gaining power over children, pedophiles display sexual interests and impulses toward children and eventually harm children to gain gratification. There are two main types of pedophiles—the fixated and the regressed (Groth &

Birnbaum, 1978). Fixated pedophiles have sexual interest mainly in children and focus on meeting their desires through children whom they can control. Regressed pedophiles may occasionally use children as substitutes for their sexual partners because of stress, convenience, psychological rationalization, or unsuccessful marital relationships.

Regardless of the type of offenders, common treatment goals include the following:

- Increasing self-control
- Understanding consequences of sexual behaviors and learning social skills to expand the social circle
- Recognizing and being aware of early signs of sexual impulses and patterns of sexual behaviors
- Being alert to aggressive behaviors and psychological distortions toward children
- Learning communication skills to express personal problems
- Finding social support and networks with others in healthy activities

Friedman (1988) discusses the use of a family systems approach to the treatment of families of incest cases when the perpetrator is in treatment. The use of individual therapy is to break down defenses, help the client admit wrongdoing, and identify treatment goals, but it must be followed by family therapy. A family intervention will help prevent new occurrences of the abuse because it will focus on what is occurring in family relationships that may trigger and perpetuate the abuse. However, in criminal case proceedings, family treatment is rarely recommended.

In individual treatment, a cognitive behavioral approach must focus on changing the behaviors and faulty thinking of the perpetrator (Handy, 1988). With this focus, two major thoughts should be challenged. The first is misuse of power, such as "I have the power over children," or "I am the center of my social world. I don't have to work on getting sexual satisfaction or intimacy from my peers because I can try sex on children." The second is consequence enjoyment, such as "I'm not getting caught, and if I get caught, I can lie or blame the situation on the child or my spouse."

Child sexual abuse in the family is usually progressive in nature. These abusers usually mistakenly think that because they were not caught, they can manipulate the world and can therefore try to abuse again with greater frequency and higher intensity. If there are no negative consequences toward self or others, they can return to the abusive behavior without thinking. To prevent future abuse, they must know that they are responsible for all of these consequences and must stop the abuse. They must instead learn social and communication skills to express themselves, expand their social lives, and correct misconceptions about sex.

In the case of child sexual abuse, the perpetrator, not the victim, should be removed from the home so that the child's well-being can be protected. The perpetrator, the nonoffending parent, the victim, and other family members should all receive treatment, with the goal of modifying behaviors to prevent future abuse.

Using cases of father-daughter incest as an example, Handy (1988) advises that, at first, each family member should be seen individually and treating the victim should be a priority. Then, the mother and victim should be seen together, with the goal of developing a positive relationship between the two. The mother is then seen with all the children. The next meeting should be with only the father and mother. In future therapeutic sessions, without court involvement, the therapist should have a session with both parents and the victim. If there will be a child protective order, the victim and the perpetrator should not meet. Finally, it is possible that it may be appropriate for the entire family to participate in a session. The unique circumstances of each family influence the sequence of therapeutic sessions. A contract should be made with the perpetrator to include his or her acknowledgement of responsibility for what happened and a pledge not to engage in any harmful behaviors. For the other family members, Handy suggests the use of assertiveness training. In many cases, this is especially important if the intent is to reunite the family. The purpose of assertiveness training is to prepare family members to block further abuse by the perpetrator.

Prevention Programs

Treatment should not be limited to an after-the-fact approach. It should also include psychoeducational information and prevention programs for families. Organizations must respond by developing and incorporating educational materials and intervention plans.

Many child welfare organizations have published leaflets and books on child sexual abuse. Books have been published for parents to explain child sexual abuse and body protection to children. For example, with the book *When I Was Little Like You*, by Jane Porett (1993), parents or teachers can discuss issues of child sexual abuse with children. In investigation processes, this book can also help children disclose abuse. Suggested questions include "Has anything happened to you that made you sad?" "What would you do if a friend (a teacher, your mom or dad) couldn't help you solve your problem?" "Tell me about a situation when you felt scared," and "What could others do or have done to help you feel safe?"

When abused children become depressed, they may express suicidal ideations. Organizations that provide care or work with children must develop a crisis intervention plan so that the staff is trained appropriately to react to traumatic disclosure of suicidal threats. The plan with specific actions can help staff and professionals handle the situation appropriately to prevent the loss of lives. Appendix 6E includes suggestions for developing a crisis plan.

In offices or places where children interact with adults, it is important for preventive measures to be established to ensure that the adults behave appropriately so that they will not abuse children or be seen as abusers. Appendix 6F provides guidelines to assist clergy in particular to be cognizant of preventing themselves from stepping into any potential abuse trap.

Julie's Case: Treatment

In the first therapeutic session, Julie was not expressive and did not want to discuss the abuse. The therapist asked her to draw her feelings, as a rapport-building step, which helped her open up and disclose her feelings about blaming herself for breaking up the family. She was torn between loving and hating her stepfather. In the first few sessions, the focus is on the client's self-relaxation; Julie chose songs from the therapist's collection to help her relax. With the song "Ask Me" by Amy Grant, Julie discussed her inner feelings with the therapist. The therapist asked Julie the following questions in song therapy:

- "Have you ever been hurt by someone you love? Who was this person, and how did he or she hurt you?"
- "Did you share this information with anyone? With whom? What was his or her reaction? How did it make you feel?"
- "Is it hard to disclose this information now? How does it make you feel now?"
- "Do you still feel like you are the only one and all alone? Do you think that you could benefit from talking to other survivors who have also been abused?"
- "When you heard the word *shame*, what came to your mind? How did it affect you? How does talking about it make you feel now?"

In this session, Julie was able to feel relaxed. She wrote the word *shame* on a piece of paper and then destroyed it by throwing it into the trash can. She took a deep breath and said, "I feel fine now."

In the following session, when the therapist used a word-association exercise, Julie associated the word *touch* with *dirty*. The therapist discussed this negative association with her and helped her gradually reach a conclusion that touches can be bad and good. Julie even showed the therapist by touching her therapist's hand that she was comfortable with the touch. The therapist used a homework assignment to help Julie relate to the good touch exercise: Julie was to use hand lotion to massage her own hands in the morning and before bedtime; to initiate good touches with her mother by hugging her and telling her, "Thank you for helping me"; and to write down feelings and thoughts associated with good touches.

In a family session with her mother, Julie was able to express her feelings and tell her mother about concerns and fears. She invited her mother to draw with her on a blank piece of paper titled "My Family." Later, her mother became a volunteer in the social service agency to organize workshops in the area of child sexual abuse and the role of parents in preparing teenagers to receive proper sex education. She said that her involvement would make Julie know her intent to help her recover from the family "problem."

Because of Julie's recantation, the judge ordered her stepfather to participate in a series of individual and family therapy sessions. In his individual session, he was able to identify his feelings but stressed the fact that he did not sexually abuse his stepdaughter. A four-step process helped him realize his role as a father (or stepfather) for a teenager: recognizing the problem, accepting his responsibility, reexamining values and attitudes toward parenting, and identifying future action to stop power misuse. He admitted that he was not a good father but also that he was angry with Julie. After discussing bad and confusing touches with him, Julie's stepfather was able to admit that he might have made Julie feel uncomfortable, and he apologized and promised to stop making fun of Julie in the future, acknowledging that Julie was no longer a young child.

In a couple's session, the stepfather came in for therapy with Julie's mother and worked on marital communication issues. Then, the entire family came in for a final reconciliation. In the family session, each family member took turns expressing his or her feelings toward other family members and identifying ways to enhance communications in the future. It was stressed that child sexual abuse could not exist in the family, and the therapist asked the parents to write down, "Adults are responsible for protecting their children." They then processed their feelings and talked about ways to protect their children.

Conclusion

Although child victims and survivors of childhood abuse may suffer from posttraumatic stress disorder as a result of sexual abuse, the trauma also psychologically affects other family members. To begin the process of healing a family afflicted by child sexual abuse, appropriate therapeutic interventions must be designed for each family member individually and the family as a whole. Because each family member possesses a different set of treatment goals, helping professionals must employ age- and role-sensitive therapeutic techniques to accomplish treatment goals for individual family members and the family as a whole.

APPENDIX 6A

Treatment Research

Treatment for child and adolescent victims

Study focus	Procedure	Results and/or conclusions	Author
Community treatment	401 community-based practitioners from the National Child Traumatic Stress Network were surveyed on their practices, attitudes, and perceived outcomes with child victims of sexual abuse.	The most common form of treatment used was cognitive behavioral. 3 common factors for achieving positive results in child sexual abuse (CSA) treatment: Cognitive restructuring, insight, and exposure.	Kolko, Cohen, Mannarino, Baumann, & Knudsen (2009)
Trauma-focused cognitive-behavioral therapy (TF-CBT)	Examined differential effects of TF-CBT with or without the trauma narrative with 210 children (age 4–11 years) referred for CSA.	Regardless of sessions and/or inclusion of trauma narrative, TF-CBT was effective at improving symptomatology and personal safety skills, and reducing number of externalizing behavioral problems.	Deblinger, Mannarino, Cohen, Runyon, & Steer, 2011
Continuum of treatment	Reviewed child sexual abuse intervention studies to more thoroughly understand need for intervention and effectiveness of treatments used, to suggest directions for further research.	Past studies have shown treatment of CSA symptoms to be effective; CBT therapy is the favored intervention model. A continuum of treatment model is needed to effectively assess and accommodate unique, various needs of each CSA victim.	Saywitz, Mannarino, Berliner, & Cohen (2000)

Group treatment for young women	24 adolescent females participated in 10-week group treatment for CSA. No control group was used.	Group treatment result: Participants indicated feeling supported and cognitive-behavioral management skills improved.	Kambouridis & Jevtic (2003)
Individual versus group therapy	71 abused females participated in an outcome study comparing effectiveness of individual or group therapy for treatment of CSA.	Both groups improved in functioning and symptom reduction, but individual treatment had the additional benefit of reducing PTSD.	Trowell & Kolvin (2002)
Individual versus group treatment	Compared effectiveness of individual therapy and combined individual and group therapy in treating CSA; 38 participants were divided into two treatment groups: individual therapy or individual therapy and group therapy.	After 6 months, all clients improved in functioning and no significant differences in treatment outcome were found between the two types of intervention.	Nolan et al. (2002)

Treatment for adult survivors

Study focus	Procedure	Results and/or conclusions	Author
Cognitive processing therapy (CPT)	To examine effectiveness of CPT, 71 adult female CSA survivors were divided into 2 groups: treatment and minimal attention.	CPT found to be more effective than receiving minimal attention when reducing CSA symptoms.	Chard (2005)
Appropriate attribution technique (AAT)	AAT is a psychoeducational, cognitive technique for individuals and groups; involves debunking myths, looking at preconditions to sexual offending, understanding sex offender cycle, examining defense mechanisms, and reattribution.	The technique worked well in clinical practice, yet needs to be confirmed by further empirical research.	Murtagh (2010)

Adult male survivors' anger management	Reviews literature on treatment techniques for adult male CSA survivors.	Many of the same techniques are used to treat male and female CSA survivors; these techniques should be adapted to reflect unique issues of male survivors, particularly anger management.	Winder (1996)
Adult female survivors: Strengths-based wellness intervention	A strengths-based wellness intervention helps develop coping skills, enhance quality of life, and increase functioning across domains (case example).	Wellness-based interventions can be helpful in survival and offer tools to positively approach future experiences.	Hodges & Myers (2010)
Group intervention for female survivors	41 adult female CSA survivors participated in a feminist approach–based intervention group; 11 women with same history were included in a control group.	Group intervention significantly reduced psychological distress and anxiety.	Hebert & Bergeron (2007)
Guideline-based treatment program	A 23-year-old woman diagnosed with PTSD and who suffered from sexual abuse as a child was treated using the HEALTH treatment model (emphasizes symptom reduction, a supportive therapist, learning to manage symptoms and daily functioning, ensuring personal safety, treating complex PTSD symptoms); she participated in 24 individual sessions and group therapy.	All PTSD symptoms improved after treatment, and the participant felt more prepared to work on CSA-related issues.	Connor & Higgins (2008)
Inpatient treatment	34 adult survivors of childhood sexual abuse with PTSD attended a 3-month inpatient treatment program.	Participants showed significant improvement in posttraumatic stress, general psychiatric symptoms, and interpersonal problems.	Jepsen, Svagaard, Thelle, Leigh, & Martinsen (2009)

Pharmaco-therapy	To examine effectiveness of pharmacotherapy (sildenafil) to treat unresolved sexual symptoms of CSA, 7 female participants with unresolved CSA symptoms were treated for 6 weeks. A control group of women with sexual response problems but without CSA history was also used.	Sildenafil did not effectively reduce sexual symptoms of women with history of CSA.	Berman, Berman, Bruck, Pawar, & Goldstein (2001)
PTSD and dissociative disorder treatment	Reviews the most commonly used treatments for CSA survivors; examines relationship between PTSD and dissociative disorders in CSA survivors.	The most commonly used treatments are effective in treating post-traumatic stress symptoms, but few studies have examined them in a CSA context. More research is needed to study the current interventions used with CSA survivors to properly inform evidence-based practice.	Lev-Wiesel (2008)

Treatment for families

Study focus	Procedure	Results and/or conclusions	Author
Cognitive behavioral psychotherapy	Reviews studies examining use of cognitive behavioral interventions to treat abuse-related PTSD in child victims and nonoffending parents; focuses on having child and parents relive and confront abuse in therapeutic setting.	Cognitive behavioral therapies that aid clients in reliving and confronting abuse can significantly reduce symptoms of abuse-related PTSD; reviews suggest that more controlled outcome studies are needed to explain why this type of therapy proves effective.	Ross & O'Carroll (2004)

Parent-involved treatment	Meta-analysis of 7 studies on parent-involved treatment for CSA.	Parent-involved treatment had more significant effects on 4 child symptom areas: internalizing, externalizing, sexualized behaviors, and posttraumatic stress; the more significant effects indicate that parent-involved treatments are favorable to other conditions, such as child-only treatment.	Corcoran & Pillai (2008)
Parent-involved treatment	Compares 2 types of CSA treatment: individual cognitive-behavioral therapy and family cognitive-behavioral therapy; 36 children with history of CSA were assigned to a treatment condition or waiting-list control group.	Significant results for both treatment groups in terms of PTSD symptoms and reduced anxiety; no significant difference between treatment groups, which suggests that parental involvement does not improve treatment.	King et al. (2000)
Combined parent-child cognitive behavioral therapy (CPC-CBT)	24 parents and their children were treated with CPC-CBT; 20 were treated with parent-only CBT.	Children and parents in the CPC-CBT group had greater improvements in positive parenting skills and posttraumatic stress symptoms; parent-only CBT reported less use of corporal punishment after treatment.	Runyon, Deblinger, & Steer (2010)
Treatment for extrafamilial sexual abuse	246 child victims of CSA and 323 parents participated in a pilot program at a university medical facility between 1984 and 1991. Parents and child received crisis counseling and individual treatment, and participated in children's treatment groups and parent support groups.	Children and parents reported positive outcomes after participating in the pilot, particularly in response to crisis counseling, children's treatment groups, and parent support groups, making parental involvement a key factor in this intervention.	Grosz, Kempe, & Kelly (2000)

Creative Therapy with Child Victims

Treatment with Puppet Therapy

Purposes

- Build rapport
- Disarm self defenses
- Use drama to build self-esteem
- Use of a safer object to aid in disclosure
- Identify secrets
- Discuss polarizations or conflict

Target groups

Children, adolescents, adults, individuals, or groups

Steps

1. Identify feeling responses
   Reflect on feelings:
   - "Who is this?" (point at the selected puppet)
   - "What comes to your mind when you see this puppet?"
   - "My name is Hope. I have story to tell. Once upon a time (story content) . . . and I feel relieved. Have you ever felt this way before? Do you want this feeling now?"

   Break defenses and validate feelings:
   - "This puppet (or name given by client) is not feeling well. Do you know what made him (her) feel this way?"

- "Hope has a reason to believe that I (therapist) can help her. She asked, 'Can you make me feel better now?'"

Express or label feelings

- "This lion does not have a home to stay. Do you know what he (she) would say to his (her) best friend about this problem?"
- "I know it's hard to talk about it. The bad guys are gone now, and the good angel is here. The angel then told the lion, 'You just feel overwhelmed. It's OK to feel overwhelmed, but you must talk about it to feel better. We are here to help.'"

2. Disclose secrets

Reflect mixed feelings

- "I know it is hard to say something to a stranger. I am here with a friend, Max, who is a good listener. Max said, 'Hello, Michelle! I am here to listen.'"
- "You seem to have something to say but don't know what to say. It's OK because I feel the same way, too. Let me tell you that I have mixed feelings about being treated the way I was treated. But I am brave to share my situation with the therapist. Now I feel better because I told her my secret."

Encourage expressions

- "I want to know what has made you upset."
- "Guess what? I have a feeling that you want to tell me something. Tell me."
- "I know you are not happy about something. Are you all right? Can I be here with you? I am a good listener."

Play roles

- "Here is a little lamb (Edward) who is willing to tell secrets to the therapist. How about you take him and let him tell what's going on?"
- "How about you take this puppet and use this pointer to show me where he touched you?"

3. Reflect motives

Identify wants: "Tell me what you want, Lion. It's not possible that you want nothing. Let's pretend Lion is you. What would Lion tell me?"

Invite the client to teach: "You're the teacher now. Can you teach Lion what he can get from seeing a counselor?"

4. Provide examples and empower the client

   Show empathy: "You seem to be sad (upset, unhappy, mad). Can we talk?"

   Validate intake information: "I heard that you are not feeling well. People usually tell me about what they've been worrying about. Can you do the same?"

   Provide a role model: "Here is Lion; he is going to tell his people that it is important to be brave. Can you tell me what brave means to you? Have you ever done something brave?"

   Use positive "I" statements: "Little Lamb has solved his problem. He said, 'I made it. I can do this now.' Take Little Lamb and repeat what he said earlier."

5. Assess relationship issues

   Establish trust
   • "Lion said, 'I am here to listen and help.' Talk to him."
   • "Take me with you while I am playing. I am here to help."

   Affirm closeness
   • "It's OK to talk like this provided that you do not hurt yourself or others."
   • "Is it OK to touch your hands?" Piggy said. "Of course, you are nice to me."

   Identify relationship issues
   • "Here is your mom. Take her. She just said something to you, Michelle. What did Mom say?"
   • "How do you feel about being Mom (or another family member)?"

6. Provide positive affirmation

   Affirm positive outcome: "I know you will be better if you tell me what's been bothering you."

   Develop next steps: "You seem to be able to do it. Try harder!"

7. Apply behavioral or cognitive strategies

   Identify solution: "I think Mr. Bird wants to make everybody feel bad. What can you do to make him go away? Use this puppet to tell me what you can do to solve this problem."

   Provide safety: "Oh, we are here to tell the therapist about a problem. Do you think it is OK to tell?" Another puppet: "Sure. It's safe here."

Resolve conflict: "Mr. and Mrs. Bird want to let you know that they are sorry. And you will say, 'I'm OK now.'"

Provide a sense of internal control: "Look at me, Little Lamb. Don't you want to tell me something? I can tell that you are ready to say something."

Correct irrational or distorted thoughts: "Do you know what? What you just said wasn't true. 'It's not your fault,' Piggy said."

Polarize and analyze conflict: "I don't like it!" Another puppet: "I like it!" (Repeat the conflicting statements until both say, "It's OK to be different. Let's work together.")

Treating Childhood Sexual Abuse Victims: Gestalt Empty-Chair Techniques

General Introduction

Expressing Emotions

After the client expresses fear, anger, or mixed emotions about a family member or a friend, introduce the exercise. In the following examples, "father" is an example only:

> "I'd like for us to do an exercise so that you could express your emotions directly to your father. Now, close your eyes for a few seconds.... I'll ask you some questions. Please answer them based on your current feelings or responses. If you don't feel comfortable at any time, just tell me to stop or say, 'I can't continue.' OK?"

Techniques

Without a chair:

> "Assuming that your father is sitting in this room, and he has just heard what you said, what do you think he might say to you?"

With a chair:

> (Pull up a chair) "Assuming that your father is sitting on this chair, I'd like for you to think about your father's presence for a few seconds. What would you want to tell him?"

(If silent for more than one minute) "How about telling him how you're feeling now?"

Direct dialogue (when the client starts talking to the therapist but not to the "father":

"Look at the chair as if he <u>is</u> sitting here and tell him directly about how you feel."

Role play (when the client does not want to look at the chair):

"I know you don't want him to be here (or you can imagine he's here). How about if you look at me as if I were your father—now tell me how you feel."

Swapping the chairs (role reversal):

"Let's try this. Now you sit on this chair. (Client sits on the empty chair.) Pretend that you are your father. What would you say to your daughter (pointing at the client's chair)?"

Client responds in father's role and tone.

"Now go back to your own chair. How do you feel about what your father just said? (Wait for answers.) Now what would you say to your father?"

Drama ("act as if"):

"Now switch your role to be your father, and repeat after me, 'Daughter, I'm sorry I did that to you.' (Encourage client to repeat after each sentence.) 'I'm sorry that I couldn't tell you. I don't know how to let you know. But I feel very bad about it.' How did that make you feel? (Encourage client to express.) Now you are yourself again. Look at the chair and think about what your father may respond to your feeling.

Telling one thing

"If your father could be here today to tell you one thing, and that he is sitting across from you, what would you want him to say? Tell him directly."

Debriefing

"Now the exercise is done, what did you learn from it? How did it make you feel? Do you feel any changes in you? Your father is actually not here today. Take a deep breath and say, "Good-bye." Now you can take the perspective you've learned today and feel OK about yourself."

Bibliotherapy

Theme	Title and author	Suggested questions
Acceptance and empathy	*Priscilla McDoodleNutDoodle McMae Asks Why*, by Janet Mary Sinke (2007)	• How is Priscilla different from you? • How do you feel about people who are different from you? • How do you share your feelings to someone who is different from you?
Anger	*I Was So Mad*, by Ron Miller (2000), illustrated by Mercer Mayer	• Who could make you angry? • When you are asked to do things that you don't like, what would you do or say? • What do you think about running away from problems?
Child sexual abuse	*When I Was Little Like You*, by Jane Porett (1993), illustrated by S. Dmitri Lipczenko	• How do you respond if someone did things to you that you dislike? • Tell me a situation that once you felt scared. What could others do or have done to help you feel safe?
Childhood anxiety	*Wemberly Worried*, by Kevin Henkes (2000)	• What could make you worry? • What or who would help you when you are worried? • What would you do when you see others feeling worried?
Conflicting feelings	*Double Dip Feelings*, by Barbara S. Cain (2001), illustrated by Ann Patterson	• What are you feeling at this moment? • Have you ever had mixed feelings about something or someone? How do those feelings affect you and that person? • What would you say to this person (or someone you trust) about those feelings?
Feelings	*Disney Winnie the Pooh: Happy, Sad, Mad, & Glad*, by Nancy Parent (2003), illustrated by Atelier Philippe Harchy	• Have you ever felt happy, sad, mad, and glad? What could make you feel each of those things? • Show me (with these cards) a happy (sad, mad, glad) face. What is your current feeling? • What would you like other people to do when you feel sad or mad? What would you like me to do to help you feel happy again?

Theme	Title and author	Suggested questions
Personal safety	*Never Talk to Strangers*, by Irma Joyce (2009), illustrated by George Buckett	• How is a stranger different from someone you know? • What would you do if a stranger asked you for help? • How about if someone you know asked you for help but you didn't feel comfortable about helping?
Physical and emotional violence	*The Berenstain Bears and the Bully*, by Stan and Jan Berenstain (1996)	• How did it make you feel when you saw someone cry? • Have you ever seen anyone get beaten up? • Who would you talk to when someone made you do something you didn't want to do?
Power	*The Little Wing Giver*, by Jacques Taravant (2001), illustrated by Peter Sis	• If you had wings to fly away, where would you want to go? • Have you ever had something very important taken away from you? What was this something? If you had a special power, how would you use it?
Safety smarts	*Personal safety*, by Elementary Safety 4 Kids (2011)	• What would you do if a stranger walks up to you and asks you to do something? • What do you think about why a stranger would want you to help him or her? • Where is a safe place and where is not?
Self-esteem and confidence	*Do Princesses Wear Hiking Boots?*, by Carmela LaLigna Coyle (2003)	• What do you think about being confident about yourself? • Is there anything you feel like doing but haven't been able to do it? • How would it make you feel if you were not able to do the things you want to do?
Self-esteem and understanding feelings	*The Soul Bird*, by Michael Snunit (2010)	• If you have a guiding soul bird, what do you want your soul bird to tell you? • If you hide your feelings for a while, how do you take these feelings out and share? • Who would you share your feelings with first?
Suicidal thoughts	*I'm Thankful for Each Day!*, by P. K. Hallinan (2003)	• How do the illustrations and words in the book make you feel? • What are you thankful for now? To whom you are thankful? • Which section(s) of the book do you like the best? Which section best describes how you feel right now?

Theme	Title and author	Suggested questions
Traumatized and grieving children	*Brave Bart*, by Caroline H. Sheppard (1998), illustrated by John Manikoff	• How did you feel about the story? • Have you ever had something bad happen to you like Bart did? • Who can you trust (like Helping Hannah)?
Value of self	*The English Roses*, by Madonna (2006), illustrated by Jeffrey Fulvimari	• Has there ever been a time when you wished you were someone else? • What would you like to be different in your own life? • What are some things that you like about your life?

What to Do When Clients Have Suicidal Thoughts

When disclosing child sexual abuse, a victim or a perpetrator may feel extremely distressed or not know what to do next. With emotions of despair, the victim or perpetrator may want to end his or her life. The professional who responds to the client must act effectively to stop suicidal thoughts or threats and/or potential actions to that end. Recognizing the need for proper suicidality assessment and treatment is the first step in addressing what to do for such clients.

Develop a Crisis Plan

It is essential to develop a crisis plan because child sexual abuse can traumatically affect the client's emotions during disclosure. By having a clear plan, the professional will know what to do when hearing a suicidal threat. First, don't overact, but stay calm and counsel the client. If the client shows extreme emotions and tries to carry out a suicidal action, then follow the crisis plan, which may include the following action items:

1. Draw the client's attention before you can call for help. For example, say, "I am listening to you. Calm down and take a deep breath before you talk again."
2. Don't use any extreme measures that may arouse the client's emotions. For example, don't blame; don't touch the client; don't raise your voice or scream; don't say, "I understand how you feel" (it's better to say, "I don't understand how you feel. You need to tell me more"); don't say, "It'll be all right" (it's better to say, "You

and I don't know what would happen next. Let's talk more so that we can plan ahead"); don't say, "Forget about the past" (it's better to say, "It's hard to forget and forgive. Let's talk about other options").

3. Address the fact that what the client has indicated is not an ultimate solution. For example, say, "I don't know what you're thinking now, but I can see that you are making a decision that I cannot support. I can help you if you calm down so that we can discuss other options."

4. Inform the supervisor or another colleague about your involvement, if feasible. For example, say, "I know you can't calm down now. Let me ask my colleague to come to help."

5. Call a supervisor to call the police to send a crisis team to the facility if needed. For example, say, "I need help here and please send a crisis team."

6. Wait for the police to arrive and make sure that the client is in a safe and calm environment. For example, say, "I'm here to listen to your concern."

7. Escort the client out when the police arrive. For example, say, "I'll go with you. Don't worry! You may need some medical attention to help you calm down."

8. Follow up with the hospital or crisis unit to determine how long the client will stay so that the family can come to visit. For example, say to the client, "Who would you like to see now? I'll check with them so that they can come to see you."

9. Clearly document all of your steps and the client's behaviors.

10. Follow up with the client and make an appointment quickly once he or she is released from the crisis unit.

Ask Appropriate Questions

Asking questions about a client's suicidal thoughts or behaviors can give you insight into his or her needs and can provide information to help you help your client stay safe. Your concern can counter a sense of shame and hopelessness and help develop a more effective helping relationship. For example:

- "You said you want to end your life. When did you start to have that thought? What had happened before that thought came about?"
- "What has made you feel that you would be 'better off dead' (or words from the client)?"
- "What options have you tried to help resolve this difficulty? Did you receive any assistance or help?"
- "When you thought about killing yourself, did you have a plan? Have you ever tried it? What is in your mind now about this thought? How can you dispute this thought?"
- "You probably know that killing yourself (or others) is not a rational action. Have you thought of other options that you can use to resolve this problem?"
- "When you feel lonely, isolated, or a lack of support, who would you talk with or turn to?"
- "Remember there are many people who care about you. How can these caring people help you release this thought (or your anxiety)?"

Important Checklist

- Continue to ask questions about rational alternatives.
- Identify the client's strengths in resolving difficulties in the past.
- Educate the client's family and/or friends about suicide and suicide prevention.
- Provide information and support.
- Follow up with the client after treatment regarding the plan to stay safe.
- Maintain self-care, including healthy eating and exercise habits.

Resources for Working with Suicidal Clients

American Association of Suicidology. (2011). *Know the warning signs.* Retrieved from http://www.suicidology.org/web/guest/home.

Berman, A. L., & Jobes, D. A. (1991). *Adolescent suicide: Assessment and intervention.* Washington, DC: American Psychological Association.

DeAngelis, T. (2001a). Intervening with family. *Monitor on Psychology,* *32*(10). Retrieved from http://www.apa.org/monitor/nov01/intervening.html.

DeAngelis, T. (2001b). Surviving a patient's suicide. *Monitor on Psychology,* *32*(10), 70. Retrieved from http://www.apa.org/monitor/nov01/suicide.html.

Goldsmith, S. K., Pellmar, T. C., Kleinman, A. M., & Bunney, W. E. (Eds.). (2002). *Reducing suicide: A national imperative.* Washington, DC: National Academies Press.

Joiner, T., & Rudd, M. D. (Eds.). (2000). *Suicide science: Expanding the boundaries.* Boston: Kluwer Academic.

Kleepsies, P. M., & Dettmer, E. L. (2000). The stress of patient emergencies for the clinician: Incidence, impact, and means of coping. *Journal of Clinical Psychology, 56*(10), 1353–1369.

Mishna, F., Antle, B. J., & Regehr, C. (2002). Social work with clients contemplating suicide: Complexity and ambiguity in the clinical, ethical, and legal considerations. *Clinical Social Work Journal, 30*(3), 265–280.

National Center for Injury Prevention and Control, Centers for Disease Control and Prevention. (2011). *Suicide prevention.* Retrieved from http://www.cdc.gov/injury/.

U.S. Air Force. (2011). *Suicide prevention.* Retrieved from http://www.af.mil/suicideprevention.asp.

Tips for Clergy for Preventing Sexual Abuse

Tip No. 1: Understand the Impact of Professional Expectations on Clergy

- Religious leaders are expected to be perfect and godly while the entire religious community watches.
- As caregivers, religious leaders often find it difficult to ask for care for themselves.
- The image of top leadership creates a personally and professionally isolated environment.
- It is important to look for counselors or therapists who are sensitive to the culture of celibacy by aiding clergy clients to explore the various aspects that lead to a healthy life.

Tip No. 2: Protect Clergy from Abuse Allegations

It is important to provide suggestions to clergy clients in five areas:

1. Implementing effective boundary strategies:
   Become intentionally balanced by connecting with friends and family outside the church.
   Do not seek emotional support from church members.
   Do not stay alone with any person without a sound reason.
   Do not provide transportation for a minor without parental permission.
   Do not touch parishioners in any way that can be misinterpreted.

Avoid spending excessive time alone with one client.

Post an open-door policy on office doors.

2. Consult with other spiritual leaders:

Participate in spiritual activities with leaders to learn from their experiences.

Review your journaling on a regular basis to identify potential issues.

Engage in personal prayers.

3. Maintain professionalism:

Use professional language.

Understand the impact of power differentials on relationships.

4. Use documentation:

Record any serious conflicts.

Share problems with religious leaders and/or other professionals on a regular basis.

5. Engage in continuous learning:

Be aware of personal limitations and maintain realistic appraisal of self.

Communicate self-awareness to professionals.

Attend professional workshops on healthy professional boundaries.

CHAPTER 7

Self-Care and Secondary Trauma

This chapter addresses some of the ways mental health professionals can be affected when working on cases involving child sexual abuse and the prosecution of alleged offenders. Professionals who are involved in child sexual abuse cases often experience stress because it is hard to talk about sexuality with a child who has been abused. When this stress gets out of hand, it is often referred to as secondary trauma or vicarious trauma. Secondary trauma can occur when professionals hear about a client's traumatic experience, either directly from a client or from secondary sources, but they cannot immediately find solutions to help the client overcome difficulties. Secondary trauma can generate feelings of helplessness and despair as a result of the professional's perceived inability to make positive and helpful changes for the client who has been affected by a traumatic experience. Because child sexual abuse usually does not involve eyewitnesses, it is particularly hard to resolve questions regarding the reality of what has occurred. Incest cases are particularly difficult for professionals because child victims are in highly vulnerable positions, and the professionals who assist the children are affected by the reality that the victims will either face a broken home if the perpetrator is sentenced or return to a dangerous home if the alleged perpetrator is released as a result of insufficient evidence. It is important that professionals pay special attention to their own self-care when these feelings of helplessness occur. This chapter identifies what has been learned from research about professionals' emotional responses and provides a range of suggestions for dealing with secondary trauma.

Professionals' Emotional Responses to Child Sexual Abuse Cases

To become attuned to their emotional responses, professionals must first understand the difference between burnout and secondary trauma. Burnout is associated with fatigue and insensitivity that results from long or continuous exposure to work that requires significant amounts of time and energy. Secondary trauma can occur when the professional is exposed to someone else's victimization for either a short or a long period. Secondary trauma may occur even when the individual's exposure to traumatic situations has not been continuous. To prevent secondary trauma, during the helping process, professionals in trauma work must be aware of their emotional responses to clients' descriptions of traumatic experiences.

In child sexual abuse training, a key curricular module is self-awareness. In counseling practice, self-awareness has many components, including knowledge of one's own emotions and limitations, assessment of the use of self-disclosure techniques, an understanding of how to separate professional roles and personal experiences, awareness of the impact of family of origin on one's own behaviors, and the practicing of consistent self-care to reduce work stress. When undergoing training in preparation for handling child sexual abuse cases, professionals must first assess their own emotional responses to the sexual molestation of children. In the past fifteen years, I have delivered many training programs to prepare professionals for their work in the area of child sexual abuse. Before discussing forensic interviewing techniques, the author usually gives a self-assessment instrument to professionals to identify their initial responses to child sexual abuse. This instrument collects information from the participants based on their first encounter with child sexual abuse, through work, media, or a case described at the start of training, before they receive the self-assessment sheet.

Cheung and Boutté-Queen (2000) reported the data from ten training programs based on this self-assessment instrument, which 188 anonymous respondents filled out. The respondents represented twenty-eight police constables or officers, eighty-six social workers, and seventy-four other professionals and graduate social work students. The instrument identified the ten most common categories of emotions felt in response to learning about child sexual abuse and asked respondents to rate the presence and intensity of those feelings when they heard the details of a child sexual abuse case involving incest. Within the ten categories of emotions, the instrument listed thirty-seven emotional responses on a five-point Likert-type scale, where 1 indicated the lowest level of emotions; 2, somewhat low; 3, neutral; 4, somewhat high; and 5, the highest level of emotions associated with each emotional response (for the emotional responses, see appendix 7A).

Findings from the study focused on comparing social workers and police and indicated significant differences between the two groups in terms of the intensity of their emotional responses to the first child sexual abuse case they heard or handled. Police were more likely to have stronger emotions in ambivalent and revenge feelings with regard to "ambivalence about rescuing a child or preserving the family," "ambivalence about helping or punishing the perpetrator," and "revenge because the behavior was bad or immoral." Social workers are different from police in the areas of "embarrassment with a perpetrator," "fear of being inadequate in handling the situation," "titillation in response to involuntary physiological responses to words and descriptions of sex acts," and "empathy with the child's plight/condition." The study suggests that professionals who handle or will handle child sexual abuse cases can have a range of feelings toward the child victim and the alleged perpetrator.

Before professionals handle child sexual abuse cases, they must first examine their emotional awareness, develop a sense of self-confidence, relate to other professionals, show mutual support with other professionals, and express concerns to a supervisor if they feel that negative images of sexual abuse or sexuality may affect their mental health because of prior experiences or lack of experience in the area. Appendix 7B provides the self-assessment form for rating emotional responses to child sexual abuse and can serve as a tool for assessing self-awareness before professionals handle these types of cases.

Because there is a high level of professional awareness about self-care, professionals who work with traumatized clients must understand the importance of taking care of themselves before taking care of clients. Much research on this awareness has focused specifically on the awareness of stress when working with traumatized patients. *Vicarious trauma* is a unique term used to describe how professionals can experience their own trauma through empathetic bonding with the client's experiences (see, e.g., Cornille & Meyers, 1999; Sexton, 1999; Steed & Downing, 1998). This places trauma professionals at an increased risk for job-related stress. However, research on vicarious trauma is mixed. Kadambi and Ennis (2004) conducted a literature review on vicarious trauma studies and found that exposure to traumatic material does not necessarily contribute to vicarious trauma; more research is needed to provide conceptual and empirical support for this construct.

Across ten research studies on vicarious trauma (or secondary trauma) among professionals, Chouliara, Hutchison, and Karatzias (2009) found that helping professionals in trauma work indicated a high level of stress with negative effects on their mental health in general, but these effects are not significantly different from professionals in counseling work that involves clients without sexual abuse issues. After surveying 152 mental health professionals, Devilly, Wright, and Varker (2009) found that exposure to traumatic materials does not necessarily contribute to vicarious trauma and that professionals' distress is highly correlated with work stress. In contrast, Way, VanDeusen, and Cottrell (2007) found that vicarious trauma affects self-esteem and predicts disrupted cognitions among professionals who work with clients with sexual abuse problems. VanDeusen and Way (2006) also found that client trauma can distort the professionals' views of trust and intimacy. With these mixed results about handling the spillover effect of client trauma, it is premature to conclude that secondary trauma does not exist; learning about a client's trauma and emotions can cause stress.

Child Abuse Victims' Emotions

Most children express emotions by crying and telling others about their feelings. After being sexually abused, however, a child victim is often clouded with mixed feelings of confusion, self-blame, guilt, inadequacy, and lack of relationship satisfaction and is fearful of the future of the abuser. Sometimes the disclosure of the sexual abuse can bring a feeling of relief mixed with a feeling of despair that children do not know how to express. MacIntosh and Johnson (2008) found that although the emotions of these victims or childhood survivors are mixed, they can move toward a positive perception of self-worth if they have fully participated in a treatment process that helps them understand the influence of mixed feelings on self-esteem evaluation. In other words, if victims and survivors have opportunities to explore personal conflicts when dealing with interpersonal issues, they will receive the benefits of releasing emotional distress, retaining self-confidence, and maintaining a positive outlook on life.

Professionals must first understand clients' feelings in order to help them analyze the sources of conflict and develop strategies to restore mental health. Common feelings of victimization include anger, denial, disbelief, distrust, fear, frustration, grief, guilt, loneliness, numbness, shock, and sorrow.

In child sexual abuse situations, the victim often feels mixed feelings that may also include a love-hate dilemma and a feeling of loss of innocence and hopelessness. Professionals cannot assume that all victims feel the same; therefore, they must validate a client's feelings by asking, "What feeling or mix of feelings came out when we talked about your stepdad (or perpetrator)?" "I feel that you are very confused about the situation; may I confirm this with . . . ?"

Liability: Certainty versus Reasonable Doubt

Recently, more lawsuits have been filed against workers and supervisors in child protection claiming that they have not been taking concerted efforts to protect children. Litigation has been sustained on the basis of reasons such as official misconduct, failure to take proper action, malpractice, neglect in public office, failure to properly investigate a case, and endangerment of a child's welfare. Other charges include failure to report or warn if legally required; unprofessional behaviors in handling cases; discrimination based on gender, age, or disability; and inability to perform duties. Many of these actions or lack of actions may result from professionals' hesitation to perform their tasks because of uncertainty.

Failure to remove a child can cause damage to the child, but on the practice side, it is also an issue of liability if the child is incorrectly removed. In child sexual abuse cases, it is hard to collect evidence or locate eyewitnesses to testify against an alleged perpetrator. Without concrete evidence, the worker is also subject to potential liability as a result of breaking client confidentiality when reporting the case to authorities. In the United States, professionals such as social workers are protected from liability because of the mandatory reporting system, which requires suspected child abuse to be reported. However, the mandatory reporting system operates in an environment that involves high caseloads that place workers in the vulnerable position of not being able to thoroughly investigate all suspected cases.

In the public child welfare field, workers are liable to three types of federal and state lawsuits: criminal, constitutional, and civil. Failure to take adequate precautions to protect a child from potential harm or failure to remove the child from danger can constitute criminal negligence or official misconduct on the part of the worker and the agency. However, the wrongful or unlawful removal of a child from his or her home can also make the worker legally liable for violating constitutional rights, such as privacy. Because the confidentiality of the client's information is not kept during the course of action (e.g., sustaining a court order to remove the child from school or home), a lawsuit may seek compensation for careless handling of a referral that violates the rights of privacy. As a result, professionals who handle child sexual abuse cases know that they must have strong evidence before they take action. However, gathering and collecting strong evidence requires time and energy and can contribute to the stress facing those who investigate and validate the case. When this stress is added to the stress that results from learning about sexual abuse incidents and acts, the professional who works closely with a child victim may be more likely to experience secondary trauma.

Symptoms of Stress

A research study conducted by VanDeusen and Way (2006) found that clinicians with less tenure in the field who treated sexual abuse survivors had a higher level of vicarious trauma than those with more experience. In addition, research has determined that work-related stress can contribute to physical as well as psychological and emotional problems. Professionals in trauma work must assess their stress symptoms. Physical symptoms can include backache or body ache, blurred vision, digestive problems, fatigue, headaches, changes in heart rate, muscular tension, skin rashes, sleep problems, and sweating. Psychological and emotional symptoms can include disturbed eating patterns, feeling distressed, decreased motivation, loneliness, helplessness, feeling pressure, difficulty concentrating, inability to perform duties, irritability and mood swings, and decreased enjoyment of work or leisure.

Although no single reason can fully explain work-related stress, research on occupational stress in social work has grown significantly during the past two decades. Research has examined a wide range of issues, including demographics, types and levels of stress, health, support in the workplace, and different treatments. Studies have proposed that mental health professionals experience several different types of stress, including burnout, compassion fatigue, and vicarious trauma. In a review of the literature on stress and burnout in social work, Lloyd, King, and Chenoweth (2002) found that lack of challenge on the job, role ambiguity, low work autonomy, low professional self-esteem, and difficulties in providing services to clients all are risk factors for stress; however, supervision and team support can protect against stress.

Dealing with Stress: Methods and Hints

One way to help alleviate the stress of working in the field of child sexual abuse is for professionals to ensure that they consistently perform their work in accordance with agency and policy guidelines that are established to prevent malpractice. Using concrete, established methods will help professionals avoid vulnerability to legal liability. The first step is to adhere to legislative mandates, agency policies, practice standards, and casework guidelines. To reduce the risk of malpractice, professionals must attend regular trainings and access current research findings related to the development of professional competence in the area of practice. Current research can provide evidence-based information to support professionals in coping with issues in practice. Training can also help refine documentation skills and update record-keeping practices. Communication must be clearly documented with the clients, collaterals, and/or other individuals and agencies associated with a case.

According to the American Association for Protecting Children (AAPC, 1988), professional competency is evidenced if case records include the following:

1. Specific assessment statements;
2. Detailed service plans with signatures of parents/clients;
3. Documentation of consultant input, supervisory concurrence, and assistance of other service providers;
4. Identification of decisions and conclusions with an explanation as to how and why they were reached as well as who is responsible for them;
5. Demonstration of worker's ability to identify problems, set priorities, and carry out case plans;
6. Systematic consideration of all available information in connection with the process of risk assessment. (p. V-111)

In addition, the AAPC (1988) recommends that supervisors practice with a high level of commitment to workers' safety and protection. These recommendations include regular supervisions and timely consultations, clear communications about practice standards, regular professional training for workers and supervisors, and periodic reviews of work performance and policy updates. These recommendations provide a concrete plan of action that outlines the importance of following the rules; however, it lacks the human side of work-emotion connections, which is more important than black-and-white guidelines. In another module suggested for training use, the AAPC outlines the importance of addressing professionals' values and attitudes before handling sensitive cases.

In other words, support provided at work should not be limited to making sure that proper documentation is completed and securely filed. It should also include emotional support from supervisors and administrators to create a psychologically comforting environment.

Two major components of self-care are commitment to self-care and continuous participation in stress reduction. Research summarized in appendix 7C indicates that secondary trauma is related to the perception of helplessness, and the most effective way to deal with that type of stress is a combined cognitive-affective intervention. This type of intervention must begin with a concerted effort to achieve self-awareness of stress symptoms and a commitment by professionals to take care of their own mental health before caring for others. The second step of the intervention is to challenge irrational thoughts and take action to participate in stress reduction. Because there are many stress reduction methods, professionals may choose to participate in a form of stress reduction that suits their lifestyle, availability, and preferences (see appendix 7D).

As Perry (2003) has suggested, to prevent problems caused by secondary trauma and work stress, professionals must recite their daily affirmations in four areas: physically healthy, psychologically balanced, emotionally strong, and creatively working in a supportive environment:

Physical	*Psychological*	*Emotional*	*Workplace*
Sleep well	Self-reflect	See friends	Take breaks
Eat well	Pleasure reading	Cry as an outlet	Set limits
Dancing	Say no!	Laugh and smile	Peer support
Walking	Smile	Praise yourself	Get supervision
Jogging	Solitude	Enjoy humor	Use vacations

Do not use "no time" as an excuse; we can use a simple statement as our personal affirmation for self-care at the beginning of your workday:

I will take care of myself today and will take the following steps, _____ and _____, to protect myself from secondary trauma (choose two from the list above every day or week).

Julie's Case: Self-Care Methods for the Professional

Julie recanted her allegation, stating that she was lying because she hated her stepdad. She privately told her social worker that she felt powerless because no one believed in her, not even her mother. She could not see her friends, and her friends tried to distance themselves from her, which caused her to feel more socially isolated. The saddest part for her was that her mother told her to stop lying so that the family could be together again.

When she was staying in foster care, she told her foster parents that she wanted to go out to see her friends, but she was not allowed to do so. After going home, she was not allowed to take part in any school activities, and she missed her boyfriend, who was the only person who believed her story of abuse. After her recantation, Julie said that her mother still complained about her. Although the social worker wanted to visit her, the parents decided not to allow anyone to visit Julie alone. The social worker advised Julie's mother to take all possible precautions to prevent abuse from happening. Nevertheless, the social worker shared with her supervisor that she felt absolutely distressed about the disposition of the case and identified the following feelings:

- *Powerlessness*: Cannot do anything else to protect the child
- *No improvement*: Feels that the work done has made no difference in Julie's life
- *Insensitivity*: Feels that people are insensitive to Julie's needs
- *Lack of motivation*: Feels unrewarded by this type of work
- *Lack of hope*: Trusts that Julie did not lie about the abuse but is fearful that she will display deviant behaviors
- *Inability to change the system*: Feels that society has not done much to help vulnerable victims

The supervisor helped the social worker dispute some of those thoughts:

- *Abuse will stop*: Although Julie's stepdad, the alleged perpetrator, would not be prosecuted, he would be unlikely to abuse Julie again knowing that someone is watching after him.
- *Improvement is based on the child*: Providing counseling support to Julie will help her rebuild confidence. Although the worker could no longer work with Julie alone, she was able to help Julie understand what she could do in the future to protect herself.
- *Mother is a protector*: Even though Julie's mother expressed her disagreement with Julie, she still has the role of protector. Julie's mother will definitely watch the situation closely because she is aware of the accusation.

- *Reward may not be immediate*: The worker must know that the most rewarding aspect of this type of work is not the immediate result. By helping Julie learn how to protect herself and educating her parents about child protection, the worker has built long-term outcomes in the family and has broken the cycle of abuse if Julie feels that she received adequate care.
- *Instill hope*: The worker should tell Julie that she trusts her and believes that she will learn to become independent and productive.
- *Continue advocacy effort*: The worker should not stop believing in the ability to mobilize the system; workers can change the system by providing expertise. Professionals in an interdisciplinary team will make social services available to Julie's family.

Conclusion

Helping professionals working with child victims are increasingly likely to experience secondary trauma or vicarious traumatization. To avoid the detrimental psychological effects and legal consequences of such trauma, professionals should remain aware of agency policies and guidelines. In addition, supervisors must maintain open and emotionally supportive relationships with their subordinates to minimize the emotional consequences of secondary trauma. Every helping professional involved with child victims should create a self-care plan and remain dedicated to actively practicing self-care on a continuous basis to provide the highest quality of service to child victims and families.

Professionals' Emotional Responses toward Intrafamilial Child Sexual Abuse

Instruction: The purpose of this survey is to promote emotional awareness for professionals when handling child sexual abuse cases. Your participation in this survey is completely voluntary. Rate your feelings or emotional responses to the first intrafamilial child sexual abuse case(s) you encountered (or the one you just heard from this lecture) on a scale from 1 (low or weak reaction) to 5 (high or strong reaction). There are no right or wrong answers. Do not put your name on the questionnaire. Your answers will be reported collectively with others' so that you can make a comparison.

Circle the most appropriate number on the scale to represent your first response to the case:

Rating of Your Response

1. Anger
Low   High
1 2 3 4 5   a. At the child for not stopping or resisting the behavior or for not telling someone about the abuse
1 2 3 4 5   b. At the perpetrator for violating community norms, or using a dependent child to meet his/her selfish needs
1 2 3 4 5   c. At the other parent or the siblings for not protecting the child

1 2 3 4 5 d. At other professionals for their lack of cooperation, knowledge, involvement, or sensitivity to the child or family

2. Embarrassment about investigating, discussing, and reporting intimate sexual behavior in explicit detail:

1 2 3 4 5 a. With a child
1 2 3 4 5 b. With a perpetrator
1 2 3 4 5 c. With other professionals
1 2 3 4 5 d. In public (e.g., court) with a person of opposite sex
1 2 3 4 5 e. Relating to the child's and the family's public exposure
1 2 3 4 5 f. When explicitly naming and discussing sexual organs (e.g., penis or vagina versus privates)

3. Hopelessness

1 2 3 4 5 a. About preventing abuse
1 2 3 4 5 b. About treating the family
1 2 3 4 5 c. About successfully treating the child
1 2 3 4 5 d. About lack of resources or time to deal with the problem
1 2 3 4 5 e. About "proving" a case legally
1 2 3 4 5 f. About inability to "rescue" child

4. Revenge

1 2 3 4 5 a. Because the behavior which occurred was unspeakable, bad, or immoral
1 2 3 4 5 b. Because those responsible deserve the worst possible fate (e.g., castration, life sentences, "an eye for an eye")
1 2 3 4 5 c. Because those responsible don't deserve to care for children

5. Fear

1 2 3 4 5 a. For the safety and recovery of the child
1 2 3 4 5 b. For the victim's siblings
1 2 3 4 5 c. Of family's or perpetrator's aggressive behavior
1 2 3 4 5 d. Of being inadequate in handling the situation

6. Ambivalence

1 2 3 4 5   a. About rescuing the child or preserving the family

1 2 3 4 5   b. About helping or punishing the perpetrator and/or family members

1 2 3 4 5   c. About community standards and/or expectations and whether these are appropriate

1 2 3 4 5   d. About intervening or not intervening

1 2 3 4 5   e. Exhibited by approach and/or avoidance behavior and characterized by revulsion and curiosity

7. Empathy

1 2 3 4 5   a. For the child's plight or condition.

1 2 3 4 5   b. For the family's predicament (e.g., separation, public censure, criminal charges)

8. Guilt

1 2 3 4 5   a. About punitive feelings

1 2 3 4 5   b. About anger generated

1 2 3 4 5   c. About inadequacy to handle the situation

1 2 3 4 5   d. About own curiosity for details

9. Titillation

1 2 3 4 5   a. In response to our own excitement from hearing explicit descriptions of sex acts

1 2 3 4 5   b. In response to our involuntary physiological responses to words and descriptions of sex acts (e.g., quickening of heart rate, facial flushing, rapid breathing)

10. Vulnerability

1 2 3 4 5   To the possible rekindling of our own victimization

How Strong Are My Emotional Reactions toward Child Sexual Abuse?

A Self-Assessment Tool

	My Rating	*Average Rating in My Class*
1. Anger	a. _____	a. _____
	b. _____	b. _____
	c. _____	c. _____
	d. _____	d. _____
2. Embarrassment	a. _____	a. _____
	b. _____	b. _____
	c. _____	c. _____
	d. _____	d. _____
	e. _____	e. _____
	f. _____	f. _____
3. Hopelessness	a. _____	a. _____
	b. _____	b. _____
	c. _____	c. _____
	d. _____	d. _____
	e. _____	e. _____
	f. _____	f. _____
4. Revenge	a. _____	a. _____
	b. _____	b. _____
	c. _____	c. _____

5. Fear   a. _____   a. _____
                   b. _____   b. _____
                   c. _____   c. _____
                   d. _____   d. _____

6. Ambivalence   a. _____   a. _____
                   b. _____   b. _____
                   c. _____   c. _____
                   d. _____   d. _____
                   e. _____   e. _____

7. Empathy   a. _____   a. _____
                   b. _____   b. _____

8. Guilt   a. _____   a. _____
                   b. _____   b. _____
                   c. _____   c. _____
                   d. _____   d. _____

9. Titillation   a. _____   a. _____
                   b. _____   b. _____

10. Vulnerability   _____   _____

Research on Dealing with Secondary Trauma

Key points	Reference
Step 1: Awareness	
Impact on professional behavior: • Disassociating from work • Distance self from others • Loss of empathy • Misuse of countertransference • Question the viability of a client's story • Retraumatizing clients in overt and subtle ways	Salston & Figley, 2003
Recognize the symptoms of secondary trauma: • Anxiety • Avoidance of people or activities • Despair • Excess vigilance • Feelings of hopelessness • Feelings of reexperiencing of the event • Having unwanted thoughts or images of traumatic events • Increased fatigue or illness • Nightmares • Reduced productivity • Social withdrawal • Persistent anger and sadness • Numb feelings	International Society for Traumatic Stress Studies, 2005; Pearlman & Saakvitne, 1995a; Salston & Figley, 2003
Step 2: Dealing with secondary trauma Steps to mediate effects of secondary trauma: • Attend professional workshops about traumatology. • Give yourself permission to accept the existence of trauma. • Relax when client recalls trauma. • Destigmatize secondary trauma through organizational recognition and acknowledgment.	Salston & Figley, 2003; Stamm, Varra, Pearlman, & Giller, 2002

Key points	Reference

Step 3: Treating secondary trauma
Treatment methods:
- *Critical incident stress debriefing (CISD)* — Armstrong, O'Callahan, & Marmar, 1991
  A 3- to 5-hour process led by a qualified mental
  health professional 24–48 hours after the incident.
  A professional leader facilitates the process.
  The CISD stages are as follows:

  1. The introductory phase—understand rules and
     confidentiality to join a CISD group; make clear the
     supportive event in which members both express
     their feelings and listen to one another.
  2. The fact phase—share facts about what one saw,
     heard, smelled, touched, and did during the incident
     (as an eyewitness of the client's trauma); or bring the
     therapist's feeling back to the here and now and share
     the connection between the client's trauma or recall
     and the therapist's feeling.
  3. The thought phase—state first thoughts in reaction
     to the most stressful part of the incident.
  4. The feeling phase—join the group to discuss emotional
     reactions about the incident; question how it was felt
     at the time of the incident as compared to the here-
     and-now feeling.
  5. The sharing phase—join other members to discuss
     particular physical or psychological symptoms since
     the incident.
  6. The normalization phase—discuss stress response
     syndrome and explain that it is typical or "normal"
     to initially have reactions or symptoms when exposed
     to a trauma event.

- *Sensory-based therapy* — Harris, 1995
  Using our five senses (hearing, vision, touch, taste, smell)
  to develop strategies to relax the body and spirit.

- *Multiple stressor debriefing* — Armstrong et al., 1991
  After handling a traumatic event, use debriefing
  sessions of 1.5 hours to address feelings and reactions.
  The model has four stages:

  1. Disclosure of events—acknowledge the stress
     experiences; identify the primary incident.
  2. Feelings and reactions—ventilate feelings about
     incidents; teach that strong feelings are a normal
     response; discuss symptoms bothering the participants.

Key points	Reference
3. Coping strategies—discuss normal and pathological responses to stress; help participants develop ways to care for themselves. 4. Termination—discuss positive aspects of incident; say good-bye; discuss transition to home.	

• *Vicarious trauma treatment approach*
  1. Personal strategies
    • Identify healing activities (e.g., creating art, playing music, keeping journal).
    • Maintain personal life.
    • Use relaxation and imagery that centers on themes of safety, trust, esteem, intimacy, and self-control.
  2. Professional strategies
    ■ Identify disrupted schemas.
    ■ Share feelings and/or thoughts with mental health professionals or debrief in personal psychotherapy.
	Pearlman & Saakvitne, 1995a

Step 4: Prevention
Prevent secondary trauma:

• Agency strategies (e.g., sufficient release time, safe physical space, access to employee assistance program) • General coping strategies (e.g., self-nurturing, seeking connection) • Personal strategies (e.g., respecting your limits, taking time for self-care) • Professional strategies (e.g., balanced caseloads, accessible supervision, planned assignment rotation) • Work-life balance between home, work, self, and others • Appropriate diet, exercise, relaxation techniques • Social support	Pearlman & Saakvitne, 1995b; Saakvitne & Pearlman, 1996; Salston & Figley, 2003

Tips for Parents and Professionals

Self-Care Tips for Parents

- Connect with nature.
- Find a balance of work, home, self, and others.
- Find a spiritual or religious connection.
- Find relationships that provide social support.
- Laugh and find ways to play.
- Learn about typical parent responses to their child being abused so that you can be aware of changes in yourself (e.g., emotional, physical).
- Maintain a healthy lifestyle: eat an appropriate diet, and get adequate exercise and sleep.
- Participate in a support group for parents whose children have been sexually abused.
- Practice positive affirmations.
- Practice relaxation techniques like yoga, meditation, and progressive relaxation.
- See a mental health professional.
- Spend time with a special pet.
- Take breaks away from your child.
- Talk to someone you trust about your experience; don't keep it inside (e.g., your family, a friend).

Self-Care Tips for Professional Interviewers

- Connect with nature.
- Find a balance of work, home, self, and others.
- Find a spiritual or religious connection.
- Find relationships that provide social support.
- Laugh and find ways to play.
- Learn to recognize the symptoms of secondary trauma and burnout.
- Limit your exposure to client trauma.
- Maintain a healthy lifestyle: eat an appropriate diet, and get adequate exercise and sleep.
- Participate in a support group for mental health workers.
- Practice positive affirmations.
- Practice relaxation techniques like yoga, meditation, and progressive relaxation.
- Spend time with a special pet.
- Take breaks during the workday.
- Talk to someone you trust at work about your cases.
- Use the workplace employee assistance program.

Self-Care for Professionals Who Work with Abused Children and Survivors

- Don't hesitate to seek support. Although you should maintain confidentiality of case information at all times, it is helpful to disclose discomfort and personal feelings of trauma to supervisors and other mental health professionals, particularly to someone who understands the impact of trauma work. This can be done through individual therapy or support groups.
- Engage in basic self-care, such as eating an adequate diet and getting exercise to address indirect trauma.
- Remember that indirect trauma is not an indication of a weak professional; it is a normal, human reaction and the result of being able to empathize with clients.

- Take part in activities and relationships that remind you of the good in humanity.
- Vary your caseload as much as possible by working with different populations or cases with varying degrees of severity.
- Working with victims of abuse shines light on negative experiences and often produces negative information about people, family, and the world. You need to integrate this new information into existing cognitive schemas, such as by receiving advanced training in sexual abuse treatment, good supervision, and personal therapy, and learning to balance your personal and professional life.

CHAPTER 8

Conclusion: Advocacy Efforts

Focused on the roles and responsibilities of professionals, parents, and the general public, this concluding chapter addresses the most recent concerns in the area of child sexual abuse. These concerns include the role of adults in preventing child molestation, recent research in recovered memory work, the use of research-based evidence to support best practices, the presentation of an advocacy plan, and the development of professional specialization in the field of child sexual abuse. The chapter concludes that prevention work should be targeted at both children and adults. Advocacy efforts should stress the importance of the commitment from all people, including helping professionals, legislators, parents, and the general public, to protecting children. The chapter provides an example agenda of a child advocacy center in Hong Kong to highlight the use of research materials to support community work to stop child sexual abuse.

Roles of Adults in Child Protection

Many policies and programs in the United States and other countries focus on preventing child sexual abuse. The most common policies include the legal definition of child sexual abuse, particularly to establish the illegality of sexual contact with children younger than a certain age even if the child agrees to such involvement. In most countries, child sexual abuse is legally defined as a criminal act against children younger than eighteen years old. However, the penalties vary depending on the age of victim, the level of force, both the relationship and the age difference between the victim and the perpetrator, and the type of sexual abuse—for example, more severe sentencing generally applies to acts against younger children, with the use of more force, in a familial relationship, and with the presence of penetration.

Because the age of the child victim is a determining factor both for the legality of the act and the penalties of the offense, the age definition of *child* and proof of age in different countries must be closely examined when the definition of sexual abuse is legally enforced. Appendix 8A outlines the various interpretations of the child's age in child sexual abuse laws and policies in selected countries. Among those countries in which reaching the sixteenth birthday represents the average age of the child's ability to give consent to have sex, a child older than sixteen but not mature enough to consent, such as those having mental or physical challenges, can be defined as a vulnerable witness in a child sexual abuse investigation (Crown Prosecution Service, 2011). Most laws protect children younger than eighteen from sexual exploitation by clearly defining child sexual abuse. For example, in Germany, sexual intercourse is legal from the age of fourteen in most cases, with the exception of cases where the older partner is older than eighteen and is "exploiting a coercive situation," or offering compensation, in which case the younger partner must be older than eighteen; if younger, he or she may be defined as a child victim. In addition, it is illegal for someone older than twenty-one to have sex with someone younger than sixteen if the older person exploits the younger person's "lack of capacity for sexual self-determination" (AVERT, 2009, n.p.). In many instances in international laws, the age of a child sexual abuse victim may not be defined by a specific age but may be considered with other factors, such as the age difference between the perpetrator and the victim or the victim's developmental and mental capacity.

Because the age of a victim is an important legal factor in determining whether a situation is child sexual abuse, adults must be responsible for knowing their legal responsibilities to prevent any wrongdoing. However, child sexual abuse prevention programs have largely focused on educating children in how to differentiate good and bad touching, how to say no to abuse, how to respond to abuse by telling adults, and how to protect their own bodies. Although they may not intend it, all these child-focused programs can place children in a defensive mode, which can generate negative internal thoughts, such as "I can't trust adults anymore," "Abuse is my fault if I didn't prevent it or escape from it," "I am responsible for my own welfare," and "I shouldn't be abused if I am smart." Such irrational thoughts result when adults do not assume their responsibilities as the primary actors in prevention. Educating children is important, but educating adults is essential to preventing criminal acts against children. To successfully combat child sexual abuse, adults must partner with members of the helping and legal profession to engage in education and prevention efforts. In addition, adults must increase their knowledge of child sexual abuse and provide reassurance to children to alleviate their fears and their tendency to engage in self-blame and negative internal thoughts.

Another aspect of prevention is educating children to respect their own bodies and those of other people. Learning to respect others' bodies will stop the vicious cycle of abuse by preventing children from using force to abuse their peers or siblings and eventually becoming adult abusers. Societal values that focus on mutual respect must be taught beginning in preschool or kindergarten and should be continued through to high school graduation. In this way, children who grow up in a supportive environment are more likely to become responsible, law-abiding adults.

Another aspect of child sexual abuse prevention lies in the correctional system. In general, when child abuse criminals are punished but not treated, they are more likely to repeat their acts because their mentality has not changed. It is important that these perpetrators be reformed through rehabilitative programs and intensive counseling processes. Without individualized therapeutic processes, jailed perpetrators will reenter society with the same attitudes toward children. However, with support from social workers, professional counselors, and peer counselors, those who have made mistakes in the past can go through a meaningful healing process for self-transformation.

To transform their mentalities, abusers must acknowledge how they misused their power and understand the differences between children and adults, including power differentials between adults and children, differential abilities in recognizing the effect of sexual acts on one's physical and mental health, differential perceptions toward sexuality, and gratification differentials. Perpetrators use irrational explanations to accept their sexual acts on children, such as "children like it, too," without realizing that the children are powerless and feel too scared to say no. Even if children do say no, perpetrators still minimize the impact of their sexual act by saying that children will learn to like it. However, perpetrators do not possess the knowledge or awareness that children are not mature enough to understand the effect of the sexual relationship on their physical and mental health. Perpetrators act out of a personal desire and rationalize that children are not aware of their right to refuse sexual advances, or they believe that children can give consent. Even in a case when an underage child agrees to a sexual act with an adult, the child who later regrets the agreement can report the incident as sexual abuse. A perpetrator, without knowing that child sexual abuse can have a long-lasting effect on victims, does not understand the impact of knowledge differentials between a child and an adult. Children may have a skewed perception about sexual gratification because of their developmental immaturity. It is also common that the adult perpetrator's sexual gratification derives from the pain of the child victim, even though the perpetrator may believe that he or she is bringing pleasure to the child.

Some organizations (e.g., the North American Man-Boy Love Association; the René Guyon Society) argue that children also possess sexual drives and should be allowed to enjoy sex with their peers and other adults. This view is not accepted by general society because it does not take into consideration the factors of adult-child differentials that place children at risk of exploitation and abuse. If all adults were to take part in child sexual abuse prevention, there would no longer be adult perpetrators in any children's lives. When children are nurtured and cared for, they learn how to respect others. Adults who care about children's normal development do not steal children's trust and love to reach their own sexual gratification.

Research in Recovered Memory Work

The most recent research in child sexual abuse is related to the controversies of false memory syndromes in abuse recalls, particularly when someone has led an adult survivor to believe that a childhood trauma experience such as sexual abuse has caused the survivor's current relationship problems. One aspect of this is the interviewer's misuse of leading questions that guide a person to disclose sexual abuse that has not actually occurred. According to McNally and Geraerts (2009), there are three categories of recovered memories: a repressed memory is a recall of an emotionally traumatic event that can be expressed in a safe environment only after a long period of time, a false memory is a recollection of wrong information based on highly suggestive or erroneous triggers, and a nontraumatic experience has not been previously perceived as a trauma but has been repressed and recollected usually with reminders outside of psychotherapy. Recovered memories are not always reliable or accurate because other facts and perceptions may "contaminate" the recall. Mixing information from other sources or using information told previously by another source may also cause false memory syndromes.

It is important to note that there is a possibility that an adult client may recall an episode of childhood sexual abuse as nontraumatic when it occurred. McNally and Geraerts (2009) point out that in many child sexual abuse cases, the abuser often makes the child believe that nothing in their relationship is abnormal, especially when the abuse does not involve physical violence or coercion. The use of bribery, for example, can make the victim feel that the sexual act is an exchange of services; therefore, the victim feels responsible for his or her own abuse as an active participant. Also, a person might perceive the sexual abuse as mutual sex play or an exploratory experiment, which he or she did not register as a traumatic event. McNally and Geraerts (2009) also state that one trigger to recall is a suspicion that "emotional problems and life difficulties are attributable to blocked memories of sexual abuse" (p. 130). In addition, individuals may be "unexpectedly reminded of events that they believe they had not thought about for many years" (p. 130). In other words, this type of recovered memory may not be a repression or perceived as a trauma, but it brings the residual effects of abuse to the surface.

Because there is a possibility that a recovered memory is not true, Geraerts et al. (2009) suggest that professionals be cautious about using recovered memory as a base to prove childhood sexual abuse. For example, professionals must follow several clinical observations and evaluations: the context of the memory recall, including when the recall was first initiated; the cognitive functioning of the individual during the recall; the individual's susceptibility to audio and visual images in memory recalls across situations; the cognitive mechanisms used in the recall and in other situations; and the clinician's assessment of individual differences in memory recall.

It is possible that once a person has verbalized the memory in detail, whether true or false, he or she perceives that the recall is absolutely true. Piper (2008) found three reasons behind false accusations: being coached by others, having a misconception about the incident, and erroneous thinking toward nonsexual abuse. When an interviewer solicits information through leading and other nonprofessional questions, those errors may lead the interviewee to believe that abuse has occurred. So, interviewers should not use leading and suggestive questions; should never use their authority to press for answers; should not use reinforcement to encourage disclosure; should not use disconfirmation to correct the child's answer, particularly when the interviewee says, "I don't know"; and should not invite the interviewee to speculate an answer. Tips for professionals in recovered memory work are provided in appendix 8B.

Trend of Research-Based Practice

Research in child sexual abuse has focused on the variety of skills used, from investigations to treatment techniques. A literature review of research conducted in the past decade along with some previously published influential research shows that research- and evidence-based data support the application of various techniques in interviewing and treating child sexual abuse victims.

The literature has demonstrated that evidence must be provided to support the skills used in the field. Although most evidence-based research projects have targeted changing the behaviors of abusers through treatment in physical abuse and neglect cases, studies on child sexual abuse focus mainly on forensic interview skills, credibility of the child's statement, and the validation of abuse. Some studies use data to connect children's credibility to the validation process. Occasionally, quantitative evidence is presented to support treatment outcomes, but few studies have directly focused on the effect of sexual abuse on abused children's future sexual behavior problems or abusive behaviors.

Chaffin and Friedrich (2004) found it difficult to disseminate evidence-based practice information in the field of child protection for several reasons:

- Lack of funding and resources to support practice-based research
- Lack of advocacy to take new and technologically advanced initiatives
- Lack of incentives that link rewards to outcomes
- That child protection agencies are not viewed as learning organizations
- Gap between practice and research
- Ineffective marketing strategies to adopt tested models
- Practitioners not being perceived as research consumers
- Lack of measurable policies to prove positive outcome delivery
- Lack of leadership that supports research in a high-caseload environment
- Lack of a work unit focusing on research development

These barriers hinder the development of research skills for practitioners and frontline workers. In addition, professionals whose caseloads are high may not see a need to further their knowledge or refine their skills when they perceive that the immediate response is to rescue the child. The importance of evidence-based practice should be communicated widely in the child welfare field and be addressed in major staff meetings and at national conferences so that professionals hear more about progress made in the field from tested data and responses directly from the client system.

Research is not limited to quantitative data analyses; it should include narratives or stories told by clients. From their voices, we can understand the perspective of those who use services. These voices should be collectively presented to protect clients' confidentiality, especially with respect to experiences of children and adolescents who need professional counseling during the process. For adult survivors, the storying method provides a chance for the clients to express concerns and suggestions through reciting past experiences and recollections of materials, to warn potential abusers, and to stop abuse. It is crucial that a systematic approach be used to recite significant findings so that information that clients provide is not considered anecdotal. In the literature, the systematic analyses of stories from survivors can provide insight for practitioners to help clients enhance their self-development (Morrison & Ferris, 2009), develop intervention strategies (Beveridge & Cheung, 2004), and identify the process toward transcendence (Hunter, 2009). According to Draucker and Martsolf (2008), story-ing steps can include the following:

1. Start the story with the pieces not yet told.
2. Unfold the story for the first time.
3. Shield the story that identifies the secrecy in the abuse.
4. Revisit the story that reexamines abuse as an account of life experience.
5. Share the story that delivers an important message to explain life forces.

These narrative steps can help survivors reexamine their suffering from different angles so that they can move on to the next stage of life and use the information they gain to help them improve their outlook on life.

Advocacy Efforts

Child sexual abuse is taboo in cultures around the world, but it is also taboo to talk about child sexual abuse publicly. In an effort to normalize the prevention and education components of child sexual abuse, this section provides an example of advocacy efforts in Hong Kong, which aim for communities to collaborate to partake in action and education to uphold and enact the principle of children's rights to protect their dignity for their physical and psychological development. The author is a member of the Advocacy Committee of Hong Kong's End Child Sexual Abuse Foundation, which facilitates discussions and actions in the process of carrying out advocacy activities to promote preventive work in child sexual abuse. The advocacy agenda presented in appendix 8C aims to encourage people around the world to begin advocacy efforts in this important area. Appendix 8D provides research support for in-depth analysis of current information related to child sexual abuse prevention and treatment.

Child Sexual Abuse as a Practice Specialization

Child sexual abuse has been a subject of study in social work, counseling, psychology, medicine, and nursing. Recently, it has become an important training subject for police, lawyers, prosecutors, judges, forensic examiners, and other professionals who work closely with children. It also draws the attention of educators, child-care workers, and pastoral personnel because of the nature of their work that involves children. Learning the skills used in child sexual abuse investigations is helpful for Child Protective Service workers whose role may or may not involve investigations, because these skills will help them understand the process of investigations, which is a step in the broader process of child protection. Before they start in this specialized area of work, professionals must learn about commitment in child protection work by reviewing relevant codes of ethics, identifying steps to protect children, being sensitive in handling abuse disclosures, and continuing a daily routine of self-care. Professionals who work with children are obligated to increase their knowledge base and skill set regarding child sexual abuse in an effort to protect children and advocate for them and their families so that they can receive sensitive and appropriate services (appendix 8E). In conclusion, the mission of this book is to bring all of us together to work to protect children. As a team, all adults—professionals and the general public—must work together to prevent and stop child sexual abuse.

Age Definitions of Child Sexual Abuse in Selected Countries

Country	Age of consent	Age of the child victim and connection to penalty
Australia	16–18, varies by state	Child sexual abuse laws vary greatly by state. For example, in Victoria, offenders who are fewer than 2 years older than victims over the age of 10 are not always prosecuted. If the perpetrator is a caregiver of the victim, then it is an offense to sexually penetrate a person under the age of 18, even though the age of consent is 16 in Victoria (Victoria Consolidated Legislation, http://www.austlii.edu.au/au/legis/vic/consol_act/ca195882/s45.html).
Canada	16	A close-in-age exemption allows youth aged 14 to 16 to consent to sexual activity with a partner within five years of age. An accused cannot use the defense of consent if that person is in a position of trust or authority over the child under the age of 18 (Victims of Violence, http://www.victimsofviolence.on.ca/rev2/index.php?option=com_content&task=view&id=331&Itemid=21).
China	14	Higher penalties apply if the victim is under age 14 (National Laws, Legislation of Interpol Member States on Sexual Offences against Children, http://www.interpol.int/Public/Children/SexualAbuse/NationalLaws/).
Hong Kong	16	Punishment for child sexual abuse in China depends on the age of the victim (under age 18), the type of abuse (i.e.: incest, rape, gross indecency), and the gender of the victim and perpetrator. Higher penalties apply if the victim is under age 13 (National Laws, Legislation of Interpol Member States on Sexual Offences against Children, http://www.interpol.int/Public/Children/SexualAbuse/NationalLaws/csaHongKongChina.pdf).

Country	Age of consent	Age of the child victim and connection to penalty
Mexico	12–18, depending on state laws	Any type of sexual act performed on a person under the age of 12 is punishable by 2 to 5 years in prison. If physical or moral violence is used or if the offense is committed through the abuse of trust, the sentence is increased by half. Laws are not as clear on consensual sex with adolescents between 12 and 18. However, if consent is obtained through deceit, punishment ranges from 3 months to 4 years in prison (Código Penal Federal, Mexico, http://www.diputados.gob.mx/LeyesBiblio/pdf/9.pdf).
New Zealand	16	In New Zealand, it is an offence to have a sexual connection with a person under the age of 16. If the perpetrator is in a position of authority, it is an offence to have a sexual connection with a person under the age of 18. Both parties can be prosecuted if under the age of 16 (Parliamentary Counsel Office, New Zealand Legislation, http://www.legislation.govt.nz/act/public/1961/0043/latest/DLM329212.html?search=ts_act_crimes+act_resel&p=1).
Singapore	16	Any person who partakes in sexual activity with a person under the age of 16 is guilty of a sexual abuse offence (Singapore Statutes Online, Attorney-General's Chambers, http://statutes.agc.gov.sg/non_version/html/homepage.html).
United Kingdom	16	CSA laws vary based on jurisdiction, although the age of consent is 16 throughout. Punishment for CSA varies based on the age differences between the perpetrator and victim, type of sexual connection, gender, and position of authority. Higher penalties apply if the victim is under 13 (Crown Prosecution Service, http://www.cps.gov.uk/legal/s_to_u/sentencing_manual/s9_sexual_activity_with_a_child/).
United States	14–18, depending on state	U.S. laws and punishments of CSA vary greatly by state. This variation includes age of consent (mostly at age 18), age difference between partners, type of sexual contact, position of authority, gender, etc. (National Laws, Legislation of Interpol Member States on Sexual Offences against Children, http://www.interpol.int/Public/Children/Sexual Abuse/NationalLaws/csaUSA.pdf).

Tips for Professionals: Recovered Memory Work

Technique to avoid	Example	Consequence	Suggested technique
Using suggestive questions to validate abuse	Avoid leading questions, such as "Do you think you may have been abused?"	Client may be directed to think there must be something in the past that explains current problems.	Use open-ended phrasing, such as "Tell me more."
Accepting the client's answer with no further validation	Avoid accepting the answer immediately when it is about sexual abuse, for example, "Wow, it must be the sexual abuse that made you feel this way."	Client does not think about how to differentiate truth from false memories.	"You said that what we just said reminded you of being sexually touched by your stepdad. When did you start to have this memory about your stepdad's behavior?" "You said you just started to recall this memory—what triggered this memory?"
Using sexual abuse scenarios to explain unexplainable symptoms	Avoid saying, "Your symptoms are very similar to a case I handled before in which the client was sexually abused."	Client may place him- or herself into scenarios and think that sexual abuse can explain similar symptoms.	"You seem to suffer from something. Let's talk more about it." Use examples that are helpful to the client, such as "I know it's hard to talk about something that bothers you."

Technique to avoid	Example	Consequence	Suggested technique
Urging to recall memories	Avoid saying, "Before you continue with your childhood story. May I ask …?"	Client who starts to recall childhood issues needs time to describe the entire incident. Do not ask questions in between description, which will interrupt the chain of thoughts and break the recalled "picture" into pieces.	If the client stops during the full account of memory recall, say, "Take a deep breath before you continue," or "I don't know what's in your mind now, but it seems to be hurtful. Tell me more."
Encouraging disclosure with reinforcement	Avoid giving the client any reinforcement or verbal praise when disclosing abuse (e.g., "You are right," "Perfect," "Wow, you are incredible").	Client may think that you agree with what he or she has said.	Use affirmative encouragers to help the client talk more: "I hear you," "I am with you," "I feel intense feelings here."
Correcting client's terminology	Avoid correcting the client's use of vocabulary to describe abuse.	Client may think that you do not understand the impact of sexual abuse on the client.	Listen to the entire story first, then clarify terminology with the client: "You said he touched your privacy. Where or what is your privacy?"
Rejecting client's answer	When a client says, "I don't know" or "I don't remember," do not reject the client's answer by saying, "You don't remember? I'm sure you do," or "You don't know? How could you not know?"	Client may think that he or she must have another answer.	"When you say 'I don't know' what do you mean?" "When people say 'I don't remember' they may actually forget, or not want to recall the memory, or feel uncomfortable talking about it. When you said, 'I don't remember' what exactly did you mean?"

Technique to avoid	Example	Consequence	Suggested technique
Not being honest about false memory syndrome	When client asks whether the professional believes the account of sexual abuse, the professional does not react to the question; when asked about reasonable doubt, the professional denies the possibility of false memory syndrome.	Client does not know whether the recall may be a false memory.	Be neutral in the assessment process (e.g., "I know you are telling me things that you strongly believe are true. You may also know that it's hard to validate abuse at this point. It's possible that other sources have contaminated your memory. Let me ask you some more information to help you validate your case." Also, ask whether the client has heard of false memory syndrome: "There has been a debate about false memory syndrome when abuse is involved in recall. Are you aware of that? Let me explain what it is."
Assessing client with hypnosis techniques	Do not use hypnosis to validate abuse. Avoid guiding the client to think about abuse if the client does not disclose the information initially.	The client is led to believe that he or she was abused.	Use free-association techniques such as writing or sharing stories about past experience. If the client discloses sexual abuse, ask the client to validate specific details.

Advocacy Agenda:
An Example from Hong Kong

The following agenda was developed by the author for the End Child Sexual Abuse Foundation.

Leadership

Comprehensive Legislative Reform

Start a Zero Tolerance to Child Sexual Abuse campaign (Zero Tolerance Campaign) for the safety of children and culturally sensitive treatment for sexual abuse victims. The Hong Kong society wishes to see legislation:

Define "child sexual abuse" in clearer terms in the crime ordinance.

Modify the presumption that a boy younger than age fourteen is incapable of sexual intercourse or penile penetration. Boys younger than fourteen should be charged with an offense for rape or incest if and when sufficient evidence is presented.

Support the creation of a new system in which professionally trained guardians (e.g., social workers) provide emotional and practical support for sexual abuse victims in criminal proceedings. Appoint a Department of Justice member to keep contact with victims to inform them what is going on and to address any concerns.

Pass a Youngsters' Act, similar to the Children's Act enacted in the United Kingdom in 1989, in which victims are given the right to have adult guardians—lawyers or social workers—speak on their behalf in court hearings.

Provide comprehensive explanations to victims or/and their families about the plea-bargain option.

Facilitate the use of the victim impact statement with clear guidelines.

Pass laws on mandatory psychotherapy and/or counseling for adolescent and adult sex offenders.

Establish a system of sex offender management in the interest of their rehabilitation and the safety of children and teenagers.

Establish a commission for children and young people to do the following:

- Study the development of youngsters' sexuality
- Advise the Education Bureau on sex education
- Improve the public's understanding of the rights of child sexual abuse victims
- Implement a "blue card" system to issue blue cards to certify the qualifications and suitability of people to work with children under the age of 18 to ensure safety for children under their care (see http://www.ccypcg.qld.gov.au/employment/index.html)

Information Collection and Dissemination

Conduct regular research studies to maintain a solid, rational, and strong advocacy agenda and position. These studies aim to maintain updated information on child sexual abuse and dispatch it to legislators, judges, police officers, school principals, social workers, teachers, and health and mental care professionals to enhance their understanding of victims' trauma and effective interventions. Information from child sexual abuse laws should be disseminated to parents.

Collaboration

- *Sex offender registry*: To work with individuals and organizations to hasten the creation of a registry and to ensure that the Security Bureau will implement it with effective measures, such as the blue card system.
- *Victims' recovery*: To collaborate with the government and coordinate with other nongovernmental organizations to ensure that the

child sexual abuse victims and their families in need of psychotherapy and/or counseling receive appropriate services, especially
when governmental services are not readily available.

- *Media influence*: To inform the local media on a regular basis
  about the advocacy position in preventing child sexual abuse so as
  to educate the public and expedite the government's action
  toward successful implementation of needed services for the prevention and treatment of child sexual abuse in our society.

Monitor and Respond

Continue to

- Work with multidisciplinary professionals in the areas of child
  sexual abuse.
- Use current literature to identify culturally sensitive measures in
  preventing child sexual abuse and provide data to support effective treatment modalities.
- Remain open to the community's needs for educational programs
  in child sexual abuse prevention.
- Respond to public policy issues that may affect child sexual abuse
  victims and their families.

Codes of Ethics: Examples Related to Child Protection

American Academy of Child and Adolescent Psychiatry. (N.d.) *Code of ethics*. Retrieved from http://www.aacap.org/galleries/AboutUs/ CodeOfEthics.PDF. (Provides clarification on the Code of Ethics and attaches case vignettes with principal references.)

American Association of Christian Counselors. (N.d.). *The hope of survivors: Excerpts from American Association of Christian Counselors (AACC) Code of Ethics*. Retrieved from http://www.thehopeof survivors.com/aacc_ethics.asp. (Identifies the most relevant pieces in the AACC Code of Ethics that directly address the prohibition of sexual relationships with former and current clients and a strong condemnation of sexual misconduct.)

American Psychological Association. (2010). *Ethical principles of psychologists and code of conduct*. Retrieved from http://www.apa.org/ethics/ code2002.html. (Standard 3 specifies sexual misconduct; standard 4 deals with privacy and confidentiality.)

Archdiocese of Los Angeles. (2005). *Report to the people of God: Clergy sexual abuse Archdiocese of Los Angeles, 1930–2003*. Retrieved from http://archdiocese.la/protecting/pdf/White_Paper-10-12-2005.pdf. (Provides the history of clergy sexual abuse of minors in the Los Angeles archdiocese and describes the archdiocese's policy for child sexual abuse treatment and prevention, which includes confidentiality, zero tolerance, and victim assistance.)

Archdiocese of St. Louis. (2003). *Code of Ethics Conduct for clergy, employees, and volunteers working with minors*. Retrieved from https://www .parishsports.net/iwaa/code-of-ethical-conduct.pdf. (Identifies a

wide range of policies relevant to helping people who work with
minors in the church, including volunteers and addresses ethical
misconduct, sexual misconduct, confidentiality, and work ethics.)

Association for the Treatment of Sexual Abusers. (2001). *Professional code
of ethics.* Retrieved from http://www.atsa.com/pdfs/COE.pdf. (This
association represents professionals committed to the welfare of
clients, the community, and colleagues. Based on a foundation of
theory and research, knowledge and skill, professions are self-regu-
lating. An inherent assumption in this process is the adoption and
adherence to a set of standards or code of ethics that facilitates evaluation of each professional act as to its positive or negative impact
on constituents. This Code of Ethics is intended to reflect scientifically informed and professionally accepted beliefs regarding professional behavior and conduct. At the same time, such a code must
also satisfy the prevailing community standards.)

Australian Hypnotherapists Association. (N.d.). *Code of ethics.* Retrieved
from http://www.philiphollingdale.com/AHA%20Code%20of%20
Ethics.pdf. (Provides basic ethical principles and guidelines for AHA
members working with clients in contexts in which issues related to
false memories of childhood sexual abuse may arise.)

Child Justice League. (2004). *The Holy See and the Convention on the
Rights of the Child in the Republic of the Philippines.* Retrieved from
http://www.catholicsforchoice.org/topics/international/documents/
2005shadowreportphilippines.pdf. (Assesses how the laws of the
Holy See affect the Roman Catholic Church in the Philippines and
compromise the laws of the Philippines that seek to protect children; presents examples of clergy abuse; shows how laws of the Holy
See undercut national laws, leaving children and young people at
risk of abuse by clergy.)

Irish Association of Humanistic and Integrative Psychotherapy. (2005).
Code of ethics and practice for psychotherapists. Retrieved from
http://www.iahip.com/pdf/Bye-Law%203%20-%20March%
202005.pdf

Kane, M. N. (2006). Risk management for Catholic priests in the United
States: A new demand from the code of pastoral conduct. *Journal of
Religion and Spirituality in Social Work, 25*(1), 47–67. (Focuses on

research on risk management strategies, aiming to supply information to priests who provide pastoral counseling, spiritual direction, and clinical-type intervention to parishioners and those seeking pastoral services.)

National Association for Social Workers. (2010). *Code of ethics.* Retrieved from http://www.socialworkers.org/pubs/Code/code.asp. (Section 1.09 specifies no sexual contact with any individuals to whom they exercise authority including clients, former clients, or workers under their supervision.)

The Society of Homeopathy: Northampton. (2004). *Code of ethics and practice.* Retrieved from http://www.homeopathy-soh.org/for-homeopaths/documents/10CodeofEthicsApr04.pdf (Describes the code of ethics for homeopathic treatment, standards that are established and maintained for professional homeopaths, and the working definition of child sexual abuse and management of cases.)

Advocacy Efforts in Child Sexual Abuse: Legislation, Policy, and Practice around the World

Monit Cheung, PhD, LCSW, Jackie Duron, LMSW, and Amanda Ford, MSW, for Advocacy Committee, End Child Sexual Abuse Foundation

In order to strengthen child protection endeavors, the ZERO TOLER-ANCE CAMPAIGN proposed by the End Child Sexual Abuse Foundation in Hong Kong aims to plan and implement advocacy efforts to stop child sexual abuse. This report summarizes recent literature in order to provide direction for advocates to examine their effort in promoting legislation, policy, and treatment practices that can prevent child sexual abuse. It is divided into nine areas: 1) defining child sexual abuse; 2) presumption regarding perpetrator's age; 3) children's advocates; 4) victim impact statements; 5) mandatory therapeutic services for offenders; 6) sexual offender registry; 7) dealing with the offender; 8) apology as an intervention; and 9) global trends.

Defining Child Sexual Abuse

Defining child sexual abuse is an important step in improving and further-ing the development of advocacy, research, and treatment (Haugaard, 2000). Statutory definitions function in a civil manner to provide protec-tion and in a criminal manner to specify prohibitions and penalties (Faller, 1993). Ost (2004) demonstrates the importance of clearly expanding on the definition of an offense by examining amendments to the United Kingdom's Sexual Offences Act of 2003, which included specific provisions regarding sexual grooming in order to extend the protection of children. In a review of legal rulings regarding the term "sexual abuse of a minor," Herat (2009) states that the definition is unambiguous because the plain meaning of the law and prior precedent supports it. Literature suggests the use of a clear and comprehensive definition of child sexual abuse in advocacy efforts in reference to a review of definitions from Australia, Canada, the United States, and United Kingdom.

In Australia, the National Child Protection Clearinghouse (2010) provides this definition:

> Sexually abusive behaviour refers to any sexual activity between a child and an adult or older person (five or more years older). Sexual activity includes fondling genitals, masturbation, oral sex, vaginal or anal penetration by a penis, finger or any other object, fondling of breasts, voyeurism, exhibitionism and exposing or involving the child in pornography. (Higgins, 1998; James, 1994; US National Research Council, 1993)

The Australian Institute of Family Studies (2009) has found the following:

> Defining sexual abuse is a complicated task. Although some behaviours are considered sexually abusive by almost everyone (e.g., the rape of a 10-year-old child by a parent), other behaviours are much more equivocal (e.g., consensual sex between a 19-year-old and a 15-year-old), and judging whether or not they constitute abuse requires a sensitive understanding of a number of definitional issues specific to child sexual abuse.
>
> A very general definition of child sexual abuse has been proposed by Tomison (1995): "the use of a child for sexual gratification by an adult or significantly older child/adolescent" (p. 2). Similarly, Broadbent & Bentley (1997) defined child sexual abuse as: "any act which exposes a child to, or involves a child in, sexual processes beyond his or her understanding or contrary to accepted community standards" (p. 14). Sexually abusive behaviours can include the fondling of genitals, masturbation, oral sex,

vaginal or anal penetration by a penis, finger or any other object, fondling of breasts, voyeurism, exhibitionism and exposing the child to or involving the child in pornography (Bromfield, 2005; US National Research Council, 1993).

However, unlike the other maltreatment types, the definition of child sexual abuse varies depending on the relationship between the victim and the perpetrator. For example, any sexual behaviour between a child and a member of their family (e.g., parent, uncle) would always be considered abusive, while sexual behaviour between two adolescents may or may not be considered abusive, depending on whether the behaviour was consensual, whether any coercion was present, or whether the relationship between the two young people was equal (Ryan, 1997). Thus, in this paper, different definitions are presented for each class of perpetrator: adults with no familial relationship to the child, adult family members of the child, adults in a position of power or authority over the child (e.g., teacher, doctor), adolescent or child perpetrators, and adolescent or child family members.

In Canada, the Department of Justice (2005) states:

Sexual abuse and exploitation of children and youth occurs when an older child, adolescent or adult takes advantage of a younger child or youth for sexual purposes, including for participation in prostitution, pornographic performances and in the production of pornography. Sexual abuse and exploitation is perpetrated on children of all ages, from infancy to adolescence.

In this fact sheet, "children" refers to individuals under the age of 12 and "youth" refers to individuals under the age of 18.

The Canadian statutes on sexual offences (2008) read as follows:

Sexual interference

151. Every person who, for a sexual purpose, touches, directly or indirectly, with a part of the body or with an object, any part of the body of a person under the age of 16 years

(a) is guilty of an indictable offence and liable to imprisonment for a term not exceeding ten years and to a minimum punishment of imprisonment for a term of forty-five days; or

(b) is guilty of an offence punishable on summary conviction and liable to imprisonment for a term not exceeding eighteen months and to a minimum punishment of imprisonment for a term of fourteen days.

R.S., 1985, c. C-46, s. 151; R.S., 1985, c. 19 (3rd Supp.), s. 1; 2005, c. 32, s. 3; 2008, c. 6, s. 54.

Invitation to sexual touching

152. Every person who, for a sexual purpose, invites, counsels or incites a person under the age of 16 years to touch, directly or indirectly, with a part of the body or with an object, the body of any person, including the body of the person who so invites, counsels or incites and the body of the person under the age of 16 years,

(a) is guilty of an indictable offence and liable to imprisonment for a term not exceeding ten years and to a minimum punishment of imprisonment for a term of forty-five days; or

(b) is guilty of an offence punishable on summary conviction and liable to imprisonment for a term not exceeding eighteen months and to a minimum punishment of imprisonment for a term of fourteen days.

R.S., 1985, c. C-46, s. 152; R.S., 1985, c. 19 (3rd Supp.), s. 1; 2005, c. 32, s. 3; 2008, c. 6, s. 54.

Sexual exploitation

153. (1) Every person commits an offence who is in a position of trust or authority towards a young person, who is a person with whom the young person is in a relationship of dependency or who is in a relationship with a young person that is exploitative of the young person, and who

(a) for a sexual purpose, touches, directly or indirectly, with a part of the body or with an object, any part of the body of the young person; or

(b) for a sexual purpose, invites, counsels or incites a young person to touch, directly or indirectly, with a part of the body or with an object, the body of any person, including the body of the person who so invites, counsels or incites and the body of the young person.

Legislation in the United Kingdom lists offenses under the Sexual Offences Act 2003 as:

Child sex offences

9. Sexual activity with a child
10. Causing or inciting a child to engage in sexual activity
11. Engaging in sexual activity in the presence of a child
12. Causing a child to watch a sexual act
13. Child sex offences committed by children or young persons
14. Arranging or facilitating commission of a child sex offence
15. Meeting a child following sexual grooming etc.

In the United States, the American Psychological Association (n.d.) finds:

There is no universal definition of child sexual abuse. However, a central characteristic of any abuse is the dominant position of an adult that allows him or her to force or coerce a child into sexual activity. Child sexual abuse may include fondling a child's genitals, masturbation, oral-genital contact, digital penetration, and vaginal and anal intercourse. Child sexual abuse is not solely restricted to physical contact; such abuse could include noncontact abuse, such as exposure, voyeurism, and child pornography. Abuse by peers also occurs.

The Child Welfare Information Gateway (2011) provides this explanation of the definition of sexual abuse/exploitation:

All states include sexual abuse in their definitions of child abuse. Some states refer in general terms to sexual abuse, while others specify various acts as sexual abuse. Sexual exploitation is an element of the definition of sexual abuse in most jurisdictions. Sexual exploitation includes allowing the child to engage in prostitution or in the production of child pornography.

Presumption Regarding Perpetrator's Age

Children and adolescents today are engaging in sexual behaviors at earlier ages. In a study of 11 to 17 year old males, Zolondek, Abel, Northey, and Jordan (2001) found that the average age of onset for sexualized behaviors was 10–12 years old. Among all 11 to 17 year olds, 60% reported engaging in the offense of child molestation (Zolondek et al., 2001). These behaviors also include earlier sexual intercourse and the capacity for use of manipulation (Noonan & Charles, 2009).

Premature coital onset for youth relates to earlier pubertal development. Several studies have found that adolescent males today are reaching puberty at earlier ages (Johnson & Tyler, 2007; Juul, Magnusdottir, Scheike, Prytz, & Skakkebaek, 2007; Karpati, Rubin, Kieszak, Marcus, & Troiano, 2002). With specific statistics, Johnson and Tyler's (2007) study found that adolescents (boys and girls) are reaching puberty by 12-13 years old and are more likely to initiate sex earlier than youths reaching puberty at later ages.

With internet and media exposure at an early age, both males and females perceive through these sexual materials that they are mature enough to engage in sexual discussions and activities, which leads to an early onset of sexual activities before puberty. A study investigating the effect of internet access on sexual initiation found that males with internet access initiated sexual intercourse at an average age of 12 years old (Kraus & Russell, 2008).

Sexual initiation at earlier ages among adolescents has many implications for policies and programs seeking to maintain the health and safety of youths. In the UK, the Sexual Offences Act of 1993 changed the common law presumption to reflect that boys under the age of 14 are capable of sexual intercourse, and therefore, sexual offenses (Sexual Offences Act, 2003; Thomas, 2009). In Australia, the government has recognized adolescent or child perpetrators by stating:

Adolescent or child perpetrators: Sexual abuse is indicated when there is non-consensual sexual activity between minors (e.g., a 14-year-old and an 11-year-old), or any sexual behaviour between a child and another child or adolescent who—due to their age or stage of development—is in a position of power, trust or responsibility over the victim. For example, any sexual activity between a 9-year-old and a 15-year-old would be considered abusive as the age difference between the two children leads not only to marked developmental differences, but also disparities in their levels of power and responsibility within their relationship. Another example of abuse due to an imbalance of power would be sexual activity between two 15-year-olds, where one suffers an intellectual disability that impairs their ability to understand the behaviours that they are engaging in. Normal sexual exploration between consenting adolescents at a similar developmental level is not considered abuse.

Adolescent or child family members: Sexual abuse occurs when there is sexual activity between a child and an adolescent or child family member that is non-consensual or coercive, or where there is an inequality of power or development between the two young people. Although consensual and non-coercive sexual behaviour between two developmentally similar family members is not considered child sexual abuse, it is considered incest, and is strongly proscribed both socially and legally in Australia. (Australian Institute of Family Studies, 2009, pp. 3–4)

Furthermore, the Australian government has found that a person's age alone does not make one incapable of sexual intercourse (Crimes Act of 1900, 2012). The law repealed the ruling that a male under the age of 14 years is unable to copulate (Crimes Act of 1958, 2012).

In Canada, the government has recognized that non-consensual sexual activity initiated by minors as young as 12 years old is criminal (Department of Justice Canada, 2005). The Canadian legislation has been amended as follows:

Bill C-7, the Youth Criminal Justice Act replaced the Young Offenders Act on April 1, 2003. The new Act holds young people (12–17 years old) accountable for their actions through interventions that are fair and in proportion to the seriousness of the offence committed. The new Act recognizes the interests and needs of victims, and the importance of rehabilitation and reintegration of young offenders (including adolescent sex offenders).

In this fact sheet, "children" refers to individuals under the age of 12 and "youth" refers to individuals under the age of 18. A child who is 12 or 13 can consent to sexual activity with another child who is 12 years of age or more but under 16, no more than two years older, and is neither in a position of trust or authority towards the younger child, nor a person with whom the younger child is in a relationship of dependency. All non-consensual sexual activity is a criminal offence, regardless of age. (Department of Justice Canada, 2005, p. 11)

In the United States, the minimum age for recognizing a juvenile sex offender ranges from 6 to 12 years of age, with some states maintaining no statutory minimum (Martin & Pruett, 1998). The Office of Juvenile Justice and Delinquency Prevention has found that 16 percent of juveniles who commit sexual offenses are younger than 12 years of age (U.S. Department of Justice, 2009). Generally, the criminal justice system is faced with reports of sexual offenses committed by youth that "increases sharply at age 12 and plateaus after age 14" (U.S. Department of Justice, 2009).

Providing prevention programs for preadolescent males and females is important so that youths can better understand their personal boundaries and responsibilities, receive adequate sex education, and prevent later risk of peer sexual abuse and later revictimization (Maker, Kemmelmeier, & Peterson, 2001; Stermac, Reist, Addison, & Miller, 2002). Efforts to prevent child sexual abuse can be strengthened by focusing on teaching self-protection skills that provide knowledge in identifying and resisting inappropriate touching (Kenny et al., 2008). Comprehensive prevention programs include offender prevention and target parents and the entire environment that surround youth (Wurtele, 2009). In a review of studies focusing on juvenile offenders in Australia and the United States, Hanser and Mire (2008) found that many juvenile offenders share a history of sexual abuse and successful intervention programs included cognitive models of therapy, groups, and a systemic model involving parents.

Children's Advocates

Children are often afraid of court proceedings because they are unaware of what will happen, who will be there, or where they are going (Tisdall, Bray, Marshall, & Cleland, 2004). In a study of children involved in legal cases, children with their own legal representation had more favorable experiences of the court process and found their interaction with the court to be less intimidating than children without individual legal representation (Tisdall et al., 2004). A child-centered approach to including children in proceedings is one that promotes their well-being, upholds children's rights, fulfills legal responsibilities, improves services, enhances decision-making, supports children's protection, and develops children's skills (Sinclair & Franklin, 2000). A child-focused perspective to children's active participation in decision-making is an integral piece in effecting lasting change and is achieved when children believe that their involvement makes a difference (Sinclair & Franklin, 2000). Legal representatives, court advocates, and guardians can strengthen the judicial process through efforts focused on supporting the child through legal proceedings.

Australia

The Child Witness Support Program in Australia is a program provided to child victims and witnesses through a community based non-profit organization (Roylance & Scanlon, 1999). The organization receives referrals from the police department and criminal justice system and provides services to children aimed at educating and supporting them through the court process (Roylance & Scanlon, 1999). Based on legislation that allows a support person to be present with a child at court while they are giving evidence, volunteers may accompany a child (Roylance & Scanlon, 1999; Evidence (Protection of Children) Act, 2003). The Australian legislature appoints a separate legal representative for any child alleged to be a victim of child abuse (Nicholson, 2003). The representative is charged with acting independently and in the best interest of the child, informing the court of the child's wishes, and supporting the child by minimizing trauma related to judicial proceedings (Parliament of Australia, 2003).

Canada

In Canada, the Office of Child and Youth Advocate (n.d.a) is mandated to provide assistance to children and youth who are receiving services under the Child, Youth & Family Enhancement Act or Protection of Sexually Exploited Children's Act. These services include representing the rights, interests, and wishes of children and youth; providing education, including an explanation of rights and proceedings; and may include legal representation (Office of Child and Youth Advocate, n.d.b).

United Kingdom

The Children and Family Court Advisory and Support System (Cafcass, 2010) in the United Kingdom has the primary purpose of protecting children, which has been outlined by several legislative acts, including the Children's Act and Criminal Justice and Court Services Act 2000. Children's guardians have the role of representing the child's best interests, considering and expressing the child's wishes, and facilitating the child's participation in proceedings (Cafcass, 2010). A children's guardian or guardian *ad litem* also has a duty to select a solicitor, a legal representative, for the child (Cafcass, 2006).

United States

In the United States, the 1974 Child Abuse and Prevention Act mandated that each child be assigned a guardian *ad litem* to act in the best interests of the child (U.S. Department of Justice, 2006). The Victims of Child Abuse Act of 1990 further required that a court-appointed special advocate (CASA) be available to every child victim in need (U.S. Department of Justice, 2006). While state legislation may vary on the roles and responsibilities of CASA volunteers, general duties include collecting case information, monitoring the case, providing mediation, identifying resources, and may include legal representation (U.S. Department of Justice, 2006). A consumer satisfaction survey of CASA volunteers found that attorneys and judges experienced high satisfaction with advocate involvement, and overall, there is a request for more volunteers to be appointed to cases (Litzelfelner, 2008). Weisz and Thai (2003) found that when CASA volunteers were involved in a case, more extensive information was provided to the court. CASA volunteers may help reduce the number of placements and court continuances a child experiences, and they help the child access more services as compared to children without CASA support (Litzelfelner, 2000).

Victim Impact Statements

A victim impact statement (VIS) is written or oral testimony describing the effect of a crime on a victim (National Center for Victims of Crime, 1999). A victim impact statement expresses the direct and indirect effects of an offense, which provides recognition of the victim in the judicial hearing and information of consideration for sentencing and most importantly, stresses the victim's need for services (van der Merwe, 2008). Victim impact statements are a tool for increasing awareness among offenders, implementing the processes of closure and healing for victims, and introducing communication in the sentencing domain (Roberts, 2003).

Australia, the United Kingdom, and the United States all follow a justice model allowing for VISs in criminal proceedings (Erez & Rogers, 1999). In Canada, a written statement provided by a victim or authorized representative reflects the physical, psychological, social, and financial consequences of the crime endured by the victim (Department of Justice Canada, 2001). In the United States, child victims may submit drawings, models, or other expressions that are appropriate to their age and development (National Center for Victims of Crime, 1999). Edwards (2009) argues that there are three principles which support the use of victim impact statements (VPS) in the United Kingdom: supporting the victim's healing, improving sentencing by facilitating appropriate compensation, and enhancing service quality by strengthening the public's confidence in the criminal justice system.

While several countries have passed legislation that allows victims of any criminal offense to present a VIS, other countries, such as Israel, limit the use of VISs. In Israel, only victims of sexual abuse are allowed to participate in a criminal case (Leichtentritt & Davidson-Arad, 2002). The Israeli law provides the victim of sexual abuse with an opportunity to indirectly participate in proceedings through the submission of a statement to a social worker (Leichtentritt & Davidson-Arad, 2002). The Israeli directive requires social workers to provide a VIS for all children who have been sexually abused (Leichtentritt & Davidson-Arad, 2006).

Victim impact statements acknowledge a victim's personal reaction to a crime and promote systemic change by linking public policies regarding victim's rights and court proceedings (Propen & Schuster, 2010). Victim impact statements contribute to collective understanding and strengthen systemic change through the facilitation of advocates, who provide guidelines for a model statement and inform victims of judicial standards (Propen & Schuster, 2010). A victim impact statement recognizes the dignity of an individual, which enhances the sensitivity and integrity of the justice system (Beukman, 2010).

Judges and prosecutors reported that VISs have helped them better understand individual experiences of crime and victimization (Erez & Rogers, 1999). The accessibility to the victim's experience through statements gives practitioners empathy for the extent of the human impact resulting from the crime (Erez & Rogers, 1999). In Canada, judicial officers find VISs to be useful and incorporate them in sentencing, but they suggest that more victims should be informed of their right to submit one (Department of Justice Canada, n.d.). A victim impact statement should be a subject of consideration in all cases of children under age sixteen because of the potential to illustrate the profound impact of the offense on the victim, including emergent needs (van der Merwe, 2008).

Mandatory Therapeutic Services for Offenders

Several studies have found that sexual offender treatment reduces recidivism (Hanson et al., 2002; Lösel & Schmucker, 2005; Reitzel & Carbonell, 2006; Scalora & Garbin, 2003). Mandatory treatment is a provision in the legislation of many countries, including Australia (Macgregor, 2008), Canada (Macgregor, 2008), the United Kingdom (Macgregor, 2008; Mandeville-Norden, Beech, & Hayes, 2008), and the United States (Schaffer, Jeglic, Moster, & Wnuk, 2010). Research comparing the effects of mandatory treatment with voluntary treatment is limited and remains an area for further exploration (Jones, Pelissier, & Klein-Saffran, 2006).

In the United States, many states follow a best-practice guideline for the type of treatment offered (Schaffer et al, 2010). Cognitive-based therapy models are the most popular and widely used in sexual offender treatment (Calley, 2007; Hanser & Mire, 2008; Macgregor, 2008). Some of the other models of treatment include the transtheoretical model of change (Patel, Lambie, & Glover, 2008), motivation counseling (Patel et al., 2008), multi-systemic therapy (Letourneau et al., 2009), and family-focused interventions (Letourneau et al., 2009).

Individuals in an outpatient program in the United States reported usefulness in treatment that targets relapse prevention and motivation for sexual behaviors (Levenson, Prescott, D'Amora, 2009). Internal and external motivators increase an offender's voluntary entrance into treatment (Jones, 2006). Implementing motivational programs that strive to enhance awareness of sexual offense issues could promote greater offender participation (Jones, 2006). Programs that are sensitive to the various cultural backgrounds of offenders are more successful in reducing sexual recidivism (Macgregor, 2008). Australia and New Zealand have moved toward more integration of family involvement (Macgregor, 2008). Treatment should focus on the individual offender's needs, which may include psychological, substance abuse, and intellectual disability issues (Hayes et al., 2009).

Treatment that views the offender as part of a system could explore system dynamics (Shursen, Brock, & Jennings, 2008). Advocates support rehabilitative approaches that are strengths-focused to really meet the need of sex offenders (Letourneau et al., 2009). Rehabilitation should target improving the offender's well-being foremost and then reducing reoffending (Birgden, 2007). Treatment focused on well-being meets the physical, social, and psychological needs of the offender and prepares them for leading a life that is socially acceptable and meaningful for them (Birgden, 2007).

When considering public policy, the cost of programs that reduce sexual recidivism should be considered alongside the benefits, specifically the reduction in sexual violence (Caldwell, 2010). Programs that provide short-term treatment to control behaviors have more probable effectiveness (Caldwell, 2010). Sex offender treatment, as a strategy for addressing sexual offenses, is effective and cost efficient (Birgden, 2007).

Sexual Offender Registry (SOR)

Although specific components vary based on the implementing country (United Kingdom, United States, France, Canada, Australia, or Republic of Ireland), sex offender registers (SORs) intend to protect the public from crimes that are sexual in nature by requiring designated offenders to register with authorities and/or report pertinent information. Failure to comply with specified standards may be associated with its own set of enforceable sanctions (Levenson, Fortney, & Baker, 2010; Murphy, Fedoroff, & Martineau, 2009; Salerno et al., 2010; Schiavone & Jeglic, 2009; Thomas, 2009).

The United Kingdom's (UK) Sexual Offences Act 2003 replaced the 1997 version with the same name. The law requires in-person notification of address changes for sex offenders within three days as well as a new annual verification meeting. Under the legislation, police officers are able to photograph and fingerprint registrants, and the time periods for registration are halved for young offenders (Roche, 2008; Thomas, 2009).

Currently, Canada maintains two registries for sex offenders: The Ontario Sex Offender Registry (2001) and the National Sex Offender Registry (2004). Placement of an offender on the registry in Canada lasts anywhere from 10 years to life and includes relevant information such as a photograph, age, address, victim characteristics, and the type of offense. Distinctive from the SORs in the United States, Canada does not make the information readily available to the general public, which may be indicative of the higher compliance with SOR orders in Canada than in the United States (Murphy et al., 2009; Petrunik & Deutschmann, 2008).

Precursors to current legislation in the United States include the Jacob Wetterling Act (1994) that required the maintenance of a sex offender name and address roster by law enforcement agencies, and Megan's Law (1996) that allowed agencies to make the aforementioned information available to the public (Bonnar-Kidd, 2010; Levenson, 2003; Levenson et al., 2010; Schiavone & Jeglic, 2009; Tregilgas, 2010).

In the United States in 2006, the Sex Offender Registration and Notification Act mandated that an online registry of sex offenders, including juvenile offenders convicted in adult criminal court and/or those at least 14 years of age involved in sex offenses with aggravating circumstances, be created by all states. Although these minimum standards apply to all states, individual state differences exist, such as North Dakota's authorization to place juveniles as young as seven years of age on SORs. In actuality, only four states—Indiana, Ohio, Oklahoma, and South Dakota—explicitly prohibit the registration of offenders under age 14. States may also differ in their classification systems and hierarchical risk levels used to cluster sex offenders into groups. Although collaborative efforts of practitioners and agencies to disseminate information through community notification may differ based on locality, the requirements listed under the Adam Walsh Child Protection and Safety Act 2006 (AWA) maintained uniform statewide requirements which necessitate the display and maintenance of online SORs with links to the national website. A uniform classification system based on offense is mandated through the act to obtain specific state funds. Additional requirements include: kidnapping as a registerable sexual offense regardless of sexual intent, registering of sex offenders in any jurisdiction (not just residence but also work, school, etc.), making failure to register a punishable felony, requiring a sex offenders' entire criminal history not just sexual offenses, and providing funds to support the enforcement of the laws (Bonnar-Kidd, 2010; Levenson, 2003; Salerno et al., 2010; Schiavone & Jeglic, 2009; Tregilgas, 2010).

Housing restrictions and buffer zones that prohibit sex offenders from living in proximity to locales where children are in attendance—daycares, parks, schools, bus stops, etc.—vary based on state legislation. Variations include the imposed distance, the terminology used, and the specific infraction (Schiavone & Jeglic, 2009). Suggestions aimed at creating successful approaches to sex offender supervision include the multi-faceted, collaborative efforts of the centrally supportive court and administrative office directives. Stemming from this hub are the auxiliary roles of pre-sentence officers, probation officers, collateral contacts, treatment providers, forensic teams, and law enforcement (Palmiotto & MacNichol, 2010). Other proposed models include the use of Child Abuse Assessment Centers (to determine if abuse has occurred) and Child Advocacy Centers (to support and advocate for the child, the family, and investigational integrity). These models implement the use of independent centers that coordinate social services and law enforcement efforts (Wiley, 2009).

Dealing with the Offender

The unique population of juvenile offenders further complicates the discussion and legal protocols pertaining to sexual offenses and the subsequent practices. Common characteristics of juvenile offenders, both in the United States and Australia, include psychological trauma, mental health diagnoses, dysfunctional family backgrounds, childhood abuse, and experiences of incest. Treatment programs that incorporated group-based efforts and family involvement were associated with the prevention of further offenses. Similar programs have been utilized in both the United States and the United Kingdom. Yet, evaluative research is still lacking in the area of juvenile sex offender treatment (Hanser & Mire, 2008).

Laws centered on maintaining public protection, such as the Parole (Extended Supervision) Amendment Act 2004 of New Zealand, provide court-imposed community supervision for sexual offenders with child victims—in this specific instance up to ten years after prison release. The specific intent of the act is to assess the risk of re-offense against children. Assessments must include considerations for the rights of the offender as well as prevention of harm to both the victim and to society. Current practices for assessment include a computer-scored measure based on official records of New Zealand offenders. Empirical measures include the Automated Sexual Recidivism Scale and the Sex Offender Need Assessment Rating, yet challenges surround the utilization of these tools and their proposed predictive accuracy (Vess, 2009; Watson & Vess, 2007).

In Australia, the Crimes (Serious Sex Offenders) Act 2006 legally allows the continued detainment of sex offenders in prison after sentence completion on the basis of predicted risk. The Crimes (Serious Sex Offenders) Act 2006 makes this allowance based upon continued community threat of an offender after release (Crimes Act 2006, 2006; Keyzer, 2009). The Serious Sex Offender Monitoring Act of 2005, introduced by the Victorian government in Australia, provided post-detention supervision of offenders through an Extended Supervision Order that enforces monitoring through the Adult Parole Board. Restrictions on residential choice, leisure activity, and place of employment are also possible through this legislation because of the high recidivism rate, which is assessed by experts in the fields of psychology and forensic psychiatry (Birgden, 2007; Ducat, Thomas, & Blood, 2009; Wood & Ogloff, 2006).

In the UK, the Children Act 1989 represents the major legislative piece aimed at promoting child welfare. Through this act, a court may grant an Emergency Protection Order (EPO) to provide safety for a child who is at risk for subsequent sexual abuse by authorizing removal from harmful locales and prevention of removal from hospitals and/or other places deemed safe. Alternatively, an exclusion requirement may be incorporated into a protective order to remove the perpetrator, rather than the child, from the home. If it appears that a child is not in need of urgent intervention, a Child Assessment Order may be requested to determine if a child's health or development warrant concern. Supervision and care orders might also be provided by the court to place a child under the supervision of local authorities, including probation officers. A supervision order is in effect for one year (may be extended to three) and does not remove a child from the family home; rather, a supervisor oversees the child and coordinates many facets, including assessments, medical proceedings, and/or treatment. Subsequently, a care order confers parental responsibility to the intended authority. These orders, which are long-term in nature, generally pertain to children who are less than eighteen years of age (Griffith & Tengnah, 2007; Keating, 2006).

The Children Act 2004 incorporated collaborative efforts of key agencies through local safeguarding children boards (LSCB), which promote child welfare to safeguard children. Abuse allegations and interventions are developed and conducted in accordance with the guidelines established by the LSCB. The act facilitates the tracking of children's progression in England and Wales through the establishment of electronic databases that include information on the areas of health, education, standard of living, social activity, and potentially criminal behavior. Overall, the aim is to improve multi-disciplinary collaboration, integrate planning, increase accountability, and coordinate services (Griffith & Tengnah, 2007; Keating, 2006; Penna, 2005; Roche, 2008).

The UK's Sexual Offences Act 2003 provides a greater degree of protection for children and other vulnerable populations by conceptualizing the terms *consent* and *sexual*, creating specific offenses, strengthening notification requirements, and managing offenders. Through this Act, the age of consent is 16 years with no distinction for sexual orientation. The term, sexual, is defined as activity that is sexual in nature (i.e., intercourse or masturbation) or that may be sexual because of the circumstances or purposes of a person in relation to it, such as touching clothing (Griffith, 2010; Perry, 2009; Roche, 2008).

The Sexual Offences Act 2003 also deals specifically with offenders who are involved in sexual exploitation (i.e., intentionally facilitating proceedings of trafficking people within or out of the UK for the purposes of sexual exploitation). Even if the intended individual is not sexually exploited, any British person involved in exploitive proceedings may be prosecuted in any country in the world with a maximum penalty of fourteen years imprisonment. The act increases the minimum duration of a restraining order to five years (Elvin, 2008; Gillespie, 2005b; Law Library of Congress, 2007; Perry, 2009; Roche, 2008).

Responses to offenders and the distribution of justice differ in European jurisdictions from that of the United States. The U.S. perspective often stems from a community protection approach from which the aforementioned legislations develop sex offender registries, community notification procedures, and civil commitment, lending itself to punitive punishment strategies. Though the UK and Canada have similar registration and notification programs, measures often stem from restorative justice initiatives. Canada, in particular, developed the Circle of Support and Accountability program that emerged as a faith-based initiative to reintegrate high-risk sex offenders into the community. The program of trained volunteers provides supports for offenders and holds them accountable to program guidelines. The UK has utilized the Thames Valley Project, developed by Quakers, which is very similar to Canada's circle program. Alternately, continental Europe often focuses on the medicalization of deviant behavior. Switzerland, an exception, utilizes the punitive-driven means of the United States blended with a hybrid of medical approaches, while German legislation provides for a 10-year sentence for dangerous recidivists (Petrunik & Deutschmann, 2008).

Apology as an Intervention

Australia, Canada, the United Kingdom, and the United States support the use of apology in judicial proceedings and have passed legislation to protect the use of apology from civil liability (Vines, 2008). The exchange of remorse and apology between an offender and a victim may be ideally suited for a mediation setting (Bibas & Bierschbach, 2004). The issuance of an apology in a civil mediation process could support an authentic apology, which could lead to victim healing (Taft, 2000).

Australian jurisdictions have legislated youth justice conferencing whereby an offender meets with a victim during a 60-90 minute conference that is structured to include introductions, narrations, and agreement negotiations (Hayes, 2006). A convener or mediator, police officer, and support persons for both victim and offender are present during the exchange, which includes the offender's acknowledgement of harm, issuance of an apology, victim's expression of impact, and agreement for restitution (Hayes, 2006). Hayes (2006) suggests that youth justice conferencing engages the offender and victim, may provide more justice than court exchanges, and may lead to reductions in offending. Mediation between victims and juvenile offenders may promote positive outcomes for victims, juveniles, and the general public (Nugent, Williams, & Umbreit, 2003).

The issuance of an apology should include an acknowledgment of the offense, willingness to admit wrongdoing, and willingness to avoid repeating such behaviors (Regehr & Gutheil, 2002). In a meta-analysis of research evaluating the use of apology, Fehr, Gelfand, and Monisha (2010) found a positive impact of apology on promoting victims' feeling of forgiveness. While forgiveness may be an outcome, Jenkins (2006) proposes that the sole of use of apology can be potentially harmful because it is a perceived tie to anticipation of forgiveness; therefore, it is suggested that the concept of restitution be used to promote a better understanding of restorative justice practices.

Restorative justice practices provide an opportunity for victims to have their voice heard while the offenders acknowledge responsibility (Choi & Severson, 2009). Sexual violence victims in one study sought an opportunity to share their story and receive public affirmation as part of their therapeutic journey (Des Rosiers, Feldthusen, & Hankivsky, 1998). It is found that an apology provides the impetus for the victims to regain their voice and may reduce recidivism among offenders (Petrucci, 2002).

Apology is considered an important practice that fosters social interactions and relationships between the offender and the victim, as well as involving their communities in the healing process (Bibas & Bierschbach, 2004).

Global Trends

Since the United Nations established the Convention on the Right of the Child, many countries have begun to address issues related to sexual abuse and the rights of one of the world's most vulnerable populations—children (Child Safe International, 2007).

Sri Lanka has tightened legislation in terms of making pedophilia a non-bailable offense and permitting child video testimony during court to minimize psychological trauma for the affected children (Fredette, 2009).

Cambodia's constitution protects children from sexual exploitation and affords children the rights to life, education, and protection during wartime. In 1996, a law was passed to suppress kidnapping, trafficking, and exploitation of children, predominantly in the area of child prostitution. Thailand has created laws protecting children, individuals under the age of 18, from being involved in prostitution. In Indonesia, the age of consent for sexual activity is 16 years old for females and 18 years old for males, and someone who forces sexual intercourse on another person may be punished with up to 12 years imprisonment (Child Safe International, 2007).

Additionally, the changing socio-cultural dynamics resulting from the influence of globalization have caused new emergent challenges related to the topic of child sexual abuse, including the disbursement of child pornography via the internet, internet grooming of abuse victims, and child sexual tourism, which all require a careful tailoring of legislative action to ensure the safety of children. The case of child pornography is illustrative of these complexities, as evidenced by discrepancies in legislative development and enforcement. Although the distribution and production of pornographic images of a child was curbed by legislation in the 1970s and 1980s, possession was not made illegal in the United Kingdom until 1988 and in many other countries until the 1990s—1992 (Norway), 1993 (Germany, France, and Canada), 1994 (Austria), and 1995 (Denmark and Belgium) (Fredette, 2009; Gillespie, 2005a; Graupner, 2004; Oswell, 2006). Although significant steps have been made to prevent the maltreatment of children, continued support and the development of relevant legislation will strengthen efforts to end sexual abuse and deal with offenders accordingly.

As with the development of any legislative documents and their subsequent decisions, balancing the role of the state in the lives of families with the rights of children to be protected from harm within families is a difficult area to navigate and requires much consideration (Bendall, 2009). As globalization presents unique challenges in the prevention and intervention of abuse, international legislation, as evidenced by the United Nations Convention on the Rights of Children with its intent to create an obligatory duty to assist the defenseless, has become a critical necessity in preserving the rights of children worldwide (Fredette, 2009; Sneddon, 2003). Individual countries utilize a variety of tactics to prevent and intervene in instances of identified sexual abuse, including information dissemination, treatment modalities, social services, court rulings, and offender registries.

Conclusion

The ZERO TOLERANCE CAMPAIGN proposed by the End Child Sexual Abuse Foundation in Hong Kong supports advocacy efforts to stop child sexual abuse. The ZERO TOLERANCE CAMPAIGN supports legislation, which will address issues discussed in this report of literature. The following actions steps are proposed:

1. Define child sexual abuse within the Crime Ordinance in terms that are clear and inclusive of all sexual offenses against minors.
2. Amend the age of presumption governing sexual ability of minors to 12 years of age. This change would recognize the ability for minors to engage in sexual intercourse and would allow youth under the age of 14 to be charged with sexual offenses and receive proper treatment.
3. Authorize independent legal representation when appropriate and advocates to be appointed for minors involved in child sexual abuse cases. The legal representative would provide a voice for the

child and act in their best interest in cases related to familial abuse that may impact guardianship. The advocate would support the child through court proceedings and ensure that the child understands the complexity of the legal system.

4. Allow victims of child sexual abuse to provide a victim impact statement or appropriate expression (drawing, model, etc.) in criminal proceedings. This measure provides the victim with an opportunity to share the impact sexual abuse has had. This will strengthen the judicial system by recognizing the victim and promoting offender reintegration in the community.

5. Improve therapeutic services and access for offenders so that treatment is available and an integral component of the offender's return to the community.

6. Implement mediation exchanges between the victim and offender, which allow the offender to express remorse for his/her actions and apologize.

7. Initiate a sexual offender registry as part of offender accountability and community protection.

Annotated Bibliography
Child Sexual Abuse, 1998–2011

To provide evidence to support the suggestions and protocols offered in this book, I have identified research-based literature to support each area of practice. The following represents the most recent (from the past decade) or most representative and influential literature in the field that addresses research and evidence-based data that support various techniques in interviewing and treating victims of child sexual abuse. The annotations are summarized from the original source and/or library abstract. Materials are organized into ten areas: (1) anatomical dolls and drawings in forensic interviews, (2) child sexual abuse assessment, (3) child sexual abuse interviews, (4) child witnesses, (5) disclosure, (6) disproportionality of minorities in child welfare, (7) false allegations in child sexual abuse, (8) law and legal actions, (9) treatment, and (10) other investigative interview literature.

These summaries closely adhere to the original abstracts. Please use the summaries here as references only and cite only from the original sources. This list is representative, not comprehensive, of research in the field between 1998 and 2011. Because research in child sexual abuse is updated constantly, readers should check their library or the Child Welfare Information Gateway (at http://www.childwelfare.gov) for additional and updated resources.

1. Anatomical Dolls and Drawings in Forensic Interviews

Anatomical Drawings

Aldridge, J., Lamb, M. E., Sternberg, K. J., Orbach, Y., Esplin, P. W., & Bowler, L. (2004). Using a human figure drawing to elicit information from alleged victims of child sexual abuse. *Journal of Counseling and Clinical Psychology*, *72*(2), 304–316.

Ninety forensic interviews were conducted with children age 4–13 who were suspected victims of child sexual abuse. Structured interviews were performed by six police officers and followed the National Institute of Child Health and Human Development procedures. The protocol consists of the introductory, rapport-building, transitional, free-recall, and directive questioning phases. Gender-neutral anatomical drawing was used with additional structured questions. Results demonstrated that the anatomical drawing yielded 18 percent of the interview details attained; educing 27 percent of the interview details among four- to seven-year olds, 19 percent among eight- to ten-year olds, and 12 percent from eleven- to thirteen-year olds. Anatomical drawings may be useful during forensic interviews, especially with younger children after disclosure, but they may affect the accuracy of the forensic details obtained.

Everson, M. D., & Boat, B. W. (2002). The utility of anatomical dolls and drawings in child forensic interviews. In M. L. Eisen, J. A. Quas, & G. S. Goodman (Eds.), *Memory and suggestibility in the forensic interview* (pp. 383–408). Mahwah, NJ: Erlbaum.

This chapter highlights the findings and limitations of several influential studies on the use of props and anatomical dolls in forensic interviews with children. It also addresses new directions in the use of mnemonic aids, such as drawings, to augment recall.

Holmes, L. S., & Finnegan, M. J. (2002). The use of anatomical diagrams in child sexual abuse forensic interviews. *National Center for the Prosecution of Child Abuse Update Newsletter*, *15*(5).

The article provides an overview of anatomical diagrams in child sexual abuse forensic interviews. Four distinct purposes of anatomical diagrams have been addressed: (1) identifying body parts; (2) concluding whether a child can distinguish between the two genders; (3) helping the child designate where sexual abuse took place; and (4) clarifying discrepancies in the child's statements. Some researchers suggest that the anatomical diagrams should portray nude male and female figures, whereas others believe that the genitalia in the diagram should be covered with a swimsuit. The use of diagrams with swimsuits as a standard tool may create an environment of shame and secrecy with the idea that genital regions should be covered.

Katz, C., & Hershkowitz, I. (2010). The effects of event drawing on children's accounts of sexual abuse. *Child Maltreatment, 15*(2), 171–179.

This study was designed to explore the effects of event drawing during investigative interviews on the detail of the accounts made by children. The sample included 125 children from age 4–14 who were alleged victims of sexual abuse. Children who used drawing disclosed more free-recall information about the abusive events, including details about people, actions, time, and location of the incidents, than did children who did not participate in drawing. The effect of drawing was evident regardless of the child's age, gender, type of abuse, and time delay. The findings suggest that event drawing can enhance children's forensic statements in child abuse investigations.

Anatomical Dolls

Boat, B., Everson, M., & Holland, J. (1990). Maternal perceptions of non-abused young children's behavior after the children's exposure to anatomical dolls. *Child Welfare, 69*(5), 389–400.

The controversy surrounding the use of anatomical dolls requires further examination of children's experiences during structured interviews. In the current study, children age 3–5 were exposed to anatomical dolls in a structured interview and, after two weeks, were observed by their mothers. Although many mothers felt that their children's awareness of body parts was increased, none reported that these behaviors could be indicative of sexual abuse rather than their experience in the interviews.

Cheung, M., & Boutte-Queen, N. M. (2010). Assessing the relative importance of the child sexual abuse interview protocol items to assist child victims in abuse disclosure. *Journal of Family Violence, 25*(1), 11–22.

This study identifies the importance of using the Child Sexual Abuse Interview Protocol for multiple disciplines to obtain detailed information of what the alleged child victims say and claim, as well as the concurrence of multiple professionals about the relevance of items in the protocol in their practice. A survey with one hundred items based on the Child Sexual Abuse Interview Protocol was self-administered by thirty-six professionals working at a child advocacy center. These respondents unanimously believed that it was very important for interviewers to complete two specific items during the course of an investigative interview: "showing the interviewer is listening to the child" and "showing patience with the child." This study identifies the importance of using a comprehensive interview protocol for multidisciplinary professionals who work with alleged victims of child sexual abuse. The use of these hundred items will enhance the effectiveness of conducting a one-time interview to avoid repeated interviews. This finding dissolves the myth that multiple disciplines brought forth diverse opinions and instead encourages the concept of working together as a team.

Dickinson, J. J., Poole, D. A., & Bruck, M. (2005). Back to the future: A comment on the use of anatomical dolls in forensic interviews. *Journal of Forensic Psychology Practice*, 5(1), 63–74.

Major concerns of using anatomical dolls with child-related crimes include level of child cognitive development, quantity and quality of information, that the demonstration of dolls may offer suggestive techniques, biases of interviewers, and possible memory distortion in the process of interpretation.

Everson, M. D., & Boat, B. W. (1997). Anatomical dolls in child sexual abuse assessments: A call for forensically relevant research. *Applied Cognitive Psychology*, 11, S55–S74.

The authors offer a critique of arguments against the use of anatomical dolls in forensic evaluations and examine the efficacy of doll use in interviews and the sexually suggestive nature of anatomical dolls. They also recommend design features for future research.

Faller, K. C. (2005). Anatomical dolls: Their use in assessment of children who may have been sexually abused. *Journal of Child Sexual Abuse*, 14(3), 1–21.

This article provides a literature review on research findings concerning anatomical dolls, advantages and disadvantages of their use in forensic interviews, and various roles of anatomical dolls during interviews. One focus of anatomical doll research is whether the use of dolls is sexually suggestive. A second focus is whether the use of such dolls brings any additional value to the forensic interview. Research studies recommend that the best-practice uses of anatomical dolls are to demonstrate what happened, as an anatomical model to be used as a body map for identification of body parts, and most commonly as a memory stimulus.

Hlavka, H. R., Olinger, S. D., & Lashley, J. L. (2010). The use of anatomical dolls as a demonstration aid in child sexual abuse interviews: A study of forensic interviewers' perceptions. *Journal of Child Sexual Abuse, 19*(5), 519–553.

This article discusses dolls as demonstration aids. Children are often willing and able to use such dolls throughout the interview process for communication, clarification, consistency, and distancing from the event.

Lam, M. E., Hershkowitz, I., & Sternberg, K. J. (1996). Investigative interviews of alleged sexual abuse victims with and without anatomical dolls. *Child Abuse and Neglect, 20*(12), 1251–1259.

This article compares responses by alleged victims of child sexual abuse during forensic interviews. In interviews with anatomical dolls, children used an equivalent number of details and words than those interviewed without the aid of anatomical dolls. When dolls were not used, the average responses of children were more detailed and significantly longer, especially in responses to open-ended invitations.

Marvasti, J. A. (2001). Using anatomical dolls psychotherapy with sexualized children. In H. G. Kaduson & C. E. Schaefer (Eds.), *101 More Favorite Play Therapy Techniques*. Lanham, MD: Aronson.

Anatomical dolls have been used for several years in the evaluation and validation of sexual abuse in children. They are generally used in forensic evaluations of child sexual abuse. It is felt that a naked anatomical doll is sexually suggestive to a child and may contaminate the process of evaluation and validation of incest and sexual abuse. These dolls are introduced only after a child verbalizes sexual victimization, in order to facilitate communication.

Nichols, K. S. (2009). Assessing sexual abuse protocols for family litigation. *American Journal of Family Law, 22*(4), 184–191.

Although awareness of child sexual abuse is increasing, false allegations are also on the rise. Consequently, the importance of an accurate process of assessment concerning protocols for family litigation, report completeness, and recognition of child susceptibility to suggestion is invaluable. The inclusion of anatomical dolls and human-figure drawings throughout the investigative process is discussed.

Samra, J., & Yuille, J. C. (1996). Anatomically-neutral dolls: Their effects on the memory and suggestibility of 4- to 6-year-old eyewitnesses. *Child Abuse and Neglect, 20*(12), 1261–1272.

The eyewitness accounts of children, age 4–6, were compared on the basis of the use of verbal interviews and verbal interviews aided by anatomically neutral dolls. After the interview process, the memories of the children were assessed using three different interviews that included three leading questions. No main effects were observed for the interview type, the participant-versus-observer condition, or overall accuracy of accounts.

Sivan, A. B. (1991). Preschool child development: Implications for investigation of child abuse allegations. *Child Abuse and Neglect, 15*, 485–493.

Research on child development and the influential components of television on preschool-age children was examined to determine the accuracy of allegations of abuse. The author concludes that play is based on experiential reality for preschool-age children.

Sivan, A. B., Schor, D. P., Koeppl, G. K., & Noble, L. D. (1988). Interaction of normal children with anatomical dolls. *Child Abuse and Neglect, 12*, 295–304.

This pilot study collected normative data about the play behaviors of nonreferred children with anatomical rag dolls. Observations of the 144 nonreferred children, age 3–8, showed that the children did not consider anatomically correct dolls any more interesting than any other toys. Therefore, aggressive and/or sexually explicit interactions with anatomically correct dolls should be taken seriously.

Thierry, K. L., Lamb, M. E., Orbach, Y., & Pipe, M.-E. (2005). Developmental differences in the function and use of anatomical dolls during interviews with alleged sexual abuse victims. *Journal of Consulting and Clinical Psychology, 73*(6), 1125–1134.

The use of anatomical dolls during forensic interviews with children who were alleged victims of sexual abuse replied to open-ended questions with a similar amount of detail both in the presence and in the absence of the anatomical dolls. Results show that younger children are more likely to engage in suggestive play and supply incongruous details with the anatomical dolls. Older children provided congruent information both with and without the anatomical dolls.

Tishelman, A. C., & Geffner, R. (2010). Forensic, cultural, and systems issues in child sexual abuse cases—Part 1: An introduction. *Journal of Child Sexual Abuse: Research, Treatment, and Program Innovations for Victims, Survivors, and Offenders, 19*(5), 485–490.

The five articles contained in this issue include diverse perspectives on approaches to extended interviews and evaluations of child sexual abuse suspicions, an exploration of the ways culture affects child sexual abuse disclosure and reporting, considerations relevant to the management of a child's mental health needs during the ongoing forensic process, and the use of anatomical dolls in forensic interviews. Several practice areas are in need of attention, including prioritizing a child's mental health needs while minimizing disruption of forensic processes and developing best practices and models of child sexual abuse assessment and evaluation when a one-session forensic interview is insufficient.

Wakefield, H., & Underwager, R. (2006). The use of anatomically detailed dolls in forensic interviews. *Issues in Child Abuse Accusations, 16*(1), 4.

There are no accepted standards for the use of anatomically detailed dolls in child sexual abuse investigations. Dolls are used to clarify details but may not add any validation points to the investigation. It is suggested that dolls not be used in forensic interviews, in order to avoid contaminating the child's account. If dolls are used, the attorney must evaluate whether their use may have compromised the reliability of the child's statement.

Weill, R., Dawson, B. L., & Range, L. M. (1999). Behavioral and verbal responses of unabused externalizing children to anatomically detailed doll interviews. *Journal of Family Violence, 14*(1), 61–70.

Results suggest that children with externalizing behaviors are more active in their play with anatomical dolls than are nonexternalizing children. Externalizing children were more sexually aggressive when initially exposed to the anatomical dolls than were nonexternalizing children.

Welsh, T. (2007). Child's play: Anatomically correct dolls and embodiment. *Human Studies, 30*(3), 255–267.

Studies have shown that anatomically detailed dolls can result in false accounts in young, preschool-age children. This problem is usually considered a cognitive one: with age, children can correctly map their bodies onto a doll because of their greater intellectual ability to represent themselves. A discussion of embodiment is required to understand the use and abuse of anatomical dolls in forensic interviews.

2. Child Sexual Abuse Assessment

Alaggia, R., & Kirshenbaum, S. (2005). Speaking the unspeakable: Exploring the impact of family dynamics on child sexual abuse disclosures. *Families in Society, 86*(2), 227–234.

This qualitative study used the long interview method to identify a range of family dynamics that may affect a child's ability to disclose sexual abuse. It is estimated that between 30 percent and 80 percent of victims do not purposefully disclose child sexual abuse (CSA) before adulthood. Data about disclosure processes were used from interviews with twenty male and female CSA survivors. Disclosure can be significantly compromised when certain conditions exist: rigidly fixed gender roles based on a patriarchy-based family structure; family violence; indirect communication patterns; and social isolation. It is important to identify disclosure barriers to deal with them effectively.

Akhtar, S., & Gilligan, P. (2006). Cultural barriers to the disclosure of child sexual abuse in Asian communities: Listening to what women say. *British Journal of Social Work, 36*(8), 1361–1377.

There is obvious underreporting of child sexual abuse in Britain's Asian communities, and professionals are responding with varied amounts of cultural competence. Professionals need to develop better understandings of cultural practices that determine behavior in those communities. Culturally competent practice and respectful dialogue are essential to the protection of children. Members of Asian communities are aware of child sexual abuse, recognize that all communities need to address the issue, and report that many of those affected in their own communities have found it difficult to access relevant services. These consultations indicate that difficulties, which appear to arise from Asian women's fears about how agencies will respond, are frequently compounded by the impact of cultural imperatives arising from *izzat* (honor or respect), *haya* (modesty), and *sharam* (shame or embarrassment), which have a considerable influence on how many will behave.

Chaffin, M., Silovsky, J., & Vaughn, C. (2005). Temporal concordance of anxiety disorder and child sexual abuse: Implications for direct versus artificial effects of sexual abuse. *Journal of Clinical Child and Adolescent Psychology, 34*(2), 210–222.

This study examined the temporal concordance between the onset of childhood anxiety disorders and the points of onset and ending of child sexual abuse (CSA). Sexually abused children were assessed with structured diagnostic interviews. Onset ages for lifetime prevalence anxiety disorders were combined and sequenced with the onset and ending of sexual abuse. The findings support the idea that CSA can have a direct link to childhood anxiety disorders, apart from confounded vulnerability factors, postabuse events, and stable family background factors. The authors contrast the findings with those from cross-sectional partial correlation studies that have suggested little direct connection between sexual abuse and mental health outcomes.

Cronch, L. E., Viljoen, J. L., & Hansen, D. J. (2006). Forensic interviewing in child sexual abuse cases: Current techniques and future directions. *Aggression and Violent Behavior, 11*(3), 195–207.

In child sexual abuse cases, skillful forensic interviews are important to ensure the protection of innocent individuals and the conviction of perpetrators. Numerous interviewing techniques have received attention in the literature, including allegation blind interviews, open-ended questioning, cognitive interviewing, the Touch Survey, truth-lie discussions, and anatomical dolls. Recent studies have examined new directions in forensic interviewing, such as structured interview protocols and the extended forensic evaluation model. The model of the child advocacy center has been established as a strategy to prevent repeated interviewing and to provide a safe, child-friendly atmosphere for children and families to receive services.

Davidson, J., Bifulco, A., Thomas, G., & Ramsay, M. (2006). Child victims of sexual abuse: Children's experience of the investigative process in the criminal justice system. *Practice, 18*(4), 247–263.

This article is a selected review of research on issues surrounding the investigation of intrafamilial child sexual abuse for children age 8 and older in the criminal justice system. Particular attention is paid to features of the investigative interview in relation to the child's level of understanding, ability to report, and likely emotional response during proceedings. Best practice by police and social care agencies involves establishing valid and reliable information from children while attending to their developmental level and emotional state. The article makes recommendations for improving the interview process and optimizing information recording in a format easily shared between agencies. Updated and ongoing training procedures are essential to successful practice, with training being shared across police and social work agencies.

Davies, M., & Rogers, P. (2009). Perceptions of blame and credibility toward victims of childhood sexual abuse: Differences across victim age, victim-perpetrator relationship, and respondent gender in a depicted case. *Journal of Child Sexual Abuse, 18*(1), 78–92.

This study investigated victim culpability, credibility, and assault severity in a hypothetical sexual abuse case. Members of the U.K. general public read the depiction of a female child assaulted by an adult male perpetrator. Respondents then completed an attributions questionnaire. Results showed that male respondents were less positive toward victims and considered the victim less credible than female respondents. Younger victims (age 5) were considered more credible than older children (age 15). Victims of strangers were viewed more positively and as more credible than victims of someone known to the victim (their father or a family friend). Suggestions for future work are proposed.

Draucker, C. B., & Martsolf, D. S. (2008). Storying childhood sexual abuse. *Qualitative Health Research, 18*(8), 1034–1048.

This article presents a theoretical framework that explains how survivors of childhood sexual abuse tell others about their abuse experiences. Data are drawn from open-ended interviews conducted with seventy-four individuals who experienced ongoing childhood sexual abuse by a family member or close acquaintance. The core psychosocial process used in response to this problem is storying childhood sexual abuse. The framework includes five processes, and the stories associated with each process vary in their nature and function. The processes and associated stories are starting the story (the story not yet told), coming out with the story (the story first told), shielding the story (the story as secret), revising the story (the story as account), and sharing the story (the story as message).

Everson, M. D., & Sandoval, J. (2011). Forensic child sexual abuse evaluations: Assessing subjectivity and bias in professional judgements. *Child Abuse and Neglect, 35*(4), 287–298.

This study attempts to identify and quantify factors that contribute to disagreements in forensic assessments of child sexual abuse. Participants included 1106 professionals in the field of child maltreatment. Each completed the Child Forensic Attitude Scale. Analysis found two subscales for emphasis on sensitivity and one each for emphasis on specificity and skepticism. Child Protective Service workers were unexpectedly more concerned about overcalling abuse and more skeptical of child disclosures than other professionals. These attitudes operate as predispositions or biases toward viewing CSA allegations as likely to be true or likely to be false. Several strategies for curbing the influence of subjective factors are highlighted, including self-awareness of personal biases and team approaches to assessment.

Faller, K. C. (2005). Anatomical dolls: Their use in assessment of children who may have been sexually abused. *Journal of Child Sexual Abuse, 14*(3), 1–21.

See annotation in the section "Anatomical Dolls."

Faller, K. C., Cordisco-Steele, L., & Nelson-Gardell, D. (2010). Allegations of sexual abuse of a child: What to do when a single forensic interview isn't enough. *Journal of Child Sexual Abuse: Research, Treatment, and Program Innovations for Victims, Survivors, and Offenders, 19*(5), 572–589.

This article describes the state of knowledge about extended assessments and forensic evaluations in situations of possible sexual abuse. It provides a critical review of the modest body of relevant research, describes two models for extended assessments, and presents descriptive survey findings of sixty-two professionals who have conducted extended assessments. Agencies should consider conducting extended assessments with young or traumatized children whose sexual abuse allegations are not resolved in a single interview and in complex child sexual abuse cases.

Finnilä-Tuohimaa, K., Santtila, P., Björnberg, L., Hakala, N., Niemi, P., & Sandnabba, K. (2008). Attitudes related to child sexual abuse: Scale construction and explorative study among psychologists. *Scandinavian Journal of Psychology, 49,* 311–323.

The Child Sexual Abuse Attitude and Belief Scale was constructed and answered by 242 child psychologists. Four CSA-related attitude and belief subscales were identified through confirmatory factor analysis: (1) The disclosure subscale, reflecting the favoring of a disclosure at any cost; (2) the pro-child subscale, reflecting unconditional belief in children's reports; (3) the intuition subscale, reflecting favoring an intuitive approach to CSA investigations; and (4) the anti-criminal-justice-system subscale, reflecting negative attitudes toward the legal system. The results suggest that some psychologists hold extreme attitudes and many inaccurate beliefs related to CSA. Female participants tended to have stronger attitudes than male participants. The more training in interviewing children the participants had, the more erroneous beliefs and stronger attitudes they had. Experience did not affect attitudes and beliefs.

Gudas, L. S., & Sattler, J. M. (2006). Forensic interviewing of children and adolescents. *Forensic mental health assessment of children and adolescents.* Oxford: Oxford University Press.

The accuracy of children's statements and testimony in the legal arena historically has been challenged. Much of the skepticism has stemmed from child sexual abuse interviews that questioned existing traditional pre-trial and trial procedures. Mental health clinicians became acutely aware of their limitations in forensic situations. Tests, techniques, and psychotherapeutic strategies developed and used in general clinical settings were found to be inadequate. The ongoing development of forensic psychology, formal training programs focusing on children and the law, and research on psycholegal issues and children have all assisted in offering sounder assessments of children. Forensic interviewing of children and adolescents is considered a task for clinicians with specialized training. This work attempts to further clinicians' awareness of the uniqueness of forensic interviewing of children and adolescents.

Gumpert, C. H., Lindblad, F., & Grann, M. (2002). A systematic approach to quality assessment of expert testimony in cases of alleged child sexual abuse. *Psychology, Crime and Law, 8*(1), 59–75.

The article describes a proposed method of translating guidelines on written expert testimony on child sexual abuse into a quality assessment protocol: the Structured Quality Assessment of Expert Testimony, or SQX-12. This would create an evaluative tool to assess written expert testimony regarding child sexual abuse. The proposed tool consists of twelve items referring to different quality aspects of written expert testimony. The authors conclude that the SQX-12 may provide the first step toward the conceptualization of quality forensic reports regarding child sexual abuse.

Hershkowitz, I. (2009). Socioemotional factors in child sexual abuse investigations. *Child Maltreatment, 14*(2), 172–181.

Two socioemotional factors are evaluated in regard to children's production of forensic information during sexual abuse investigations: rapport building and interviewer's support. The study tested to what extent (a) the length and questioning style in the rapport-building session and (b) the level of support interviewers provided to the children were associated with the amount of forensic details that children provided. The associations were explored for more talkative and less talkative children, and for children of two groups (age 4–6 and age 7–9). The results suggest that richer information in children's responses is associated with a short and open rapport-building session, as well as with a greater level of interviewer's support.

Hershkowitz, I., Fisher, S., Lamb, M. E., & Horowitz, D. (2007). Improving credibility assessment in child sexual abuse allegations: The role of the NICHD investigative interview protocol. *Child Abuse and Neglect, 31*(2), 99–110.

The study was designed to explore whether the credibility of children's statements regarding their alleged experiences of child sexual abuse could be assessed in a more valid and reliable way when investigative interviews were conducted using the NICHD protocol rather than in an unstructured manner. More nonprotocol than protocol interviews were rated as "no judgment possible" rather than as either credible or incredible. Allegations made in protocol interviews were more accurately rated as credible or incredible. Levels of interrater reliability were also higher when protocol interviews were rated. The use of the NICHD protocol facilitated the assessment of credibility by child investigators, although incredible allegations remained difficult to detect.

Hershkowitz, I., Horowitz, D., Lamb, M. E., Orbach, Y., & Sternberg, K. J. (2004). Interviewing youthful suspects in alleged sex crimes: A descriptive analysis. *Child Abuse and Neglect, 28*(4), 423–438.

Seventy-two alleged perpetrators age 9–14 were interviewed by one of thirteen experienced youth investigators about incidents that alleged victims had reported. All interviews followed the structured interview guide appended to this article. The total number of details alleged perpetrators provided did not vary depending on age or whether they fully or partially admitted to the allegations. In both cases, more information was elicited using invitations rather than suggestive or option-posing prompts. Contrary to expectations, alleged perpetrators who at least partially admitted their involvement provided considerable amounts of information and were responsive to free-recall prompts, although interviewers used riskier (potentially error-inducing) prompts when interviewing suspects rather than alleged victims.

Hershkowitz, I., Lanes, O., & Lamb, M. (2007). Exploring the disclosure of child sexual abuse with alleged victims and their parents. *Child Abuse and Neglect, 31*(2), 111–123.

The goal of the present study was to examine how children disclosed sexual abuse by alleged perpetrators who were not family members. Six experienced investigators interviewed thirty alleged victims of sexual abuse and their parents using the NICHD Investigative Interview Protocol. The disclosure process varied depending on the children's ages, severity and frequency of abuse, parents' expected reactions, suspects' identities, and strategies suspects had used to foster secrecy. The children's willingness to disclose abuse to their parents promptly and spontaneously decreased when they expected negative reactions, especially with more serious abuse. There was a strong correlation between predicted and actual parental reactions.

Korkman, J., Santtila, P., & Sandnabba, N. K. (2006). Dynamics of verbal interaction between interviewer and child in interviews with alleged victims of child sexual abuse. *Scandinavian Journal of Psychology*, *47*(2), 109–119.

Investigative interviews with children were analyzed with a view to explore the verbal dynamics between interviewer and child. Different types of interviewer statements and child responses were defined, and the interrelationships between these were explored. Invitations and directive utterances were associated with an increase in informative responses by the child, the adverse being true for option-posing and suggestive utterances. Even after the child had provided an informative answer, interviewers continued to rely on focused and leading interviewing methods.

Korkman, J., Santtila, P., Westeråker, M. A., & Sandnabba, N. K. (2008). Interviewing techniques and follow-up questions in child sexual abuse interviews. *European Journal of Developmental Psychology*, *5*(1), 108–128.

The quality of a representative sample of forty-three forensic interviews with alleged victims (age 3–8) of child sexual abuse (CSA) in Finland was investigated. Interviews were coded for type of interviewer utterance, type of child response, details in the child response, and number of words in each utterance. The interviewers continued to rely on leading and suggestive questions even after the child had provided significant information. Longer questions often rendered no reply from the child, whereas shorter questions rendered descriptive answers. Interviewers seemed to fail in discussing the topic of sexual abuse in an appropriate way, frequently employing long and vague unspecific suggestive utterances.

Korkman, J., Santtila, P., Westeråker, M. A., & Sandnabba, N. K. (2008). Failing to keep it simple: Language use in child sexual abuse interviews with 3-8-year-old children. *Psychology, Crime and Law*, *14*(1), 41–60.

Previous studies have found that legal interviews with children often are conducted in a language that exceeds the cognitive level of interviewed children. The present study carried out investigative interviews with 3- to 8-year-old children in cases of suspected child sexual abuse (CSA). Results showed that the language used during the interviews included long and complex sentences, multiple questions before the child was allowed to answer, and unclear references to persons and situations. This raised concerns about the credibility of the information gained in the interviews. The issue of how to more properly and age-appropriately conduct CSA interviews needs further attention.

Kooiman, C. G., Ouwehand, A. W., & Kuile, M. M. (2002). The Sexual and Physical Abuse Questionnaire (SPAQ): A screening instrument for adults to assess past and current experiences of abuse. *Child Abuse and Neglect, 26*(9), 939–953.

This study used the Sexual and Physical Abuse Questionnaire to assess sexual and physical abuse during childhood and later life. The criterion validity of the questionnaire was investigated in a population of psychiatric outpatients using the Structured Trauma Interview as the gold standard for assessing sexual and physical abuse. The questionnaire may be a useful screening instrument in research and in clinical practice to assess sexual abuse during childhood and later years. As a screening instrument for physical abuse it is less satisfactory.

Lindahl, M. W. (2009). Beyond Munchausen by proxy: A proposed conceptualization for cases of recurring, unsubstantiated sexual abuse allegations. *Journal of Child Sexual Abuse, 18*(2), 206–220.

In the emerging literature, cases involving recurring, unsubstantiated allegations of child sexual abuse have generally been categorized as Munchausen by proxy. Recent scholars have recommended restricting the label to the original conceptualization, involving purposeful deception motivated by the psychological need for medical attention. This leaves many cases unclassified that do not fit the Munchausen-by-proxy criteria. This article presents a reconceptualization of such cases, proposing the labeling of them as "recurring sexual abuse allegation" cases. Defining the set of cases more clearly can aid child protection workers in case management and can encourage research on prevalence, consequences to children, treatment strategies, and needed legal reforms.

Lowenstein, L. F. (2011). The complexity of investigating possible sexual abuse of a child. *American Journal of Family Therapy, 39*(4), 292–298.

The author evaluates three important issues in relation to child sex abuse allegations: the potential signs in the behavior of children who might have suffered sexual abuse, how an evaluation of an allegedly sex abused child can be carried out, and the possible long-term effects on a child who has suffered from sexually abuse. The complexities of coming to the right conclusions are considered when there are false positives as a result of the overlap of evidence between sexually abused and nonabused children.

Mart, E. R. (2010). Common errors in the assessment of allegations of child sexual abuse. *Journal of Psychiatry and Law*, *38*(3), 325–343.

The assessment of child sexual abuse (CSA) allegations is a complex, challenging, and high-stakes undertaking. The consequences of sloppy assessments that lead to a false-positive or a false-negative court decision are clearly severe. Despite this, many professionals and paraprofessionals who undertake such assessments continue to perform substandard CSA investigations. This article presents some of the common errors made by CSA investigators and suggests the use of research-based investigative protocols and ongoing training as ways to improve the situation.

3. Child Sexual Abuse Interviews

Castelli, P., Goodman, S., & Ghetti, S. (2005). Effects of interview style and witness age on perceptions of children's credibility in sexual abuse cases. *Journal of Applied Social Psychology*, *35*(2), 297–319.

The present study concerns the effects of interview style and victim age on perceptions of child victims and witnesses and defendant guilt based on two experiments. In experiment 1, child age (age 4 versus age 7) did not significantly influence guilt ratings. Mock jurors were less likely to convict the alleged perpetrator and less likely to rate the child as credible when testimony was taken through a highly leading interview. The effects of interview style on guilt ratings were similar in experiment 2 for a 4-year-old victim or witness but not a 7-year-old victim or witness. In both studies, women were more likely than men to convict the defendant and to believe the child.

Cheung, M. (2008). Promoting effective interviewing of sexually abused children: A pilot study. *Research on Social Work Practice*, *18*(2), 137–143.

This study is centered on interviewing techniques with alleged child sexual abuse victims. Ninety randomly selected videotapes were reviewed, and the interviewing techniques recorded on the sixty-nine-item Child Sexual Abuse Interviewing Skills Instrument. The analysis of the instrument indicates the use of more what and how questions in disclosure cases, whereas more closing questions are used in nondisclosure cases. Interviewers should maintain an attitude that they can obtain additional information from other sources, which will help demonstrate patience and understanding rather than leading the child to disclosure or false allegation.

Cheung, M., & Boutte-Queen, N. M. (2010). Assessing the relative importance of the child sexual abuse interview protocol items to assist child victims in abuse disclosure. *Journal of Family Violence, 25*(1), 11–22.

See annotation in the section "Anatomical Dolls."

Colangelo, J. J. (2007). Recovered memory debate revisited: Practice implications for mental health counselors. *Journal of Mental Health Counseling, 29*(2), 93–120.

The article discusses key reform options to address the difficulties associated with prosecuting child sex offenses in Australia. The simplest and cheapest approach would be to adopt a model based on the New South Wales Pilot Program, but reforms can be deceptive because vulnerable witness protections do not seem to influence trial processes and outcomes. The challenge in formulating an alternative model for prosecuting child sex offenses involves several considerations, such as how the prosecution process and outcomes will affect the safety of the victim and other children.

Collings, S. J. (2007). Non-supportive disclosure in child sexual abuse: Confidants' characteristics and reactions. *Psychological Reports, 100*(3), 768–770.

In a sample of 856 South African child victims of sexual abuse, 26 percent experienced nonsupportive reactions at initial disclosure, for two reasons: ignoring the child (16 percent of cases) and punishing or silencing the child (10 percent of cases). Nonsupportive disclosure was equally likely when the confidant was a nonoffending guardian, another family member, or a professional person. It was significantly more likely when the confidant was a community member.

Cross, T. P., Jones, L. M., Walsh, W. A., Simone, M., & Kolko, D. (2007). Child forensic interviewing in children's advocacy centers: Empirical data on a practice model. *Child Abuse and Neglect, 31*(10), 1031–1052.

Children's advocacy centers (CACs) aim to improve child forensic interviewing following allegations of child abuse by coordinating multiple investigations, to provide child-friendly interviewing locations, and to limit redundant interviewing. This analysis presents one of the first rigorous evaluations of CACs' implementation of these methods. Case abstractors collected data on investigation methods in 1069 child sexual abuse cases with forensic interviews by reviewing case records from multiple agencies. The CAC cases were more likely than comparison cases to feature police involvement in CPS cases, multidisciplinary team interviews, case reviews, joint police and Child Protective Services (CPS) investigations, and video- and audiotaping of interviews. The CACs appear to have increased coordination on investigations and child forensic interviewing. The CAC setting was the location for most CAC child interviews, whereas comparison communities often used settings that many consider undesirable.

DeVoe, E. R., & Faller, K. C. (2002). Questioning strategies in interviews with children who may have been sexually abused. *Child Welfare, 81*(1), 5–31.

This article examines the number and types of questions employed in clinical and computer-assisted interviews with children referred for sexual abuse evaluation. This research was part of a larger study to assess the efficacy of a computer-assisted protocol in the evaluation of child sexual abuse allegations. Interviews were analyzed from forty-seven girls and twenty-nine boys, age 5–10, who had been referred to a multidisciplinary clinic for sexual abuse assessment. Findings suggest that many children are able to describe sexual abuse with careful questioning that includes nonleading but focused inquiry.

Faller, K., Grabarek, M., Nelson-Gardell, D., & Williams, J. (2011). Techniques employed by forensic interviewers conducting extended assessments: Results from a multi-site study. *Journal of Aggression, Maltreatment and Trauma, 20*(3), 237–259.

This study uses multisite data from assessments of 137 children suspected of sexual abuse to examine which interview techniques yield information related to sexual abuse. Frequently used techniques were general assessment activities; touching education; nonleading, abuse-focused questions; and prevention education. Infrequently used techniques were anatomical dolls, standard anatomical drawings, and narrative elaboration. The techniques that saw greater yields of confirmatory details about sexual abuse were anatomical dolls, cognitive interviews, and narrative elaboration. Lower-yield techniques were general assessment activities,

touch education, hand-drawn anatomical drawings, and prevention education. Techniques associated with a rating of sexual abuse likely were the
use of anatomical dolls and anatomical drawings.

Finnilä-Tuohimaa, K., Santtila, P., Sainio, M., Niemi, P., & Sandnabba, K.
(2009). Expert judgment in cases of alleged child sexual abuse: Clinicians' sensitivity to suggestive influences, pre-existing beliefs and base
rate estimates. *Scandinavian Journal of Psychology, 50*(2), 129–142.

Clinicians' expertise in child sexual abuse (CSA) cases was explored by
giving a questionnaire covering clinical experience and self-evaluated
expertise, beliefs, and attitudes about CSA to 320 child mental health professionals. Participants were sensitive to the presence of leading questions
but not to the presence of other suggestive techniques. Experience affected
only sensitivity to leading questions. Strong attitudes and beliefs decreased
sensitivity to leading questions and made participants more prone to wanting the case to be prosecuted even though other suggestive influences than
leading questions were present.

Jülich, S. (2005). Stockholm syndrome and child sexual abuse. *Journal of
Child Sexual Abuse, 14*(3), 107–129.

This article, based on an analysis of unstructured interviews, identifies
that the emotional bond between survivors of child sexual abuse and the
people who perpetrated the abuse against them is similar to that of the
powerful bidirectional relationship central to Stockholm syndrome.
Aspects of Stockholm syndrome could be identified in the responses of
adult survivors of child sexual abuse, which appeared to affect their ability
to criminally report offenders. An emotional bond, which has enabled the
sexual abuse of children, serves to protect the offender long after the abuse
has ceased. The implications of Stockholm syndrome could offer valuable
insights to those working in the field of child sexual abuse.

Kim, T., Choi, S., & Shin, Y. (2011). Psychosocial factors influencing competency of children's statements on sexual trauma. *Child Abuse and Neglect, 35*(3), 173–179.

The objectives of this study were to assess children's competence in stating their traumatic experience and to determine psychosocial factors influencing the competency of children's statements in Korean child sex abuse

victims. The study included 214 children who had experienced sexual abuse. The children's parents were surveyed using questionnaires (Beck Depression Inventory and State-Trait Anxiety Inventory). Children completed psychological measures including the Children's Depression Inventory and the Revised Children's Manifest Anxiety Scale. The modified-Criteria-Based Content Analysis (CBCA) was used to assess children's statements. Children with parents who showed supportive reactions scored significantly higher on the modified-CBCA scores than did those with unsupportive parents. The competence of statements in Korean child sex abuse victims is related to parental emotional states and support. Therefore, promoting parental support through psychoeducation is among the most important factors in helping children overcome psychological trauma.

Korkman, J., Santtila, P., Drzewiecki, T., & Sandnabba, N. K. (2008). Failing to keep it simple: Language use in child sexual abuse interviews with 3-8-year-old children. *Psychology, Crime and Law, 14*(1), 41–60.

See annotation in the section "Child Sexual Abuse Assessment."

Korkman, J., Santtilla P., Westeraker, M., & Sandnabba, N. K. (2008). Interviewing techniques and follow-up questions in child sexual abuse interviews. *European Journal of Developmental Psychology, 5*(1) 108–128.

See annotation in the section "Child Sexual Abuse Assessment."

Lamb, M. E., & Garretson, M. E. (2003). The effects of interviewer gender and child gender on the informativeness of alleged child sexual abuse victims in forensic interviews. *Law and Human Behavior, 27*(2), 157–171.

Forensic investigators in three countries used either the NICHD structured interview protocol or local standard interview practices to interview 672 alleged victims age 4–14. Children's responses varied depending on their gender and age, gender of the interviewer, and type of question asked. Girls of all ages provided more information in response to directive questions from female rather than male interviewers, whereas boys did not respond differently to male and female interviewers. The oldest girls provided more information in response to option-posing questions from male interviewers. More information was provided by the younger children in response to suggestive prompts from interviewers of the opposite gender.

Lamb, M. E., Orbach, Y., Hershkowitz, I., Esplin, P. W., & Horowitz, D. (2007). A structured forensic interview protocol improves the quality and informativeness of investigative interviews with children: A review of research using the NICHD Investigative Interview Protocol. *Child Abuse and Neglect, 31*(11–12), 1201–1231.

This study shows how the results of research on children's memory, communicative skills, social knowledge, and social tendencies can be translated into guidelines that improve the quality of forensic interviews of children. Controlled studies have repeatedly shown that the quality of interviewing reliably and dramatically improves when interviewers employ the NICHD Protocol. No other technique has proved similarly effective. Use of the structured NICHD Protocol improves the quality of information obtained from alleged victims by investigators, thereby increasing the likelihood that interventions will be appropriate.

Lamb, M. E., Orbach, Y., Sternberg, K. L., Aldridge, J., Pearson, S., Stewart, H., et al. (2009). Use of a structured investigative protocol enhances the quality of investigative interviews with alleged victims of child sexual abuse in Britain. *Applied Cognitive Psychology, 23*(4), 449–467.

One hundred alleged victims of child sexual abuse, age 4–13, were interviewed by police investigators about their experiences. Half the children were interviewed using the National Institute of Child Health and Human Development Protocol for structured interviews, whereas the other children were interviewed by investigators following the Memorandum of Good Practice. Protocol-guided interviews elicited more information using free-recall invitations and less information using directive, option-posing, and suggestive questions than did standard Memorandum interviews.

Legault, E., & Laurence, J. R. (2007). Recovered memories of childhood sexual abuse: Social worker, psychologist, and psychiatrist reports of beliefs, practices, and cases. *Australian Journal of Clinical and Experimental Hypnosis, 35*(2), 111–133.

Canadian psychiatrists, psychologists, and social workers were surveyed regarding their endorsement of beliefs and techniques thought to be associated with cases of memory recovery of child sexual abuse (CSA) and regarding the number of CSA cases seen. Support for recovered memory validity was associated with use of more memory recovery techniques, including hypnosis and related techniques, and more reports of recovered memory. Psychiatrists were the most skeptical of recovered memory validity and social workers the least. The study suggests that there is not an epidemic of recovered memories of CSA. Care must be exerted when exploring clients' past history.

Lippert, T., Cross, T. P., Jones, L., & Walsh, W. (2009). Telling interviewers about sexual abuse: Predictors of child disclosure at forensic interviews. *Child Maltreatment, 14*(1), 100–113.

This study aims to identify characteristics that predict full disclosure by victims of sexual abuse during a forensic interview. Data came from agency files for 987 cases of sexual abuse between December 2001 and December 2003 from children's advocacy centers and comparison communities in four U.S. states. Cases of children fully disclosing abuse when interviewed were compared with cases of children believed to be victims who gave no or partial disclosures. The likelihood of disclosure increased for female victims, when a primary caregiver was supportive, and when a child's disclosure instigated the investigation. The likelihood of disclosure was greater for children who were older at abuse onset and at forensic interview (each age variable had an independent effect).

Nichols, K. S. (2009). Assessing sexual abuse protocols for family litigation. *American Journal of Family Law, 22*(4), 184–191.

The article discusses the assessment of sexual abuse protocols for U.S. family litigation. It notes that although awareness of child sexual abuse has increased, false allegations related to such abuse are also increasing in child custody battles. The accuracy, completeness of the reports, and susceptibility of the child to suggestions are given attention during child interviews. The article examines how human-figure drawings and anatomical dolls are used in child sexual abuse investigations.

Orbach, Y., & Lamb, M. E. (2007). Young children's references to temporal attributes of allegedly experienced events in the course of forensic interviews. *Child Development, 78*(4), 1100–1120.

Developmental differences in references to temporal attributes of allegedly experienced events were examined in 250 forensic interviews of 4- to 10-year-old alleged victims of sexual abuse. The findings documented age-related increases in 4- to 10-year-olds' references to temporal attributes, using the appropriate relational terminology, both spontaneously and in response to temporal requests. More references to temporal attributes were elicited from recall than from recognition memory, which highlights spontaneous reporting capabilities.

Oxburgh, G., Williamson, T., & Ost, J. (2006). Police officers' use of emotional language during child sexual abuse investigations. *Journal of Investigative Psychology and Offender Profiling*, 3(1), 35–45.

This article examined the use of emotional language by police officers who interview child victims as well as suspects during sexual offense investigations. Thirty-four interview transcripts of investigative interviews with alleged sex offenders were analyzed. The results revealed a significant effect of prior acquaintance with the victim, in that a greater number of negative emotional utterances (e.g., contempt, disgust and anger) were used by interviewers who had not previously interviewed the victim. The study found that, despite recent recommendations, most police officers had not received specialist investigative interviewing specific to sex offenders.

Perona, A. R., Bottoms, B. L., & Sorenson, E. (2006). Research-based guidelines for child forensic interviews. *Journal of Aggression, Maltreatment and Trauma*, 12(3–4), 81–130.

This article presents important considerations for conducting forensic interviews with children who are witnesses to or alleged victims of crime— specifically, to present the basic principles of the forensic interview and review some of the best structured forensic protocols currently available; to provide a detailed, practical blueprint for conducting a structured forensic interview; and to discuss special considerations for interviews with children of different age groups and children who have special needs or circumstance. Also included are suggestions to assist legal and social service professionals in accessing the social science research literature that should inform forensic interview techniques.

Santtila, P., Korkman, J., & Sandnabba, N. K. (2004). Effects of interview phase, repeated interviewing, presence of a support person, and anatomically detailed dolls on child sexual abuse interviews. *Psychology, Crime and Law*, 10(1), 21–35.

A nonrepresentative sample of twenty-seven investigative interviews with suspected victims of child sexual abuse (CSA) in Finland were analyzed. The number of new details the child reported was higher in the beginning, whereas the number of focused and suggestive question types increased toward the end of the interviews. Repeated interviews contained more words and descriptive answers by the child, and contained more suggestive questions. Another person attending the interview led to the child being less informative, and the interviewer posed more suggestive questions than when another person was not present. Similar effects were found to be associated with the use of anatomically detailed dolls.

Smith, D. W., Witte, T. H., & Fricker-Elhai, A. E. (2006). Service outcomes in physical and sexual abuse cases: A comparison of child advocacy center-based and standard services. *Child Maltreatment, 11*(4), 354–360.

Child advocacy centers (CACs) were developed to improve child abuse investigative services provided by Child Protective Services (CPS) agencies. Until recently, there has been little research comparing CAC-based procedures and outcomes to those in CPS investigations not based in CACs. The current study tracked seventy-six child abuse cases reported to authorities and investigated through either a private, not-for-profit CAC or typical CPS services in a mid-South rural county. Comparisons between CAC and CPS cases were made in terms of involvement of local law enforcement in the investigation, provision of medical exams, abuse substantiation rates, mental health referrals, prosecution referrals, and conviction rates. Analyses revealed higher rates of law enforcement involvement, medical examinations, and case substantiation in the CAC-based cases than in the CPS cases. This study found preliminary support for the assumptions underlying the establishment of CACs.

Wakefield, H. (2006). Guidelines on investigatory interviewing of children: What is the consensus in the scientific community? *Issues in Child Abuse Accusations, 16*(1), 1–5.

Research over the past several years dramatically demonstrates how child witnesses are susceptible to misleading information given to them in leading and suggestive interviews. As a result of this research, professionals agree on the basic ways children must be interviewed to get accurate, uncontaminated, forensically useful information. Interviewers must avoid preexisting conceptions about what happened and encourage children to tell about relevant events in their own words—and interviews should be taped.

Wakefield, H., & Underwager, R. (2006). The use of anatomically detailed dolls in forensic interviews. *Issues in Child Abuse Accusations, 16*(1), 4. See annotation in the section "Anatomical Dolls."

Westcott, H. L., & Kynan, S. (2004). The application of a "story-telling" framework to investigative interviews for suspected child sexual abuse. *Legal and Criminological Psychology, 9*(1), 37–56.

Transcripts of seventy interviews with children up to age 12, from England and Wales, were coded using a scheme devised specifically for the purpose of the study. The results suggest that even though, superficially, the accounts adhered to a story structure, they were often incomplete and disordered to a degree that would affect understanding. Implications for practice include the importance of careful questioning and the value of a second interviewer monitoring the interview. The storytelling framework was a useful tool for suggesting where difficulties may arise for children in presenting their account and for an observer (e.g., juror) in making sense of the child's experience as elicited in the interview.

Westcott, H. L., & Kynan, S. (2006). Interviewer practice in investigative interviews for suspected child sexual abuse. *Crime and Law, 12*(4), 367–382.

Transcripts of seventy videotaped Memorandum interviews from England and Wales were coded using a specifically developed scheme. Children were age 7–12. Recorded aspects of interviewer practice included implementation of the different phases of the interview, interviewer distortions, and other problematic interviewer behaviors. Several problems were noted in the transcripts. Discussions of truth and lies in the rapport phase were at a basic level that did not include intention to deceive. More than half the sample included interviewer distortions, and other instances of problematic behaviors were noted. The importance of interviewer training is highlighted, and further discussion is required as to why such training does not appear to be implemented in practice.

Vandervort, F. E. (2006). Videotaping investigative interview of children in cases of child sexual abuse: One community's approach. *Journal of Criminal Law and Criminology, 96*(4), 1353–1416.

Legal scholars have long debated the efficacy and necessity of videotaping investigative interviews with children with allegations of child sexual abuse. This debate has failed to consider how other investigative tools might be used in conjunction with videotaping to advance community interests. The debate about videotaping has taken place with little actual data. This article seeks to consider the interests of the broader community to present both quantitative and qualitative data from a single county's long-standing use of protocol. The author concludes that videotaping, when one element of an integrated protocol for investigating child sexual abuse, can serve the interests of the community.

4. Child Witnesses

Bala, N., Lee, K., Lindsay, R. C. L., & Talwar, V. (2010). The competency of children to testify: Psychological research informing Canadian law reform. *International Journal of Children's Rights, 18*(1), 53–77.

Recent psychological research establishes that the ability of children to answer questions about the meaning of such concepts as truth and promise is not related to whether they will actually tell the truth. However, the act of promising to tell the truth increases the likelihood that children will tell the truth. Informed by this research, Canada significantly reformed its laws governing the process for determining the competence of child witnesses. The last section of this article briefly surveys laws that govern the competency of child witnesses in other jurisdictions and offers proposals for reform.

Cheung, M., & Boutte-Queen, N. M. (2010). Assessing the relative importance of the child sexual abuse interview protocol items to assist child victims in abuse disclosure. *Journal of Family Violence, 25*(1), 11–22.

See annotation in the section "Anatomical Dolls."

Faller, K. C., & Nelson-Gardell, D. (2010). Extended evaluations in cases of child sexual abuse: How many sessions are sufficient? *Journal of Child Sexual Abuse, 19*(6), 648–668.

This article provides new findings from a national study involving eighteen forensic interview sites of 137 children who were randomly assigned to a four- or eight-session extended evaluation. Cases assigned to the eight-session protocol were significantly more likely to be classified as "credible disclosure" of sexual abuse than cases assigned to the four-session protocol and significantly less likely to be classified as "credible nondisclosure" of sexual abuse than cases in the four-session protocol. Variables that predicted the likelihood of sexual abuse were eight-session protocol, older victim age, and caretaker belief that the child had been sexually abused. When new disclosures were examined in the eight-session protocol, 95 percent of new disclosures occurred by the sixth session.

Finn, T. R. (2011). The Massachusetts child hearsay statute and the admissibility of non-testimonial out-of-court statements describing sexual abuse. *New England Journal on Criminal and Civil Confinement, 37*(1), 33–53.

This article addresses the issue concerning the move of Massachusetts to enact a special child hearsay exception. The statute directs the proponent of a child's hearsay statement to establish both the unavailability of the declarant and guides of reliability that are comparable to those of firmly rooted hearsay exceptions. It affirms that the exception is grounded on the basis that child hearsay can be as necessary and trustworthy as traditional hearsay exceptions.

McGregor, K., Julich, S., Glover, M., & Gautum, J. (2010). Health professionals' responses to disclosure of child sexual abuse history: Female child sexual abuse survivors' experiences. *Journal of Child Sexual Abuse, 19*(3), 239–254.

This study reports on a postal questionnaire, conducted in 2004, with female survivors of child sexual abuse. The questionnaire explored their experiences of health professionals' responsiveness to disclosure of child sexual abuse history. Of sixty-one participants, age 22–65, 69 percent had disclosed to health professionals. Those who had not disclosed reported that they would have liked to but were not asked about child sexual abuse. Most participants related a fear of common medical examination procedures to their experience of child sexual abuse, and 64 percent said this stopped them from attending regular health checks. The current study suggests that the development of guidelines for dealing with possible child sexual abuse survivors would be useful for health professionals.

Motzkau, J. F. (2010). Speaking up against justice: Credibility, suggestibility and children's memory on trial. In J. Haaken & P. Reavey (Eds.), *Memory matters: Contexts for understanding sexual abuse recollections* (pp. 63–85). New York: Routledge/Taylor and Francis.

Child witnesses have always posed a challenge to legal practice, testing the laws of evidence and necessitating special rules and procedures. In this chapter, I suggest that the scientific and public debate on memories of sexual abuse could benefit from a detailed examination of how legal systems negotiate the tensions and ambiguities surrounding children's memory of sexual abuse. This means examining memory in terms of the concrete practices through which its expression is negotiated and exploring the dynamic and shifting conditions under which credibility is assessed and established. The chapter draws on interview data from a larger research project that has compared child witness practice in England and Wales and Germany against the backdrop of a genealogy of suggestibility research (Motzkau, 2006).

Myklebust, T., & Bjørklund, R. A. (2010). Factors affecting the length of responses in field investigative interviews of children (FIIC) in child sexual abuse cases. *Psychiatry, Psychology and Law, 17*(2), 273–289.

One hundred field investigative interviews of children are analyzed. Analysis of variance showed that of all the variables, interviewer's utterances had the most impact on the children's responses, with the open questions eliciting the longest answers. The variable to follow was the children's age, with the oldest children yielding longer responses than the younger children to the open questions. Contrary to the hypothesis, the interviewer's competence, children's gender, and time of interview had little impact on the length of the children's responses.

Powell, M. B., & Hughes-Scholes, C. H. (2009). Evaluation of the questions used to elicit evidence about abuse from child witnesses: Australian study. *Psychiatry, Psychology and Law, 16*(3), 369–378.

The interviews included 136 videotaped child witness statements, conducted between 2001 and 2007 by police officers from two jurisdictions of Australia. The results indicated many positive aspects of the interviewers' performance, including use of ground rules at the start of the interview, encouraging of a free-narrative account by seeking the children's understanding of the purpose of the interview, and avoidance of suggestive questions. The interviewers tended to raise issues of contention when the child did not provide an initial disclosure. Many closed questions raised specific details not yet mentioned by the child.

Roma, P., Martini, P., Sabatello, U., Tatarelli, R., & Ferracuti, S. (2011). Validity of Criteria-Based Content Analysis (CBCA) at trial in free-narrative interviews. *Child Abuse and Neglect, 35*(8), 613–620.

This study was designed to investigate the reliability of Criteria-Based Content Analysis (CBCA) in allegations of child sexual abuse during court hearings, by comparing CBCA results with the court's final sentence. Also investigated were whether CBCA scores correlated with age and which criteria were better in distinguishing cases of confirmed and unconfirmed abuse. From 487 child sexual abuse cases, a study sample of 60 confirmed and 49 unconfirmed cases were used. Two expert raters applied the fourteen-item version of CBCA to child witness testimony. The criteria that best distinguish the two groups are quantity of details, interactions, and subjective experience. The CBCA scores correlate positively with age, independent of abuse. Given its ability to distinguish between confirmed and unconfirmed cases of suspected child abuse, the CBCA could be a useful tool for expert opinion.

5. Disclosure

Alaggia, R. (2004). Many ways of telling: Expending conceptualization of child sexual abuse disclosure. *Child Abuse and Neglect, 28*(11), 1213–1227.

This study examined twenty-four female and male survivors of child sexual abuse by using the long-interview method to trace disclosure processes. The results of the investigation identified several patterns of disclosure. Prolonged engagement, persistent observation, negative case analysis, and peer debriefing were among the techniques used to ensure the trustworthiness of data. Results of the study facilitated expanding conceptualization of additional disclosure patterns to include behavioral and indirect verbal attempts, disclosures intentionally withheld, and disclosures triggered by recovered memories. The author concludes that the supplementary definitions integrate complex facets of disclosure derived from the context of human development, memory, and environmental influences.

Alaggia, R. (2005). Disclosing the trauma of child sexual abuse: A gender analysis. *Journal of Loss and Trauma, 10*(5), 453–470.

This study qualitatively explored dynamics that impede or promote disclosure of child sexual abuse. Findings on the impact of gender on disclosure are reported from data from thirty in-depth interviews of adult survivors. Noteworthy differences connected to gender and disclosure emerged. The overall trend was toward delaying disclosure, and for those who tried to disclose in childhood, attempts were often made in behavioral or indirect verbal ways. However, males reported difficulty disclosing because they feared being viewed as homosexual and as victims. Women's difficulties centered on feeling conflicted about responsibility, and they strongly anticipated being blamed or not believed. Findings are linked to therapeutic work with traumatic loss.

Alaggia, R., & Kirshenbaum, S. (2005). Speaking the unspeakable: Exploring the impact of family dynamics on child sexual abuse disclosures. *Families in Society, 86*(2), 227–234.

See annotation in the section "Child Sexual Abuse Assessment."

Fontes, L. A., & Plummer, C. (2010). Cultural issues in disclosures of child sexual abuse. *Journal of Child Sexual Abuse: Research, Treatment, and Program Innovations for Victims, Survivors, and Offenders, 19*(5), 491–518.

Cultural norms affect the likelihood that an adult will discover or a child will disclose child sexual abuse. Cultural norms also affect whether abused children's families will report child sexual abuse to authorities. This article explores ways that ethnic and religious culture affect child sexual abuse disclosure and reporting, both in the United States and internationally. Guidelines for culturally sensitive child abuse interviewing are provided to facilitate disclosures of abuse from culturally diverse children in formal settings.

Hunter, S. V. (2011). Disclosure of child sexual abuse as a life-long process: Implications for health professionals. *Australian and New Zealand Journal of Family Therapy, 32*(2), 159–172.

An objective of this research project was to gain a better understanding of the disclosure process of child sexual abuse. Face-to-face in-depth interviews were conducted with twenty-two men and women age 25–70 who had an early sexual experience at age 15 or younger. Narrative inquiry methodology was used, and data analyzed using Rosenthal and Fischer-Rosenthal's (2004) process of data analysis. Most participants did not make a selective disclosure until adulthood. The main barriers to disclosure and possible gender differences are discussed. The author suggests that family therapists manage the challenges inherent in disclosure of child sexual abuse at every age.

Jensen, T. K., Gulbrandsen, W., Mossige, S., Reichelt, S., & Tjersland, O. A. (2005). Reporting possible sexual abuse: A qualitative study on children's perspectives and the context for disclosure. *Child Abuse and Neglect, 29*(12), 1395–1413.

The study investigated the context in which children were able to report their child sexual abuse experiences and the children's views as to what made it difficult to talk about abuse and what helped them in the disclosing process. The goal was to study disclosures as they were occurring in their natural settings. Qualitative analysis was conducted to capture the children's and caregivers' perspectives of the disclosure process. The results indicate that disclosure is a fundamentally dialogic process that becomes less difficult if the children perceive an opportunity to talk and a purpose for speaking, and if a connection has been established to what they are talking about. It is difficult for children to initiate a conversation about something secret and confusing, especially when there are few conversational routines in a family. Children need a supportive structure to reveal their experiences of child sexual abuse.

Jonzon, E., & Lindblad, F. (2004). Disclosure, reactions, and social support: Findings from a sample of adult victims of child sexual abuse. *Child Maltreatment, 9*(2), 190–200.

Information about abuse characteristics, disclosure, and current social support was collected through semistructured interviews and questionnaires from 122 adult women. Women who used an active disclosure strategy in childhood reported more physical and violent abuse. Women who reported more severe abuse had more often received negative reactions from their social network. A relationship was found between current social support and positive, rather than negative, reactions.

Jonzon, E., & Lindblad, F. (2005). Adult female victims of child sexual abuse: Multitype maltreatment and disclosure characteristics related to subjective health. *Journal of Interpersonal Violence, 20*(6), 651–666.

This study examined the impact of child sexual abuse and disclosure characteristics on adult psychological and psychosomatic symptoms. Data on abuse characteristics, disclosure-related events, and subjective health were collected from 123 adult women. The results indicate that disclosure-related events have a stronger relation than abuse characteristics to long-term consequences of childhood sexual abuse.

London, K., Bruck, M., Ceci, S. J., & Shuman, D. W. (2005). Disclosure of child sexual abuse: What does the research tell us about the ways that children tell? *Psychology, Public Policy, and Law, 11*(1), 194–226.

The empirical basis for child sexual abuse accommodation syndrome is a theoretical model that suggests that sexually abused children frequently display secrecy, tentative disclosures, and retractions of abuse statements. Two data sources were evaluated: studies of adults' reports of having been abused as children and chart-review studies of children undergoing evaluation or treatment for sexual abuse. The evidence indicates that most abused children do not reveal abuse during childhood. However, the evidence fails to support the notion that denials, tentative disclosures, and recantations characterize the disclosure patterns of children with confirmed histories of sexual abuse.

London, K., Bruck, M., Wright, D., & Ceci, S. (2008). Review of the contemporary literature on how children report sexual abuse to others: Findings, methodological issues, and implications for forensic interviewers. *Memory, 16* (1), 29–48.

Methods used during forensic interviews with children are driven by beliefs about how children recall and report child sexual abuse (CSA) to others. Summit (1983) proposed a theory (child sexual abuse accommodation syndrome) contending that, because of the specific traumatic characteristics of CSA, children often delay disclosing abuse or altogether fail to disclose during childhood, deny abuse when asked, and often recant abuse allegations. In this article, the authors review and critique the contemporary literature from two main sources: retrospective accounts from adults reporting CSA experiences and studies of children undergoing forensic evaluation for CSA. They conclude that children often delay abuse disclosure, but denial and recantation are not common.

Lovett, B. B. (2004). Child sexual abuse disclosure: Maternal response and other variables impacting the victim. *Child and Adolescent Social Work Journal, 21*(4), 355–371.

Disclosure of childhood sexual abuse is a process unique to each victim and may be influenced by factors of race, ethnicity, culture, religion, and gender. The response by caregivers and professionals affects disclosure and can be responsible for recantation. Maternal responses that show protection and support can be associated with victims' improved mental health and social functioning. Nonabusive caregivers are often marginalized by the child welfare system in its attempt to secure physical safety for the child. This article summarizes the literature regarding sexual abuse disclosure and maternal response and discusses the areas for future research.

Parent, S. (2011). Disclosure of sexual abuse in sport organizations: A case study. *Journal of Child Sexual Abuse, 20*(3), 322–337.

The disclosure of sexual abuse in the world of sports is a process that has not been widely documented or reviewed. This article presents the results of a document analysis of sport organization policies and interviews conducted with twenty-seven sport stakeholders. The interviews focus on these stakeholders' perceptions of how the disclosure process would unfold if a case of sexual abuse were to arise in their organization. The results reveal several problems affecting the disclosure of sexual abuse in sport organizations.

Schaeffer, P., Leventhal, J. M., & Asnes, A. (2011). Children's disclosures of sexual abuse: Learning from direct inquiry. *Child Abuse and Neglect, 35*(5), 343–352.

This study inquires into the process of a child's disclosure to a forensic interview protocol, determines whether children will discuss the process of their disclosure, and describes the factors that children identify as leading them to disclose their sexual abuse or causing them to delay disclosure. Over one year, 191 forensic interviews were reviewed of child sexual abuse victims age 3–18, who spoke about the reasons they either disclosed their abuse or delayed disclosure. The reasons children identified for choosing to tell were classified into three domains: disclosure as a result of internal stimuli, disclosure facilitated by outside influences, and disclosure due to direct evidence of abuse. The barriers to disclosure identified by the children were categorized into five groups: (1) threats made by the perpetrator, (2) fears, (3) lack of opportunity, (4) lack of understanding, and (5) relationship with the perpetrator. Understanding why children disclose their abuse and why they wait to disclose will assist both professionals and families.

Sjöberg, R. L., & Lindblad, F. (2002). Delayed disclosure and disrupted communication during forensic investigation of child sexual abuse: A study of 47 corroborated cases. *Acta Paediatrica, 91*(12), 1391–1396.

This study examined the factors in understanding disclosure of child sexual abuse. Cases from a Swedish district court were studied in which a confession from the defendant corroborated allegations of child sexual abuse. The results showed that delayed disclosure was related to a close relationship with the abuser and young age at the first experience of abuse. The findings highlight the importance of social factors in children's disclosure of sexual abuse.

Shalhoub-Kevorkian, N. (2005). Disclosures of child abuse in conflict areas. *Violence against Women, 11*(10), 1263–1291.

Analyzing legal policies requires an in-depth understanding of the sociopolitical contexts in which sexual abuse is disclosed. Data presented in this study are based on a larger study of 628 Palestinian Israeli girls age 14–16. The contextual analyses of the interviews focused on how young girls perceived disclosure, social support, and legal intervention to their abuse. Data revealed that the girls' attitudes not only conformed to general findings on disclosure of sexual abuse but also reflected sociopolitical fears and stressors. The study reveals how decontextualizing child protection laws and policies can keep sexually abused girls from seeking help.

Sorsoli, L., Kai-Keating, M., & Grossman, F. (2008). "I keep that hush-hush": Male survivors of sexual abuse and the challenges of disclosure. *Journal of Counseling Psychology, 55*(3), 333–345.

Disclosure is a prominent variable in child sexual abuse research, but little research has examined male disclosure experiences. Sixteen male survivors of childhood sexual abuse were interviewed about their experiences of disclosure. Techniques included a grounded theory approach to coding and use of conceptually clustered matrices. Participants described distinct personal, relational, and sociocultural reasons for their struggles with disclosure. The results highlight that barriers to disclosure exist in multiple domains of experience and are encountered across all ages.

Springman, R. E., Wherry, J. N., & Notaro, P. C. (2006). The effects of interviewer race and child race on sexual abuse disclosures in forensic interviews. *Journal of Child Sexual Abuse, 15*(3), 99–116.

This study examined the impact of interviewer and child race on disclosures by alleged child sexual abuse victims during forensic interviews. Previous studies have failed to examine race as a variable affecting disclosure in a real-world setting. The study examined 220 cases from an archive of reports generated from forensic interviews in an urban setting. The reports were reviewed and coded for degree of disclosure, focusing on

African American and Caucasian children and interviewers. The results indicate that interviewer race alone failed to serve as a significant predictor. The interaction between child and interviewer race was not in the predicted direction, with cross-race dyads disclosing more than same-race dyads.

Ullman, S. B. (2003). Social reactions to child sexual abuse disclosures: A critical review. *Journal of Child Sexual Abuse, 12*(1), 89–121.

This article reviews the current empirical literature on disclosure and reactions to adult survivors to assess what is known about the process of disclosure and the outcome. Most studies assessing social reactions in detail have focused on adult survivors reporting their disclosures of child sexual abuse as children. Research suggests that few victims tell anyone about child sexual abuse as children and that the type of reactions to disclosure vary according to when disclosure occurs (childhood or adulthood), the nature of the disclosure, and the person to whom one discloses. Evidence shows that negative social reactions are harmful to survivors' well-being, but better assessments of specific reactions are needed in theoretically based studies to evaluate how the responses affect survivors' recovery in other contexts.

Walker-Descartes, I., Sealy, Y. M., Laraque, D., & Rojas, M. (2011). Caregiver perceptions of sexual abuse and its effect on management after a disclosure. *Child Abuse and Neglect, 35*(6), 437–447.

The study aimed to examine caregiver management strategies for child sexual abuse (CSA) when presented with hypothetical scenarios. To do so, 153 caregivers were given three CSA scenarios with seven management strategies presented in the twenty-one-item Taking Action Strategies (TAS) scale. Caregivers were asked to rate strategies according to their willingness to carry out each action (5 = greater likelihood of carrying out the action specified; 1 = a lower likelihood of carrying out that action). The CSA scenarios included exposure to pornography or masturbation, fondling, and penetration, whereas management strategies included fighting the accused, blaming the child, and outreach to the authorities. Results suggest that several factors influence caregiver management of sexual abuse. Other implications include the need for educational efforts for caregivers. Despite criticisms of the child protective systems, caregivers with past encounters with CPS view the agencies as valuable resources.

6. Disproportionality of Minorities in Child Welfare

Annie E. Casey Foundation. (2008). *Undercounted, underserved, immigrant refugee families in the child welfare system.* Retrieved from http://www .aecf.org/upload/PublicationFiles/IR3622.pdf.

This report focuses on the needs of immigrant and refugee children in the child welfare system. It is a result of extensive research and the recommendations from a consultative session with national experts and child welfare practitioners.

Ayon, C., & Lee, C. D. (2005). A comparative analysis of child welfare services through the eyes of African American, Caucasian and Latino parents. *Research on Social Work Practice, 15*(4), 257–266.

The purpose of this study was to determine whether differences exist among African American, Caucasian, and Latino families who received child welfare services. A secondary data analysis of cross-sectional survey data employing standardized measures was used. The results showed that minority clients were likely to have more children and lower incomes, and to receive public assistance. African American and Latino parents reported more positive outcomes on children's academic adjustment and symptomatic behavior than Caucasian parents when receiving services. When recommending child welfare services, workers need to take ethnicity into account, as culturally sensitive and community-based programs may be more effective when serving ethnic or racial minority groups.

Casey Family Programs. (2009). *Disproportionality in the child welfare system: The disproportionate representation of children of color in foster care.* Retrieved from http://www.ncsl.org/print/cyf/fostercarecolor.pdf.

This work reports statistics on groups who are over- and underrepresented in foster care as well as maltreatment rates. On September 30, 2003, more than 50 percent of the 523,085 children in foster-care placements were children of color, although they represented only 41 percent of the child population in the United States.

Center for the Study of Social Policy. (2004). *Fact sheet 1: Basic facts on disproportionate representation of African Americans in the foster care system—The race + child welfare project.* Retrieved from http://www.cssp.org/uploadFiles/factSheet1.pdf.

The U.S. child welfare system is entangled in an epidemic involving race and poor child and family outcomes. African American children and families are significantly more likely to be torn apart by the local child welfare agency than any other racial group in the country. This situation has resulted in severe levels of overrepresentation of African American children in the country's child welfare system.

Center for the Study of Social Policy. (2004). *Fact sheet 2: State-by-state statistical profile of racial overrepresentation in foster care—The race + child welfare project.* Retrieved from http://www.cssp.org/uploadFiles/statOR FactSheet2.pdf.

Currently, there is no widely used method for calculating racial overrepresentation or racial disparity in the foster-care system. This fact sheet offers one approach to quantifying the extent of this problem. The project calculated a racial disproportionality ratio by dividing the proportion of black (or non-Hispanic white) children in foster care by the proportion of black (or non-Hispanic white) children in the state population younger than age 18. A table indicates the statistical overrepresentation of African American children and black-white disparity among children in foster care in the fifty states for the year 2000.

Chibnall, S., Dutch, N. M., Jones-Harden, B., Brown, A., Gourdine, R., Smith, J., et al. (2003). *Children of color in the child welfare system: Perspectives from the child welfare community.* Washington, DC: Department of Health and Human Services, Children's Bureau and Administration for Children and Families. Retrieved from http://www.child welfare.gov/pubs/otherpubs/children/children.pdf.

Because of concerns about the overrepresentation of minority children in the child welfare system, particularly African American children, the Children's Bureau sponsored an exploratory qualitative study of the child welfare system's response to children of color. The project was intended to gain insight into the issue of overrepresentation from the perspective of the child welfare community and to describe the strategies used by child

welfare agencies to meet the needs of children and families. The information presented here can be used to inform policy makers about overrepresentation and potentially promising practices, strategies, and programs
to reduce it. The information can educate and inform the child welfare
community.

Child Welfare League of America. (2005). *Children of color in the child welfare system.* Retrieved from http://ndas.cwla.org/Include/text/Children
%20of%20Color05.pdf.

This article gives an overview of racial disproportionality in the child
welfare system, including relevant research, statistics, and initiatives to
address this issue.

Chipungu, S. S., & Bent-Goodley, T. B. (2004). Meeting the challenges of
contemporary foster care. *Future of Children, 14*(1), 74–93.

This article discusses the current status of the foster-care system and
finds that agencies often have difficulty providing adequate, accessible, and
appropriate services for families in their care. Children of color, particularly African American children, are disproportionately represented in foster care. Foster families can find the experience overwhelming and frustrating, which causes many to leave foster parenting within the first year.
Organizational problems such as large caseloads, high staff turnover, and
data limitations compromise efforts to adequately serve and monitor families. The authors believe that promising policies and practices aimed to
strengthen families, support caseworkers, provide timely and adequate
data, and infuse cultural competency throughout the system can move the
foster-care system forward in the coming years.

Church, W. T., Gross, E., & Baldwin, J. (2005). Maybe ignorance is not
always bliss: The disparate treatment of Hispanics within the child welfare system. *Children and Youth Services Review, 27*(12), 1279–1292.

Previous studies have indicated that the proportion of culturally diverse
children to white children is increasing in public social service agencies.
Culturally diverse children are more likely to receive more intensive and
punitive services, are more likely to stay in the system for longer periods of
time, and are reported more often to Child Protective Services. The purpose of the study was to explore how child welfare practices with Hispanic

children are different from those with white non-Hispanic children. The study was a retrospective, two-year, longitudinal survival analysis of differential child welfare placement outcomes of white non-Hispanic and Hispanic children and families. Findings demonstrate that Hispanic children are more likely to be placed out of the home more quickly and for longer periods of time than their white non-Hispanic counterparts. The current study demonstrates the need for increased cultural awareness among child welfare professionals, especially in terms of assessment and case decision making.

Clegg & Associates. (2004). *Racial disproportionality in child welfare system in King County, Washington.* Retrieved from http://www.chs-wa.org/KingCountyReportonRacialDisproportionality.pdf.

This article discusses factors that contribute to disproportionality at different points in the child protective services process and proposes action steps to address them.

Coakley, T. M. (2008). Examining African American fathers' involvement in permanency planning: An effort to reduce racial disproportionality in the child welfare system. *Children and Youth Services Review, 30*(4), 407–417.

Children of color are disproportionately represented in the child welfare system. This study examines the extent to which African American fathers' involvement in permanency planning influences children's placement outcomes using a secondary data analysis of eighty-eight children's child welfare case records. Findings show that children were reunited with birth families more often and had shorter stays in foster care when their fathers were involved. Recommendations are provided for child welfare policy, practice, and research.

Crampton, D., & Jackson, W. L. (2007). Family group decision making and disproportionality in foster care: A case study. *Child Welfare, 86*(3), 51–69.

Research on the disproportionate number of children of color in the child welfare system suggests that we should focus on investigations, substantiations, and placements to understand how experiences of children vary by race and ethnicity. This article describes one community's efforts to use family group decision making in placement decisions to reduce disproportionality in foster care by diverting children from regular foster-care services and keeping them in their extended families.

Denby, R. W., Curtis, C. M., Alford, K. A., & Nielsen, K. (1998). Family preservation services and special populations: The invisible target. *Families in Society, 79*(1), 3–14.

Children of color are especially vulnerable for a devastating outcome as a result of their living environment and are disproportionately represented in the child welfare system. Social workers perpetuate the injustices associated with the child welfare system by ignoring the special needs of children of color when administering family preservation services. The authors present results from a national study that examined the attitudes, beliefs, and behaviors of family preservation workers. Results indicate a significant bias against targeting family preservation services to children of color.

Derezotes, D., & Hartnett, M. A. (2005). *Child welfare system involvement of African Americans: Jones County, Illinois.* Retrieved from http://www.racemattersconsortium.org/docs/whopaper6.pdf.

This report was developed by the Race Matters Consortium as an example of the first step that administrators should take when considering alternatives to address racial disproportionality in the child welfare system. Once this type of analysis is complete, further examination of the points in the system where disproportionality occurs is necessary. Various approaches can be used, including case-file reviews, child welfare professional interviews, client focus groups, and examination of court procedures.

Dougherty, S. (2003). *Practices that mitigate the effects of racial/ethnic disproportionality in the child welfare system.* Retrieved from http://www.casey.org/NR/rdonlyres/F2CF350A-1A46-4E02-80EA-3746F2A70F20/132/casey_mitigating_disproportionality.pdf.

This report focuses on practices that might moderate the effects of disproportionality on children and families who are already involved with the out-of-home care system. It also explores ways that other systems (education, health care, and juvenile justice) are seeking to mitigate disproportionate representation of children of color. The author examines the work of systems as they affect children in out-of-home care who attend school, are served by the health-care system, and often have interaction with the juvenile justice system.

Fulcher, L. C. (2002). Cultural safety and the duty of care. *Child Welfare*, *81*(5), 689–708.

This report examines the notion of cultural safety in relation to the duty-of-care mandate assigned to child welfare workers when the state intervenes in family life. The focus is on the vulnerabilities of rural and indigenous youth in New Zealand to cultural racism. The assertion is that child welfare professionals have a professional obligation to enhance their cultural competencies, including those related to effective work with rural families and children.

Green, M. Y. (2002). *Minorities as majority: Disproportionality in child welfare and juvenile justice.* Retrieved from http://www.cwla.org/articles/cv0211minorities.htm.

In 1992, Congress amended the Juvenile Justice and Delinquency Prevention Act to make it a core requirement for states to demonstrate their efforts to reduce disproportionate minority confinement. After a decade of data gathering, statistics confirmed what child welfare professionals suspected all along: far too many children of color pass from protection to punishment. In this two-part series, *Children's Voice* examines the seemingly intractable problem. The first article defines the scope and nature of the problem, looks at emerging research, and explores perspectives from all sides. The second article focuses on several local jurisdictions that are meeting challenges with promising programs and practices.

Green, M. Y. (2002). *Balancing the scales: Targeting disproportionality in child welfare and juvenile justice.* Retrieved from http://www.cwla.org/articles/cv0301balancing.htm.

Juvenile crime is decreasing significantly, but the number of juveniles in confinement continues to grow. The juvenile justice system confines far more minority youth than their offense rates can justify. African American children show up more often and stay far longer in child welfare systems than do white children. Several communities nationwide are addressing the problems of disproportionality with promising results. Three different communities are using a mix of strategies, including interagency collaboration, systems rethinking, accurate data collection and analysis, cultural competency, and community involvement.

Harris, M. S., & Hackett, W. (2008). Decision points in child welfare: An action research model to address disproportionality. *Children and Youth Services Review*, *30*(2), 199–215.

Researchers who conducted secondary analysis of data collected in community-based focus groups convened to analyze the key points at which racial disproportionality grew wider in child welfare. Analysis confirms findings that point to referral bias, unclear or problematic policies related to engaging kin, the confounding role of poverty, and racial disparities in the availability of services to improve family problems. The authors assert that professionals who believe the court system is fair and rational will not be vigilant in seeking out checks and balances to racial bias and may be less likely to seek training or consciousness-raising experiences to address their own bias. The research methodology used serves as an example of the ways university-based researchers can team with community-based action planning coalitions to stimulate systems change.

Hill, R. B. (2006). *Synthesis of research on disproportionality in child welfare: An update.* Retrieved from http://www.casey.org/NR/rdonlyres/ 053CD4C6-300D-402A-8C18-7E476C929D2A/990/0226_CC_BobHill Paper_FINAL.pdf.

This research paper focuses on information about black children and families. The following questions are reviewed: Does a child's or family's race influence the decisions that child welfare professionals make about that child or family? Are white and black children in the child welfare system treated differently? What other research is needed to help us understand why there is disproportionality and disparity in the child welfare system, how it happens, and what happens as a result?

Klingner, J. K., Harry, B., & Felton, R. K. (2003). Understanding factors that contribute to disproportionality: Administrative hiring decisions. *Journal of Special Education Leadership*, *16*(1), 23–33.

A study involving twelve elementary schools investigated hiring and placement decisions of school district-level personnel and principals. The research findings indicate inequities in the quality of leadership and instruction in inner-city schools. This leads to impaired efforts to reduce disproportionate placements of culturally and linguistically diverse children into special education.

Lemon, K., D'Andrade, A., & Austin, M. J. (2005). *Understanding and addressing disproportionality in the front end of the child welfare system.* Retrieved from http://cssr.berkeley.edu/bassc/public/DISPRO_PDF.pdf.

This literature review, commissioned by the Bay Area Social Services Consortium, examines the nature of disproportionality in the front-end child welfare system. The first section outlines the problem and describes several theories about its cause. The second section describes interventions that have been developed on the basis of those theories and assesses the effectiveness of the interventions.

Michigan Department of Human Services. (2006). *Equity: Moving toward better outcomes for all of Michigan's children.* Retrieved from http://www.michigan.gov/documents/DHS-Child-Equity-Report_153952_7.pdf.

This report discusses the overrepresentation of children of color in the child welfare system in Michigan and presents recommendations for addressing this issue.

Minnesota Department of Human Services. (2002). *Report to the legislature on the study of outcomes for African American children in Minnesota's child protection system.* Retrieved from http://edocs2.dhs.state.mn.us/lfserver/Legacy/MS-1943-ENG.

This report complies with the legislative mandate in the 2001 Minnesota Session Laws to study why African American children in Minnesota are disproportionately represented in out-of-home placements. The committee used the experience of child welfare experts and academics to develop an understanding of the over representation of African American children. Several causes have been found, including racism, practices of child welfare professionals, and reporting patterns of mandated reporters and others. This report provides a review of the data, an abbreviated look at child welfare decision points, local and national research about racial disparities of African American children and their families in the out-of-home placement system, and full recommendations of the committee.

Minnesota Department of Human Services. (2009). *The role of the case-worker in identifying, developing and supporting strengths in African American families involved in Child Protective Services: A practice guide.* Retrieved from http://www.friendsnrc.org/download/06confpres/disporportionality.pdf.

This practice guide was developed as a tool for social workers to help them address the systemic issue of the overrepresentation and racial disparity of African American children and their families involved in Child Protective Services. It is anticipated that the guide will be a resource and reference manual for caseworkers as they engage African American families in effective service delivery.

Murphy, S. M., & Bryant, D. (2002). The effect of cross-cultural dialogue as child welfare parenting classes: Anecdotal evidence in Black and White. *Child Welfare, 81*(2), 385–405.

The child welfare system indicates that evidence of successful completion of parenting classes is instrumental in determining whether parents are actively engaged in the process of permanency planning. Such classes vary in length and intensity, with topics ranging from how to raise healthy families to how to discipline your child. Two social workers chronicle their efforts to create a class format that recognizes the psychosocial and cultural influences inherent in facilitating these classes.

Park, R. P. (2003). Child abuse report decision-making: The role of ethnicity and other factors in a psychologist's decision to report physical abuse. *Dissertation Abstracts International: Section B: The Sciences and Engineering, 64*(5-B), 2397.

The goal of this study was to explore the relationship that psychologists' ethnicity and other characteristics have on their decisions to report physical child abuse. Surveys containing a short questionnaire and a hypothetical vignette were mailed to eight hundred psychologists, two hundred in each of four ethnic groups: African American, Asian American, Latino, and Caucasian. After the surveys were returned, a fifth multiracial ethnic group was created. Results indicated that Caucasian psychologists were slightly but significantly more likely to report. A factor significantly related to the decision to report was the level of certainty that abuse was occurring. Results indicated that African American respondents had significantly more favorable beliefs about corporal punishment than did Caucasian and multiracial respondents.

Roberts, D. E. (2003). Child welfare and civil rights. *University of Illinois Law Review.* Retrieved from http://home.law.uiuc.edu/lrev/publications/2000s/2003/2003_1/Roberts.pdf.

Although child welfare receives considerable media and scholarly attention, it is seldom treated as a civil rights issue. The child welfare system is overwhelmed by an alarming racial disparity, with black children especially representing a disproportionate share of the foster-care population. The author ties the child welfare system's racial disparity to broader economic and racial inequities. She concludes that viewing the disparity as a group-based civil rights violation calls for transforming the state's focus from punishing impoverished parents to providing increased, not coercive, support for vulnerable families.

Salend, S. J., & Garrick, D. L. (2002). A comprehensive approach to identity and addressing issues of disproportionate representation. *Remedial and Special Education, 23*(5), 289.

Reasons for the disproportionate representation of students from culturally and linguistically diverse backgrounds in special education are multifaceted and shaped by the cultural experiences of students and professionals. This article presents a comprehensive approach to identifying and addressing issues of disproportionate representation. Included are a list of questions for examining the extent to which issues and factors of disproportionality exist, as well as strategies to address the needs of students from culturally and linguistically diverse backgrounds.

Texas Health and Human Services Commission and Texas Department of Family and Protective Services. (2006). *Disproportionality in Child Protective Services: Statewide reform effort begins with examination of the problem.* Retrieved from http://www.dfps.state.tx.us/Documents/about/pdf/2006-01-02_Disproportionality.pdf.

Senate Bill 6, passed by the Seventy-Ninth Texas Legislature, requires comprehensive reform of Texas's Child Protective Services system. One aspect of that reform is to address issues of disproportionality or overrepresentation of a particular race or ethnic group in a program or system.

Too many children of color in foster care? (2004). *Policy and Practice of Public Human Services, 62*(1), 7.

In response to the widespread concern of the overrepresentation of children of color in the foster-care system, this article looks at practices that may alleviate this disproportionality, including family group conferencing, placement with relatives, diligent recruitment, and maintenance of family connections. Strategies for recruiting foster and adoptive families include identifying the right communities to target, using child-specific recruitment efforts, and team decision making.

Walker, S. (2002). Culturally competent protection of children's mental health. *Child Abuse Review, 11*(6), 380–393.

This article describes and discusses the concept of culturally competent practice and ways practitioners can better understand the needs of children in a multicultural, diverse society and intervene in more effective ways. It summarizes the components of a culturally competent practice to support families in the protection of children's mental health, with implications for practice.

7. False Allegations in Child Sexual Abuse

Ahlgrim-Delzell, L., & Dudley, J. R. (2001). Confirmed, unconfirmed, and false allegations of abuse made by adults with mental retardation who are members of a class action lawsuit. *Child Abuse and Neglect, 25*(8), 1121–1132.

The purpose of this article is to explore differences in confirmed, unconfirmed, and false allegations of abuse from clients with mental retardation in regard to type of abuse and perpetrator. Interviews were conducted with 1220 people with mental retardation who were part of a class-action lawsuit in North Carolina. A content analysis of abuse allegations was performed. Unconfirmed claims are the most frequent. Females made more allegations of abuse than males in general, and more allegations of rape. Other clients with mental retardation are most frequently accused of confirmed assaults. Staff members are most frequently accused in false allegations. Ability of the alleged victim to report information and timing of the investigation are important factors in substantiating abuse. Awareness of client-to-client violence and prevalence of false accusations against staff necessitates increased safeguards for both clients and staff.

Anderson, E. M., & Levine, M. (1999). Concerns about allegations of child sexual abuse against teachers and the teaching environment. *Child Abuse and Neglect, 23*(8), 833–843.

The major objective of this article was to determine teachers' awareness of the potential for child abuse allegations against themselves and the effects on the teaching environment. In response to a vignette, 42 percent advised a new teacher against being alone in a room with a student, 62 percent advised against casual touching, and 70 percent advised against hugging or putting an arm around a student. The more teachers expressed concern about abuse allegations against themselves, the more teachers advised against contact. Fear of abuse allegations is prominent among teachers. Fears may cause teachers to limit contact with students with potentially adverse consequences for students and the teaching environment.

Baker, R. A. (Ed.) (1998). *Child sexual abuse and false memory syndrome.* New York: Prometheus Books.

This book consists of six parts, including memory and its recovery; repression and amnesia; hypnosis, suggestion, and iatrogenesis; professional problems and ethical issues; research, needed research, and legal implications; and summary and conclusion. Baker warns therapists and other helping professionals about the consequences of making quick judgments.

Bala, N. M. C., Mitnick, M., Trocmé, N., & Houston, C. (2007). Sexual abuse allegations and parental separation: Smokescreen or fire? *Journal of Family Studies, 13*(1), 26–56.

If allegations of sexual abuse of a child are made after parents separate, the challenges of resolving custody and visitation issues greatly increase. These are high-conflict cases, and settlement may be difficult to arrange. The involvement of several agencies and professionals, with overlapping responsibilities and potentially conflicting opinions, may complicate case resolution. This article discusses how parental separation affects the making of child sexual abuse allegations, with particular emphasis on how separation may contribute to unfounded allegations. Recent research is reviewed, and national data from Canada on allegations of abuse and neglect when parents have separated are presented.

Boakes, J. (1999). False complaints of sexual assault: Recovered memories of childhood sexual abuse. *Medicine, Science, and the Law, 39*(2), 113–120.

False claims are easily made and carry serious consequences for the accused; however, many who make false claims genuinely believe the truth of what they report. Some, though, lie for their own gain. A special type of false allegation is false memory syndrome, which typically surfaces in therapy. People report that they recover memories of previously unknown childhood sexual abuse. The influence practitioners have on eliciting false memories and false complaints cannot be ignored.

Bornstein, B. H., & Muller, S. L. (2001). The credibility of recovered memory testimony: Exploring the effects of alleged victim and perpetrator gender. *Child Abuse and Neglect, 25*(11), 1415–1426.

The purpose of this study was to explore the effects of victim-complainant and perpetrator-defendant gender on the impact of recovered memory testimony in criminal sexual abuse trials. Recovered memory testimony results in a lowered view of the defendant's culpability and adds to the defendant's credibility. The complainant with recovered memory was viewed as less credible and less likely to be telling the truth. These effects of testimony type (i.e., recovered versus remembered) were qualified by an interaction with complainant and defendant gender, such that testimony type exerted an effect in cases of alleged heterosexual but not homosexual abuse.

Cannell, J., & Pope, H. (2001). Standards for informed consent in recovered memory therapy. *Journal of the American Academy of Psychiatry and the Law, 29*(2), 138–147.

Malpractice suits have garnered large rewards against therapists for instilling or recovering false memories of sexual abuse. Failing to inform patients concerning the risk of recovering false memories, is an increasingly made allegation against therapists. The article concludes that the risk or cluster of risks that must be disclosed to a patient recovering repressed memories in psychotherapy should include warnings about recovering false memories.

Carnes, C. N., Nelson-Gardell, D., & Wilson, C. (1999). Addressing challenges and controversies in child sexual abuse interviewing: The forensic
evaluation protocol and research project. *Journal of Aggression, Maltreatment and Trauma, 2*(2), 83–103.

The article describes a forensic evaluation protocol demonstrated in
gathering facts to validate true abuse, in determining when initial concerning statements of children are actually not due to sexual abuse, and in
uncovering false allegations and vindicating the falsely accused. A multisite
research project is currently under way that involves more than forty children's advocacy centers across the United States. This will further test the
efficacy of the model and further refine practice. The multisite project will
also include data on the evaluators' own abuse history and whether this
affects evaluation outcomes.

Dammeyer, M. D. (1998). The assessment of child sexual abuse allegations:
Using research to guide clinical decision making. *Behavioral Sciences and
the Law, 16*(1), 21–34.

The article addresses the issue of which sources of information clinicians should rely on when conducting child sexual abuse assessments.
Specifically, the commonly used indicators and procedures for assessing
allegations of abuse are identified and then examined in light of their
respective empirical literatures. It is concluded that medical examinations
and the child's report are among the best sources of information and
should therefore be most heavily relied on to arrive at accurate decisions.
Clinicians are encouraged to adopt a scientist's mind-set in conducting an
a priori, hypothesis-driven research investigation. This approach should
help clinicians avoid the temptation of post hoc analyses, which reflect personal biases more than actual data.

Davis, S. L. (1998). Social and scientific influences on the study of children's suggestibility: A historical perspective. *Child Maltreatment, 3*(2),
186–194.

Previous discussions stemming from research on the suggestibility of
children are examined against a historical backdrop treating the relationship between societal beliefs and scientific study of the suggestibility of
children. Modern research concerns the treatment of issues that result
from children having the role of victim or witness in court and the rights
of the accused. The approach to these and related issues was different

before the twentieth century, when there was less social concern about the sexual abuse of children.

Fish, V. (1998). The delayed memory controversy in an epidemiological framework. *Child Maltreatment, 3*(3), 204–222.

This study shows the delayed memory of child sexual abuse using an epidemiological framework. Potential problems of false positives include estimates for epidemiological variables, rate of false negatives, and effects of therapist characteristics.

Gunter, M., du Bois, R., Eichner, E., Rocker, D., Boos, R., Klosinski, G., et al. (2000). Allegations of sexual abuse in child custody disputes. *Medicine and Law, 19*(4), 815–825.

Allegations of sexual abuse are increasingly made in the context of divorce proceedings. The study aimed to describe ideal typical patterns of family dynamics when sexual abuse is alleged in divorce proceedings. Development of an assessment plan according to the methods of the qualitative descriptive social sciences and retrospective assessment of twenty-four legal cases of custody and visitation right proceedings in which allegations of sexual abuse ($N = 30$ children) were made. The results show significant incidence of sexual deviations of a parent. With respect to allegations of sexual abuse in divorce cases, four types of family dynamics were identified. The qualitative assessment of the data showed that distinguishing between actual abuse and false allegations cannot adequately clarify family dynamics. Rather, it tends to conceal that even a false allegation usually originates from a sexualized atmosphere in the family. The main family structures observed without exception in the sample already existed before the separation phase and had corresponding effects on the child which must be considered in the evaluation.

Hershkowitz, I. (1999). The dynamic of interviews involving plausible and implausible allegations of child sexual abuse. *Applied Developmental Science, 3*(2), 86–91.

This article focuses on interviews involving plausible and implausible allegations of child sexual abuse among Jews in Israel, responses of children to open-ended utterances in plausible statements, and accuracy assessments of the obtained information. It compares the dynamics of the interviews and discusses the effect of suggested prompts on children providing implausible accounts.

Hershkowitz, I. (2001). A case study of child sexual false allegation. *Child Abuse and Neglect, 25*(10), 1397–1411.

The first objective of the article was to follow the path by which a naive suggestion made in the course of a mother-child conversation transformed into an allegation of severe sexual abuse. The second objective was to analyze the child's interview scientifically and explore the limitations of scientific tools for detecting implausible allegations. The event the child described was "very unlikely to have happened," but the credibility assessment failed to detect its implausibility. Comparison of the two statements revealed that the child fabricated central details but incorporated them into a description of an event she really experienced, and most of the information provided was truthful.

Malloy, L. C., Lyon, T. D., & Quas, J. A. (2007). Filial dependency and recantation of child sexual abuse allegations. *Journal of the American Academy of Child and Adolescent Psychiatry, 46*(2), 162–170.

Controversy abounds regarding the process by which child sexual abuse victims disclose their experiences, particularly the extent to which and the reasons why some children recant their allegations. This study examined the prevalence and predictors of recantation among child sexual abuse victims age 2–17. Case files ($n = 257$) were randomly selected from all substantiated cases resulting in a dependency court filing in a large urban county between 1999 and 2000. A 23.1 percent recantation rate was observed. Multivariate analyses supported a filial dependency model of recantation, whereby abuse victims who were more vulnerable to familial adult influences (i.e., younger children, those abused by a parent figure and who lacked support from the nonoffending caregiver) were more likely to recant. An alternative hypothesis that recantations resulted from potential inclusion of cases involving false allegations was not supported.

McCauley, M. R., & Parker, J. F. (2001). When will a child be believed? The impact of the victim's age and juror's gender on children's credibility and verdict in a sexual-abuse case. *Child Abuse and Neglect, 25*(4), 523–539.

The study aimed to provide insight into the central dimensions jurors use when deciding on a child victim's credibility and verdict. Participants

($N = 573$) read a simulated trial (robbery or sexual assault case in which the defendant was a stranger or an acquaintance) in which the alleged victim was a girl age 6 or age 13. The trials were constructed to be as similar as possible with only minimal differences in the child's testimony. The defendant was more likely to be found guilty in the sexual assault cases than in the robbery case. The child was perceived as more credible, honest, and as having a better memory in the sexual assault cases than in the robbery case. Perceptions of memory and honesty predicted verdict and punishment. The child's age did not affect credibility or verdict. Finally, women were more likely than men to perceive the child as more credible.

Oates, R. K., Jones, D. P., Denson, D., Sirotnak, A., Gary, N., & Krugman, R. D. (2000). Erroneous concerns about child sexual abuse. *Child Abuse and Neglect, 24*(1), 149–157.

The purpose of this study is to evaluate the nature of concerns about sexual abuse, with particular reference to false reports of sexual abuse made by children. A review of case notes of all child sexual abuse reports to the Denver Department of Social Services over twelve months were evaluated, with 551 cases in four groups: substantiated, not sexual abuse, inconclusive, and erroneous accounts by children. Of cases, 43 percent were substantiated, 21 percent were inconclusive, 34 percent were not considered abuse cases, and 2.5 percent were considered erroneous accounts.

Pillai, M. (2002). Allegations of abuse: The need for responsible practice. *Medicine, Science, and the Law, 42*(2), 149–159.

The current U.K. child protection process has evolved reactively out of scandals, which has led to a culture of support for those making the allegations of abuse and has not provided proper ways to identify false claims. Information was collected from twenty-two families that were the subject of criminal or civil proceedings when a female adolescent or young adult developed a mental health problem. The results were mostly disastrous for the young person and the family. Claims of innocence were taken as evidence of guilt, and information was interpreted to fit this presumption while ignoring factual evidence to the contrary. The reasons underlying this professional behavior are considered. It is not clear that families and alleged victims will fare any better under recently revised guidance and framework.

Poole, D. A., & Lindsay, D. S. (1998). Assessing the accuracy of young children's reports: Lessons from the investigation of child sexual abuse. *Applied and Preventive Psychology, 7*(1), 1–26.

The procedures for investigating allegations of child sexual abuse have come under intense scrutiny by social critics, researchers, and the courts. Concerns about under- and overidentification have led to two approaches to evaluation: the indicator approach, which seeks to specify symptoms to identify sexually abused children, and the assessments approach, which analyzes conditions associated with accurate and inaccurate event reports. A review of research reveals inconsistencies between empirical results and commonly cited practices about how to discriminate between true and false reports. Four principles for designing studies and communicating findings are suggested to improve the interface between research and practice.

Trocme, N., & Bala, N. (2005). False allegations of abuse and neglect when parents separate. *Child Abuse and Neglect, 29*(12), 1333–1345.

This article provides an in-depth summary of the characteristics associated with intentional false reports of child abuse and neglect in the context of parental separation. Child maltreatment investigations conducted in selected sites during the months of October through December of 1998 were tracked, yielding a final sample of 7672 child maltreatment investigations. Canadian Incidence Study of Reported Child Abuse and Neglect (CIS-98) data indicate that more than one-third of maltreatment investigations are unsubstantiated, but only 4 percent of all cases are considered intentionally fabricated. Results of this analysis showed that neglect is the most common form of intentionally fabricated maltreatment. Of the intentionally false allegations of maltreatment tracked, custodial parents (usually mothers) and children were least likely to lie about reports of abuse or neglect. These results raise important clinical and legal issues, which require further consideration.

Werner, J., & Werner, M. C. M. (2008). Child sexual abuse in clinical and forensic psychiatry: A review of recent literature. *Current Opinion in Psychiatry, 21*(5), 499–504.

The purpose of this review is to evaluate recent literature on child sexual abuse and to highlight the clinical and forensic issues raised. The relationship between child sexual abuse and victims' mental health is increasingly being proven, which underlines the importance of correct clinical and forensic diagnosis of abuse. Forensic child and adolescent practitioners need to be highly trained. Evaluation of sexually abused children and adolescents must be accurate to ensure legal validity and must be performed with diligence so that alleged victims do not experience recurrence. Practitioners' actions must be referenced against appropriate instruments, and they must be prepared for the ethical and forensic dilemmas and new demands that arise in the field.

8. Law and Legal Actions

Bertram, R. (2008). Establishing a basis for multi-system collaboration: System team development. *Journal of Sociology and Social Welfare, 35*(4) 9–27.

Reports of child sexual abuse require police, Child Protective Services, forensic and medical evaluators, prosecutors, family court and treatment providers to negotiate complementary, overlapping roles with children and families. Administrators from these agencies in Kansas City, Missouri, clarified this multisystem response by applying a theory-based model for team development. This was previously studied in direct practice with families. The article presents the model and an exploratory case study. Findings suggest the model's efficacy for resolving interagency conflict, and it may contribute to constructing logic models in multisystem collaboration.

Buck, J. A., Warren, A. R., & Brigham, J. C. (2004). When does quality count? Perceptions of hearsay testimony about child sexual abuse interviews. *Law and Human Behavior, 28*(6), 599–621.

This study assessed how the quality of a sexual abuse investigative interview with a child and the age of the child influence jurors' reactions to either the original interview with the child or to testimony by an adult hearsay witness. Jurors in the child interview conditions were more likely to find the defendant guilty if they read the good interview than if they read either the poor or the typical interview. In the hearsay conditions verdicts did not significantly differ by interview quality. The findings suggest that there is a significant loss of information when the testimony of a hearsay witness is used in place of the actual interview with the child. This can call into question the appropriateness of allowing hearsay testimony.

Cossins, A. (2002). The hearsay rule and delayed complaints of child sexual abuse: The law and the evidence. *Psychiatry, Psychology and Law, 9*(2), 163–176.

This article evaluates the traditional legal significance of delayed disclosure with psychological literature, which shows that most children delay disclosure. Rather than being an unusual feature of child sexual abuse, delay is a typical response of sexually abused children. Several self-report studies of offenders confirm that grooming processes create a relationship of power between the child and offender so that delayed disclosure reflects the position of powerlessness of the sexually abused child. The author challenges the narrow legal approach to the admissibility of hearsay evidence of delayed disclosure and recommends that a special exception be made for hearsay statements of a child's delayed disclosure in child sexual assault trials.

Cossins, A. (2006). Prosecuting child sexual assault cases: Are vulnerable witness protections enough? *Current Issues in Criminal Justice, 18*(2), 299–317.

The article analyzes the effectiveness of the reforms that have been introduced to protect children when giving evidence in court during child sexual assault (CSA) cases in Australia. Numerous studies have used the degree of secondary victimization experienced by complainants as a method to assess the impact of the criminal justice system and the efficiency of particular law reform measures. If the only aim of reform is to improve the experiences of child complainants, the evidence suggests that this can be reached by prosecuting CSA cases in the same jurisdiction as other criminal cases. The prevention of CSA is just as significant as making the experiences of child victims less traumatic in court.

Courtin, J. (2006). Judging the judges: How the Victorian Court of Appeal is dealing with appeals against conviction in child sexual assault matters. *Current Issues in Criminal Justice, 18*(2), 266–298.

The article presents a study of how the Victorian Court of Appeal in Australia deals with appeals against conviction in child sexual assault matters. The complexities of the child sexual assault trial, combined with the threat of appellate scrutiny, are not the only factors to consider in understanding the source of significant trial judge error. The data in this study confirm that in Victoria, warnings to the jury in such trials are problematic and judicial error is significant.

Cramer, R. J., Adams, D. D., & Brodsky, S. L. (2009). Jury selection in child sex abuse trials: A case analysis. *Journal of Child Sexual Abuse, 18*(2), 190–205.

The article offers an analysis of psychological constructs for jury selection in child sex abuse cases from the defense perspective. The authors specifically define general and case-specific jury selection variables. General variables include authoritarianism, rigidity, need for cognition, pretrial knowledge, and race and socioeconomic status. Case-specific variables include sexual attitudes, homonegativity, juror abuse history, and beliefs about children. The article provides a factual background of a representative case, incorporates relevant case law, identifies sources for voir dire and juror questionnaire items, and discusses lessons from the primary author's first experience as a trial consultant for the defense.

Croxen, E. (2004). Dig deep into child abuse allegations. *Family Advocate, 26*(4), 24–27.

This article presents guidelines for use in litigating domestic relations cases with allegations of child abuse. Domestic relations litigators must remember that the domestic relations judge does not hear a divorce case from the perspective of protecting children. During the initial client interview, the litigator must always be a skeptic and should put the client through the most critical cross-examination possible, so as to explore weaknesses in the allegations before they are made part of the case. Every lawyer who expects to litigate such issues must become educated in the basic mechanisms of psychological evaluations and the diagnoses of mental disorders. The attorney has an obligation to address the course of action the client should take in the event that further allegations by a child are made.

Geraerts, E., Raymaekers, L., & Merckelbach, H. (2008). Recovered memories of childhood sexual abuse: Current findings and their legal implications. *Legal and Criminological Psychology, 13*(2), 165–176.

Recent research on recovered memories of childhood sexual abuse has shown that there are at least two types of recovered memory experiences: those that are gradually recovered in the context of suggestive therapy and those that are spontaneously recovered. We were able to find different origins for these recovered memory experiences. People recovering memories through suggestive therapy are more prone to forming false memories. People reporting spontaneously recovered memories are more prone to forgetting prior incidences of remembering. Memories recovered spontaneously, outside of suggestive therapy, are more likely to correspond to genuine abuse events. In this article, the authors summarize recent research on recovered memories and argue that these scientific findings should be applied in the justice system and in clinical practice.

Goodman, G. S. (2006). Children's eyewitness memory: A modern history and contemporary commentary. *Journal of Social Issues, 62*(4), 811–832.

This article provides a modern historical overview of child eyewitness research, as well as an evaluative commentary on the field, with special emphasis on children's eyewitness memory and suggestibility in child sexual abuse cases. Examples of legal cases that inform scientific research are described; discussion of relevant laws is presented, as is a selected studies review. Although a great deal has been learned about children's eyewitness memory and suggestibility over the past few decades, answers are evasive and much more research is needed.

Hutchfield, J., & Coren, E. (2011). The child's voice in service evaluation: Ethical and methodological issues. *Child Abuse Review, 20*(3), 173–186.

This article examines the ethical issues that arose from a qualitative study with children who had experienced sexual abuse. Also addressed are the implications of these ethical issues for the methodology and conduct of the study. The ethical dimensions discussed include protection of the therapeutic relationship, anonymity, confidentiality, consideration of the sensitivity of the issue, informed consent, the right to withdraw, and storage of data. The article highlights the importance of conducting research that follows ethical guidelines and reflects on the process of designing a study which incorporates them.

Lyon, T. D., & Saywitz, K. J. (2006). From post-mortem to preventive medicine: Next steps for research on child witnesses. *Journal of Social Issues, 62*(4), 833–861.

This article proposes five directions for future child witness research: the refinement of developmentally sensitive questioning aids that increase completeness without increasing suggestibility, the development of approaches to non-disclosure and recantation, the construction of interventions that meet mental health needs of child-victim witnesses without creating false memories or tainting testimony, a focus on details of children's narratives that are often lacking, and expanding our attention beyond child sexual abuse allegations in criminal court while considering the many contexts in which child witnesses are questioned.

Motzkau, J. F. (2007). Matters of suggestibility, memory and time: Child witnesses in court and what really happened. *Forum: Qualitative Social Research, 8*(1), 1–20.

This article examines how the English legal system employs special measures designed to manage children's apparent deficiencies while also guaranteeing the accuracy of their evidence in court. Using courtroom observations and data from interviews with legal professionals, the author follows the path of the video from its planning and recording by the police to its presentation in court. The author shows that the collision of the different time zones creates circumstances under which the video itself can become an ambiguous agent and ultimately a fanciful witness.

Payne, B. K., & DeMichele, M. (2011). Sex offender policies: Considering unanticipated consequences of GPS sex offender monitoring. *Aggression and Violent Behavior, 16*(3), 177–187.

This article describes unanticipated consequences as defined by Robert K. Merton and describes five unanticipated consequences of recent legislation mandating the use of GPS monitoring for sex offenders. Criminal justice researchers should analyze the wide-reaching policy effects of GPS sex offender laws. The authors argue that the use of GPS tracking for sex offenders is an underresearched and theorized criminal justice policy that should not be considered a way to solve sex-related crimes. Instead, it should be seen as another tool that may enhance community supervision.

Piper, A. (2008). Investigating child sex abuse allegations: A guide to help legal professionals distinguish valid from invalid claims. *Journal of Psychiatry and Law, 36*(2), 271–317.

This article aims to help prosecutors gain more knowledge about the process of child sex abuse allegations. Increased knowledge reduces professionals' doubts about handling such complex cases. The author reviewed the pertinent literature to find the following: clinicians' judgments about the veracity of unconfirmed CSA allegations may lack a firm scientific basis; no psychological test or method reliably indicates whether a child has been sexually mistreated; children sometimes falsely accuse; the concepts of memory repression and recovered memory are not scientifically sub-stantiated; medical evaluations are often inadequate to determine the pres-ence or absence of sex abuse; the most reliable indicator of sexual mistreat-ment is often not the physical examination but the child's own report; and certain features of the child's account suggest that the accusation is valid. It is concluded that conducting such interviews is of vital importance. Sug-gestions are also made to improve these interviews' quality.

Scher, J. (2009). Out-of-court statements by victims of child sexual abuse to multidisciplinary teams: A confrontation clause analysis. *Family Court Review*, *47*(1), 167–189.

This research note advocates a limited exception to the blanket hearsay ban on out-of-court statements set out by the Supreme Court decision in *Crawford v. Washington*. *Crawford* requires that hearsay evidence that is tes-timonial in nature be deemed inadmissible if the witness is unavailable and the defendant does not have a prior opportunity to cross-examine the wit-ness. Where nontestimonial hearsay is at issue, cross-examination may not be necessary. When a sexual abuse victim makes statements during a foren-sic interview to a member of a multidisciplinary team, these statements should be deemed nontestimonial and thus admitted into evidence, with-out requiring cross-examination of the child. Allowing for this exception to the general hearsay ban in *Crawford* will promote public policy and limit the negative impact such abuse has on society.

Watters, T., Brineman, J., & Wright, S. (2007). Between a rock and a hard place: Why hearsay testimony may be a necessary evil in child sexual abuse cases. *Journal of Forensic Psychology Practice*, *7*(1), 47–57.

In a criminal case in which a child is the alleged victim, the legal system has struggled with the issue of whether that child should be subjected to testifying on the stand or whether hearsay testimony is a reliable alterna-tive. This commentary addresses the criticisms against hearsay testimony and discusses problems with children testifying in court. It argues that the emotional damage resulting from allowing a child to testify far outweighs any criticism of hearsay testimony. Other concerns about unreliable testi-mony of children are addressed. By creating standards in which to allow it, hearsay testimony can be a credible way to translate the information ensuring the defendant's right to a fair trial.

Wiley, T. R., & Bottoms, B. L. (2009). Effects of defendant sexual orientation on juror's perceptions of child sexual assault. *Law and Human Behavior, 33*(1), 46–60.

Mock jurors' reactions to a sexual abuse case involving a male teacher and a 10-year-old child were examined. Because gay men are sometimes stereotyped as child molesters, the defendant's sexual orientation was portrayed as either gay or straight and the victim as either a boy or girl. Jurors made more pro-prosecution decisions in cases involving a gay than a straight defendant, especially when the victim was a boy. In boy-victim cases, jurors' emotional feelings of moral outrage toward the defendant determined these effects. The results have implications for understanding social perceptions of cross- and same-gender child sexual abuse and juror decision making in child sexual assault cases perpetrated by homosexual and heterosexual men.

9. Treatment

Anderson, K. M., & Hiersteiner, C. (2007). Listening to the stories of adults in treatment who were sexually abused as children. *Families in Society, 88*(4), 637–644.

This qualitative study examines the healing and recovery stories of twenty-seven adult sexual abuse survivors. Results from the study highlight the importance of creating a baseline for mental health treatment and services in the words, style, content, and form of client stories. Narrative theory holds promise as a guiding model for understanding the stories of adults who experienced sexual abuse in childhood.

Anderson, S., & Miller, R. (2006). The effectiveness of therapy with couples reporting a history of childhood sexual abuse: An exploratory study. *Contemporary Family Therapy: An International Journal, 28*(3), 353–366.

The purpose of this pilot study was to explore the impact of childhood sexual abuse (CSA) on couple's therapy. Participants were couples seeking therapy who were screened for CSA before therapy. Groups were compared using self-report and therapist-rated measures of individual and relational distress. Results indicate that, although therapists report significant differences between CSA couples and couples not reporting abuse at the onset of therapy, those reports do not translate into significant differences.

Arnold, E. M., Kirk, R. S., Roberts, A. C., Griffith, D. P., Meadows, K., & Julian, J. (2003). Treatment of incarcerated, sexually-abused adolescent females: An outcome study. *Journal of Child Sexual Abuse*, *12*(1), 123–139.

This study examined the psychosocial functioning of one hundred adolescent females (age 12–17) sentenced to secure care and the impact of a gender-specific, cognitive-behavioral therapy (CBT) intervention on the psychosocial functioning of subjects who reported a history of sexual abuse. The Multidimensional Adolescent Assessment Scale was used to assess psychosocial functioning. Results show that incarcerated female adolescents who reported a history of sexual abuse demonstrated more impairment in their functioning than did those without a reported history of sexual abuse. They also responded positively to a gender-specific, CBT-based intervention.

Avinger, K. A. (2007). Group treatment of sexually abused adolescent girls: A review of outcome studies. *American Journal of Family Therapy*, *35*(4), 315–326.

This article provides a review of outcome studies in regard to group treatment for adolescent victims of child sexual abuse (CSA). A review of outcome studies from 1985 to 2005 revealed only ten studies that specifically addressed group therapy for sexually abused girls age 11–18. Only four used comparison or control groups. Seven of the groups took place in outpatient settings, and three took place in inpatient or residential settings. Although none of the studies reported significant changes in externalizing behavior, several group models resulted in significant reductions in group members' self-reported anxiety symptoms and increases in self-reported self-esteem.

Beveridge, K., & Cheung, M. (2004). A spiritual framework in incest survivor's treatment. *Journal of Child Sexual Abuse*, *13*(2), 105–120.

This article highlights the theoretical concept of integration during the treatment process for adult female incest survivors. Spirituality as a therapeutic foundation is discussed, with examples of therapeutic techniques. A case study illustrates the psychospiritual process of treating a twenty-nine-year-old female incest survivor and describes how self-integration has helped her heal from trauma. Noteworthy outcomes of treatment include the client gaining self-awareness as well as being freed from emotional blindness. The recommended practice framework includes a three-step healing process of building alliance with the client in a safe environment, disputing faulty religious assumptions, and supporting the needs for reconnection and continuous spiritual support

Carr, A. (2004). Interventions for post-traumatic stress disorder in children and adolescents. *Pediatric Rehabilitation, 7*(4), 231–244.

Clinical features, epidemiology, and etiology of post-traumatic stress disorder (PTSD) are outlined. Also reviewed are outcome studies involving children with PTSD who have survived traumatic accidents, natural disasters, and child sexual abuse. Key components of effective treatment are psychoeducation about trauma reactions, continued exposure to trauma-related cues until habituation occurs, coping skills training, and parent training to equip parents with the skills needed to facilitate their children's recovery.

Chard, K. M. (2005). An evaluation of cognitive processing therapy for the treatment of posttraumatic stress disorder related to childhood sexual abuse. *Journal of Consulting and Clinical Psychology, 73*(5), 965–971.

This study compared the effectiveness of cognitive processing therapy for sexual abuse survivors (CPT-SA) with that of the minimal attention (MA) given to a wait-listed control group. Seventy-one women were randomly assigned to one of two groups. Participants were assessed at pretreatment and three times post-treatment: immediately after treatment and at a three-month and one-year follow-up. Analyses suggested that CPT-SA is more effective than MA in reducing trauma-related symptoms, and the results were maintained for at least one year.

Chop, S. M. (2003). Relationship therapy with child victims of sexual abuse placed in residential care. *Child and Adolescent Social Work Journal, 20*(4), 297–301.

Behaviors exhibited by child sexual abuse victims placed in residential care are difficult to understand and treat. This article focuses on understanding the behaviors from a relationship perspective. Staff should recognize that a child's relationship problems are not the result of interventions but are residual effects of the child's past abuse. Understanding the relationship problems these youths experience allows for reframing these behaviors and directing interventions.

Chouliara, Z., Karatzias, T., Scott-Brien, G., Macdonald, A., MacArthur, J., & Frazer, N. (2011). Talking therapy services for adult survivors of childhood sexual abuse (CSA) in Scotland: Perspectives of service users and professionals. *Journal of Child Sexual Abuse, 20*(2), 128–156.

This study aimed to elicit perceptions and experiences of talking therapy services for CSA survivors and professionals using qualitative interviews and analyzing transcripts with the Interpretative Phenomenological Analysis. Participants included thirteen adult survivors and thirty-one professionals in statutory and voluntary services in Scotland. The main themes found were benefits and challenges of the therapeutic process. Benefits included a trusting therapeutic relationship, feeling safe to disclose, breaking isolation, enhancing self-esteem and self-worth, contextualizing the abuse, and moving toward recovery. Challenges included trauma-focused work, supportive contact, continuity and consistency of services, accessibility during acute episodes, hearing and managing disclosures, child protection issues, and availability and accessibility of services. The findings support a greater emphasis on relational models, supervision, and training.

Cobia, D. C., Sobansky, R. R., & Ingram, M. (2004). Female survivors of childhood sexual abuse: Implications for couples' therapists. *Family Journal, 12*(3), 312–318.

There is a well-established relationship between childhood sexual abuse and adult sexual functioning. Couples with a partner who is a survivor of childhood sexual abuse are at heightened risk of relationship problems that accompany or result in unsatisfying or dysfunctional sexual relationships. Couples' therapists need an understanding of the long-term impact of such trauma and knowledge about interventions that might minimize the possibly damaging effects on intimate relationships.

Cohen, J. A., Deblinger, E., Mannarino, A. P., & Steer, R. A. (2004). A multisite randomized controlled trial for children with sexual abuse–related PTSD symptoms. *Journal of the American Academy of Child and Adolescent Psychiatry, 43*(4), 393–402.

This study aimed to examine the differential efficacy of trauma-focused cognitive-behavioral therapy (TF-CBT) and child-centered therapy for treating posttraumatic stress disorder (PTSD) and related emotional and behavioral problems in children who have suffered sexual abuse. For each of the two treatments, 229 children age 8–14 and their primary caretakers were randomly assigned. The children had significant symptoms of PTSD, with 89 percent meeting full *DSM-IV* PTSD diagnostic criteria. Results indicated that children assigned to TF-CBT, compared to those assigned to child-centered therapy, showed significantly more improvement with regard to PTSD, depression, behavior problems, shame, and abuse-related attributions. Correspondingly, parents assigned to TF-CBT showed greater improvement in their own self-reported levels of depression, abuse-specific distress, support of the child, and effective parenting practices. This study suggests the efficacy of this treatment for children who have experienced multiple traumas.

Cohen, J. A., Mannarino, A. P., & Knudsen, K. (2005). Treating sexually abused children: 1 year follow-up of a randomized controlled trial. *Child Abuse and Neglect, 29*(2), 135–145.

This study measures the improvement in response to two alternative treatments for sexually abused children. Eighty-two sexually abused children age 8–15 and their primary caretakers were randomly assigned to trauma-focused cognitive-behavioral therapy (TF-CBT) or nondirective supportive therapy delivered over twelve sessions. The TF-CBT group showed significantly greater improvement in anxiety, depression, sexual problems, and dissociation at the six-month follow-up and in PTSD and dissociation at the twelve-month follow-up. This study gives additional support for the effectiveness of TF-CBT.

Colangelo, J. J. (2007). Recovered memory debate revisited: Practice implications for mental health counselors. *Journal of Mental Health Counseling, 29*(2), 93–120.

See annotation in the section "Child Sexual Abuse Interviews."

Cole, K. L., Sarlund-Heinrich, P., & Brown, L. S. (2007). Developing and assessing effectiveness of a time-limited therapy group for incarcerated women survivors of childhood sexual abuse. *Journal of Trauma and Dissociation, 8*(2), 97–121.

The purpose of this preliminary investigation was to implement and evaluate the efficacy of a time-limited, trauma-focused group intervention with a group of recently incarcerated women who had experienced CSA. Five women completed the group plus pre- and posttest measures; a wait-list control group completed measures at the same intervals. Results were mixed for the effectiveness of treatment; women in the control group showed consistent declines in scores during the wait-list period. This suggests that the intervention may have helped them adjust.

Corcoran, J. (2004). Treatment outcome research with the non-offending parents of sexually abused children: A critical review. *Journal of Child Sexual Abuse, 13*(2), 59–84.

Potentially harmful effects arise from the experience of childhood sexual abuse, but maternal support has been identified as a crucial factor. This article attempts to provide a critical review of the treatment outcomes reported for these new interventions. Studies have been organized according to the sexually abused child's stage of development: preschool, school age, and adolescence. Also included are recommendations for service delivery and research.

Cunningham, C., Fill, K., & Al-Jamie, L. (1999). Sand tray play with traumatized children: A comparison study. In K. C. Faller (Ed.), *Maltreatment in early childhood: Tools for research-based intervention* (pp. 195–205). New York: Haworth Maltreatment and Trauma Press.

This study examines the patterns of play in latency-age males to determine whether the play of boys with sexual abuse trauma differs from other types of trauma play. Three groups of five boys each were assessed using sand-tray play. The first were victims of sexual abuse, the second were being treated for chronic or terminal health conditions, and the third had no known trauma. Despite the small number of subjects, the findings reflected distinct patterns in the groups examined. Differences included the average number of figures used, organization in trays, whether they were chosen deliberately or randomly, the central figure, and the ability to find resolution.

Daigneault, I., Cyr, M., & Tourigny, M. (2007). Exploration of recovery trajectories in sexually abused adolescents. *Journal of Aggression, Maltreatment and Trauma, 14*(1–2), 165–184.

This study documents recovery status and symptom changes from a one-year follow-up of sexually abused adolescent girls in child protection services in Québec, Canada. Sixteen participants completed questionnaires assessing symptoms, types of maltreatment endured, and services received. They were interviewed using the Multidimensional Trauma Recovery and

Resiliency Interview (MTRR-I), which was in turn rated by interviewers using the companion rating scale, the MTRR. Analyses of one-year follow-up data revealed statistically significant changes toward better functioning on multiple domains and less symptomatology for most of the girls interviewed. The recovery status of a minority of research participants seems to have worsened in the interval. The discussion considers these findings and addresses relevancy of the MTRR measures in cases of sexually abused adolescents.

Daigneault, I., Hébert, M., & Tourigny, M. (2006). Attributions and coping in sexually abused adolescents referred for group treatment. *Journal of Child Sexual Abuse, 15*(3), 35–59.

This study aims to assess the predictive value of self-attributions and coping behaviors on sexually abused teenagers' functioning. A total of 103 female adolescents completed self-report measures to assess their psychological functioning in terms of anxiety, depression, posttraumatic stress disorder, sexual concerns, dissociation, anger, self-injurious behaviors, antisocial behaviors, and drug use. Attributions and coping behaviors did not significantly explain additional variance for scores of antisocial behaviors and drug use. Personal attributions of blame for negative events were the strongest predictors of adolescents' functioning.

Deblinger, E., Mannarino, A. P., Cohen, J. A., & Steer, R. A. (2006). A follow-up study of a multisite, randomized, controlled trial for children with sexual abuse–related PTSD symptoms. *Journal of the American Academy of Child and Adolescent Psychiatry, 45*(12), 1474–1484.

The article concentrates on the study of the effectiveness of two controlled trials in treating children with sexual abuse–related posttraumatic stress disorder (PTSD) symptoms. Trauma-focused, cognitive-behavioral therapy (TF-CBT) and child-centered therapy were used to determine the differential responses of the patients. Children treated with TF-CBT have fewer symptoms of PTSD using the mixed-model repeated analyses.

Deblinger, E., & Runyon, M. K. (2005). Understanding and treating feelings of shame in children who have experienced maltreatment. *Child Maltreatment, 10*(4), 364–376.

This article conceptualizes the development and maintenance of shame after experiencing child sexual and/or physical abuse. The authors review research on the impact of shame, with an emphasis on understanding how this type of painful emotional suffering can be prevented and/or treated. Trauma-focused interventions that have demonstrated efficacy in helping children overcome feelings of shame are described. Also suggested are directions for future research that may further understanding of the development, impact, and treatment of feelings of shame.

Deblinger, E., Stauffer, L. B., & Steer, R. A. (2001). Comparative efficacies of supportive and cognitive behavioral group therapies for young children who have been sexually abused and their non-offending mothers. *Child Maltreatment, 6*(4), 332–343.

The differential efficacies of supportive and cognitive-behavioral group therapy models designed for young children (age 2–8) who have experienced sexual abuse and their nonoffending mothers were compared. Forty-four mothers and their children participated in either supportive or cognitive-behavioral therapy groups. Results indicated that, compared to mothers in support groups, mothers who participated in cognitive behavioral groups reported greater reductions at posttest in their intrusive thoughts and their negative parental emotional reactions regarding the sexual abuse. The children treated with cognitive-behavioral therapy demonstrated greater improvement in their knowledge regarding body safety skills at posttest than did children who received supportive therapy.

Duane, Y., Carr, A., Cherry, J., McGrath, K., & O'Shea, D. (2003). Profiles of the parents of adolescent CSA perpetrators attending a voluntary outpatient treatment program in Ireland. *Child Abuse Review, 12*(1), 5–24.

A group of twenty-two parents of adolescent sexual offenders (PASO) was compared with a group of nineteen normal controls (NC) and ten clinical controls (CC) on demographic, developmental, personal adjustment, and family environment variables. The assessment protocol included the General Health Questionnaire-12, the Culture-Free Self-Esteem Inventory, the Child Behavior Checklist, the Family Assessment Device, the Parent Satisfaction Scale, and the Multidimensional Scale of Perceived Social Support. Compared with clinical and normal controls, more parents in the PASO group reported that they had been arrested or charged for a criminal offense; had personally experienced child abuse; and more of their adolescents had experienced child abuse. More adolescents of parents in the PASO group had witnessed parental drug or alcohol abuse and had been placed in care outside their home. However, the groups did not differ significantly in their levels of perceived social support.

Dufour, S., & Chamberland, C. (2004). The effectiveness of selected interventions for previous maltreatment: Enhancing the well-being of children who live at home. *Child and Family Social Work, 9*(1), 39–56.

The authors critically assessed reviews of the literature published between 1984 and 2002 to describe the state of knowledge about the effectiveness of interventions aimed to protect or improve the welfare of child victims of maltreatment and who remain in the family home. The interventions studied target children, parents, or families. The intervention effectiveness indicators measure changes in parents' and children's knowledge, attitude, emotion, and behavior.

Edmond, T., & Rubin, A. (2004). Assessing the long-term effects of EMDR: Results from an 18-month follow-up study with adult female survivors of CSA. *Journal of Child Sexual Abuse, 13*(1), 69–86.

This eighteen-month follow-up study builds on the findings of a randomized experimental evaluation that found qualified support for the short-term effectiveness of eye-movement desensitization and reprocessing (EMDR) in reducing trauma symptoms among adult female survivors of childhood sexual abuse (CSA). The current study provides preliminary evidence that the therapeutic benefits of EMDR for adult female survivors of CSA can be preserved over an eighteen-month period. There is support for the suggestion that EMDR did so more efficiently and provided a greater sense of trauma resolution than did routine individual therapy.

Edmond, T., Sloan, L., & McCarty, D. (2004). Sexual abuse survivors' perceptions of the effectiveness of EMDR and eclectic therapy. *Research on Social Work Practice, 14*(4), 259–272.

This article examines survivor perspectives of the effectiveness of two different treatments for trauma symptoms among adult female survivors of childhood sexual abuse: eye-movement desensitization and reprocessing (EMDR) and eclectic therapy. Qualitative interviews in a mixed-methods study were conducted with thirty-eight adult female survivors of childhood sexual abuse. Two major differences in outcomes between the two treatment approaches were observed. There were significant distinctions between the two treatment groups in terms of the importance and effect of the client-therapist relationship, as well as depth of change. Survivor's narratives indicate that EMDR produces greater trauma resolution while in eclectic therapy; survivors value their relationship with their therapist, through whom they learn effective coping strategies.

Farmer, E., & Pollock, S. (2003). Managing sexually abused and/or abusing children in substitute care. *Child and Family Social Work, 8*(2), 101–112.

This article reports on research of the characteristics, management, and therapeutic treatment of sexually abused and/or abusing children in substitute care. Of the forty sexually abused and/or abusing young people age 10 or older in the interview sample, two-thirds showed sexual behaviors in the placement studied, but one-third did not. Analysis of the findings shows that four key components of effective management are supervision, adequate sex education, modification of inappropriate sexual behavior, and therapeutic attention to the needs that motivate this behavior. Supervision includes planning for safe care before placement, preparing other children in the setting, teaching young people how to keep themselves safe when out on their own, and careful monitoring contact with birth family members.

Freshwater, K., Ainscough, C., & Toon, K. (2002). Confronting abusers: Three opinions of clinicians and survivors. *Journal of Child Sexual Abuse, 11*(4), 35–52.

This article explores direct and symbolic forms of survivors confronting their abusers through a review of the current literature and the self-report of twelve female survivors, after therapy. Six of the survivors had chosen to directly confront their abusers and six had not. Their experiences and opinions are presented together with a discussion of important issues in this area and the need for further research. One hundred eighty-eight female participants (44 victims and 144 nonvictims of CSA) from a four-year university were recruited for this study.

Fritsch, R. C., & Warner, R. R. (2004). Commentary on a first-person account of sexual abuse: From experience to theory and treatment. *Psychiatry: Interpersonal and Biological Processes, 67*(3), 239–245.

This article focuses on Penelope Hollander's first-person account of the outcome of sexual trauma that provides an important opportunity to view how a sophisticated writer with knowledge of psychoanalytical theory can understand the experience of sexual abuse. She also recounts how her experience of the sexual abuse produced a powerful erotic striving while crippling her relationship with men. A review on some ideas on the treatment of patients who are survivors of trauma is looked at.

Geraerts, E., Lindsay, D. S., Merckelbach, H., Jelicic, M., Raymaekers, L., Arnold, M., et al. (2009). Cognitive mechanisms underlying recovered-memory experiences of childhood sexual abuse. *Psychological Science, 20*(1), 92–98.

People sometimes report recovering long-forgotten memories of childhood sexual abuse. The memory mechanisms that lead to such reports are not well understood, and the authenticity of recovered memories has often been challenged. Two subgroups of people are identified. The subgroups differed dramatically in their cognitive profiles: People who recovered memories of abuse through suggestive therapy exhibited a heightened predisposition to the construction of false memories. Conversely, people who recovered memories of abuse spontaneously showed a heightened proneness to forget prior incidences of remembering but exhibited no increased likelihood of false memories. This points to mechanisms that underlie recovered-memory experiences and indicates that recovered memories may at times be false and at other times be authentic.

House, A. S. (2006). Increasing the usability of cognitive processing therapy for survivors of child sexual abuse. *Journal of Child Sexual Abuse, 15*(1), 87–103.

This article describes a modification of cognitive processing therapy for child sexual abuse (CPT-SA) that reduces the number of individual therapy sessions required. Modifications are based on the developing literature on stage-based approaches to the treatment of CSA. Initial pilot data on modified CPT-SA suggests that the therapy may be effective for the treatment of posttraumatic stress disorder and depression.

Hovey, A., Stalker, C. A., Schachter, C. L., Teram, E., & Lasiuk, G. (2011). Practical ways psychotherapy can support physical healthcare experiences for male survivors of childhood sexual abuse. *Journal of Child Sexual Abuse, 20*(1), 37–57.

This article summarizes the findings of a multiphase qualitative study about survivors' experiences in health-care settings. The study used the *Handbook on Sensitive Practice for Health Care Practitioners: Lessons from Adult Survivors of Childhood Sexual Abuse*. This article discusses what psychotherapists can learn from the health-care experiences of the male

survivors who participated in this project. It also offers practical suggestions for supporting male clients who experience difficulty seeking treatment for physical health concerns.

Hyman, S. M., Gold, S. N., & Cott, M. A. (2003). Forms of social support
    that moderate PTSD in childhood sexual abuse survivors. *Journal of
    Family Violence, 18*(5), 295–300.

This study sought to distinguish the specific types of perceived social
support of posttraumatic stress disorder (PTSD) in victims of childhood
sexual abuse (CSA). One hundred seventy-two adult females reporting
CSA were administered the Interpersonal Support Evaluation List (ISEL)
and the Impact of Events Scale (IES). The ISEL measures the perceived
availability of four support types. The IES measures core PTSD symptoms
of intrusion and avoidance. Analysis indicated that social support significantly buffered PTSD development. The best model contained self-esteem
and appraisal support. Self-esteem support was identified as the most
important variable in preventing PTSD development.

Kessler, M. R. H., Nelson, B. S., Jurich, A. P., & White, M. B. (2004). Clinical
    decision-making strategies of marriage and family therapists in the
    treatment of adult childhood sexual abuse survivors. *American Journal
    of Family Therapy, 32*(1), 1–10.

Therapists are likely to treat sexual abuse survivors in their clinical work.
A modified Delphi study was used to collect data to determine how American Association of Marriage and Family Therapy–approved supervisors
make treatment decisions following client disclosures of CSA. Three
rounds of data were collected. The results suggested that there are several
issues to address in therapy regardless of treatment model and type of disclosure. Suggestions for treatment are provided.

Kessler, M. R. H., White, M. B., & Nelson, B. S. (2003). Group treatments
    for women sexually abused as children: A review of the literature and
    recommendations for future outcome research. *Child Abuse and Neglect,
    27*(9), 1045–1061.

This article provides a critique of the outcome research of thirteen studies on the treatment of adults who suffered childhood sexual abuse. Also
discussed are specific methodological strategies that can enhance the quality of research in the future. Although many of the studies contain methodological limitations, the results generally indicate that group treatment

helps reduce symptomatology in the short term and at follow-up. Several outcome studies have found group treatment to be effective in the recovery of female CSA survivors.

King, N. J., Heyne, D., Tonge, B. J., Mullen, P., Myerson, N., Rollings, S., et al. (2003). Sexually abused children suffering from post-traumatic stress disorder: Assessment and treatment strategies. *Cognitive Behaviour Therapy, 32*(1), 2–12.

This review addresses recent advances in the assessment and treatment of sexually abused children with posttraumatic stress disorder. Outlined are the diagnostic criteria for PTSD and variables in the development of PTSD. Also addressed is the clinical assessment of PTSD in sexually abused children. A familywide cognitive-behavioral treatment framework for sexually abused children with PTSD is suggested. The results of recent evaluation studies supportive of cognitive-behavioral therapy in the treatment of sexually abused children are examined. Also given are conclusions for clinical practice and directions for future research.

Kouyoumdjian, H., Perry, A., & Hansen, D. (2009). Nonoffending parent expectations of sexually abused children: Predictive factors and influence on children's recovery. *Journal of Child Sexual Abuse, 18*(1), 40–60.

This study examined the influence of parental expectations on the functioning of sexually abused children. Participants included sixty-seven sexually abused youths and sixty-three of their nonoffending primary caregivers. Parental expectations about how sexual abuse affects children predicted parents' ratings of children's behavior at pretreatment. Parental expectations of children's overall future functioning did not predict parents' ratings of children's behavior. Results highlight the influential role the sexual abuse label has in shaping parental expectations about children's functioning.

Lau, M., & Kristensen, E. (2007). Outcome of systemic and analytic group psychotherapy of adult women with history of intrafamilial childhood sexual abuse: A randomized controlled study. *Acta Psychiatrica Scandinavica, 116*(2), 96–104.

This study compared the effects of analytic and systemic group psychotherapy on CSA. One hundred fifty-one women with intrafamilial CSA were randomly put into two groups. Quality of life, psychosocial function, psychological distress, and flashbacks were assessed before and after treatment. Eighty-two patients completed group therapy. Both therapies led to improved quality of life, fewer psychopathological symptoms, and better overall functioning. Longer-term follow-up data are required for conclusions on maintenance of therapeutic gains.

Lescano, C. M., Brown, L. K., Puster, K. L., & Miller, P. M. (2004). Sexual abuse and adolescent HIV risk: A group intervention framework. *Journal of HIV/AIDS Prevention in Children and Youth*, 6(1), 43–57.

Adolescents with a history of sexual abuse are at particular risk for HIV because of difficulties with affect regulation and dysfunctional thinking. These difficulties can lead to impulsivity and failure to set limits in sexual situations. Cognitive-behavior therapy has frequently been employed in the treatment of abused children and adolescents. A variant of this, dialectical behavior therapy (DBT), has been applied with abused adults, which may be useful as a framework for addressing affect dysregulation and dysfunctional thinking specific to sexuality in and HIV prevention for abused adolescents. Important factors in the application of DBT to HIV prevention are developmental factors, use of experiential training, and environment of the intervention.

Longo, R. E. (2004). An integrated experiential approach to treating young people who sexually abuse. *Journal of Child Sexual Abuse*, 13(3–4), 193–213.

This article promotes the use of an integrated (holistic) approach to treating juvenile sexual offenders. An integrated model takes into account that youths are resilient; youths progress through various stages of development; those stages are often arrested as a result of trauma, child abuse and neglect, and attachment disorders; humanistic approaches and the therapeutic relationship are essential to the healing and recovery process; youths learn and work with various learning styles; many traditional assessment and treatment approaches can be modified with an integrated approach; and the use of experiential treatments can have a positive, deep impact in treating youths with sexual behavior problems.

Lovett, B. (2007). Sexual abuse in the preschool years: Blending ideas from object relations theory, ego psychology, and biology. *Child and Adolescent Social Work Journal*, 24(6), 579–589.

This article uses concepts from relational psychodynamic theories and findings from neurobiology to conceptualize a young child's experience of sexual abuse. Selected developmental tasks are discussed using an integrated theoretical framework. Literature that highlights the importance of the child's environment is reviewed. It is recommended that social work practitioners expand on the biology domain when conducting a bio-psychosocial assessment. Social work students may benefit from additional content on biology in social work curricula.

Martsolf, D. S., & Draucker, C. B. (2005). Psychotherapy approaches for adult survivors of childhood sexual abuse: An integrative review of outcomes research. *Issues in Mental Health Nursing, 26*(8), 801–825.

This review synthesized results of twenty-six outcomes research studies and two meta-analyses that evaluated abuse-focused psychotherapy techniques for survivors of childhood sexual abuse. Different therapeutic approaches delivered in individual, group, or combination formats were evaluated with pre- and posttest, quasi-experimental, or randomized control designs. Accumulated research findings suggest that abuse-focused psychotherapy for adults sexually abused as children is generally beneficial in reducing psychiatric distress, depression, and trauma-specific symptoms. There was little evidence about the effectiveness of individual versus group therapy or the ideal treatment length.

McKay, A. (2006). Cognitive-behavioural treatment of children with sexual behaviour problems can have long-term beneficial impact. *Canadian Journal of Human Sexuality, 15*(2), 113–114.

The article presents a discussion on sexual behavior problems (SBP) among children with an emphasis on the result of a study by Carpentier, Silovsky, and Chaffin. Among children, SBP is considered a progressive behavior pattern that leads to adolescent and adult sexual offenses. Previous studies revealed that a child with SBP is not likely to commit adolescent or adult sexual offenses. It pointed out that the social and legal policy assumes that childhood SBPs are difficult to establish and modify.

McGregor, K., Thomas, D. R., & Read, J. (2006). Therapy for child sexual abuse: Women talk about helpful and unhelpful therapy experiences. *Journal of Child Sexual Abuse, 15*(4), 35–59.

Women with a history of childhood sexual abuse (CSA) were asked to describe what was helpful and unhelpful to them in therapy. The sample of 191 completed postal questionnaires, and a subsample of 20 participants was interviewed. This article focuses on three specific areas of therapy mentioned by interviewees: establishing a therapeutic relationship, talking about experiences and effects of CSA, and dealing with errors in therapy. Findings suggest that to avoid making serious therapy errors, therapists need special skills to be aware of the dynamics and effects of CSA and of abuse-focused therapy and to deal with abuse-related material, and they need to develop an equal and open therapy relationship that includes ongoing consultation with clients about their experiences of therapy.

McLean, L. M., Toner, B., Jackson, J., Desrocher, M., & Stuckless, N. (2006). The relationship between childhood sexual abuse, complex post-traumatic stress disorder and alexithymia in two outpatient samples: Examination of women treated in community and institutional clinics. *Journal of Child Sexual Abuse, 15*(3), 1–17.

Relationships between trauma variables, complex posttraumatic stress disorder (complex PTSD), affect dysregulation, dissociation, somatization, and alexithymia were studied in seventy women with early onset sexual abuse. Women were treated either in community-based private or clinic outpatient settings. Measures were the Toronto Alexithymia Scale-20 and the Psychological Trauma Assessment Program. Compared with the community sample, the clinic sample met diagnostic criteria for both lifetime and current complex PTSD; showed correlations among current affect dysregulation, dissociation, and somatization with alexithymia; and had higher levels of alexithymia. Results suggest the clinic sample continued to experience current forms of suffering, risk, and vulnerability. The findings show possible implications regarding types of treatment available in community versus clinic settings.

Miller, B. J., Cardona, J., & Hardin, M. (2006). The use of narrative therapy and internal family systems with survivors of childhood sexual abuse: Examining issues related to loss and oppression. *Journal of Feminist Family Therapy, 18*(4), 1–27.

The emerging trend in society is one that facilitates healthier grieving and the ability to story the losses brought on by trauma. This article seeks to address the need to better understand how to engage clients in the therapeutic experiences of healing and the liberation of their histories. Informed by narrative and internal family systems theories, the authors propose unique interventions that better inform clinicians how to assist clients in making a meaning out of their losses related to CSA.

Nenad, P. (2002). Prolonged exposure counterconditioning (PEC) as a treatment for chronic post-traumatic stress disorder and major depression in an adult survivor of repeated child sexual and physical abuse. *Clinical Case Studies, 1*(2), 148–169.

Prolonged exposure counterconditioning (PEC) was tested as a treatment for chronic post-traumatic stress disorder (PTSD) in an adult survivor of repeated child sexual and physical abuse. PEC uses images evocative of reliving very pleasurable life moments to weaken traumatic conditioned emotional responses (CERs). A higher-order conditioned stimuli (CS) is used as a traumatic CER elicitor. Prolonged imaginal reliving of pleasurable CSs is used as a counterconditioner to the traumatic CERs. A statistical technique for analyzing single-case subject designs based on classical test theory was used to evaluate the client's progress in treatment. Results showed that PEC effectively decreased the client's PTSD symptoms, depression, and anxiety. The client's negative cognitions became considerably more positive. Other clinically observed symptoms also showed improvement. All results were maintained at a three-month follow-up.

Nickel, R., & Egle, U. T. (2005). Influence of childhood adversities and defense styles on the 1-year follow-up of psychosomatic-psychotherapeutic inpatient treatment. *Psychotherapy Research, 15*(4), 483–494.

The current study explores the connection between reported sexual abuse and physical maltreatment during childhood and immature defense styles affecting the one-year follow-up of inpatients that had undergone psychodynamic group therapy. Early trauma was assessed using a structured patient interview, and the defense styles were assessed with a questionnaire on defense styles. At the one-year follow-up, the entire sample showed a distinct improvement. The effect sizes for health-related quality of life ranged from 0.82 to 1.21, and that for psychological distress was 0.81. Patients with early traumatization were significantly more impaired both before treatment and at follow-up, yet they profited from treatment comparably to patients without early traumatization. The quality of life among patients with highly immature defense styles was significantly lower than for those with fewer immature defense styles.

Nolan, M., Carr, A., Fitzpatrick, C., O'Flaherty, A., Keary, K., Turner, R., et al. (2002). A comparison of two programmes for victims of child sexual abuse: A treatment outcome study. *Child Abuse Review*, *11*(2), 103–123.

This study aimed to evaluate the comparative effectiveness of individual therapy and combined individual and group therapy in the psychological treatment of child sexual abuse victims. The Child Behaviour Checklist (CBCL), the Youth Self Report form (YSR), the Children's Depression Inventory (CDI), and the Trauma Symptom Checklist for Children (TSCC) were administered before treatment and six months later to a group of twenty young people who participated in individual therapy (IT) programs and to a group of eighteen young people who participated in programs that involved combined individual and group therapy (IGT). For both types of programs, statistically significant improvement occurred. From this study, it can be concluded that after six months, individual therapy and combined individual and group therapy were equally effective in the psychological treatment of child sexual abuse victims.

Oellerich, T. (2007). Rethinking the routine provision of psychotherapy to children/adolescents labeled "sexually abused." *International Journal of Behavioral Consultation and Therapy*, *3*(1), 123–144.

Sexually abused children are routinely offered treatment at considerable financial cost. A result of this is that mental health professionals are being accused of exploiting the problem of child sexual abuse (CSA). Is the routine provision of psychotherapy for sexually abused children warranted? This article argues that the evidence indicates it is not warranted. Its provision is not in the best interests of either the children or mental health professionals. It is argued that it is time to rethink the routine provision of psychotherapy to children and adolescents labeled sexually abused. Recommendations are given based on the evidence.

Ownbey, M. A., Jones, R. J., Judkins, B. L., Everidge, J. A., & Timbers, G. D. (2001). Tracking the sexual behavior-specific effects of a foster family treatment program for children with serious sexual behavior problems. *Child and Adolescent Social Work Journal*, *18*(6), 417–436.

Few treatment programs exist for very young children with serious sexual behavior problems, and even fewer have produced data relating to their effectiveness. The scarce data that have emerged focus on global social adjustment or improvement rather than on sexual behavior-specific changes. This study tracked both frequency of problem sexual behaviors and caregiver estimates of the propensity to reoffend of six initial clients referred to a treatment-intensive foster-care program for sexually reactive children and preadolescent sexual offenders. A simple pre-post (base point–treatment) design was used, and in-treatment data gathered over a two-year interval. Initial results indicate that the problem sexual behaviors of most of these clients were effectively and immediately suppressed in the context of their treatment intensive foster placements. Recommendations are given concerning the viability of foster-care intervention for sexualized and offending children.

Palmer, S., Stalker, C. A., Harper, K., & Gadbois, S. (2007). Balancing positive outcomes with vicarious traumatization: Participants' experiences with group treatment for long-term effects of childhood abuse. *Social Work with Groups, 30*(4), 59–77.

A total of thirty adult survivors of childhood abuse were interviewed approximately six months after completing a six-week inpatient program for traumatic stress recovery. Their progress was assessed by standardized instruments that measured PTSD symptoms, general psychiatric symptoms, trauma-related beliefs, and self-esteem at discharge. Most interviewees spoke positively about their treatment experience and were maintaining gains at six-month follow-up. Six (20 percent) of the interviewees, however, reported some negative effects from their participation in process groups, including vicarious traumatization.

Parker, A., Fourt, A., Langmuir, J. I., Dalton, E. J., & Classen, C. C. (2007). The experience of trauma recovery: A qualitative study of participants in the Women Recovering from Abuse Program (WRAP). *Journal of Child Sexual Abuse, 16*(2), 55–77.

The aim of this qualitative study was to understand how women with a history of child maltreatment experienced the Women Recovering from Abuse Program (WRAP), an existing intensive group-treatment program. Seven women were interviewed following their participation in WRAP. The three themes that emerged were breaking trauma-based patterns, doing therapy, and the healing journey as a continuous process. The findings strengthen the understanding about how participants view the recovery process.

Paul, L. A., Gray, M. J., Elhai, J. D., Massad, P. M., & Stamm, B. H. (2006). Promotion of evidence-based practices for child traumatic stress in rural populations. *Trauma, Violence and Abuse, 7*(4) 260–273.

Although most abused children exhibit striking resiliency in the face of such harrowing experiences, childhood trauma translates into the need of clinical services to address resultant unremitting distress. Several effective interventions for child traumatic stress have been developed in the past several years, and these services are increasingly available in urban areas. Unfortunately, residents of rural regions may remain underserved despite the existence of effective treatments. This article briefly reviews the prevalence of childhood trauma and shows the numerous barriers to effective treatment faced by rural populations. Some promising evidence-based interventions are also reviewed for child traumatic stress.

Plummer, C. A. (2006). Non-abusive mothers of sexually abused children: The role of rumination in maternal outcomes. *Journal of Child Sexual Abuse, 15*(2), 103–122.

This study of 125 nonabusive mothers confirmed that ruminative cognition plays a role in maternal emotional and behavioral outcomes subsequent to the discovery of the sexual abuse of their children. Abuse severity, a maternal history of child abuse experiences, and life stressors were shown to be predictors of negative outcomes. The central finding was that these factors, many of which are not controllable, were less likely to predict poor maternal outcomes than rumination, a cognitive process that may be alterable. The effects of most predictors on outcomes in this study were mediated by a ruminative cognitive style. This study asserts that rumination is the main component for understanding maternal outcomes in the postdiscovery phase of sexual abuse cases. Rumination should be routinely assessed both for research and treatment purposes.

Poon, W. L. (2007). The value of using hypnosis in helping an adult survivor of childhood sexual abuse. *Contemporary Hypnosis, 24*(1), 30–37.

This report describes the successful treatment of a thirty-three-year-old Chinese woman who had affect dysregulation and trauma symptoms resulting from familial childhood sexual abuse. A strategically phased treatment plan fit specifically to the needs of the client was used. The treatment framework consisted of three phases: training on affect management, strengthening the ego, and reprocessing the trauma. Hypnosis was used for these phases. Data indicate a significant reduction in the trauma symptoms.

Porter, C., Lawson, J., & Bigler, E. (2005). Neurobehavioral sequelae of child sexual abuse. *Child Neuropsychology*, *11*(2), 203–220.

This study examined intellectual and memory functioning in a sample of sexually abused children compared with a demographically and age-matched control group. The severity of abuse and other important factors were also examined in relation to cognitive performance. Elevated levels of psychopathology were observed in the abused children, as well as diminished performance on tasks influenced by attention or concentration. Significant differences in memory function were not found.

Price, C. (2005). Body-oriented therapy in recovery from child sexual abuse: An efficacy study. *Alternative Therapies in Health and Medicine*, *11*(5), 46–57.

This study examines body-oriented therapy—an approach focused on body awareness and involving the combination of bodywork and the emotional processing of psychotherapy. The objective was to examine the efficacy and the perceived influence on abuse recovery of body-oriented therapy. The outcomes reflected three key constructs—psychological well-being, physical well-being, and body connection. Results were gathered at six time points: baseline, two times during intervention, post-intervention, and at one month and three months follow-up. To examine the experiential perspective of the study process, written questionnaires were administered before and after intervention and at one month and three months.

Price, J. L., Hilsenroth, M. J., Callahan, K. L., Petretic-Jackson, P. A., & Bonge, D. (2004). A pilot study of psychodynamic psychotherapy for adult survivors of childhood sexual abuse. *Clinical Psychology and Psychotherapy*, *11*(6), 378–391.

The purpose of this study was to evaluate the effectiveness of an open trial of individual short-term, psychodynamic psychotherapy of adult survivors of childhood sexual abuse. Sexual abuse survivors demonstrated significant improvement in symptomatic distress, level of functioning, and dynamic personality variables according to self-report measures and clinical rating scales. Abuse survivors developed positive therapeutic alliances, which remained high throughout the course of treatment. Sexual abuse survivors' response to treatment was similar to that of nonabused patients, with the potential for greater change in feelings about the self. The findings demonstrate that psychodynamic psychotherapy may be useful for childhood sexual abuse survivors.

Rellini, A. (2008). Review of the empirical evidence for a theoretical model to understand the sexual problems of women with a history of CSA. *Journal of Sexual Medicine, 5*(1), 31–46.

The main aim of this article was to illustrate a theoretical model to understand sexual problems in CSA survivors. A second aim was to discuss the definition of CSA adopted in research projects. Vaginal photoplethysmography, sexual self-schemas, and implicit sexual associations to sexual stimuli were the focus of the studies reviewed. The studies showed that during exposure to sexual stimuli, CSA survivors experienced more inhibitory responses and less excitatory responses than women in the comparison groups. In situations when sexual stimuli were not present, CSA survivors showed a greater excitation of sexual responses than women in the comparison groups. The CSA survivors showed a potential difficulty inhibiting intrusive sexual thoughts. The ability to guide the selection of cognitive and behavioral interventions for patients is an advantage over other studies.

Ribner, D. S. (2006). The dead little girl. *Sexual and Relationship Therapy, 21*(1), 71–85.

This article describes the treatment of a woman whose complaint was the absence of desire for sexual contact with her husband. As the case evolved, she began to recall childhood traumatic experiences that had remained long repressed. Her literary talent allowed a level of expression not often available in the therapy setting. Excerpts from her writings provide a unique element to this case description.

Romano, E., & De Luca, R. V. (2005). An individual treatment programme for sexually abused adult males: Description and preliminary findings. *Child Abuse Review, 14*(1), 40–56.

The present study describes an individual treatment program developed for adult males who have experienced childhood sexual abuse. The treatment program focused on three areas related to sexual abuse, specifically feelings of self-blame, anger, and anxiety. Also presented are preliminary findings on treatment effects. Overall findings indicated improvements in behavioral self-blame, anger, state anxiety, and trait anxiety. Treatment did not appear to have an effect on long term self-blame. Findings should be viewed as a contribution to the currently limited data on treatment effects for sexually abused adult males.

Romano, E., & De Luca, R. (2006). Evaluation of a treatment program for sexually abused adult males. *Journal of Family Violence, 21*(1), 75–88.

This study evaluated the effectiveness of an individual treatment program for five adult males who experienced childhood sexual abuse. A treatment manual focusing on abuse-related self-blame, anger, and anxiety was developed. Daily self-blame, anger, and anxiety self-ratings were completed before and throughout treatment. A multiple-baseline approach was used to evaluate treatment effects. The findings indicated that most participants saw significant reductions in self-blame, anger, and anxiety as a result of their involvement in the sexual abuse treatment program. Feelings of self-blame and anger also saw decreases. The study made an important initial contribution to the development of systematic treatment outcome research for a population of individuals who have received relatively little attention. The results have implications for future clinical and research efforts with sexually abused adult males.

Ross, G., & O'Carroll, P. (2004). Cognitive behavioural psychotherapy intervention in childhood sexual abuse: Identifying new directions from the literature. *Child Abuse Review, 13*(1), 51–64.

This article reviews outcome studies for the treatment of child sexual abuse where a posttraumatic stress disorder (PTSD) conceptualization was used to plan treatment interventions. The article concludes that sexually abused children and their nonabusing caregivers can significantly benefit from cognitive behavioral interventions that use reliving and confrontation of the abusive experience. There is a need for further controlled outcome research of cognitive behavioral interventions using reliving techniques to explore how and why these interventions help in reducing abuse-related PTSD symptoms.

Schlesinger, N. J. (2006). Treatment implications of a female incest survivor's misplaced guilt. *Psychoanalytic Social Work*, *13*(2), 53–66.

This article discusses treatment of an incest survivor who suffered from guilt. The process of discovering and understanding the unconscious fantasies that accompanied the patient's early traumatic experiences led to the ease of her misplaced guilt. It is necessary to understand and address the unconscious fantasies attached to the incest.

Schneider, K. M., & Phares, V. (2005). Coping with parental loss because of termination of parental rights. *Child Welfare*, *84*(6), 819–842.

This article addresses the process in which children and adolescents cope with acute stress of parental loss from causes other than divorce or death. Participants were sixty children and adolescents from a residential treatment facility. Most had experienced neglect, physical abuse, and sexual abuse, and their parents had their parental rights terminated. Measures indicated that children reported low levels of depressive symptoms, whereas caregivers reported the children to be experiencing significant psychological problems. Children used avoidant coping strategies more often than emotion-focused coping strategies.

Thun, D., Sims, P. L., Adams, M. A., & Webb, T. (2002). Effects of group therapy on female adolescent survivors of sexual abuse: A pilot study. *Journal of Child Sexual Abuse*, *11*(4), 1–16.

Treatment interventions for female sexual abuse survivors were explored through a pilot study examining the relationship between group treatment and adolescent self-image. Participants were thirteen female adolescent high school dropouts with a history of sexual abuse who participated in the National Guard Youth Challenge Program at Camp Shelby in Mississippi. Participants completed the Offer Self-Image Questionnaire for Adolescents. Because this was a pilot study, mean trends were observed to see directional changes that may assist future researchers. Participants who received group therapy increased in levels of impulse control, whereas the group that did not receive group therapy remained the same. The experimental group had a decrease in self-reliance, whereas the control group maintained their levels of self-reliance.

Tjersland, O. A., Mossige, S., Gulbrandsen, W., Jensen, T. K., & Reichelt, S. (2006). Helping families when child sexual abuse is suspected but not proven. *Child and Family Social Work, 11*(4), 297–306.

This article reports from a project investigating reactions in families when intrafamilial child sexual abuse was suspected, as well as family members' responses to a therapeutic approach. Data were obtained from therapeutic sessions and follow-up interviews with mothers, children, and alleged perpetrators. In most cases after treatment the conflicts had been reduced, the children had few symptoms, supervised contact had been established, and the clients were satisfied with the treatment. One conclusion is that therapeutic sessions, in which family members share information about concerns and take part in the decisions of how to protect children, seem relevant and helpful to the clients in unclear abuse cases.

Tourigny, M., Hébert, M., Daigneault, I., & Simoneau, A. C. (2005). Efficacy of a group therapy for sexually abused adolescent girls. *Journal of Child Sexual Abuse, 14*(4), 71–93.

The effects of a group therapy program for teenage girls reporting child sexual abuse were evaluated by means of a pretest and posttest design with a control group. The psychoeducational intervention consisted of an average of twenty weekly two-hour meetings. Results of the repeated analyses of variance showed a significant improvement in youths participating in the therapy compared with the control group. Comparisons were made on measures of posttraumatic stress, internalizing and externalizing behavior problems, coping strategies, relationship with the mother, and sense of empowerment. The findings suggest that the group therapy offered by the Centre d'Intervention en Abuse Sexuels pour la Famille was effective in reducing symptoms for sexually abused teenagers.

Wagner, A. W., Rizvi, S. L., & Harned, M. S. (2007). Applications of dialectical behavior therapy to the treatment of complex trauma-related problems: When one case formulation does not fit all. *Journal of Traumatic Stress, 20*(4), 391–400.

In this article, effective treatment of complex trauma-related problems depends on a reliance on theory, idiographic assessment, and empirically supported principles of change. Dialectical behavior therapy (DBT) is used to demonstrate the applicability of this approach to the treatment of multiproblem, heterogeneous populations in general. Two case studies are presented that highlight the utility of DBT principles to complex trauma-related problems specifically.

Woody, J. D. (2002). Media coverage of child sexual abuse: An opportunity for family therapists to help families and communities. *American Journal of Family Therapy, 30*(5), 417–426.

The recent media coverage of child sexual abuse charges involving priests is likely to lead to various needs among the public for professional services. Family therapists should prepare to respond effectively to the high anxiety that these media stories trigger. Family therapists with expertise in human sexuality should use such reports to promote a broader understanding of all aspects of sexuality for individuals and families. Professionals can integrate aspects of sexuality education in dealing with the mass media, in crisis intervention for persons at risk, and in therapy that centers on child or adult experiences of sexual abuse.

Wright, D. C., Woo, W. L., Muller, R. T., Fernandes, C. B., & Kraftcheck, E. R. (2003). An investigation of trauma-centered inpatient treatment for adult survivors of abuse. *Child Abuse and Neglect, 27*(4), 393–406.

The purpose of this study was to examine a comprehensive inpatient treatment program designed for adult survivors of childhood abuse with posttraumatic stress disorder (PTSD). One hundred thirty-two formerly abused individuals completed clinician-administered and self-administered measures of PTSD symptomatology at admission and discharge. Analyses revealed that the program was effective in reducing symptoms from admission to discharge. The findings suggest that the current intensive inpatient group treatment program reduces PTSD symptoms effectively for a sample of adult survivors of abuse.

Wurtele, S. (2009). Preventing sexual abuse of children in the twenty-first century: Preparing for challenges and opportunities. *Journal of Child Sexual Abuse, 18*(1), 1–18.

This article briefly describes the range and consequences of child sexual abuse and briefly critiques child-focused personal safety educational programs designed to prevent sexual victimization. Also offered are suggestions for expanding the focus of child-directed efforts and recommendations for alternative approaches to primary prevention.

10. Other Investigative Interview Literature

Čėsnienė, I., & Grigutyt, N. (2006). Child investigative interviews in Lithuania: Problems and perspectives. *Socialinis Darbas*, 5(1), 58–62.

There are two child interview rooms in Lithuania at present. An interview room at the nongovernmental organization Child House in Vilnius is mainly designed to conduct investigative interviews in child sexual abuse cases. Although conducting investigative interviews differs greatly in child interview room and police office or courtroom, there are still some problems in child sexual abuse investigative interviews. The purpose of this article is to present the most current problems in Lithuania. Focus is given to problems such as recording the testimony, cross-examination, interviewing the child in a presence of a suspect, and negative attitudes of police officers toward child-witnesses.

Cheung, M., & Boutté-Queen, M. N. (2010). Assessing the relative importance of the child sexual abuse interview protocol items to assist child victims in abuse disclosure. *Journal of Family Violence*, 25(1), 11–22.

Multiple disciplines benefit from obtaining information through the Child Sexual Abuse Interview Protocol. Professionals from a variety of fields self-administered the survey, unanimously reporting that "showing that the interviewer is listening" and "showing patience with the child" were very important to complete during the course of an investigative interview. Four major considerations resulted in the context of use of the interview guide: flexibility, appropriate use of anatomical dolls, age-appropriate psychological assessment, and ordering of questions based on incident severity.

Colangelo, J. J. (2009). The recovered memory controversy: A representative case study. *Journal of Child Sexual Abuse*, 18(1), 103–121.

The recovered-memory controversy has been an ongoing debate in the mental health profession for the past two decades. Disagreement remains in the field over the validity of "forgotten" memories of childhood sexual abuse that are recalled or recovered during therapy. At the center of the controversy are the concepts of repression. Provided is an overview of the central factors in the debate.

Daly, L. W. (2005). Police officers do not receive adequate training to prepare them to handle child sexual abuse investigations. *Issues in Child Abuse Accusations, 15*(1), 1–13.

This study examined 250 police academies who responded to a questionnaire regarding their typical police training. The responses indicated that officers receive training in investigations, interviewing, and interrogation that prepared them only for generalized areas of duty. Also reported was that most state authorities did not mandate specialized training for child sexual abuse investigations. They were not prepared to handle child sexual abuse investigations. This is also true for those assigned to child protection units.

Denov, M. S. (2005). The long term effects of child sexual abuse by female perpetrators: A qualitative study of male and female victims. *Journal of Interpersonal Violence, 19*(10), 1137–1156.

This qualitative study explores the experience and long-term impact of sexual abuse by women. The data derived from in-depth interviews with fourteen adult victims (seven men and seven women) of child sexual abuse by females. Most respondents reported severe sexual abuse by their mothers. As a result of the sexual abuse, male and female respondents reported long-term difficulties with substance abuse, self-injury, suicide, depression, rage, and strained relationships with women, self-concept and identity issues, and discomfort with sex.

Draucker, C., Martsolf, D. S., Roller, C., Knapik, G., Ross, R., & Stidham, A. (2011). Healing from childhood sexual abuse: A theoretical model. *Journal of Child Sexual Abuse, 20*(4), 435–466.

The purpose of this study was to develop a theoretical model to describe how adults heal from childhood sexual abuse. A subsample of forty-eight women and forty-seven men who had experienced childhood sexual abuse was used. During semistructured, open-ended interviews, they were asked to describe their experiences with healing from childhood sexual abuse and other victimization throughout their lives. Several analytic techniques were used to synthesize the findings from these frameworks to develop a theoretical model that included four stages of healing, five domains of functioning, and six enabling factors that facilitate movement from one stage to the next. The model can be used to educate clinicians about various processes that facilitate healing guide discussions.

Forbes, F., Duffy, J. C., Mok, J., & Lemvig, J. (2003). Early intervention service for non-abusing parents of victims of child sexual abuse: Pilot study. *British Journal of Psychiatry, 18*(1), 66–72.

In this study, thirty-nine parents of thirty-one children completed scales at the baseline assessment; eighteen repeated them following interventions. Initially, parents reported high rates of psychopathological symptoms in themselves and their children, which were reduced following the intervention. The response of nonabusing parents to disclosure of abuse may influence the child's outcome. The findings confirmed the high rates of psychopathological symptoms found in parents of children following disclosure of sexual abuse. Children clinically identified for intervention had higher measured levels of psychopathological symptoms.

Kane, M. N. (2006). Risk management for Catholic priests in the United States: A new demand from the code of pastoral conduct. *Journal of Religion and Spirituality in Social Work, 25*(1), 47–67.

This article focuses on a research on risk management strategies, similar to those used by social workers and other mental health practitioners. It reports that after the disclosures of Episcopal cover-ups of child sexual abuse by Catholic clergy, the U.S. Conference of Catholic Bishops announced the Charter for the Protection of Children and Young People, which requires that all U.S. dioceses and eparchies identify a code of conduct for clergy, employees, and volunteers. The study intends to supply important information for priests who provide pastoral counseling, spiritual direction, or any clinical-type intervention to parishioners and to those seeking pastoral services.

Lamb, M. E., Sternberg, K. J., Orbach, Y., Hershkowitz, I., & Horowitz, D. (2003). Differences between accounts provided by witnesses and alleged victims of child sexual abuse. *Child Abuse and Neglect, 27*(9), 1019–1031.

The objective of this article is to determine whether child witnesses of sexual abuse were more or less informative about the alleged incidents than alleged victims when interviewed similarly. Twenty-six alleged victims of child sexual abuse (age 5–14) and twenty-six children who had witnessed but not experienced similar events were interviewed. All children were interviewed using the NICHD investigative interview protocol. Interviewers used more open-ended invitations and elicited more information using open-ended prompts from witnesses than from victims, whereas they used suggestive prompts when interviewing victims. The results indicate that young children can be informative witnesses about events that they have either experienced or witnessed.

McNally, R. J., & Geraerts, E. (2009). A new solution to the recovered memory debate. *Perspectives on Psychological Science, 4*(2), 126–134.

The controversy regarding recovered memories of childhood sexual abuse (CSA) has been characterized by two perspectives. Some people repress their memories of abuse because the experiences have been so emotionally traumatic and can recover memories only when it is psychologically safe to do so many years later. According to the other perspective, many reports of recovered memories of sexual abuse are false memories, often inadvertently fostered by therapists. This article provides evidence for a third interpretation that applies to another group of people who did not experience their CSA as traumatic; they either failed to think about their abuse for years or forgot their previous recollections, and they recalled their CSA spontaneously after encountering reminders outside of psychotherapy. Therefore, recalling CSA after many years is not the same thing as having recalled a previously repressed memory of trauma.

Nichols, K. S. (2009). Assessing sexual abuse protocols for family litigation. *American Journal of Family Law, 22*(4), 184–191.

See annotation in the section "Anatomical Dolls."

Schreiber, N., Bellah, L. D., Martinez, Y., McLaurin, K. A., Strok, R., Garven, S., et al. (2006). Suggestive interviewing in the McMartin Preschool and Kelly Michaels daycare abuse cases: A case study. *Social Influence, 1*(1), 16–47.

In the present study, quantitative analyses were performed on a total of fifty-four interview transcripts from two highly publicized day-care cases (McMartin Preschool and Kelly Michaels) and a comparison group of child sexual abuse cases from Child Protection Services (CPS). Systematic analyses showed that interviews from the two day-care cases were highly suggestive. Compared with the CPS interviews, the McMartin and Michaels interviewers were significantly more likely to introduce new suggestive information into the interview; provide praise, promises, and positive reinforcement; express disapproval, disbelief, or disagreement with children; exert conformity pressure; and invite children to pretend or speculate about supposed events.

Walsh, C., Jamieson, E., MacMillan, H., & Trocme, N. (2004). Measuring child sexual abuse in children and youth. *Journal of Child Sexual Abuse*, *13*(1), 39–68.

This article reviews the psychometric properties of the questions or instruments that have measured exposure to child sexual abuse directly. A search of four electronic databases using descriptors "child sexual abuse" and "measurement" or "instrumentation" yielded four telephone administered tools, thirteen face-to-face interviews, and thirty-two self-administered questionnaires. A limited amount of instruments have been subjected to in-depth evaluation. It is critical to establish the validity and reliability of instruments measuring child sexual abuse and other forms of victimization to enhance the growth and expansion of the field.

Yiming, C., & Fung, D. (2003). Child sexual abuse in Singapore with special reference to medico-legal implications: A review of 38 cases. *Medicine, Science, and the Law*, *43*(3), 260–266.

This study reviews the trends of child sexual abuse in Singapore and discusses the medico-legal considerations in the identification, assessment, and management of these cases. It is a retrospective case review of thirty-eight consecutive cases of child sexual abuse at a child guidance clinic in Singapore. Most of the children in this study were young (74 percent younger than age 9) and female (78.9 percent), with abusers who are males and usually known to the victims. Sufficient support of the victims in the form of specialized handling during the court proceedings and in the use of new technology for obtaining the child's testimony may be necessary. A child's capability to testify is determined by the child's credibility and competence.

References

Adoption Assistance and Child Welfare Act, P.L. 96-272 (1980).

Alaggia, R. (2004). Many ways of telling: Expending conceptualizations of child sexual abuse disclosure. *Child Abuse and Neglect, 28*(11), 1213–1227.

Alaggia, R., & Kirshenbaum, S. (2005). Speaking the unspeakable: Exploring the impact of family dynamics on child sexual abuse disclosures. *Families in Society, 86*(2), 227–234.

American Academy of Child and Adolescent Psychiatry. (2009). *Facts for families: Child sexual abuse.* Retrieved from http://www.aacap.org/cs/root/facts_for_families/child_sexual_abuse.

American Association for Protecting Children. (1988). *Child sexual abuse curriculum for social workers.* Denver, CO: Author.

American Professional Society on the Abuse of Children. (2002). *Practice guidelines: Investigative interviewing in cases of alleged child abuse.* Chicago: Author.

American Psychological Association. (N.d.). *Understanding child sexual abuse: Education, prevention, and recovery.* Retrieved from http://www.apa.org/pubs/info/brochures/sex-abuse.aspx#.

Anagnostaki, L., Wright, M. J., & Bourchier-Sutton, A. J. (2010). The semantics of secrecy: Young children's classification of secret content. *Journal of Genetic Psychology, 171*(4), 279–299.

Armstrong, K., O'Callahan, W., & Marmar, C. R. (1991). Debriefing Red Cross disaster personnel: The multiple stressor debriefing model. *Journal of Traumatic Stress, 4*(4), 581–593.

Australian Institute of Family Studies. (2009). *What is child abuse and neglect?* Retrieved from http://www.aifs.gov.au/nch/pubs/sheets/rs6/rs6.html.

Australian Institute of Family Studies, National Child Protection Clear-
    inghouse. (2010). *Australian legal definitions: When is a child in need
    of protection?* Retrieved from http://www.aifs.gov.au/nch/pubs/
    sheets/rs12/rs12.pdf.
AVERT. (2009). *Worldwide ages of consent.* Retrieved from http://www
    .avert.org/age-of-consent.htm.
Baker, K. (2009). *Preventing child sexual abuse: A national directory and
    handbook.* Retrieved from http://www.asiaing.com/preventing-child-
    sexual-abuse-a-national-resource-directory-and-handbook.html.
Baker, R. A. (Ed.) (1998). *Child sexual abuse and false memory syndrome.*
    New York: Prometheus Books.
Bendall, C. (2009). The demise of the enhanced standard of proof in
    child protection cases: re B [2008] ukhl 35. *Journal of Social Welfare
    and Family Law, 31*(2), 185–191.
Berman, L., Berman, J., Bruck, D., Pawar, R. V., & Goldstein, I. (2001).
    Pharmacotherapy or psychotherapy? Effective treatment for FSD
    related to unresolved childhood sexual abuse. *Journal of Sex and
    Marital Therapy, 27*(5), 421–425.
Bernstein, D. E., & Jackson, J. D. (N.d.). *The* Daubert *trilogy in the States*
    (George Mason Law and Economics Research Paper No. 04-06).
    Arlington, VA: Law and Economics Center, George Mason Univer-
    sity School of Law.
Beukman, B. A. (2010). Victim impact statements and the role of the
    South African criminologist. *US-China Law Review, 7*(3), 47–53.
Beveridge, K., & Cheung, M. (2004). A spiritual framework in incest sur-
    vivors treatment. *Journal of Child Sexual Abuse, 13*(2), 105–120.
Bibas, S., & Bierschbach, R. A. (2004). Integrating remorse and apology
    into criminal procedure. *Yale Law Journal, 114*(1), 85–148.
Bilchik, S. (2001). *Forming a multidisciplinary team to investigate child
    abuse.* Washington, DC: U.S. Department of Justice. Retrieved from
    http://www.ncjrs.gov/pdffiles1/ojjdp/170020.pdf.
Birgden, A. (2007). Serious Sex Offenders Monitoring Act 2005 (Vic): A
    therapeutic jurisprudence analysis. *Psychiatry, Psychology, and Law,
    14*(1), 78–94.

Bligh, S., & Kupperman, P. (1993). Facilitated communication evaluation procedure accepted in a court case. *Journal of Autism and Developmental Disorders, 23*(3), 553–557.

Bolen, R., & Scannapieco, M. (1999). Prevalence of child sexual abuse: A corrective meta analysis. *Social Service Review, 73,* 281–313.

Bonanno, G. A., Keltner, D., Noll, J. G., Putnam, F. W., Trickett, P. K., LeJeune, J., et al. (2002). When the face reveals what words do not: Facial expressions of emotion, smiling, and the willingness to disclose childhood sexual abuse. *Journal of Personality and Social Psychology, 83*(1), 94–110.

Bonnar-Kidd, K. K. (2010). Sexual offender laws and prevention of sexual violence or recidivism. *American Journal of Public Health, 100*(3), 412–419.

Bottoms, B. L., Najdowski, C. J., & Goodman, G. S. (Eds.) (2009). *Children as victims, witnesses, and offenders: Psychological science and the law.* New York: Guilford Press.

Boyer, D., & Fine, D. (1992). Sexual abuse as a factor in adolescent pregnancy and child maltreatment. *Family Planning Perspectives, 24*(1), 1.

Broadbent, A., & Bentley, R. (1997). *Child abuse and neglect Australia 1995–96* (Child Welfare Series No. 17). Canberra: Australian Institute of Health and Welfare.

Bromfield, L. M. (2005). *Chronic child maltreatment in an Australian statutory child protection sample* (Unpublished doctoral dissertation). Deakin University, Geelong, Australia.

Brown, S. D., Brack, G., & Mullis, F. Y. (2008). Traumatic symptoms in sexually abused children: Implications for school counselors. *Professional School Counseling, 11*(6), 368–379.

Calley, N. G. (2007). Integrating theory and research: The development of research-based treatment programs for juvenile male sex offenders. *Journal of Counseling and Development, 85,* 131–142.

Caldwell, M. F. (2010). Study characteristics and recidivism base rates in juvenile sex offender recidivism. *International Journal of Offender Therapy and Comparative Criminology, 54*(2), 197–212.

Cammaert, L. P. (1988). Nonoffending mothers: A new conceptualization. In L. E. A. Walker (Ed.), *Handbook on sexual abuse of children: Assessment and treatment issues* (pp. 309–325). New York: Springer.

Canfield, J., & Hansen, M. V. (1998). *Chicken soup for the teenage soul II.* Deerfield Beach, FL: Health Communications.

Centers for Disease Control and Prevention. (2002). *CDC injury research agenda.* Atlanta: Department of Health and Human Services. Retrieved from http://www.cdc.gov/ncipc/pub-res/research_agenda/Research%20Agenda.pdf.

Chaffin, M., & Friedrich, B. (2004). Evidence-based treatments in child abuse and neglect. *Children and Youth Services Review, 26*(11), 1097–1113.

Chard, K. M. (2005). An evaluation of cognitive processing therapy for the treatment of posttraumatic stress disorder related to childhood sexual abuse. *Journal of Consulting and Clinical Psychology, 73*(5), 965–971.

Cheung, K. M. (1997). Developing the interview protocol for video-recorded child sexual abuse investigations: A training experience with police officers, social workers and clinical psychologists in Hong Kong. *Child Abuse and Neglect: The International Journal, 21*(3), 273–284.

Cheung, K. M., Leung, P., & Alpert, S. (1997). A model for family preservation case assessment. *Family Preservation Journal, 2*(2), 1–20.

Cheung, M. (2003). Utilization of questioning techniques in forensic child sexual abuse interviews. *Journal of Brief Therapy, 3*(1), 45–57.

Cheung, M. (2008). Promoting effective interviewing of sexually abused children: A pilot study. *Research on Social Work Practice, 18*(2), 137–143.

Cheung, M., & Boutté-Queen, N. M. (2000). Emotional responses to child sexual abuse: A comparison between police and social workers in Hong Kong. *Child Abuse and Neglect: The International Journal, 24*(12), 1613–1621.

Cheung, M., & Boutté-Queen, N. M. (2009). Assessing the relative importance of the child sexual abuse interview protocol items to assist child victims in abuse disclosure. *Journal of Family Violence, 25*(1), 11–22.

Child Abuse Prevention and Treatment Act. 42 U.S.C. §§ 5101 et seq., 42
    U.S.C. §§ 5116 *et seq.* (1974 and as amended). Retrieved from
    http://www.acf.hhs.gov/programs/cb/laws_policies/cblaws/capta/
    index.htm.

Child Safe International. (2007). *International laws.* Retrieved from
    http://childsafe-international.org/InternationalLaws.asp.

Child Welfare Information Gateway. (2010). *Clergy as mandatory reporters
    of child abuse and neglect.* Retrieved from http://www.childwelfare
    .gov/systemwide/laws_policies/statutes/clergymandated.cfm.

Child Welfare Information Gateway. (2011). *State statutes search.*
    Retrieved from http://www.childwelfare.gov/systemwide/laws_
    policies/state/.

Child Welfare League of America. (2009). *Access the data: Child abuse
    and neglect.* Retrieved from http://ndas.cwla.org/data_stats/access/
    predefined/home.asp?MainTopicID=1.

Children and Family Court Advisory and Support Service. (2006).
    Practice guidance for guardians appointing a solicitor for the child.
    Retrieved from http://www.cafcass.gov.uk/pdf/Practice_Guidance_
    for_Guardians_Appointing_a_solicitor_for_the_child%20[2].pdf.

Children and Family Court Advisory and Support Service. (2010).
    *Cafcass safeguarding framework: August 2010 working together
    update.* Retrieved from http://www.cafcass.gov.uk/pdf/Cafcass%20
    Safeguarding%20Framework%20Working%20Together%2012-
    08-10.pdf.

Children's Bureau, U.S. Department of Health and Human Services.
    (2009). *Child maltreatment 2007.* Retrieved from http://www.acf.hhs
    .gov/programs/cb/pubs/cm07/index.htm.

Choi, J.J., & Severson, M. (2009). "What! What kind of apology is this?":
    The nature of apology in victim offender mediation. *Child and
    Youth Services Review, 31,* 813–820.

Chouliara, Z., Hutchison, C., & Karatzias, T. (2009). Vicarious traumati-
    sation in practitioners who work with adult survivors of sexual vio-
    lence and child sexual abuse: Literature review and directions for
    future research. *Counselling and Psychotherapy Research, 9*(1), 47–56.
    doi:10.1080/14733140802656479.

Clark County Prosecuting Attorney. (2011). *Victim/witness services: Effective courtroom performance by witnesses in a criminal case.* Retrieved from http://www.clarkprosecutor.org/html/victim/wtips.htm.

Clifford, R. C. (2008). *Qualifying and attacking expert witnesses.* Costa Mesa, CA: James.

Cohen, J., Berliner, L., & Mannarino, A. (2010). Trauma focused CBT for children with co-occurring trauma and behavior problems. *Child Abuse and Neglect, 34*(4), 215–224.

Cohen, J., Deblinger, E., Mannarino, A., & Steer, R. (2004). A multisite, randomized controlled trial for children with sexual abuse–related PTSD symptoms. *Journal of the American Academy of Child and Adolescent Psychiatry, 43*(4), 393–402.

Cohen, J., & Mannarino, A. (2008). Trauma-focused cognitive behavioural therapy for children and parents. *Child and Adolescent Mental Health, 13*(4), 158–162.

Colangelo, J. J. (2007). Recovered memory debate revisited: Practice implications for mental health counselors. *Journal of Mental Health Counseling, 29*(2), 93–120.

Community Protection Act of 1990 (Washington State). Retrieved from http://www.co.cowlitz.wa.us/sheriff/rso/cpa.htm.

Connor, P., & Higgins, D. J. (2008). The "HEALTH" model: Part 2—Case study of a guideline-based treatment program for complex PTSD relating to childhood sexual abuse. *Sexual and Relationship Therapy, 23*(4), 401–410.

Corcoran, J., & Pillai, V. (2008). A meta-analysis of parent-involved treatment for child sexual abuse. *Research on Social Work Practice, 18(5),* 453–464.

Cornille, T. A., & Meyers, T. W. (1999). Secondary traumatic stress among child protective workers: Prevalence, severity, and predictive factors. *Traumatology, 5,* art. 2. Retrieved from http://www.fsu.edu/%7Etrauma/art2v5i1.htm.

Crimes Act of 1900. (2012). Section 68: Australian Capital Territory Consolidated Acts. Retrieved from http://www.austlii.edu.au/au/legis/act/consol_act/ca190082/s68.html.

Crimes Act of 1958. (2012). Section 464ZF: Victorian Consolidated Legislation. Retrieved from http://www.austlii.edu.au/au/legis/vic/consol_act/ca195882/sch8.html.

Crimes (Serious Sex Offenders) Act 2006. (2006). Australia (NSW): Criminal law. *Commonwealth Law Bulletin, 32*(2), 275–319.

Criminal Procedure Ordinance Cap 221. Retrieved from http://www.legislation.gov.hk/blis_pdf.nsf/6799165D2FEE3FA94825755E0033E532/AB95385D2FD2C236482575EE004ED4BB?OpenDocument&bt=0.

Cronch, L. E., Viljoen, J. L., & Hansen, D J. (2006). Forensic interviewing in child sexual abuse cases: Current techniques and future directions. *Aggression and Violent Behavior, 11*, 195–207.

Crown Prosecution Service. (2011). *Special measures: Principles*. Retrieved from http://www.cps.gov.uk/legal/s_to_u/special_measures/.

Daubert v. Merrell Dow Pharmaceuticals, 509 U.S. 579 (1993).

Davies, D., & Cole, J. (1996). A model for conducting forensic interviews with child victims of abuse. *Child Maltreatment, 1*(3), 189–200.

Dayan, J., & Minnes, P. (1995). Ethical issues related to the use of facilitated communication techniques with persons with autism. *Canadian Psychology/Psychologie Canadienne, 36*(3), 183–189.

Deblinger, E., Mannarino, A. P., Cohen, J. A., Runyon, M. K., & Steer, R. A. (2011). Trauma-focused cognitive behavioral therapy for children: Impact of trauma narrative and treatment length. *Depression and Anxiety, 28*(1), 67–75.

Deblinger, E., Mannarino, A., Cohen, J., & Steer, R. (2006). A follow-up study of a multisite, randomized, controlled trial for children with sexual abuse–related PTSD symptoms. *Journal of the American Academy of Child and Adolescent Psychiatry, 45*(12), 1474–1484.

Deblinger, E., Thakkar-Kolar, R. R., Berry, E. J., & Schroeder, C. M. (2010). Caregivers' efforts to educate their children about child sexual abuse. *Child Maltreatment, 15*(1), 91–100.

Department of Justice Canada. (2001). *Summary report on victim impact statement focus groups*. Retrieved from http://www.justice.gc.ca/eng/pi/rs/rep-rap/2000/rr00_vic21/rr00_vic21.pdf.

Department of Justice Canada. (2005). *Sexual abuse and exploitation of children and youth: A fact sheet*. Retrieved from http://www.justice.gc.ca/eng/pi/fv-vf/facts-info/sex_abu.pdf.

Department of Justice Canada. (N.d). *Victim impact statements at sentencing: Experiences and perceptions a survey of three jurisdictions*. Retrieved from http://www.justice.gc.ca/eng/pi/rs/rep-rap/2006/rr06_vic3/p0.html.

Des Rosiers, N., Feldthusen, B., & Hankivsky, O. (1998). Legal compensation for sexual violence: Therapeutic consequences and consequences for the judicial system. *Psychology, Public Policy, and Law,* *4*(1), 433–451.

Devilly, G. J., Wright, R., & Varker, T. (2009). Vicarious trauma, secondary traumatic stress or simply burnout? Effect of trauma therapy on mental health professionals. *Australian and New Zealand Journal of Psychiatry, 43*(4), 373–385. doi:10.1080/00048670902721079.

DeVoe, E. R., & Faller, K. C. (2002). Question strategies in interviews with children who may have been sexually abused. *Child Welfare, 81*(1), 5–31.

Draucker, C. B., & Martsolf, D. S. (2008). Storying childhood sexual abuse. *Qualitative Health Research, 18*(8), 1034–1048.

Ducat, L., Thomas, S., & Blood, W. (2009). Sensationalising sex offenders and sexual recidivism: Impact of the Serious Sex Offender Monitoring Act 2005 on media reportage. *Australian Psychologist, 44*(3), 156–165.

Eberlin, M., McConnachie, G., Ibel, S., & Volpe, L. (1993). Facilitated communication: A failure to replicate the phenomenon. *Journal of Autism and Developmental Disorders, 23*(3), 507–530.

Edwards, I. (2009). The evidential quality of victim personal statements and family impact statements. *International Journal of Evidence and Proof, 13*, 293–320.

Elvin, J. (2008). The concept of consent under the Sexual Offenses Act 2003. *Journal of Criminal Law, 72*, 519–536.

End Child Sexual Abuse Foundation. (2008). *Annual report.* Retrieved from http://www.ecsaf.org/images/upload_images/file/Annual%20 Report%2008-09.pdf.

Erez, E., & Rogers, L. (1999). Victim impact statements and sentencing outcomes and processes: The perspectives of legal professionals. *British Journal of Criminology, 39*(2), 216–239.

Evidence (Protection of Children) Amendment Act 2003. (2003). Retrieved from http://www.legislation.qld.gov.au/LEGISLTN/ACTS/2003/ 03AC055.pdf.

Faller, K. C. (1993). *Child sexual abuse: Intervention and treatment issues.* Retrieved from http://www.childwelfare.gov/pubs/usermanuals/ sexabuse/sexabuse.pdf.

Faller, K. C. (1996). *Evaluating children suspected of having been sexually abused: The APSAC Study Guides 2.* American Professional Society on the Abuse of Children. Thousand Oaks, CA: Sage.

Faller, K. C. (2002). *Understanding and assessing child sexual maltreatment* (2nd ed.). Thousand Oaks, CA: Sage.

Faller, K. C. (2006). *Interviewing children about sexual abuse: Controversies and best practice.* New York: Oxford University Press.

Faller, K. C., Cordisco-Steele, L., & Nelson-Gardell, D. (2010). Allegations of sexual abuse of a child: What to do when a single forensic interview isn't enough. *Journal of Child Sexual Abuse, 19*(5), 572–589.

Faller, K. C., & Nelson-Gardell, D. (2010). Extended evaluations in cases of child sexual abuse: How many sessions are sufficient? *Journal of Child Sexual Abuse, 19*(6), 648–668.

Federal Rules of Civil Procedure. *Rule 26: Duty to disclose.* Retrieved from http://www.law.cornell.edu/rules/frcp/Rule26.htm.

Federal Rules of Evidence. P.L. 93-595, § 1, Jan. 2, 1975, 88 Stat. 1937 (December 1, 2011). *Rule 702: Rules of evidence on expert testimony.* Retrieved from http://www.law.cornell.edu/rules/fre/rule_702.

Fehr, R., Gelfand, M. J., & Monisha, N. (2010). The road to forgiveness: A meta-analytic synthesis of its situational and dispositional correlates. *Psychological Bulletin, 136*(5), 894–914.

Finkelhor, D., Ormrod, R. K., & Turner, H. A. (2009). The developmental epidemiology of childhood victimization. *Journal of Interpersonal Violence, 24*(5), 711–731.

Fontes, L. A., & Plummer, C. (2010). Cultural issues in disclosures of child sexual abuse. *Journal of Child Sexual Abuse, 19*(5), 491–518.

Fredette, K. (2009). International legislative efforts to combat child sex tourism: Evaluating the council of Europe convention on commercial child sexual exploitation. *Boston College International and Comparative Law Review, 32*(1), 1–43.

Friedman, S. (1988). A family systems approach to treatment. In L. E. A. Walker (Ed.), *Handbook on sexual abuse of children: Assessment and treatment issues* (pp. 326–349). New York: Springer.

Gardner, R. A. (1995). *Protocols for the sex-abuse evaluation.* Cresskill, NJ: Creative Therapeutics.

General Electric Co. v. Joiner, 522 U.S. 136 (1997).

Geraerts, E., Lindsay, D. S., Merckelbach, H., Jelicic, M., Raymaekers, L., Arnold, M. M., et al. (2009). Cognitive mechanisms underlying recovered-memory experiences of childhood sexual abuse. *Psychological Science, 20*(1), 92–98. doi:10.1111/j.1467-9280.2008.02247.x.

Gillespie, A. A. (2005a). Child pornography: Balancing substantive and evidential law to safeguard children effectively from abuse. *International Journal of Evidence and Proof, 9,* 29–49.

Gillespie, A. A. (2005b). Sex Offenders Act 1997: Restraining orders. *Journal of Criminal Law, 69*(5), 377–380.

Goldstein, S. L. (1999). Interviewing the offender. *The sexual exploitation of children: A practical guide to assessment, investigation, and intervention.* Washington, DC: CRC Press.

Gorman, B. J. (1999). Facilitated communication: Rejected in science, accepted in court—a case study and analysis of the use of FC evidence under Frye and Daubert. *Behavioral Sciences & the Law, 17*(4), 517–541.

Graupner, H. (2004). The 17-year-old child: An absurdity of the late 20th century. *Journal of Psychology and Human Sexuality, 16*(2–3), 7–24.

Griffith, R. (2010). Sexual Offences Act 2003: Key concepts. *British Journal of Midwifery, 18*(8), 524–525.

Griffith, R., & Tengnah, C. (2007). Protecting children: The role of the law—2. Legal powers to safeguard children. *British Journal of Community Nursing, 12*(4), 175–180.

Grosz, C. A., Kempe, R. S., & Kelly, M. (2000). Extrafamilial sexual abuse: Treatment for child victims and their families. *Child Abuse and Neglect, 24*(1), 9–23.

Groth, A. N., & Birnbaum, H. J. (1978). Adult sexual orientation and the attraction to underage persons. *Archives of Sexual Behavior, 7*(3), 175–181.

Handy, L. C. (1988). A developing behavioral treatment model: One therapist's perspective within a community's evolving response. In L. E. A. Walker (Ed.), *Handbook on sexual abuse of children: Assessment and treatment issues* (pp. 350–383). New York: Springer.

Hanser, R. D., & Mire, S. M. (2008). Juvenile sex offenders in the United States and Australia: A comparison. *International Review of Law, Computers and Technology, 22*(1–2), 101–114.

Hanson, R. K., Gordon, A., Harris, A. J. R., Marques, J. K., Murphy, W., Quinsey, V. L., et al. (2002). First report of the collaborative outcome data project on the effectiveness of psychological treatment for sex offenders. *Sexual Abuse: A Journal of Research and Treatment, 14,* 169–194.

Harris, C. J. (1995). Sensory-based therapy for crisis counselors. *Compassion fatigue* (pp. 101–114). New York: Brunner/Mazel.

Haskins, C. (2003). Treating sibling incest using a family system approach. *Journal of Mental Health Counseling, 25*(4), 337–350.

Haugaard, J. (2000). The challenge of defining child sexual abuse. *American Psychologist, 55*(9), 1036–1039.

Hayes, H. (2006). Apologies and accounts in youth justice conferencing: Reinterpreting research outcomes. *Contemporary Justice Review, 9*(4), 369–385.

Hayes, R., Barnett, M., Sullivan, D. H., Nielssen, O., Large, M., & Brown, C. (2009). Justifications and rationalizations for the civil commitment of sex offenders. *Psychiatry, Psychology and Law, 16*(1), 141–149.

Health Canada, Family Violence Prevention Division. (1994). *Sibling sexual abuse: A guide for parents.* Vancouver, BC: Author.

Hebert, M., & Bergeron, M. (2007). Efficacy of a group intervention for adult women survivors of sexual abuse. *Journal of Child Sexual Abuse, 16*(4), 37–61.

Hembree, E. A., & Brinen, A. P. (2009). The prolonged exposure (PE) for treatment of childhood sexual abuse–related PTSD: Do we need to augment it? *Pragmatic Case Studies in Psychotherapy, 5*(2), 35–44.

Herat, E. (2009). *Ninth Circuit v. Board of Immigration Appeals*: Defining "sexual abuse of a minor" after *Estrada-Espinoza v. Mukasey. Washington Law Review, 84*(3), 523–553.

Hernandez, A., Ruble, C., Rockmore, L., McKay, M., Messam, T., Harris, M., et al. (2009). An integrated approach to treating non-offending parents affected by sexual abuse. *Social Work in Mental Health, 7*(6), 533–555.

Hershkowitz, I. (2002). The role of facilitative prompts in interviews of alleged sex and abuse victims. *Legal and Criminological Psychology, 7*(1), 63–72.

Hershkowitz, I., Orbach, Y., Lamb, M. E., Sternberg, K. J., & Horowitz, D. (2006). Dynamics of forensic interviews with suspected abuse victims who do not disclose abuse. *Child Abuse and Neglect, 30*(7), 753–769.

Hershkowitz, I., & Terner, A. (2007). The effects of repeated interviewing on children's forensic statements of sexual abuse. *Applied Cognitive Psychology, 21*(9), 1131–1143.

Higgins, D. J. (1998). *Multi-type maltreatment: Relationships between familial characteristics, maltreatment and adjustment of children and adults* (Unpublished doctoral dissertation). Deakin University, Burwood, Australia.

Hindman, J. (1989). *Just before dawn.* Ontario, OR: AlexAndria.

Hlavka, H. R., Olinger, S. D., & Lashley, J. L. (2010). The use of anatomical dolls as a demonstration aid in child sexual abuse interviews: A study of forensic interviewers' perceptions. *Journal of Child Sexual Abuse, 19*(5), 519–553.

Hodges, E. A., & Myers, J. E. (2010). Counseling adult women survivors of childhood sexual abuse: Benefits of a wellness approach. *Journal of Mental Health Counseling, 32*(2), 139–153.

Hollely, K. (2002, April). Children in court: The role and scope of the support person. *CARSA, 3*(1), 14–18. Retrieved from http://child advocacy.wikispaces.com/file/view/Support+for+children+in+court .pdf.

Hopper, J. (2008). *Sexual abuse of males: Prevalence, possible lasting effects, and resources.* Retrieved from http://www.jimhopper.com/male-ab/.

Horton, C. B. (1996). Children who molest other children: The school psychologist's response to the sexually aggressive child. *School Psychology Review, 25*(4), 540–558.

Howlin, P., & Jones, D. H. (1996). An assessment approach to abuse allegations made through facilitated communication. *Child Abuse and Neglect, 20*(2), 103–110.

Hunter, S. V. (2009). Beyond surviving: Gender differences in response to early sexual experiences with adults. *Journal of Family Issues, 30*(3), 391–412.

Hurley, P., Lashbrook, D., Cunningham, A., & Stevens, L. (2006). *My day in court.* Retrieved from http://www.lfcc.on.ca/my_day_in_court_ project.pdf.

In re Gault, 387 U.S. 1 (1967).

In re Winship, 397 U.S. 358 (1970).

International Society for Traumatic Stress Studies. (2005). *Indirect traumatization in professionals working with trauma survivors.* Retrieved from http://www.istss.org/resources/indirect_trauma.cfm.

James, M. (1994). Child abuse and neglect: Incidence and prevention. *Family Matters, 37*, 80–85.

Jenkins, A. (2006). Shame, realization and restitution: The ethics of restorative practice. *Australian and New England Journal of Family Therapy, 27*(3), 153–162.

Jepsen, E. K., Svagaard, T., Thelle, M. I., Leigh, M. E., & Martinsen, E. W. (2009). Inpatient treatment for adult survivors of childhood sexual abuse: A preliminary outcome study. *Journal of Trauma and Dissociation, 10*(3), 315–333.

Johnson, K., & Tyler, K. (2007). Adolescent sexual onset: An intergenerational analysis. *Journal of Youth and Adolescence, 36*(7), 939–949.

Jones, N., Pelissier, B., & Klein-Saffran, J. (2006). Predicting sex offender treatment entry among individuals convicted of sexual offense crimes. *Sexual Abuse: A Journal of Research and Treatment, 18*(1), 83–98.

Jones, W. G. (2006). *Working with the courts in child protection.* Child Welfare Information Gateway. Retrieved from http://www.child welfare.gov/pubs/usermanuals/courts/chapterseven.cfm.

Juul, A., Magnusdottir, S., Scheike, T., Prytz, S., & Skakkebaek, N. (2007). Age at voice break in Danish boys: Effects of pre-pubertal body mass index and secular trend. *International Journal of Andrology, 30*(6), 537–542.

Kadambi, M. A., & Ennis, L. (2004). Reconsidering vicarious trauma: A review of the literature and its limitations. *Journal of Trauma Practice, 3*(2), 1–21.

Kambouridis, H., & Jevtic, D. (2003). Group treatment and sexual abuse: Young women share their experience. *Australian Journal of Psychology, 55*, 188–192.

Karpati, A. M., Rubin, C. H., Kieszak, S. M., Marcus, M., & Troiano, R. P. (2002) Stature and pubertal stage assessment in American boys: The 1988–1994 Third National Health and Nutrition Examination Survey. *Journal of Adolescent Health, 30*(2), 205–212.

Keating, H. (2006). Protecting or punishing children: Physical punishment, human rights and English law reform. *Legal Studies, 26*(3), 397–413.

Kenny, M. C., Capri, V., Thakkar-Kolar, R. R., Ryan, E. E., & Runyon, M. K. (2008). Child sexual abuse: From prevention to self-protection. *Child Abuse Review, 17*(1), 36–54.

Kent v. United States, 383 U.S. 541 (1966).

Kerig, P. K., Sink, H. E., Cuellar, R. E., Vanderzee, K. L., & Elfstrom, J. L. (2010). Implementing trauma-focused CBT with fidelity and flexibility: A family case study. *Journal of Clinical Child and Adolescent Psychology, 39*(5), 713–722.

Kessler, M. R. H., & Goff, B. S. N. (2006). Initial treatment decisions with adult survivors of childhood sexual abuse: Recommendations from clinical experts. *Journal of Trauma Practice, 5*(3), 33–56. doi:10.1300/J189v05n03_03.

Keuhn, D., Vericker, T., & Capps, R. (2007). *Child sexual abuse: Removals by generation and ethnicity* (Child Welfare Research Program Brief No. 2). Washington, DC: Urban Institute. Retrieved from http://www.urban.org/uploadedpdf/311460_child_abuse.pdf.

Keyzer, P. (2009). The "preventive detention" of serious sex offenders: Further consideration of the international human rights dimensions. *Psychiatry, Psychology and Law, 16*(2), 262–270.

King, N. J., Tonge, B. J., Mullen, P., Myerson, N., Heyne, D., Rollings, S., et al. (2000). Treating sexually abused children with posttraumatic stress symptoms: A randomized clinical trial. *Journal of the American Academy of Child and Adolescent Psychiatry, 39*(11), 1347–1355.

Kolko, D. J., Cohen, J. A., Mannarino, A. P., Baumann, B. L., & Knudsen, K. (2009). Community treatment of child sexual abuse: A survey of practitioners in the National Child Traumatic Stress Network. *Administration and Policy in Mental Health and Mental Health Services Research, 36,* 37–49.

Konstantareas, M., & Gravelle, G. (1998). Facilitated communication. *Autism, 2*(4), 389–414.

Kools, S., & Kennedy, C. (2001). Child sexual abuse treatment: Misinterpretation and mismanagement of child sexual behaviour. *Health and Development, 28*(3), 211–218.

Korkman, J., Santtila, P., Drzewiecki, T., & Sandnabba, N. (2008). Failing to keep it simple: Language use in child sexual abuse interviews with 3-8-year-old children. *Psychology, Crime and Law, 14*(1), 41–60.

Korkman, J., Santtila, P., & Sandnabba, N. K. (2006). Dynamics of verbal interaction between interviewer and child in interviews with alleged victims of child sexual abuse. *Scandinavian Journal of Psychology, 47*(2), 109–119.

Krahenbuhl, S. J., Blades, M., & Westcott, H. (2010). "What else should I say?" An analysis of the question repetition practice in police interviews of 4-11-year-olds. *Police Practice and Research, 11*(6), 477–490.

Kraus, S. W., & Russell, B. (2008). Early sexual experiences: The role of Internet access and sexual explicit material. *Cyber Psychology and Behavior, 11*(2), 162–168.

Kuehnle, K., & Connell, M. (2010). Child sexual abuse suspicions: Treatment considerations during investigation. *Journal of Child Sexual Abuse, 19*(5), 554–571.

Kumho Tire Co. v. Carmichael, 526 U.S. 137 (1999).

Lamb, M. E., & Fauchier, A. (2001). The effects of question type on self-contradictions by children in the course of forensic interviews. *Applied Cognitive Psychology, 15*, 483–491.

Lamb, M. E., Hershkowitz, I., Sternberg, K. J., Esplin, P. W., Hovav, M., Manor, T., & Yudilevitch, L. (1996). Effects of investigative utterance types of Israeli children's responses. *International Journal of Behavioral Development, 19*(3), 627–637.

Lamb, M. E., Orbach, Y., Hershkowitz, I., Esplin, P. W., & Horowitz, D. (2007). A structured forensic interview protocol improves the quality and informativeness of investigative interviews with children: A review of research using the NICHD Investigative Interview Protocol. *Child Abuse and Neglect, 31*(11–12), 1201–1231.

Lamb, M. E., Orbach, Y., Sternberg, K. J., Aldridge, J., Pearson, S., Stewart, H. L., et al. (2009). Use of a structured investigative protocol enhances the quality of investigative interviews with alleged victims of child sexual abuse in Britain. *Applied Cognitive Psychology, 23*(4), 449–467.

Lamb, M. E., Sternberg, K. J., Orbach, Y., Esplin, P. W., Stewart, H., & Mitchell, S. (2003). Age differences in young children's responses to open-ended invitations in the course of forensic interviews. *Journal of Consulting and Clinical Psychology, 71,* 926–934.

Law Library of Congress. (2007). *United Kingdom: England and Wales: Children's rights.* (Publication No. 2007-04112). Washington, DC: Law Library of Congress.

Leichtentritt, R. D., & Davidson-Arad, B. (2002). Construction of the victim impact statement for sexually abused minors: A dramaturgy approach. *British Journal of Social Work, 32*(8), 1067–1087.

Leichtentritt, R. D., & Davidson-Arad, B. (2006). The impact of sexual abuse as portrayed by Israeli social workers through the victim impact statement. *Families in Society, 87*(1), 123–132.

Letourneau, E. J., Henggeler, S. W., Borduin, C. M., Schewe, P. A., McCart, M. R., Chapman, J. E., et al. (2009). Multisystemic therapy for juvenile sexual offenders: 1-year results from a randomized effectiveness trial. *Journal of Family Psychology, 23*(1), 89–102.

Lev-Wiesel, R. (2008). Child sexual abuse: A critical review of intervention and treatment modalities. *Children and Youth Services Review, 30,* 665–673.

Levenson, J. S. (2003). Policy interventions designed to combat sexual violence: Community notification and civil commitment. *Journal of Child Sexual Abuse, 12*(3–4), 17–52.

Levenson, J. S., Fortney, T., & Baker, J. N. (2010). Views of sexual abuse professionals about sex offender notification policies. *International Journal of Offender Therapy and Comparative Criminology, 54*(2), 150–168.

Levenson, J. S., Prescott, D. S., & D'Amora, D. A. (2009). Sex offender treatment: Consumer satisfaction and engagement in therapy. *International Journal of Therapy and Comparative Criminology, 54*(3), 307–326.

Levine, K., Shane, H. C., & Wharton, R. H. (1994). What if . . . : A plea to professionals to consider the risk-benefit ratio of facilitated communication. *Mental Retardation, 32*(4), 300–304.

Litzelfelner, P. (2000). The effectiveness of CASAs in achieving positive outcomes for children. *Child Welfare, 79*(2), 179–193.

Litzelfelner, P. (2008). Consumer satisfaction with CASAs (court appointed special advocates). *Children and Youth Services Review, 30*(2), 173–186.

Lloyd, C., King, R., & Chenoweth, L. (2002). Social work, stress and burnout. *Journal of Mental Health, 11*(3), 255–265.

London, K., Bruck, M., Wright, D. B., & Ceci, S. J. (2008). Contemporary literature on how children report sexual abuse to others: Findings, methodological issues, and implications for forensic interviewers. *Memory, 16*(1), 29–47.

Lösel, F., & Schmucker, M. (2005). The effectiveness of treatment for sexual offenders: A comprehensive meta-analysis. *Journal of Experimental Criminology, 1*, 117–146.

Lyon, T. D. (2005). *Ten step investigative interview.* Retrieved from http://works.bepress.com/thomaslyon/5/.

Lyon, T. D. (2010). Investigative interviewing of the child. In D. N. Duquette & A. M. Haralambie (Eds.), *Child welfare law and practice* (2nd ed.). Denver, CO: Bradford.

Lyon, T. D., & Ahern, E. C. (2010). Disclosure of child sexual abuse. In J. E. B. Myers (Ed.), *The APSAC handbook on child maltreatment* (3rd ed.). Los Angeles: National Institute of Child and Human Development.

Lyon, T. D., & Matthews, M. (2006). *Model brief: Questioning of child witnesses.* Los Angeles: University of Southern California.

Lyon, T. D., Saywitz, K. J., Kaplan, D. L., & Dorado, J. S. (2001). Reducing maltreated children's reluctance to answer hypothetical oath-taking competency questions. *Law and Human Behavior, 25*(1), 81–92.

Macgregor, S. (2008, April). *Sex offender treatment programs: Effectiveness of prison and community based programs in Australia and New Zealand* (Issue Brief No. 3). Retrieved from http://www.indigenous justice.gov.au/briefs/brief003.pdf.

MacIntosh, H. B., & Johnson, S. (2008). Emotionally focused therapy for couples and childhood sexual abuse survivors. *Journal of Marital and Family Therapy, 34*(3), 298–315. doi:10.1111/j.1752-0606.2008 .00074.x.

Maker, A. H., Kemmelmeier, M., & Peterson, C. (2001). Child sexual abuse, peer sexual abuse and sexual assault in adulthood: A multi-risk model of revictimization. *Journal of Traumatic Stress, 14*(2), 351–369.

Malloy, L. C., Lyon, T. D., & Quas, J. A. (2007). Filial dependency and recantation of child sexual abuse allegations. *Journal of the American Academy of Child and Adolescent Psychiatry, 46,* 162–170.

Mandeville-Norden, R., Beech, A., & Hayes, E. (2008). Examining the effectiveness of a UK community-based sexual offender treatment programme for child abusers. *Psychology, Crime and Law, 14*(6), 493–512.

Mapes, B. E. (1995). *Child eyewitness testimony in sexual abuse investigations.* Brandon, VT: Clinical Psychology.

Martin, E. F., & Pruett, M. (1998). The juvenile sex offender and the juvenile justice system. *American Criminal Law Review, 35*(2), 279–332.

Martone, M., Jaudes, P. K., & Cavins, M. R. (1996). Criminal prosecution of child sexual abuse cases. *Child Abuse and Neglect, 20*(5), 457–464.

Marx, S. P. (1996). Victim recantation in child sexual abuse cases: The prosecutor's role in prevention. *Child Welfare, 75*(3), 219–233.

McNally, R. J., & Geraerts, E. (2009). A new solution to the recovered memory debate. *Perspectives on Psychological Science, 4*(2), 126–134. doi:10.1111/j.1745-6924.2009.01112.x.

Mellor, A., & Dent, H. R. (1994). Preparation of the child witness for court. *Child Abuse Review, 3*(3), 165–176.

Mesibov, G. B. (1995). Facilitated communication: A warning for pediatric psychologists. *Journal of Pediatric Psychology, 20*(1), 127–130.

Minnes, P. (1993). Facilitating communication about facilitated communication. *Journal of Autism and Developmental Disorders, 23*(2), 416–419.

Morrison, A., & Ferris, J. (2009). The Satir model with female adult survivors of childhood sexual abuse. *Satir Journal, 3*(2), 73–100.

Mostert, M. P. (2001). Facilitated communication since 1995: A review of published studies. *Journal of Autism and Developmental Disorders, 31*(3), 287–313.

Mostert, M. P. (2010). Facilitated communication and its legitimacy—twenty-first-century developments. *Exceptionality, 18*(1), 31–41.

Murphy, L., Fedoroff, J. P., & Martineau, M. (2009). Canada's sex offender registries: Background, implementation, and social policy considerations. *Canadian Journal of Human Sexuality, 18*(1–2), 61–72.

Murtagh, M. P. (2010). The Appropriate Attribution Technique (AAT): A new treatment technique for adult survivors of sexual abuse. *North American Journal of Psychology, 12*(2), 313–334.

Myers, J. B. (1992). *Legal issues in child abuse and neglect.* Newbury Park, CA: Sage.

Myers, J. B. (1994). The tendency of the legal system to distort scientific and clinical innovations: Facilitated communication as a case study. *Child Abuse & Neglect, 18*(6), 505–513.

National Center for Victims of Crime. (1999). *Victim impact statements.* Retrieved from http://www.ncvc.org/ncvc/main.aspx?dbName= DocumentViewer&DocumentID=32515.

National Children's Advocacy Center. (2002). *Forensic interview structure.* Retrieved from http://xpedio02.childrensmn.org/stellent/groups/ Public/@Manuals/@MRCAC/@Interv/documents/PolicyReference Procedure/085427.pdf.

National Children's Advocacy Center. (2009). *Forensic interview structure.* Retrieved from http://xpedio02.childrensmn.org/stellent/groups/ Public/@Manuals/@MRCAC/@Interv/documents/PolicyReference Procedure/085427.pdf.

National Children's Alliance. (2011). *Regional children's advocacy centers.* Retrieved from http://www.nationalchildrensalliance.org/index .php?s=63.

National Training Program on Effective Treatment Approaches in Child Sexual Abuse. (1993). [Unpublished training manual]. Huntsville, AL: Author.

Neoh, J., & Mellor, D. (2009). Professional issues related to allegations and assessment of child sexual abuse in the context of family court litigation. *Psychiatry, Psychology and Law, 16*(2), 303–321. doi:10.1080/13218710902852883.

Nichols, K. S. (2009). Assessing sexual abuse protocols for family litigation. *American Journal of Family Law, 22*(4), 184–191.

Nicholson, A. (2003, June 21). *Children and children's rights in the context of family law.* Address presented at the conference of the Law Association for Asia and the Pacific, Brisbane, Australia.

Nolan, M., Carr, A., Fitzpatrick, C., O'Flaherty, A., Keary, K., Turner, R., & Tobin, G. (2002). A comparison of two programmes for victims of child sexual abuse: A treatment outcome study. *Child Abuse Review, 11*(2), 103–123.

Noonan, R. K., & Charles, D. (2009). Developing teen dating violence prevention strategies: Formative research with middle school youth. *Violence against Women, 15*(9), 1087–1105.

Nordberg, P. (2006). *Resolving Daubert challenges.* Retrieved from http://www.daubertontheweb.com/Summary%20Judgment.htm.

Nugent, W. R., Williams, M., & Umbreit, M. S. (2003). The practice of restorative justice: Participation in victim-offender mediation and the prevalence and severity of subsequent delinquent behavior—A meta-analysis. *Utah Law Review, 1,* 137–166.

Oates, R. K., Jones, D. P., Denson, D., Sirotnak, A., Gary, N., & Krugman, R. D. (2000). Erroneous concerns about child sexual abuse. *Child Abuse and Neglect, 24*(1), 149–157.

Office of Child and Youth Advocate. (N.d. a). *Mandate, scope and authority.* Retrieved from http://advocate.gov.ab.ca/home/Mandate.cfm.

Office of Child and Youth Advocate. (N.d. b). *Advocacy services.* Retrieved from http://advocate.gov.ab.ca/home/Advocacy_Services_home.cfm.

Orbach, Y., Hershkowitz, I., Lamb, M. E., Sternberg, K. J., Esplin, P. W., & Horowitz, D. (2000). Assessing the value of structured protocols for forensic interviews of alleged child abuse victims. *Child Abuse and Neglect, 24*(6), 733–152.

Ost, S. (2004). Getting to grips with sexual grooming? The new offence under the Sexual Offences Act 2003. *Journal of Social Welfare and Family Law, 26*(2), 147–159.

Oswell, D. (2006). When images matter: Internet child pornography, forms of observation and an ethics of the virtual. *Information, Communication and Society, 9*(2), 244–265.

Owens, G. P., Pike, J. L., & Chard, K. M. (2001). Treatment effects of cognitive processing therapy on cognitive distortions of female child sexual abuse survivors. *Behavior Therapy, 32*(3), 413–425.

Paine, M. L., & Hansen, D. J. (2002). Factors influencing children to self-disclose sexual abuse. *Clinical Psychology Review, 22*(2), 271–295.

Palmiotto, M., & MacNichol, S. (2010). Supervision of sex offenders: A multi-faceted and collaborative approach. *Federal Probation, 74*(2), 27–30.

Parliament of Australia. (2003). *Separate representation of children.* Retrieved from http://www.aph.gov.au/senate/committee/legcon_ctte/completed_inquiries/199699/legalaid/report/c08.htm.

Patel, S. H., Lambie, G. W., & Glover, M. M. (2008). Motivational counseling: Implications for counseling male juvenile sex offenders. *Journal of Addictions and Offender Counseling, 28,* 86–100.

Patterson, T., & Pipe, M. (2009). Exploratory assessments of child abuse: Children's responses to interviewer's questions across multiple interview sessions. *Child Abuse and Neglect, 33*(8), 490–504.

Pearlman, L. A., & Saakvitne, K. W. (1995a). Treating therapists with vicarious traumatization and secondary traumatic stress disorders. In C. R. Figley (Ed.), *Compassion fatigue* (pp. 150–177). New York: Brunner/Mazel.

Pearlman, L. A., & Saakvitne, K. W. (1995b). *Trauma and the therapist: Countertransference and vicarious traumatization in psychotherapy with incest survivors.* New York: Norton.

Penna, S. (2005). The Children Act 2004: Child protection and social surveillance. *Journal of Social Welfare and Family Law, 27*(2), 143–157.

Perona, A. R., Bottoms, B. L., & Sorenson, E. (2006). Research-based guidelines for child forensic interviews. *Journal of Aggression, Maltreatment and Trauma, 12*(3–4), 81–130.

Perry, A. D. (2009). Unlucky Section 13: Sexual activity between children and the Sexual Offences Act 2003. *King's Law Journal, 20*, 327–337.

Perry, B. (2003). *The cost of caring: Secondary traumatic stress and the impact of working with high-risk families and children.* Retrieved from http://www.childtrauma.org/ctamaterials/SecTrma2_03_v2.pdf.

Peters, J. K. (2001). *Representing children in child protective proceedings: Ethical and practical dimensions.* New Haven, CT: Yale Law School, Jerome N. Frank Legal Services Organization.

Petrucci, C. J. (2002). Apology in the criminal justice setting: Evidence for including apology as an additional component in the legal system. *Behavioral Sciences and the Law, 20*(4), 337–362.

Petrunik, M., & Deutschmann, L. (2008). The exclusion-inclusion spectrum in state and community response to sex offenders in Anglo-American and European jurisdictions. *International Journal of Offender Therapy and Comparative Criminology, 52*(5), 499–519.

Piper, A. (2008). Investigating child sex abuse allegations: A guide to help legal professionals distinguish valid from invalid claims. *Journal of Psychiatry and Law, 36*(2), 271–317.

Porett, J. (1993). *When I was little like you.* Washington, DC: Child Welfare League of America.

Prior, M., & Cummins, R. (1992). Questions about facilitated communication and autism. *Journal of Autism and Developmental Disorders, 22*(3), 331–338.

Propen, A. D., & Schuster, M. L. (2010). Understanding genre through the lens of advocacy: The rhetorical work of the victim impact statement. *Written Communication, 27*(1), 3–35.

Protection of Children against Sexual Exploitation Act of 1977, P.L. 95-225 (1977).

Protective Services for Children and Young People. (1993). *Child sexual abuse: Non-offending parent.* Washington, DC: Department of Health and Community Services. Retrieved from http://www.ccoso .org/library%20articles/CP_csa_non-offending_vol3.pdf

Regehr, C., & Gutheil, T. (2002). Apology, justice, and trauma recovery. *Journal of the American Academy of Psychiatry Law, 30*, 425–430.

Reitzel, L. R., & Carbonell, J. L. (2006). The effectiveness of sex offender treatment for juveniles as measured by recidivism: A meta-analysis. *Sexual Abuse: A Journal of Research and Treatment, 18*, 401–421.

Roberts, J. V. (2003). Victim impact statements and the sentencing process: Recent developments and research findings. *Criminal Law Quarterly, 47*(3), 365–396.

Roche, J. (2008). Children's rights, confidentiality and the policing of children. *International Journal of Children's Rights, 16*, 431–456.

Rodgers, T. (2004). *Safety activities for kids.* Indianapolis, IN: JIST.

Romano, E., & De Luca, R. V. (2001). Male sexual abuse: A review of effects, abuse characteristics, and links with later psychological functioning. *Aggression and Violent Behavior, 6*, 55–78.

Ross, G., & O'Carroll, P. (2004). Cognitive behavioural psychotherapy intervention in childhood sexual abuse: Identifying new directions from the literature. *Child Abuse Review, 12*(1), 51–64.

Routh, D. K. (1994). Commentary: Facilitated communication as unwitting ventriloquism. *Journal of Pediatric Psychology, 19*(6), 673–675.

Roylance, R., & Scanlon, C. (1999, June 17–18). *The child witness: Preparation and support.* Paper presented at the meeting of the Australian Institute of Criminology, Brisbane, Australia.

Runyon, M. K., Deblinger, E., & Steer, R. A. (2010). Group cognitive behavioral treatment for parents and children at-risk for physical abuse: An initial study. *Child and Family Behavior Therapy, 32*(3), 196–218.

Rusinoff, J., & Gerber, P. N. (1990). Crossing typological boundaries in treating the shame cycle. In M. Hunter (Ed.), *The sexually abused male: Application and treatment strategies* (Vol. 2, pp. 99–115). Lexington, MA: Lexington Books.

Ryan, G. (1997). Sexually abusive youth: Defining the population. In G. Ryan & S. Lane (Eds.), *Juvenile sexual offending: Causes, consequences, and correction* (pp. 3–9). San Francisco: Jossey-Bass.

Saakvitne, K. W., & Pearlman, L. A. (1996). *Transforming the pain: A workbook on vicarious traumatization.* New York: Norton.

Salerno, J. M., Najdowski, C. J., Stevenson, M. C., Wiley, T. R. A., Bottoms, B. L., & Pimentel, P. S. (2010). Psychological mechanisms underlying support for juvenile sex offender registry laws: Prototypes, moral outrage, and perceived threat. *Behavioral Sciences and the Law, 28,* 58–83.

Salston, M., & Figley, C. R. (2003). Secondary traumatic stress effects of working with survivors of criminal victimization. *Journal of Traumatic Stress, 16*(2), 167–174.

Sayfan, L., Mitchell, E. B., Goodman, G. S., Eisen, M. L., & Qin, J. (2008). Children's expressed emotions when disclosing maltreatment. *Child Abuse and Neglect, 32*(11), 1026–1036.

Saywitz, K. J., & Goodman, G. S. (1996). Interviewing children in and out of court: Current research and practice implications. In L. Berliner, J. Briere, & J. Bulkey (Eds.), *APSAC handbook on child maltreatment.* Newbury Park, CA: Sage.

Saywitz, K. J., Lyon, T. D., & Goodman, G. S. (2010). Interviewing children. In J. E. B. Myers (Ed.), *The APSAC handbook on child maltreatment* (3rd ed.). Los Angeles: National Institute of Child and Human Development.

Saywitz, K. J., Mannarino, A., Berliner, L., & Cohen, J. A. (2000). Treatments for sexually abused children and adolescents. *American Psychologist, 55*(9), 1040–1050.

Scalora, M. J., & Garbin, C. (2003). A multivariate analysis of sex offender recidivism. *International Journal of Offender Therapy and Comparative Criminology, 47,* 309–323.

Schaffer, M., Jeglic, E. L., Moster, A., & Wnuk, D. (2010). Cognitive-behavioral therapy in the treatment and management of sex offenders. *Journal of Cognitive Psychotherapy: An International Quarterly, 24*(2), 92–103.

Schetky, D. H., & Green, A. H. (1998). *Child sexual abuse: A handbook for health care and legal professions.* New York: Brunner/Mazel.

Schiavone, S. K., & Jeglic, E. L. (2009). Public perception of sex offender social policies and the impact on sex offenders. *International Journal of Offender Therapy and Comparative Criminology, 53*(6), 679–695.

Scottish Government Publications. (2004). *Guidance on child witness court familiarisation visits.* Retrieved from http://www.scotland.gov .uk/Publications/2004/05/19308/36511.

Sexton, L. (1999). Vicarious traumatization of counselors and effects on their workplaces. *British Journal of Guidance and Counseling, 27,* 393–414.

Sexual Offences, Criminal Code, Department of Justice Canada §§ 151– 153. (2008). Retrieved from http://laws.justice.gc.ca/eng/C-46/ 20110107/page-4.html?rp2=HOME&rp3=SI&rp1=sexual%20abuse &rp4=all&rp9=cs&rp10=L&rp13=50#anchorbo-ga:l_V-gb:s_150_1.

Sexual Offences Act, ch. 42 UK Public General Acts § pt. 1. (2003). Retrieved from http://www.legislation.gov.uk/ukpga/2003/42/contents.

Sgroi, S. M. (1982). *Handbook of clinical intervention in child sexual abuse.* Lexington, MA: Lexington Books.

Shane, H. C. (1993). The dark side of facilitated communication. *Topics in Language Disorders, 13*(4), ix–xv.

Shields, R. E., & Bryan, L. J. (2005). Georgia's new expert witness rule: Daubert & more. *Georgia Bar Journal, 11*(2), 18–21.

Shursen, A., Brock, L. J., & Jennings, G. (2008). Differentiation and intimacy in sex offender relationships. *Sexual Addiction and Compulsivity, 15,* 14–22.

Siegel, B. (1995). Assessing allegations of sexual molestation made through facilitated communication. *Journal of Autism and Developmental Disorders, 25*(3), 319–326.

Sinclair, R., & Franklin, A. (2000). *Quality projects research briefings: Young people's participation.* Retrieved from http://www.keele.ac.uk/ research/lcs/makingresearchcount/briefings/pb3.pdf.

Smith, S. K. (2007). *Mandatory reporting of child abuse and neglect.* Retrieved from http://www.smith-lawfirm.com/mandatory_reporting.htm.

Smith, M., Haas, P. J., & Belcher, R. G. (1994). Facilitated communication: The effects of facilitator knowledge and level of assistance on output. *Journal of Autism and Developmental Disorders, 24*(3), 357–367.

Sneddon, H. (2003). The effects of maltreatment on children's health and well-being. *Child Care in Practice, 9*(3), 236–250.

Social Welfare Department. (2009). *Child witness 5 to 9.* Retrieved from http://www.swd.gov.hk/vs/doc/Child_Witness_5to9.pdf.

Spataro, J., Moss, S. A., & Wells, D. L. (2001). Child sexual abuse: A reality for both sexes. *Australian Psychologist, 36*(3), 177–183.

Stamm, H., Varra, E., Pearlman, L., & Giller, E. (2002). *The helper's power to heal and to be hurt—or helped—by trying.* Washington, DC: National Register of Health Service Providers in Psychology.

Steed, L. G., & Downing, R. (1998). A phenomenological study of vicarious traumatisation amongst psychologists and professional counselors working in the field of sexual abuse/assault. *Australian Journal of Disaster and Trauma Studies, 2.* Retrieved from http://www.massey.ac.nz/~trauma/issues/1998-2/steed.htm.

Stermac, L., Reist, D., Addison, M., & Miller, G. M. (2002). Childhood risk factors for women's sexual victimization. *Journal of Interpersonal Violence, 17*(6), 647–671.

Sternberg, K. J., Lamb, M. E., Davies, G. M., & Westcott, H. L. (2001). The Memorandum of Good Practice: Theory versus application. *Child Abuse and Neglect, 25*(5), 669–681.

Stevenson, K. M., Leung, P., & Cheung, K. M. (1992). Competency-based evaluation of interviewing skills in child sexual abuse cases. *Social Work Research and Abstracts, 28*(3), 11–16.

Taft, L. (2000). Apology subverted: The commodification of apology. *Yale Law Journal, 109*(5), 1135–1160.

Terry, K. J., & Tallon, J. (2004). *Summarizes findings about the prevalence and nature of sexual abuse in the general population and within the Catholic Church.* Retrieved from http://www.usccb.org/nrb/john jaystudy/litreview.pdf.

Thomas, T. (2009). Children and young people on the UK sex offender register. *International Journal of Children's Rights, 17*, 491–500.

Tisdall, E. K. M., Bray, R., Marshall, K., & Cleland, A. (2004). Children's participation in family law proceedings: A step too far or a step too small? *Journal of Social Welfare and Family Law, 26*(1), 17–33.

Tishelman, A. C., & Geffner, R. (2010). Forensic, cultural, and systems issues in child sexual abuse cases—Part 1: An introduction. *Journal of Child Sexual Abuse, 19*, 485–490.

Tjaden, P. G., & Anhalt, J. (1994). *The impact of joint law enforcement–child protective services investigations in child maltreatment cases.* Denver, CO: Center for Policy Research.

Tomison, A. M. (1995). *Update on child sexual abuse* (Issues Paper No. 5). Melbourne, Australia: National Child Protection Clearinghouse.

Tregilgas, K. (2010). Comments—Sex offender treatment in the United States: The current climate and an unexpected opportunity for change. *Tulane Law Review, 84*, 729–757.

Trowell, J., & Kolvin, I. (2002). Individual vs. group therapy for sexual abuse treatment. *Brown University Child Adolescent Behavior Letter, 18*(4), 5–9.

U.S. Conference on Catholic Bishops. (2002). *Promise to protect, pledge to heal: Charter for the Protection of Children and Young People, essential norms, statement of Episcopal commitment.* Retrieved from http://www.usccb.org/ocyp/charter.pdf.

U.S. Conference on Catholic Bishops. (2009). *Diocese policies on dealing with sexual abuse of minors.* Retrieved from http://www.usccb.org/comm/kit3.shtml.

U.S. Department of Health and Human Services. (2008a). *Child maltreatment 2006.* Retrieved from http://www.childwelfare.gov/can/prevalence/stats.cfm.

U.S. Department of Health and Human Services. (2008b). *Mandatory reports of child abuse and neglect.* Retrieved from http://www.childwelfare.gov/systemwide/laws_policies/statutes/manda.pdf.

U.S. Department of Health and Human Services, Child Welfare Information Gateway (2009). *Definitions of child abuse and neglect: Summary of state laws.* Retrieved from http://www.childwelfare.gov/systemwide/laws_policies/statutes/define.pdf.

U.S. Department of Justice. (2006). *National court-appointed special advo-cate program.* Retrieved from http://www.justice.gov/oig/reports/OJP/a0704/final.pdf.

U.S. Department of Justice, Office of Juvenile Justice and Delinquency Prevention (2009). *Juveniles who commit sex offenses against minors.* Retrieved from http://www.ncjrs.gov/pdffiles1/ojjdp/227763.pdf.

U.S. National Research Council. (1993). *Understanding child abuse and neglect.* Washington, D.C.: National Academy Press.

van der Merwe, A. (2008). Addressing victim's harm: The role of impact reports. *Thomas Jefferson Law Review, 30*(2), 391–406.

VanDeusen, K. M., & Way, I. (2006). Vicarious trauma: An exploratory study of the impact of providing sexual abuse treatment on clini-cians' trust and intimacy. *Journal of Child Sexual Abuse, 15*(1), 69–85. doi:10.1300/J070v15n01-04.

Vess, J. (2009). Risk assessment of sexual offenders for extended supervi-sion orders in New Zealand: Basic principles and current practice. *Journal of Child Sexual Abuse, 18,* 174–189.

Vieth, V. (2008). The development of forensic interview training models: A reply to Lamb, Orbach, Hershkowitz, Esplin, and Horowitz (2007). *Child Abuse and Neglect, 32,* 1003–1006.

Vines, P. (2008). Apologies and civil liability in the UK: A view from else-where. *Edinburgh Law Review, 12*(2), 200–230.

Wakefield, H., & Underwager, R. (1988). *Accusations of child sexual abuse.* Springfield, IL: Thomas.

Washington State Criminal Justice Training Commission & Harborview Center for Sexual Assault and Traumatic Stress. (2006). *Child inter-view guide.* Retrieved from http://centerforchildwelfare.fmhi.usf .edu/kb/trpi/Child%20Interview%20Guide.pdf

Watson, T., & Vess, J. (2007). Risk assessment of child-victim sex offend-ers for extended supervision in New Zealand. *Journal of Forensic Psychiatry and Psychology, 18*(2), 235–247.

Way, I., VanDeusen, K., & Cottrell, T. (2007). Vicarious trauma: Predic-tors of clinicians' disrupted cognitions about self-esteem and self-intimacy. *Journal of Child Sexual Abuse, 16*(4), 81–98.

Weisgram v. Marley Co., 528 U.S. 440 (2000).

Weisz, V., & Thai, N. (2003). The court-appointed special advocate (CASA) program: Bringing information to child abuse and neglect cases. *Child Maltreatment, 8*(3), 204–210.

Wells, R., McCann, J., Adams, J., Voris, J., & Dahl, B. (1997). A validational study of the structured interview of symptoms associated with sexual abuse (SASA) using three samples of sexually abused, allegedly abused, and nonabused boys. *Child Abuse and Neglect, 21*(12), 1159–1167.

Westcott, H. L., & Kynan S. (2006). Interviewer practice in investigative interviews for suspected child sexual abuse. *Psychology, Crime and Law, 12*(4), 367–382.

Wharff, E. A. (1998). A study of decision-making criteria in child sexual abuse evaluations. *Dissertation Abstracts International Section A: Humanities and Social Sciences, 59*(1-A), 0326.

Wheeler, D. L., Jacobson, J. W., Paglieri, R. A., & Schwartz, A. A. (1993). An experimental assessment of facilitated communication. *Mental Retardation, 31*(1), 49–59.

Wiley, T. R. A. (2009). Legal and social service responses to child sexual abuse: A primer and discussion of relevant research. *Journal of Child Sexual Abuse, 18,* 267–289.

Wilson, A. (2005). Expert testimony in the dock. *Journal of Criminal Law, 69*(4), 330–348.

Winder, J. H. (1996). Counseling adult male survivors of childhood sexual abuse: A review of treatment techniques. *Journal of Mental Health Counseling, 18*(2), 123–134.

Wood, M., & Ogloff, J. R. P. (2006). Victoria's Serious Sex Offenders Monitoring Act 2005: Implications for the accuracy of sex offender risk management. *Psychiatry, Psychology, and Law, 13*(2), 182–198.

Wurtele, S. K. (2009). Preventing sexual abuse of children in the twenty-first century: Preparing for challenges and opportunities. *Journal of Child Sexual Abuse, 18*(1), 1–18.

York County, Virginia. (2011). *General District Court: Court appearance tips.* Retrieved from http://www.yorkcounty.gov/DistrictCourt/CourtAppearanceTips/tabid/4433/default.aspx.

Youth Justice and Criminal Evidence Act 1999. Retrieved from http://www.legislation.gov.uk/ukpga/1999/23/contents.

Zolondek, S. C., Abel, G. G., Northey, W. F., Jr., & Jordan, A. D. (2001). The self-reported behaviors of juvenile sexual offenders. *Journal of Interpersonal Violence, 16*(1), 73–85.

Index

About the Author

Monit Cheung, MA, MSW, PhD, LCSW, is a professor at the Graduate College of Social Work, University of Houston. She is the principal investigator of the Child Welfare Education Project, a state partnership program for training child welfare social workers that is funded federally by Title IV-E, and she is the associate director of the Child and Family Center for Innovative Research. She has been a social worker for thirty-five years and is currently a licensed clinical social worker specializing in play therapy, family counseling, child and adolescent counseling, child protection, sexual and domestic violence, and incest survivor treatment. She has practiced as a volunteer clinician, providing counseling and case consultation with Asian American Family Services, and she has served as a consultant trainer for the Hong Kong Social Welfare Department and the Hong Kong Police Force. Using an experiential and practice-oriented approach in teaching, Cheung has taught at the graduate level for twenty-five years. She has presented at 212 workshops and conferences and has written 426 articles, books, book chapters, and research reports on child protection and parenting issues in both English and Chinese. Her research interests are related to treatment effectiveness in the areas of child sexual abuse, creative family therapy, therapeutic touch, and immigrant adjustment. Cheung currently serves on the Diocesan Review Board for the Protection of Children and Young People at the Diocese of Galveston-Houston, she is an advisory board member of Catholic Charities and Asian American Family Services, and she is a board member and lifetime member of the End Child Sexual Abuse Foundation in Hong Kong. Cheung has received the following awards: 2010 Alumni Hall of Fame from the Ohio State University; 2010 Outstanding Faculty Award; 2009 Best Reviewer Award from the Council on Social Work Education; Research Associate at the Center for Public Policy; 2006–2009 Honorary Professorship, University of Hong Kong; 2006 Favorite Faculty Award; 2005 Unsung Hero Award from Channel 39 KHWB-TV; 2004 Golden Harvest Award from the Asian American Family Counseling Center; 2002 YWCA Outstanding Woman Award in Education; 2001 Ervan Chew Award for Community Leadership from the Girl Scout Council; 2000 Outstanding Faculty Award; and 1999–2001 Honorary Research Fellowship with the School of Social and Administrative Studies at Cardiff University, in the United Kingdom.